Off The Beaten Track
Scandinavia

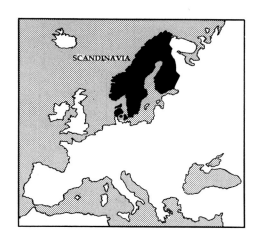

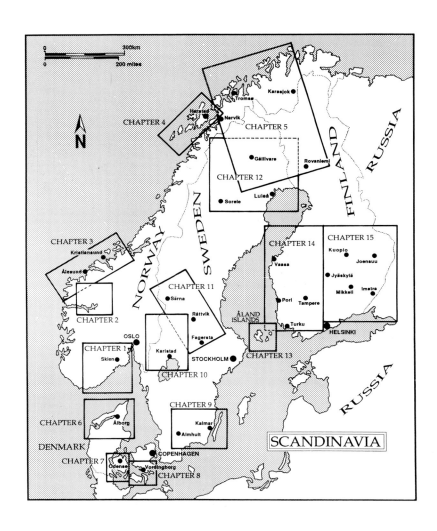

Off the Beaten Track
SCANDINAVIA

Margaret & Robin Rogers

MOORLAND PUBLISHING

The Globe Pequot Press

Published by:
Moorland Publishing Co Ltd,
Moor Farm Road West, Ashbourne,
Derbyshire, DE6 1HD England

ISBN 0 86190 500 8 (UK)

The Globe Pequot Press,
6 Business Park Road,
PO Box 833, Old Saybrook,
Connecticut 06475-0833

ISBN 1-56440-303-3 (USA)

First published 1992
Revised 2nd edition 1994
© Margaret & Robin Rogers 1994

Front Cover: Heddal stave church,
Norway (*MPC Picture Collection*).

All the illustrations in this book have
been taken by Robin Rogers.

Printed in Hong Kong by:
Wing King Tong Co Ltd

British Library Cataloguing in Publication Data:
A catalogue record for this book is available from the British Library.

Library of Congress Cataloging-in-Publication Data
Rogers, Margaret.
    Off the beaten track. Scandinavia/Margaret & Robin Rogers. — Rev. 2nd ed.
        p.   cm.
    Includes Index.
    ISBN 1-56440-303-3 (USA). — ISBN 0-86190-500-8 (UK)
    1. Scandinavia — Guidebooks.   I. Rogers, Robin. II Title. III. Title: Scandinavia.
DL4.R6 1994
914.804'88 — dc20   93-10709
                                                                                        CIP

Contents

Key to Maps

● 🏠	Town /City	～～	River
▬▬▬	Main Road	🔵	Lake
══════	Motorway	—.—.—.—	Boundary

Note on Maps and Placenames

The maps for each chapter, while comprehensive, are not designed to be used as route maps, but rather to locate the main towns, villages and places of interest.

Placenames in Denmark, Norway and Sweden often include an abbreviation, which appears on maps and road signs. The common ones are:

N	north	St	large (big, great)
S	south	Ll	small (little)
V	west	Gl	old
Ö	east		

A Note to the Reader

We hope you have found this book informative, helpful and enjoyable. It is always our aim to make our publications as accurate and up to date as possible. With this in mind, we would appreciate any comments that you might have. If you come across any information to update this book or discover something new about the area we have covered, please let us know so that your notes may be incorporated in future editions.

As it is the publisher's principal aim to produce books that are lively and responsive to change, any information that readers provide will be a valuable asset in maintaining the highest possible standards.

Introduction

Western Europe is a continent of great diversity, well visited not just by travellers from other parts of the globe but by the inhabitants of its own member countries. Within the year-round processes of trade and commerce, but more particularly during the holiday season, there is a great surging interchange of nationalities as one country's familiar attractions are left behind for those of another.

It is true that frontiers are blurred by ever quicker travel and communications, and that the sharing of cultures, made possible by an increasingly sophisticated media network, brings us closer in all senses to our neighbours. Yet essential differences do exist, differences which lure us abroad on our annual migrations in search of new horizons, fresh sights, sounds and smells, discovery of unknown landscapes and people.

Countless resorts have evolved for those among us who simply crave sun, sea and the reassuring press of humanity. There are, too, established tourist 'sights' with which a country or region has become associated and to which clings, all too often, a suffocating shroud — the manifestations of mass tourism in the form of crowds and entrance charges, the destruction of authentic atmosphere, cynical exploitation. While this is by no means typical of all well known tourist attractions, it is familiar enough to act as a disincentive for those of more independent spirit who value personal discovery above prescribed experience and who would rather avoid the human conveyor belt of queues, traffic jams and packed accommodation.

It is for such travellers that this guidebook has been written. In its pages, no more than passing mention is made of the famous, the well documented, the already glowingly described — other guidebooks will satisfy the appetite for such orthodox tourist information. Instead, the reader is taken if not to unknown then to relatively unvisited places — literally 'off-the-beaten-track'. Through the specialist knowledge of the author, visitors using this guidebook are assured

7

of gaining insights into the country's heartland whose heritage lies largely untouched by the tourist industry. Occasionally the reader is urged simply to take a sideways step from a site of renowned tourist interest to discover a place perhaps less sensational, certainly less frequented but often of equivalent fascination.

Scandinavia — the land of the Vikings— is ideal for those wishing to get off-the-beaten-track. There is a great diversity of scenery from the mighty mountains, fjords and glaciers of Norway to the grandeur of Swedish Lappland and the countless lakes of Finland. This book will enable you to discover the spectacular scenery and the quiet fishing villages of the Lofoten islands, the Jotunheim mountains, Telemark, and Jutland as well as the glassblowers, windmills and churches of Småland.

1 • Vestfold and Telemark

Introduction to Norway

Norway is scenically the most interesting of the Scandinavian countries, a land of broad rivers, high waterfalls and lakes, its interior dominated by high mountain ranges capped with permanent snowfields including Europe's second largest glacier, the Jostedalbreen. Such mountains used to hamper communications in all but the three summer months but now a network of all year roads tunnels through them and travel is possible at any time. Practically all through routes, including the 'old' roads over the mountains are surfaced: it is only the local and toll roads, used in this book for some of the diversions, that are not. Even traversing the mountains is easy for the roads climb gently in a series of hairpin bends and traffic is very light indeed in this underpopulated country. In Norway drive on the right-hand side of the road. Road and bridge building is an ongoing preoccupation of the Norwegian government, with new routes starting to supersede some of the old ferries. However the deeply indented coastline, with its steep-sided fjords and complex of offshore islands make ferries a necessary part of many routes. BAS Overseas Publications Ltd, 48-50 Sheen Lane, London SW14 8LQ, can supply either a booklet of the main ferries, or for those travelling off the beaten track, the complete *Rutebok for Norge* which includes timetables for every public ferry, bus and train service. It does not include the handful of private ferries that still operate, mainly on inland lakes. It is not necessary or indeed possible to book a passage but a timetable is useful when planning a day's route.

Attractions include a wide variety of museums ranging from the modern and specialist, like the Mining Museum in Kongsberg and the Polar Museum in Tromsø, to the *bygdetuns* or preserved farms that are common throughout the country. The season for these smaller attractions can be very short — just the 6 weeks from late June to early August when the Norwegians themselves are on holiday. Some of the original stave churches (the name refers to the method of construction) still exist with simple rose paintings on their walls

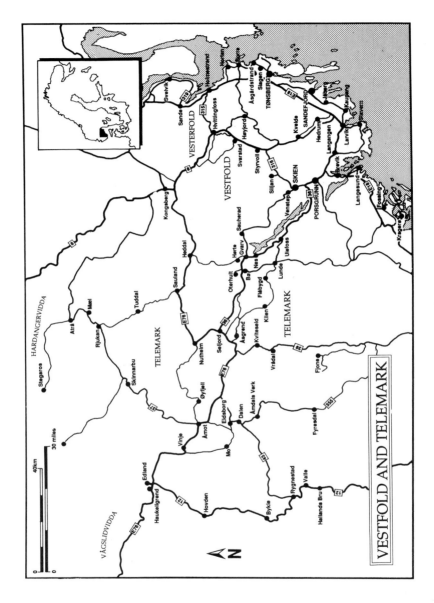

and the more sophisticated eighteenth- and nineteenth-century style of this can be seen in later churches and homesteads. Some summer dairy farms or *seters*, where the women used to spend the summer months on the high mountain pastures with the cows and goats,

milking and making butter and cheese, are still maintained as working environments and welcome visitors. Gastronomically the Norwegian *smorgåsbord* is a treat. A cold table of fishes, meats, cheeses,
and desserts, all beautifully presented with salads and breads, it also
includes some simple hot dishes. The larger hotels often present this
as their evening meal and no visit to Norway is complete without
sampling it at least once!

Vestfold and Telemark

These two areas cover the west coast of the Oslofjord and the hinterland through the rolling countryside of inner Vestfold to the long
lakes and majestic heights of the high fells in northern Telemark. It
includes sea bathing and marinas along the shore, salmon fishing on
the larger rivers, a wide range of scenery and outdoor activities and
the Telemark canal which leads one into the heart of the mountains.
Telemark was the scene of one of the most famous Resistance stories
in World War II, recorded in the Vemork Museum at Rjukan. There
are also naval and maritime, car and photographic museums and
even a silver mine. Many places possess their own *bygdetun* or
collection of farm buildings, often preserved on their original sites.
Two stave churches, with early rose paintings, also remain, while
Bykle church is a wonderful example of the later flourishing of this
style of decoration. Lying side by side, the two districts together
produce one of the most varied regions covered in this book — and
one that is easy to reach. From Oslo, it is an hour's drive to Kongsberg
or $1^1/_2$ hours to Horten. Alternatively north from Gothenberg, there
are ferries from Strømsund to Sandefjord and from Moss to Horten.
The itinerary followed here criss-crosses the terrain, covering the
best of the scenic routes but there is no hard and fast law saying this
is the way it should be done. At several points, near Dalen and Seljord
for example, routes almost cross and alternative combinations are
easily possible.

Beginning in Vestfold, the sea front is the Oslofjord and its
branches, a broad stretch of water dotted with islands and backed by
good farmland. In no sense is it a steep-sided rocky finger like the
most famous fjords on the west coast. Arriving from Oslo via
Drammen, the 319 takes one round the coast to busy little **Svelvik**
and the area of bathing and boats along the shore towards Sande.
Alternatively one can drive straight down the E18 to **Holmestrand**,
with its large marina and rose gardens along the front. From this
point south, a succession of towns sit beside the water, each with its
own individual character. Horten in the north is a naval and ferry

town with industry spoiling its waterfront. One arrives first at **Løvøy** island whose rebuilt medieval chapel overlooks a typical coastal scene of small marina, holiday homes with private jetties, and bathing in the sea. The island beyond is a naval precinct and **Karljohansvern** to the north of Horten has a comprehensive naval museum housed in an old barracks. This includes the world's first torpedo boat as well as over 100 model ships. **Horten** also possesses Norway's first, small lifeboat museum opposite the ferry port, a car museum in the beer hall of the former brewery and a unique photomuseum including a turn of the century photographic studio and many unusual and interesting cameras.

South of Horten one passes Borrehaugene, the Viking kings' graves in Norway's oldest National Park. They are a reminder that this coast of Norway is rich in Viking remains. Two world famous ship burials were discovered here — the *Oseberg* ship in one of the mounds at Slagen church just north of Tønsberg and the *Gokstadt* ship near Sandefjord. There are also innumerable burial sites, the oldest trading post in Norway at Kaupang near Larvik and Tønsberg itself was a royal seat from the ninth century onwards.

Before reaching here one passes **Åsgårdstrand**, famous in the nineteenth century as the artists' town from the many Norwegian painters who lived and worked here. Most famous was Edvard Munch who bought a yellow cottage at the north end of town in 1897 and called it 'House of Happiness'. To enjoy a short stroll through the town, park at the quay. The preserved linden tree to the right features in Munch's *Girls on the Bridge*. From the breakwater one can admire whitewashed houses rising up the hillside. Walk along the front to the sailing club and up through the garden of Munch's house which is now a museum, then back along the narrow street where roses scramble up the white woodwork and past Kiøsterudgården with its art exhibitions, to regain the harbour.

Where Åsgårdstrand is a mere 400 years old, **Tønsberg** is Scandinavia's oldest city, founded in AD871 as the seat of the Ynglinge clan from whom Vestfold's royal family descended. The north end of town is dominated by the rocky mass on which Castrum Tunbergis was built in the thirteenth century by King Håkon Håkonsson. Though now only scraps of walls remain it was once Norway's largest medieval castle. A pleasant 3km (2 mile) stroll from the quay, following green signs, leads through the oldest street, Nordbyen, nestling beneath the Slottsfjellet. Beyond here, the blue trail forks left round the water to the birdtower and in an 8km (5 mile) loop through the countryside, but the green one circles up the far side of

The whaling monument at Sandefjord

Slottsfjellet, passing through the open-air museum on the way. The Vestfold Folkmuseum of which this is part is just to the left down the hillside. On top the remains of St Michael's Church (destroyed with the castle in 1503) are laid out like a ground plan beside the view-tower. The route back to the quay descends past the church and through the memorial park with its unusual glass mosaic by Per Vigeland and typical Gustav Vigeland mother and child statue — he is the artist who created the Vigeland sculpture park in Oslo.

Sandefjord, the next town south, is characterised by its connections with the whaling industry. These are epitomised in the magnificent whaling monument on the waterfront and the Whaling Museum with its exhibition of whale hunting from Stone Age man to modern research and protective techniques. Its Maritime Museum shows the town's wider interests with displays of ship designs from Viking longboats to supertankers, while the Town Museum has room settings and workshops from various periods. South of Sande–fjord on the Jåberg road one can visit several age old attractions. There are Bronze Age rock carvings of boats and spiral figures at **Haugen** (just beyond the first farm along Haugenveien) and across the railway at **Jåberg** the 'interest' signs lead to Istrehaugen grave–field, a complex of standing stones in circles and ship shapes. Other graves and the old trading settlement are on the coast at **Kaupang** beyond Viksfjord.

Larvik, the last of the Vestfold coastal towns is a ferry port with connections to Frederikshavn in Denmark. As often happens, the most interesting part of town is on the waterfront. Here an old customs building contains the Nautical Museum with material relating to both Colin Archer, the local shipbuilder who constructed the polar ship *Fram* and to Thor Heyerdahl's expeditions. Follow the road as it curls upwards to reach the church, built by Duke Ulrik Frederik Gydenløve in 1677. Circle past the 'hospital', an eighteenth-century stone building that was Larvik's first old people's home and across the main road at the roundabouts to the Herregården which he also built. This is one of Norway's best preserved wooden buildings with interesting and unusual interiors. Hewn into a rock opposite, a series of inscriptions commemorate various royal visits to Larvik. The other point of interest is King Håkons Spring, beside the Farris Hotel. It is Norway's only mineral spring, bottled and sold by the factory next door.

It is possible to connect these coastal towns into a loop using the Lågen river valley for the return route. Return from Larvik on the E18 towards Sandefjord, turning left on the minor road beyond the river. This leads north to **Hedrum**'s early medieval church. The south door reflects those early origins with its two carved heads; the lower is Frøy, the Viking god of fertility, upturned to represent the devil. Inside there are several medieval wooden figures but the 1589 pulpit and 1664 altar are more striking. Where this road joins the 304, **Meløstranda** is a bathing place on the Astrumvatnet and where the 304 turns across the Lågen towards **Kvelde**, salmon fishing is a popular activity in the rapids, either from the flat rocks of the shore or from hired rowing boats anchored midstream. Hedrum Bygdetun in Kvelde has a well-furnished house, weaving exhibitions, domestic and farm equipment and a picture of Winston Churchill.

Join the 8 here and head north towards **Styrvoll** where at the Trollfoss falls beside the road there are flat rocks for sunbathers and safe pools for paddlers. Further on at **Svarstad** an interesting loop can be made through typical hinterland scenery. Turn left up the Hærlandselva valley, rising steadily to Surila and beyond. The tollroad to Olmholtfjell leads to an area of lakes and walks. Beyond here one drops quite steeply down to Passebekk and the Lågen valley again. Go right for Hvittingfoss, admiring **Komnes** church where it sits high across the valley. This is a pretty section passing through small farms and between verges rich with summer flowers. Do not cross the river but continue south to **Brufoss** with its camping and picnic sites. This is the northern end of a 5km (3 mile) stretch of salmon fishing — permits and details from the information centre on

Høyjord has the only stave church in Vestfold

site. Now join the 8 going north to Skjerven, then right and right and right again to reach **Høyjord** and Vestfold's only stave church. The main body dates from 1150; the ship or chancel from 1275. The chancel has a restored barrel roof decorated with Biblical medallions — Old Testament one side, New Testament the other. From here the 306 takes you back across country to Kirkebakken on the outskirts of Horten.

To connect instead from Vestfold into Telemark, leave Larvik on the 301 for the interesting little town of **Stavern**. Park in the centre for a cultural walk. Immediately beyond the shops lies the eighteenth-century naval base of Fredriksvern wharf. Although still used today — as an airforce training school — one can walk through in summer, past modern barrack huts beautiful with roses, across the water to the original yellow wood complex of protected buildings. One of them houses a small museum to local naval hero, Tordenskiold. Across the harbour one can see the citadel built to provide extra seaward defence. Immediately outside the far perimeter fence one turns right for the Minnehallen or Hall of Remembrance to Norway's merchant seamen who died during both World Wars. Circling outside the fence leads to the road back into the centre of Stavern. On rocks beyond the road stand two blockhouses built to protect the wharf from landward attack. The church's eighteenth-century interior includes galleries all round, with glassed-in boxes including one for royal visitors. The altar is elaborate Baroque and there is a most unusual clock over the centre aisle above the patterned brick floor. Turn down beside the church to reach the small park with the old watering pumps at its centre, surrounded by more eighteenth-century garrison buildings. It is then just a step back to the carpark.

Nevlunghavn, on the final point of Vestfold, is also worth visiting. A fishing port of whitewashed houses and colourful gardens, its picturesque harbour is host to pleasure craft. It is a pleasant place for strolls and there is camping and bathing nearby. Leaving on the 302, just north of the Tvedalen turning, **Halle** *mølle* (mill) has been restored and opens summer weekends for special events — but the Tvedalen road is the one that leads into Telemark. At Langangen it passes under the toll bridges up the old corkscrew road to eventually join the E18 some kilometres further on.

Before exploring the interior of Telemark one can look at its brief stretch of coast. The E18 towards Kristiansand takes one to **Brevik**, another narrow wooden coastal town with pretty gardens. A map from the tourist office is essential. The eighteenth-century Rådhus on the island at the end is now Brevik's Town Museum containing an old shop, items from sailing ships and a home front section from World War II. Behind the town is a *dammene* area of old water supply lakes, now a nature reserve with walks and a lookout point over the Eidsfjord. It is similar to the one at Kristiansund though less neat.

Over the suspension bridge and immediately right takes one to Langesund, past the Bamble Museum at **Eikgård** to **Langesund**. This town is a smaller version of Brevik with a tiny crafts exhibition and fishing museum in Cudrio's boathouse. Similar again but by far the busiest of the three is **Kragerø**. For a scenic route to it, leave the E18 when signposted Fossing. This road passes lakes and fjords with rocks, trees, abundant wild flowers and bright homesteads. The coast at Kragerø is both rocky and islanded. The town itself is closely packed and hilly, its 'suburbs' built upwards. The viewpoint overlooking it is reached from the *stadion*. A small car ferry crosses from here to Stabbestad and one could circle back from there. Alternatively return on the 38, pausing perhaps at the Berg Kragerø Museum on the way out of town. In a lovely manor house overlooking the Hellefjord, there are seventeenth- and eighteenth-century objects to admire. Cross the E18 and continue towards Drangedal. The views

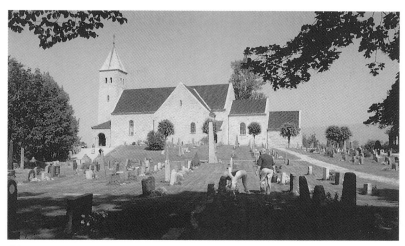

Gjerpen

over Nedre Tokke are especially lovely. Circle round its top on the 356 for Porsgrunn, twisting and undulating through rocky treeclad hills and past lakes.

This road eventually reaches **Porsgrunn** along a waterfront spoilt by industry, past the porcelain factory where groups can have guided tours. Most of Porsgrunn's attractions are in this area. The west church this side of the river and the east beyond are both mid-eighteenth century and the latter contains a unique collection of church chairs. Also beyond the bridge are the Maritime and Town Museums, both well worth a visit. **Skien** is the next town north and makes much of its connections with the playwright Henrik Ibsen. He was born in the centre of town in 1828 and lived as a child on a farm to the north called Venstøp. This is now a museum furnished in period and containing mementoes of his family. More are to be found in the Historical Museum in the manor house in Brekkeparken, overlooking the town. This is set in landscaped gardens with flowers, pavilions and delightful statues ranging from chickens to a bear. Ibsen also lived for a few months in a house in Snipetorp before leaving Skien, only ever to return once more. A statue of him stands in the park before the twin-spired church which flaunts a wealth of internal decoration.

While in the Skien area one could also make a diversion north on the 316 to Siljan church, passing **Gjerpen** church on the way and also Holtesletta campsite with its bathing area in an inlet of the lake.

Siljan church is medieval, with a font from AD950. The chancel has two unique red ship paintings probably from AD1200 and a blue ship painting in the nave of a 1600 sailing vessel. But the real purpose of going to Skien is to follow the Telemark canal northwards into the heart of that district. By means of lakes, rivers and locks it is possible to travel 150km (93 miles) from the sea at Brevik to the high mountain plateau of the north. From Skien daily passenger services on the 1882 *Victoria* travel to Dalen and the more modern 'Telemark' cruises to Notodden. They can be joined at various points along the way and bus services link with the boats. The best place to see the locks is the Ulefoss area. **Ulefoss** is an industrial town with sawmills, power-plants and an iron industry spoiling the waterfront but it does have redeeming features. The poorly signed Holla church ruins on a hill above the town give good views over the Norsjø whose northern shore is covered in apple blossom in the spring.

Øvre Verket, just before the new bridge, is a preserved workers' quarter with one cottage furnished as it might have been when housing an ironworker, his wife and ten children. Others stage craft sales. Beyond the bridge Hovedgård manor, the home of local indus-trial magnates, the Aall family, is possibly Norway's best Empire style house. In gleaming white, capped with a black dome it sits high above the river. Visiting is by guided tour. Nearby Lille Ulefoss, once the dower house, now holds art exhibitions and cultural activities. Returning over the old bridge, Ulefoss's three locks are down below, helping craft past the dam of the Aall powerplant, but the best locks are northwards at **Vrångfoss** where a flight of five raise river traffic past the next dam. From here either continue on the unsurfaced road or return to the 359. The latter passes more locks at **Lunde** (leave the 359 here) and **Kjeldal** before the two routes join at the pretty village of **Flåbygd**. From here a new road teeters high along the mountainside to Kilen.

The next stop is Kviteseid old church and *bygdetun* and there are two routes to reach them. One can turn left at Kilen and head for the ferry to Fjågesund but these are infrequent, particularly in the morn-ings. Alternatively follow the Seljord road as it climbs up to Dalsvatn and beyond, turning left for Åsgrend when signed. Only parts of this route are surfaced but it is true off-the-beaten-track territory; high rock walls, tiny lakes, and isolated farms drying their hay in lines across the fields before storing it in the overhanging stilted store-houses that are often seen in *bygdetun* collections. Left on the E76 and then on the 39 takes one south past **Kviteseid** harbour, over the two bridges and then left to the old church and *bygdetun* . The first dates

Boats moored at Kviteseid

from 1150, a time when Christianity was but a veneer over pagan traditions, as the embattled dragons round the original porch suggest but it also contains an early eighteenth-century decorated ceiling. The museum has some splendidly carved storehouses — look for the eighteenth-century man complete with tailcoat, knee breeches and wig. There is also a sculpture display in the Utsondhalli commemorating local artist Gunnar Utsond.

Just south of here, **Vrådal** is a good centre from which to tour. The jointly owned hotels run activity programmes including trips to special events and cruises on the steam ship *Fram* along Lake Nisser as well as serving a good value *smorgåsbord* with plenty of choice, particularly of cold fish. Lake Nisser is long and thin with rather bare mountains on the far side. An interesting way to cut west across to Fyresdal in the next valley is to take the ferry to Fjone. However, it only runs on the hour between 7am and 6pm or 7am and 9pm depending on the season. One can drive all the way round the south of the lake and back but apart from camping and bathing there is little to do anywhere except at **Nisset**, just south of the Fyresdal turning and only a few kilometres short of **Fjone**. Here there is a nature trail, a fishing pond, an old road between burial mounds and the Nygård School Museum. The much signed *urløype* are ski tracks. Take the toll road to Fyresdal (it is in comparatively good condition). Where it turns over a bridge, follow the Jettegryte sign to a series of potholes in the smooth rocks leading down to the river. The water in them is crystal clear. It is a shame that the lakes further on have been dammed as unless the water level is high the banks appear scarred below the treeline. Arriving at the main road, turn right for **Fyresdal** where the *bygdetun* has labelled buildings including an open hearth home from about 1400 and a store hut from 1350. Just north of town, the tiny rune stone in a heathery compound is one of four that once marked a ring where local fights were held. The *gamal kyrkegård* soon after is an old cemetery.

When you meet the 38 at Krossli, take it towards Dalen pausing first at **Åmdalsverk** for a newly established mining museum. Coffee and waffles are served in the exhibition building where mining equipment and methods are displayed from as far back as 1540. There are also guided tours of the old copper mine. Beyond here, one of the most spectacular roads is the 45. Follow it right down into Dalen and up the other side to Eidsborg just for the views. Telemark is joined along Lake Bandak (the last stretch of the Telemark canal route), down to **Dalen** with its restored nineteenth-century hotel and across to the snow-capped mountains to the west. Even though a glance at the map will show that **Eidsborg** is very close to points reached later in this tour and need not be included here, it should not be omitted. The stave church is delightfully situated on a hillside above the lake. Behind it the Lårdal Museum has a comprehensive collection of old farm buildings and a purpose-built exhibition hall with painted furniture, traditional jewellery and costumes, and workshops once belonging to local tradesmen. The homemade fiddles are beautiful. A guided tour of the church is included in the ticket price.

For a large circle that takes in part of the Setesdal valley on its way to the north of Telemark and the Hardangervidda, return on the 45, admiring the views in the opposite direction, and head for Valle. At **Skafså** one passes the memorial museum to the sculptress Anna Grimdalen, a point to which one could cut across from the 38 without descending to Dalen. The scenery as the 45 cuts crosscountry is what most people envisage when they talk about Norway. It passes alongside lakes between mountains rising to well over 1,000m (3,280ft). Just before the descent to Rygnestad, watch for Gloppefoss to the right of the road. As is so often the case in these days of hydroelectricity it is only truly spectacular in the spring but it is still worth a glance. Soon after there are excellent views of snowy mountains and of the River Otra in the Setesdal valley way below.

On reaching the 12, the real aim is to travel north but a short loop south to Valle gives one a good idea of Setesdal and includes several

Sixteenth-century store house at the Rygnestad farm, Setesdal Museum

attractions. Take the new road as far as **Valle** where the suspension bridge across the river makes an adventure, especially for children, as it sways with every step. Just to the south, Tveitetunet, in a lovely sheltered site up the hillside, is one part of the Setesdal museum. It was once the home of the local sheriff, hence the prison hut! Almost opposite the Tveitetunet turning Hallandsbru spans a waterfall with potholes where the River Otra forces its way through harder rock. Return north from here on the old road, past the unusual domed rock north of Homme, rejoining the 12 towards Hovden. At **Flateland**, the **Rygnestad** farm is also part of the Setesdal museum. Occupied as a site from the fourteenth century, the main buildings are sixteenth century. Note the huge logs used to construct the first storehouse and the paucity of windows in the three storey house. It is hard to envisage it still being lived in as late as 1940.

Continuing north the next stop is at **Bykle**. The Byklestigen signposted before and between the tunnels, is the old packhorse trail that went steeply over the mountains the road now cuts through. Bykle itself has two quite different attractions. The tiny church looks nothing from the outside but the inside is beautifully rose painted. The fronts of the two galleries (one for men and one for young girls) are decorated with carved and painted Olav's roses. Earlier, simpler roses decorate the floorboards in the galleries and the ceiling is a sky with stars and clouds and God looking down on the congregation. Outside, a third part of the Setesdal museum perches high above

The snow-capped peaks of the Vågslidvidda from the old road

Bykle at Huldreheimen, 150m (492ft) up from the carpark. These six buildings are not in their original sites. While pausing to get breath back from the climb imagine the labour involved in re-erecting them here! The view is magnificent, from snowfields opposite to the valley floor below.

From here to Hovden the countryside is remarkably unoccupied, just the high plateau and the Otra river and its lakes. **Hovden** is set on the Hartevatn lake. There are boats and canoes for hire, fish to be caught and a network of hiking tracks in the neighbourhood. For the less energetic a culture trail has been laid round the Viking bog iron area which includes a museum with a Viking hut rebuilt on genuine foundations and a display on how they worked the iron. There is also a chair lift to Nos Peak for the views. It is in operation between mid-June to mid-August, Tuesday, Thursday 12noon-2pm, Sunday 11am-1pm. All around here are the high fells. Hovden lies at over 800m (2,624ft) — the surrounding peaks rise 4-500m (1,312-1,640ft) higher. Continuing north, the road runs between very modern snow poles and electric signs indicate conditions in winter. Every so often the roads drop into valleys as the 12 does here down to the E76 to Haukeligrend and one has spectacular views from the hairpin bends. The E76 is worth following westwards just to the first tunnel. Notice the number of trails (with official white signs) and paths (small brown boards) to either side. Any are worth exploring though the latter are poorly signed. Vinje tourist office can supply details. On

The church at Vinje

approaching the tunnel take the 60kph limit road to the right. This is the old road which has been repaired and leads up to magnificent views of snow-capped peaks. Either return the same way or through the tunnels. Back at **Edland**, the Haukeli exhibition shows artefacts and handicrafts around a central theme. Further on at **Mjonøy** there are regular handicraft demonstrations and at **Vinje** the church is interesting. The font dates from the twelfth century and the floorboards formed the walls of the original stave church. They are painted on what is now the underside as can be seen by the one standing in the vestry behind the altar. The other paintings in the cruciform church (ceiling, galleries, altar) all date from 1932.

From Vinje return north just to the Mo turning as it is time to leave the main Oslo/west coast highway and take to the byeways for a scenic detour. The road to Mo is delightful, a peaceful route beside Byrtevatnet. Beyond, go left for Liosvingen, then left and right across the 38 for Gøytil. This unsurfaced road hairpins high up the mountainside through flowering verges until, just before the 7km (4 miles) post, Ravnejuv (ravine gorge) is signed to the left. Follow the path but take care, particularly with children. It emerges onto a precipice with only a low rock wall between oneself and a sheer drop to the valley deep below. There is a strong up current. Continue through to the E76 again, going left for Åmot, then right on the 37 towards Rjukan and right again at Hyllandsfoss for Øyfjell, back on minor roads again. On reaching a T-junction, go towards Høydalsmo but only to the far edge of Øyfjell where there is a collection of everyday objects in the *bygdetun* ranging from a device to stop calves drinking their mother's milk to a huge wooden swan that would be filled with beer, with little swans swimming in it. The actual drinking was done with painted wooden bowls. Return through Øyfjell to the Nutheim turning. This road is lush early on with wild flowers.

On reaching the E76 again, go right for Seljord and right again into Flatedal village. Its closely packed farms, with barns and houses crowded together, is unusual for Norway. At **Seljord** it is possible to drive along either side of the lake on surfaced roads which rejoin at the far end for Bø district where there are a number of attractions. In **Bø** itself St Olav's church is the first of a trio of medieval churches that repay visiting. The interior is sixteenth and seventeenth century with painted gallery and altar and some puzzle paintings in the chancel referring to specific Bible verses. Two kilometres (1 mile) north at Oterhult Åheim General Store has been preserved as part of Bø district museum. Continue then on the 38 turning into **Gvarv** on the Notodden road. Here nineteenth-century wooden houses are preserved just off the main road to the right. The second church to visit is at **Nes** to the right through the Norsjø apple orchards. Its chancel has been called Scandinavia's Sistine Chapel for its wealth of medieval frescoes. There is a mid-seventeenth-century pulpit and altar and outside, pagan symbols decorate the old south entrance. Slightly further towards Notodden, **Sauherad** completes the trio. Although its construction is medieval the interior is mid-seventeenth century. The cartoon-like devils' heads all over the reverse of the chancel arch probably commemorate a fire which gutted the interior as frescoes, altar, pulpit all postdate 1660. The only older artefacts are a font cover and a stone sun with a cross inside it.

Return towards Gvarv and take the second road signposted to Hørte stopping at **Evju** *bygdetun*. Here there are guided tours of the main house with its collections of porcelain from Porsgrunn, Holland and England. Continue and go right, past the System-blokk factory, on a forest road that cuts through to the Skien/Notodden road; then right for Strupa. On meeting the E76 again, go left for **Heddal**. The *bygdetun* has a beautiful rose-painted guestchamber in the farmhouse with an interesting story attached to the girl's face painted inside a flower above the stove. Also on show is a cottar's

Gaustatoppen, Telemark's highest mountain

cottage demonstrating the contrasting way of life of the poor. Just down the road, Norway's largest stave church is a stopping-off point for all the coach tours.The interior has been painted twice — originally with processional figures and later with rose paintings.

The object now is to reach Rjukan in the north. At Sauland take the unnumbered (but surfaced), road across the mountains. There is another *bygdetun* at **Tuddal** with grass-roofed cottages and storehouses but the real joy of this road is the scenery as one climbs upwards to the bleakly lichened mountains that surround Telemark's highest peak, **Gaustatoppen**. It is possible to walk to the top of this 1,883m (6,176ft) mountain. Park at Heddersvatn information board for the 4km (2 mile) track that rises some 700m (2,296ft) on the way. The views from the top are magnificent. From here the road winds down to the steep and narrow valley where **Rjukan** was purpose-built by Norsk Hydro early in the twentieth century. In winter it must be a depressing place to live as for five whole months the sun never reaches the valley floor. To counteract this, in 1928 Norsk Hydro built the first cableway in northern Europe, to take workers up to the mountain plateau for the winter sun. In summer the area around the upper station burgeons into flower. A round walk of 8km (5 miles) is possible here on what in winter is a cross-country ski trail. In World War II Rjukan became famous for the Vemork power plant where heavy water was made by the Germans for their atom bomb programme. The plant now houses a national

The view from road 37 to Kongsberg

industrial workers' museum with a walk-through section devoted to the resistance story, another to workers' life in Rjukan and a whole series of work-it-yourself models on forms of energy. It is a good museum and worth the 15 minute climb from the bridge if the buses have stopped running for the day. Returning through Rjukan in the Kongsberg direction, the Tinn Museum, with twenty-seven buildings, has costumes as well as fully equipped houses from the Middle Ages up to this century, and a wide selection of tools.

Rjukan is also the gateway to the **Hardangervidda**. Two particular routes use boats to take one to the very edge of the National Park. The first, cruising up Møsvatn from Skinnarbu some 20km (12 miles) west of Rjukan, has the advantage of a quay right beside the main road. The object of the boat is to carry hikers to Mogen from where they can spend days at a time on the plateau. Scenically this is the best area to visit but there are few overnight huts. If a hiking holiday is too strenuous, one can taste the scenery 4 days a week when the cruise up the lake and back gives a couple of hours at the top. The other trip involves a 40km (25 mile) drive on the Kalhovd road from Atrå (east of Rjukan) to Stegaros for the boat to Marbu. The day trip here gives longer at the top and there are more overnight huts for hikers. Check timetables for both routes at the Rjukan tourist office or local hotels.

From Rjukan the 37 goes all the way to Kongsberg. Where it passes **Mael** church one can see the train ferries on the other side of Lake Tinnsjø, a reminder that this was where the Resistance workers blew up the heavy water train in the last war — the tourist cinema in Rjukan usually shows the film 'Heroes of the Telemark' twice weekly in the summer season. The road circles the north of the lake, then cuts higher across the hills and past lakes to **Kongsberg**. Although out of Telemark, this city is the obvious exit point towards Oslo and a major attraction in its own right. The name means King's City and dates back to the official discovery of silver, a royal metal, in 1623. (Official because a young cowherd accidentally finding some, revealed in his excitement what had previously been a well kept local secret.) The old mine at Saggrenda is now a very interesting museum where a mine train takes you 1km ($^1/_2$ mile) into the mountain to tour both old and newer workings. The Mining Museum in the centre of town has a wonderful treasure room with lumps of raw silver in imaginatively named shapes. It also houses a Mint Museum and the National Ski Museum. Look out for the unusual statues on the old bridge and in the park by the river. Do not miss the skijumper in mid air! The Lågsdal Folk Museum is also imaginative with excellent detail. From here, Oslo is only an hour's drive away on the E76/E18.

Further Information

— Vestfold and Telemark —

Åmdalsverk
Mine Museum
Open: June to August daily 10am-5pm.

Åsgårdstrand
Munch's House
Open: May to September, Saturday and Sunday 1-7pm. June to August, Tuesday to Sunday 1-7pm.

Bø
Åheim General Store
Open: mid-June to mid-August daily 12noon-6pm.

Brevik
Town Museum
Open: mid-July to early August, Monday to Saturday 11am-2pm.

Bykle
Church
Open: mid-June to mid-August, Monday to Friday 10am-5pm. Saturday and Sunday 12noon-5pm.

Huldreheimen
Open: mid-June to mid-August, Monday to Friday 10am-6pm. Saturday and Sunday 12noon-6pm.

Edland
Haukeli Exhibition
Open: June to early August daily 10am-7pm.

Eidsborg
Lårdal Museum and Stave Church
Open: June to August daily 11am-5pm.

Eikgård
Bamble Museum
Open: June to early August Tuesday,
Friday to Sunday 1-6pm.

Evju
Bygdetun
Open: late May to mid-August daily
12noon-5pm.

Fyresdal
Bygdetun
Open: late June to end August,
Monday to Friday. Tours at 11am,
1pm, 3pm. Saturday 11am- 2pm.
Sunday 3-6pm.

Halle
Mill
Open: July to mid-August, Saturday
10am-5pm. Sunday 12noon-5pm.

Heddal
Bygdetun
Open: July to mid-August daily
11am-5pm.

Stave Church
Open: mid-May to late June and late
August to mid-September, Monday
to Saturday 10am-5pm. Sunday
12.30-5pm. Late June to late August
9am-7pm. Sunday 12.30-7pm.

Hedrum
Church
Open: late June to mid-August daily
10am-7pm.

Horten
Lifeboat Museum
Open: April to September, Friday to
Sunday 12noon-4pm.

Naval Museum
Open: May to September, Monday to
Friday 12noon-3pm. Saturday and
Sunday 12noon-4pm.

Preus Fotomuseum
Open: all year Monday to Friday
10am-2pm. Sunday 12noon-2pm.

Veteran Car Museum
Open: mid-June to mid-August daily
12noon-2pm. Mid-August to end
September, Sunday 12noon-3pm.

Hovden
Bog Iron Museum
Open: mid-June to mid-August daily
11am-6pm.

Kongsberg
Lågsdal Folk Museum
Open: mid-May to end June and
August daily 11am-3.30pm. July,
Thursday to Tuesday 11am-3.30pm.
Wednesday 11am-7pm.

*Norwegian Mining, Mint and Ski
Museums*
Open: mid-May to end June and mid
to end August daily 10am-4pm. July
to mid-August, Monday to Friday
10am-6pm. Saturday and Sunday
10am-4pm.

Silver Mine
Open: mid to end May and mid to
end August. Tours daily at 12.30pm.
June to mid-August at 11am,
12.30pm, 2pm.

Kragerø
Berg Kragerø Museum
Open: mid-May to late June and mid-
August to mid-September, Sunday
12noon-5pm. Late June to mid-
August, Tuesday to Friday 12noon-
3pm. Sunday 12noon-5pm.

Kvelde
Hedrum Bygdetun
Open: July to August, Sunday 1-6pm.

Kviteseid
Old Church and Bygdetun
Open: June to August daily 12noon-
5pm. July daily 10am-5pm.

Langesund
Cudrio's Fishing Museum
Open: mid-June to mid-August,

Monday to Friday 11am-4pm. Saturday 11am-2pm.

Larvik
Church
Open: all year Tuesday to Friday 10am-12noon.

Herregården
Open: mid-May to mid-June and rest August, Sunday 1-7pm. Mid-June to early August, Monday to Friday 3-7pm. Saturday 1-5pm. Sunday 1-7pm.

Nautical Museum
Open: mid-June to late August daily 2-6pm.

Mjonøy
Culture Centre
Open: July to early August, Monday to Saturday 10am-6pm. Sunday 1-7pm.

Øyfjell
Bygdetun
Open: July to early August, Monday to Saturday 11am-5pm. Sunday 1-6pm.

Porsgrunn
Maritime and Town Museums
Open: June to August, Monday to Friday 10am-1pm. Saturday 12noon-2pm. Sunday 12noon-3pm.

Rjukan
Krossobanen Cablecar
Open: May to late June and late August to end September daily 10am-5pm. Late June to late August daily 10am-7pm.

Tinn Museum
Open: late June to early August daily 12noon-6pm.

Vemork Industrial Workers Museum
Open: May to mid-June and mid-August to end September, Monday

to Friday 10am-4pm. Saturday and Sunday 10am-6pm. Mid-June to mid-August daily 10am-6pm.

Rygnestad
Bygdetun
Open: mid to end June and early August daily 11am-5pm. July daily 10am-6pm.

Sandefjord
Maritime, Town and Whaling Museums
Open: May to September, Monday to Saturday 11am-4pm. Sunday 11am-5pm. Thursday also 3-7pm.

Skafså
Anna Grimdalen Memorial Museum
Open: June to August daily 10am-5pm.

Skien
Brekkeparken
Open: mid-May to late August daily 12noon-8pm.

Church
Open: June to August, Monday to Saturday 9.30am-3.30pm.

Historical Museum
Brekkeparken
Open: mid-May to late June, Monday to Friday 10am-2pm. Saturday 12noon-4pm. Sunday 12noon-4pm. Sunday 12noon-6pm. Late June to late August, Monday to Saturday 12noon-4pm. Sunday 12noon-6pm.

Ibsen's Venstøp
Open: June to August daily 12noon-4pm.

Stavern
Fredriksvern Wharf
Open: June to August daily 9am-8pm.

Marine Museum
Open: June to August daily 12noon-4pm.

Minnehallen
Open: mid-May to end August daily
11am-6pm.

Tønsberg
Slottsfjellet Tower
Open: May to midsummer, Monday
to Friday 10am-3pm. Saturday and
Sunday 12noon-5pm. Midsummer to
end August daily 11am-6pm.

Vestfold Folkmuseum
Open: mid-May to mid-September,
Monday to Saturday 10am-5pm.
Sunday 12noon-5pm.

Tuddal
Bygdetun
Open: late June to early August,
Monday to Saturday 11am-6pm.
Sunday 12noon-7pm.

Ulefoss
Hovedgård
Open: mid-June to mid-August,
Monday to Friday 2-4pm. Saturday
12noon-3pm. Sunday 12noon-6pm.

Øvre Verket
Open: mid-June to mid-August daily
11am-6pm.

Valle
Tveitetunet
Open: July daily 11am-5pm.

Vinje
Church
Open: July to early August, Monday
to Saturday 11am-6pm. Sunday 1-
7pm.

Tourist Information Centres

Brevik
Fisketorget
3950 Brevik
☎ (035) 70200
Open: summer only.

Horten I Borre
Torvet 6A
3190 Horten
☎ (033) 43390

Hovden
Hovden Ferie
4695 Hovden
☎ (043) 39630

Kongsberg
Schwabes Gate 1
3600 Kongsberg
☎ (037) 31526

Larvik
Storgate 20
3250 Larvik
☎ (034) 82623

Rauland
Austbø Hotel
3864 Rauland
☎ (036) 73425

Rjukan/Tinn
3660 Rjukan
☎ (036) 91290

Sandefjord
Rådhuset
3200 Sandefjord
☎ (034) 65300

Skien
Kverndalen 8
3700 Skien
☎ (03) 528227

Tønsberg
Storgate 55
3100 Tønsberg
☎ (033) 14819

Valle
4690 Valle
☎ (043) 31056

Vrådal
Toms Sportservice
3853 Vrådal
☎ (036) 56302

Vinje
3890 Ytre Vinje
☎ (036) 71300

2 • Norwegian Glaciers and Mountains

The Jostedal glacier and the Jotunheim mountains are, with the Sogne and Hardanger fjords, the best known areas of Norway. With the largest glacier in mainland Europe and mountains rising to over 2,000m (6,560ft), the scenery is spectacular. Transport by road and water is good and access comparatively easy with Oslo and Bergen each only a day's drive away. No wonder its major attractions have long been part of the tourist trail. It has nevertheless been included here for the less well known routes and activities that are also available but do not yet feature on the average coach tour.

Many of these activities are necessarily connected to the glacier — guided glacier walks, summer skiing and plane or helicopter flights over it, for example. Rock climbing and mountain hikes are other obvious possibilities with hang gliding for the bird's eye view. Boat trips, boat hire, canoeing and wind-surfing are available on the fjords along with swimming and fishing. There are several stave churches, some excellent museums, and a selection of farms that open their premises to visitors once or twice a week. However the main attraction is the scenery, with a good pair of waterproof boots a prerequisite for enjoying this at close quarters!

The whole area can nowadays be circumnavigated, the Fjærland to Skei road having completed the circle in the late 1980s. But although one can hike over the centre, there are no traffic routes across. Thus exploration involves diversions into the interior and out again on the same route so allow plenty of time for each excursion. The starting point for this chapter is Lom, because of its road access from Oslo but from Bergen one could well start at Hella on the Sognefjord, or if arriving by fast boat, at Leikanger, a few kilometres away.

Lom has a large stave church with a beautifully constructed roof bound together with St Andrew's crosses beneath Norman arches. There are wood carvings, a painted ceiling in the choir, and a collection of early eighteenth-century religious paintings. Outside the wall stands a monument to Olav, who in 1021 converted his people to Christianity. There is also an open-air museum with twenty-one

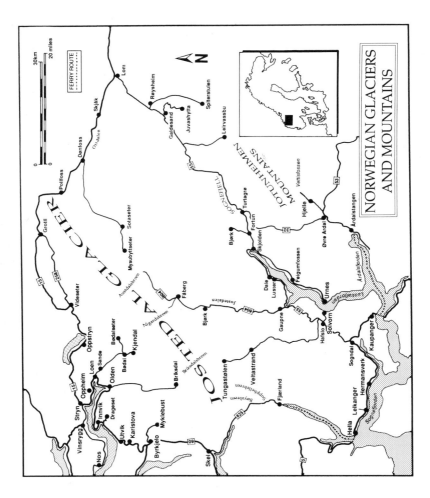

different buildings, a geological museum and a very good tourist shop — one wonders how many people take time to follow the Soleggen footpath behind the commune centre, climbing to 1,000m (3,280ft) up the hillside!

From Lom the 55 goes all the way through to Sogndal. Further down the valley there are a number of toll roads leading up into the Jotunheim mountains. The first, from Røisheim, follows the Visdal valley to the Spiterstulen seter complex. This is a well-labelled road, naming hills and bridges. At Smiugjelsøygården, where a waterfall passes under the road, paths in the woods lead to the edge of the river, rushing through a small gorge. The 18km (11 miles) long road,

*The waterfront at
Åsgårdstrand, Vestfold
(Chapter 1)*

*A carved wooden storehouse at
Kviteseid Open Air Museum in
Telemark (Chapter 1)*

The Briksdal arm of the Jostedal glacier, Norway (Chapter 2)

Barnesfjord near Sogndal, Norway (Chapter 2)

Barnesfjord near Sogndal

once the route from Lom to Oslo, gradually climbs to 1,100m (3,608ft). Here a number of old buildings have been gathered together and are let out as rooms and cottages. The main one, the Hugubygnaden, was one built in 1934. Inside all sorts of curiosities and mementoes hang on the walls. The main activities are fell walking, with Norway's highest mountain, Galdhøpiggen, a mere 4 hours away on a good path and sixteen other mountains all over 2,300m (7,544ft) high within a days trip. Glacier hikes with a local guide are also provided. Although this is not the main Jostedal glacier, the same rules apply here. All glaciers are living and potentially dangerous. Although they may seem unmoving, sections can suddenly break off and crevasses appear. One should never walk under the edge of one nor venture onto it without a guide.

The second toll road, from Galdesand, is signed to the **Galdhøpiggen** summer ski centre and to Juvashytta. This climbs much higher, to 1,840m (6,035ft), making it the highest road in northern Europe and giving panoramic views over the mountains of the Jotunheim. Here Knut O. Vole, a pioneer in mountain guiding, built the first lodge in 1884. Enlarged several times since, this is now a centre for guided glacier excursions to the summit of Galdhøpiggen and for the nearby summer ski school. It also has rooms to let and a cafeteria. Incidentally, clouds across the road on the way up do not necessarily mean that the mountain tops are shrouded too. The very cold of the glacier frequently prevents them hanging on it. The third toll road goes to Leirvassbu Fjellstua.

Beyond here the 55 traverses bleak Breiseterdalen climbing to 1,434m (4,704ft) and then maintaining similar height for up to 20km (12 miles) through the summer wonderland of snow patches and icy lakes that is **Sognefjell**. Here there can be snow walls 4 to 5m (13 to 16ft) high beside the road in August and cross country skiing throughout the year. Eventually it drops, with views, of course, through a series of hairpins to the Turtagrø hotel from where an interesting mountain road travels the 32km (20 miles) to Årdal. It is a toll road but surfaced all the way. Early on one can see the Sognefjell road zig-zagging up the hillside. The panorama of snowy peaks ahead are the Hurrungane, some of the wildest of the Jotunheim range, and the Jostedal glacier is also visible to the north-west as the road climbs to 1,315m (4,313ft). At the far end it drops down an impressive succession of hairpins into Øvre Årdal, a town that loses its charm the nearer one gets! Heading for the 53, the Hjelle road to the left just before the bridge goes up to the Vettis farm — a trip that in season can be done by horse and buggy. From here a half hour's walk brings one to the 275m (902ft) free fall of the **Vettisfossen** — a worthwhile hike provided one's footwear is sound! A drier walk can be had by following the 53 in the Tyin direction until just after the third tunnel. Park here and follow the old road up the hillside opposite, admiring the construction of its hairpin bends constructed by migrant workers long ago, as well as the magnificent views across the Jotunheim mountains and down to the fjord far below.

The through route, however, to bring one back to glacier territory is the 53 in the other direction, for **Årdalstangen**. While, waiting for the ferry to Kaupanger, one can admire the outside of the stave-style church. The Dagfinn stone by its main gate was probably found under the step of the original stave church. It dates back to the fourteenth century. There is also a copper exhibition in the eighteenth-century turf-roofed house down by the quay. Note the names in the glass windows. The ferry trip along Årdalsfjord takes $1^1/_2$ hours so the ferries are infrequent and you need to time your journey. Arriving on the quay at **Kaupanger**, the new Sognefjord Boat Museum is immediately to the left. Purpose-built round its largest exhibit, a merchant sloop that traded with Bergen, it contains a varied collection of boats from the posh 'carriages' of the rich (the fjords were their roads) to the practical ice sled that would float if the ice cracked beneath it. Just along the road is the stave church. The staves are the columns that support the roof and here there are eight each side, giving the church a far longer nave than was usual, but then, the whole church is large for its type, possibly because Kaupanger was an important market in the Middle Ages. The pulpit, altar and wall paintings are all seventeenth century. A few kilometres up the road, one passes the Sogn Folkemuseum. Here farms and individual houses have been rebuilt to produce a living museum environment complete with animals. The modern exhibition building contains a comprehensive series of displays ranging from the farming year, to women's life, to village shops and an early bank. Don't miss the English notes hung up at intervals. From here the road continues just a short way north to Sogndal where it meets the following alternative route.

While the Turtagrø-Årdal-Kaupanger route is interesting in its own right, it bypasses the first accessible stretch of glacier, therefore one might prefer to continue down the 55 from Turtagrø. As it drops beyond Oppheim, watch for the appearance of **Fortun** below in the valley bottom. With its white church and the milky turquoise river running through, it is one of the prettiest villages in Norway. **Bjørk**, which is signed from Fortun, is one of several farms taking part in a new venture to introduce the tourist to Norwegian farming. Bjørk specialises in milk and berry production and a trip there includes a traditional farmhouse lunch. The excursion only operates one day a week and should be booked through the Sogndal tourist office. On reaching the fjordside at Skjolden, a diversion can be made to Urnes stave church passing Feigumfoss on the way; however the ferry that links across to Solvorn is privately owned and only runs twice a day. It is simpler to stick to the 55 and take the boat trip from Solvorn which is discussed later on in this chapter. Stop first in **Luster** for Dale church. Built in 1250, its stone walls are 1.5m (5ft) thick, with corners, windows and door frames made of soapstone. This is softer, allowing the beautiful carving round the old main entrance. Look for the early medieval crucifix on the chancel wall and the three stages of fresco painting. While in Luster one can also take trips in a Viking boat on the fjord and possibly by cable car up the hillside. Further on, watch for Feigumfoss to appear on the far side of the fjord. Its 218m (715ft) fall, with drift of spray, is clearly visible from Høyheimsvik, and in season boat trips from Solvorn take one across for a closer look.

At **Gaupne** the tiny dark wooden church also contains murals or, for something more modern, try a helicopter flight over the glacier! For Gaupne is the gateway to this side of the Jostedalsbreen. From Gaupne the 604 travels through **Jostedalen**, which still boasts a broad river with waterfalls dropping down the mountainsides to it,

The tongue of the Nigardsbreen glacier

despite Statkraft's many HEP projects in the valley. Their Jostedal power station, half way up the valley, has guided tours and their construction roads are open to the public. The one just beyond Bruheim church (over the second bridge and fork right at the construction sign) hairpins for 9km (6 miles) up the mountainside to bring you level with the mountain tops and the Jostedal snowfield behind their peaks. It goes without saying that there are also stupendous views down into the valley. Just a little beyond where their road forks up the hill, the valley road bridges the **Geisfossen**. This gives close-ups of the main fall at the bottom — the triple falls that combine to make it can best be seen further along the 604. From Gjerde, it is possible to reach the **Bergsetbre**. As one drives along the road one can see its impressive 1,000m (3,280ft) wall of glacial ice hanging at the end of the valley. From the Bergset farm it takes about an hour to walk to its foot along quite an easy but boggy path. Back on the 604 the next turning left leads, via a toll road, to **Nigardsbreen**, where a variety of glacier walks, including family specials, take place every day, properly guided with full equipment provided for participants. All one needs is solid enough shoes for the crampons to be fixed on safely. There is also a regular boat service across the lake to this sprawling tongue of the glacier. The information boards by the roadside show the retreat of the glacier over the past two centuries but for the last 10 years it has been almost stationary and, with more snow falling in winter than is melting in summer, scientists estimate that by the year 2000 it should have crept back down to its lake. At present, however, one should allow 25 minutes from the landing stage to the glacier and longer to work along to the best vantage points from which to study its imposing blue frontage — let alone to find one's way back across the rocks to the boat! Beyond the Nigardsbreen turning, one can continue to Fåberg and then turn left for the Stygevatn dam on the construction road from where one can see the Austdalbre reaching into the edge of the lake. To accomplish all these activities and include the Turtagrø-Årdal-Kaupanger route as well — one really needs to stay in the area for several days.

South of Gaupne, at **Hafslo**, one last expedition can be made to this side of the glacier. Follow the Veitastrond road through the Hafslo farmlands, along the boulder-strewn shore of Veitastrondsvatnet, through several long tunnels and past a farm offering boats for hire and fishing licences, through the connected villages beyond the lake to the toll road to **Tungastølen**. This is another of the farms now open to tourists, like Bjørk. Twice a week it offers goat farming with the production of cheese in the old way. In addition, any day of the week, one may park at the farm and follow the track over easy moraine territory to the Austerdalsbreen. Allow 4 to 5 hours for the round walk.

Back on the 55 travelling south, the **Solvorn** turning is soon reached. This unspoilt sea village is the place to catch the motor launch for **Urnes** stave church. Invisible from this side of the fjord, it is Norway's oldest stave church, containing a medieval altar, bishop's chair and chandelier; decorations and pews from the Reformation, and seventeenth-century murals. It is included on Unesco's World Heritage list, along with the rock carvings at Alta. The next town, where the 55 meets the 5 and the route up from Kaupanger, is Sogndal; then it is along the Sogndalsfjord to join the longest tourist attraction of them all, the **Sognefjord**. Leikanger kommune is one of Norway's major fruit growing areas, with trees in blossom at the end of May. The climate here is mild and this is probably the reason for the size and age of the oak by the roadside in front of the *Tinghus* (Council House). It is 25m (79ft) high, almost 5m (16ft) round its trunk and supposedly 400 years old! In the vicarage garden behind the church even rarer trees grow. On the way to Hella, to catch the ferry for Fjærland one also passes the Kvinnefoss waterfall, right beside the main road.

Fjærland is the gateway to more branches of the glacier. Six ferries a day leave Hella for the trip up the long narrow valley. A glacier centre opened in Fjaerland in June 1991. Its two local branches of the

Fjærland valley looking towards Bøyabreen

Jostedalbreen are the **Supphellebreen** and the **Bøyabreen**. The former has retreated so high up the mountain face that although its upper edge is a beautiful blue, it is disappointingly out of reach and spoilt by its dirty skirt of snow. The latter, just before the tunnel on the new through road, is a much more imposing sight, descending the rock wall in good tones of blue, though it too stops short, with bare rock and the grey skirt below. The tunnel is 6,385m (4 miles) long, bringing one out the far side of the mountains for Skei. Turn right here for Byrkjelo through steepsided Våtedalen with its broad river and herds of goats. In Byrkjelo, go right for Utvik and right again for Myklebust. This minor road passes some very good waterfalls dropping down the mountainsides to **Sandal** where, on a still day, the snowfields are reflected in the lake. One can walk at the end of the road on the climbing track that gives views over the lake, or from Sandal there are signed walks of 3, 4, and 10km (2, 3 and 6 miles). There is also fishing in the lake.

Back on the 60, the road climbs out over the hills towards the

A timber road above Utvik

Nordfjord. The views down and towards the mountains and snow-fields are, of course, excellent. At the 600m mark, the monument on the right is to Gabriel Reed, skiing pioneer. Pause next at the Kari-stova café for the first views down into the Innvikfjord from its terrace. This a lovely stretch of road giving view after view as it sweeps down the hillside. For a pleasant walk, park at the second hairpin and stroll along the timber road opposite. Clustered round the church at the bottom of the hill is **Utvik**, with the priest's tithe barn dating from 1719 still standing at the end of the row of sheds opposite the church. Its cut under shape is typical of the older barns one usually finds in open-air museums. Along the fjord at Innvik, the local road rising up the valley also gives views but Innvik itself is not as pretty a village. There are more views to be had from the Singer monument, commemorating American millionaire painter William Singer and his wife, who lived in Olden for many years. Their home is signed behind the Yris hotel on the Briksdalbreen road. Given by Mrs Singer as a holiday home for nurses, the studio cottage below it houses an exhibition of his work.

The Briksdalbreen is what everyone associates with **Olden**. It is the prettiest glacier in Norway (some would say in Europe and beyond) and deserves to be on the tourist trail, with its coach parties to the café and the option beyond of a jaunting car pulled by the Norwegian *fjording*. Alternatively one can walk up the track, remembering a mackintosh for the waterfall's spray. There is still a kilometre ($^1/_2$

mile) to walk past where the jaunting cars stop but the walk (allow 45 minutes from the café) is worth it for the sight of the glacier filling the end of the valley with a fat paw of palest blue. The path signed Kattanakken that you pass goes up to the edge of the glacier at 1,800m (5,901ft). It is about 3 to 4 hours each way.

Less visited is the **Kjendal** glacier, reached along Lodalen from Loen. A lot of walks are signed off this road and the information at Loen or at the various camp sites should give details of these. Notice the white scar high up the rock face of Ramnefjell across the valley. Two disastrous rock falls took place here, the first in 1905 and the second in 1936. Both caused huge tidal waves that crushed boats and houses and killed a total of 135 people. A plaque on the cliff wall commemorates the deaths. Opposite the remains of the pleasure steamer are still visible among the trees. Just beyond there one has to pay a toll. Watch out for the Jørpe rock to the left (20 tons of boulder moved by the wind off avalanches) and for the bent down silver birch. The glacier, curling blue-edged down the valley, is prettier from a distance than close up. From the parking it takes 15 minutes to reach the warning sign but beyond there the blue upper area disappears and one is left with grey-topped ice!

On the return down the valley a possible diversion is up the toll road to Bodalseter. No toll roads are particularly good as they are private roads with no state maintenance. This is a poor example although it does have the compensation of running beside an excellent tumbling river with several good waterfalls and of giving views of the edge of Bodalsbreen rising jagged between the peaks. Park after about 4.2km (3 miles) — walking boots are essential to complete the last kilometre to the *seter* (summer pasture).

Beyond Loen, take the minor road up to Oppheim. This gives splendid views across to Olden and less splendid ones to Loen which is nowhere near as picturesque a place! The next town, the north-westerly point of this circular tour, is Stryn but before turning east to return to Lom it is worth going beyond the town along the north shore of the Innvikfjord, first on the 15, then left on the 613 for Hopland. This is a high road, rising to 300m (984ft) just before the viewpoint at Nos. From there one can see along the Utfjord. Returning the same way there are views from Bergset across to Utvik, just before the pine 'Vetestova' sign. This points up a toll road but it is not too far to park at the bottom and walk. The 'Vetestova' is the last remaining vestige of King Håkon's tenth-century system of warning beacons. In very good repair, it is the shelter used by the beacon minders. The visitors' book inside gives details of age and usage. The

Breag in the Loen valley

path, apart from the boggy entrance gate, is not too difficult and is very well signed. Allow 45 minutes for the round trip. Also good for views is the side road to Vinsrygg off the 15 on the way back to Stryn. There is a lovely view over the Stryn valley from the parking at the start of the toll road, which leads to Vinsrygg *seter* and Lodalseter further up the valley.

Stryn itself has a good assortment of shops and a helpful tourist office that produces an excellent booklet on the area. The 15 heads through the Stryn valley in the direction of Otta. When passing beside Stryn lake watch for the surfaced road up the hillside whose small wooden signpost reads Brekke and Åning. These two farms give excellent views across to the orchards of Flo and along to Fosnes, with Oppstryn church, not to mention the ice fields and the mountains all around. The road in the right hand corner of the lake is the first stage of an old route over the Jostedalbre whose blue fingers crawl down the mountains. The 15 climbs out of the valley at the other corner. Where it hairpins across a double bridge, stop at the picnic spot and walk onto the old one for views down into the gorge and from the new one to where it curves out of the hills. As the road climbs on, there are excellent views down over the valley and to the snowfields beyond. When the Otta road disappears into the mountainside — it is one of the new all year roads that tunnel through the hills — fork right for Grotli. This is the old road, climbing eventually to 1,139m (3,736ft). At the Videseter hotel one can walk to a viewing platform at the top of the waterfall that has been visible beside the road. Climbing on, note the height of the snow poles, mute testimony to the need for an all year road. At the top, one passes the Stryn summer ski school, with a gondola lift to the slopes right beside the road. Snow walls stand 2 to 3m (7 to 10ft) deep still in late August, and there are ice floes on the lakes.

Ottadalen, where the old road rejoins the 15 at Grotli, is another world, a pleasant valley of conifers beside the rushing Otta river. At **Pollfoss** these become proper falls. A path beside the hotel leads onto the private road and bridge over the main falls — 100m (328ft) further on a footpath cuts back through the trees for views of the lower ones. Further on, **Dønfoss** camping have created a swimming pool in the rocks by the rapids and a walk past a pothole. The best fall here is on the far side over the bridge. The right turn from there to Sotaseter is the nearest any road comes to crossing this mountain area. A toll road goes a further 7km (4 miles) to Mysubyttseter, from where a 4 hour walk reaches the highest point of the construction road for the Styggevatn dam which leads down to Gaupne and the Sognefjord. The valley from Dønfoss to Lom is in the sheltered lee of the mountains, which drain the water from the clouds and leave **Skjåk**, with its wooden stave-style church, the driest place in Norway. Here they spray the fields in even the wettest summer. This dryness is reflected in the fountain sculpture, based on old irrigation systems, which graces the centre of Lom. It is here that the circumnavigation of this area ends.

Further Information
— Norwegian Glaciers and Mountains —

Fjærland
Glacier Centre
Open: April, May, September daily 11am-5pm. June, July, August daily 9am-7pm.

Fortun
Bjørk Farm (milk and berries)
Open: Thursday 11am-2pm July to mid-August.
Book at Sogndal tourist office.

Gaupne
Church
Open: 10.30am-4.30pm. June to mid-August.

Jostedalen
Power Station
Guided tours at 10am, 12noon, 2pm. Mid-June to mid-August.

Kaupanger
Sognefjord Boat Museum and Sogn Folkemuseum
Open: May and September, Monday to Friday 9am-3pm. Saturday and Sunday 12noon-6pm. June to August, Monday to Friday 9am-6pm. Saturday and Sunday 12noon-6pm.

Stave Church
Open: June to August, 9.30am-6.30pm.

Kjendal Glacier
Boat and coach trips from Sande camping. June to August 10.30am and 3pm daily.

Lom
Bygdemuseum
Open: mid-June to mid-August, 10am-8pm daily. Guided tours every hour, 1-5pm.

Stave Church
Open: June to August, 9am-9pm.

Luster
Dale Church
Open: June to August, 9am-8pm daily.

Nigardsbreen
Early June to end August. Boat trips 10am-6pm daily.

Solvorn
Sightseeing boat trips June to August, Monday and Thursday 1.15pm and 4.15pm.
Boats to Urnes stave church daily. Extra boats mid-June to mid-August, Friday, Saturday and Sunday.

Urnes
Stave Church
Open: mid-June to mid-August, 10.30am-5.30pm daily.

Veitastrond
Tungestølen (Goat Farm)
Open: mid-June to mid-August, Wednesday, Friday and Sunday. Guided tours at 10am, 12noon, 1pm and 4pm. Book at tourist office. Late June to end July full day glacier trips Wednesday, Saturday 10am.

Tourist Information Centres

Årdal
Årdal Prosjektutvikling
5875 Årdalstangen
☎ (056) 61177

Balestrand og Fjærland
PO Box 57
5850 Balestrand
☎ (056) 91255

Jolster
6850 Skei i Jolster
☎ (057) 28126

Leikanger
5842 Leikanger
☎ (056) 54055

Lom-Jotunheim
2686 Lom
☎ (062) 11286

Luster
Rådhuset
5820 Gaupne
☎ (056) 81211

Sogndal
PO Box 222
5801 Sogndal
☎ (056) 71161

Sogn og Fjordane
Parkvegen 2
PO Box 299
5801 Sogndal
☎ (056) 72300

Turistinformasjonen i Stryn
6880 Stryn
☎ (057) 71526

3 • The Coast from Florø to Hitra

The Norwegian coast is an area of islands and fjords connected and crossed by highly efficient ferry services. An up-to-date timetable is a pre-requisite, for although one is unlikely to be left behind, planning is necessary to avoid long waits. The longer trips normally offer café facilities and all make a pleasant break from driving but inevitably they put the cost up and it is worth enquiring about a punch card, though not all ferries accept these. While most places on the coast are small, there are several towns that repay longer visits and fuller exploration — notably Florø, Ålesund, Molde and Kristiansund. All have airports and can be reached on internal flights from Bergen or Oslo. All are also ports of call for the coastal steamers, as is Måløy, and there is an increasing network of express boats. North Sea ferries also go to Ålesund and Molde and of course, Bergen.

With so much coast it is not surprising that fishing in sea, river and lake is available throughout the area. There are boats for hire and sight-seeing boat trips; windsurfing and diving to registered wrecks and some notable bird sanctuaries. But there is far more to do and see than just water-based activities. The whole area is a scenic delight for the coast is both rocky and mountainous and, by circling round inland (at most only 50km [31 miles] away from the sea), one can include the mountains of Møre and Romsdal too. Walking is a major activity here, with Alpine skiing in winter. Rock climbing is also available and in some areas, hang-gliding. Some of the hydro-electric plants are open to visitors and there are plenty of museums, ranging from the *bygdetun* (preserved farm) to fishing, coastal, or district museums. Hunting and shooting of small game, grouse and even deer is also possible for some of Norway's largest deer populations live just in from the shore.

For this chapter the starting point is Ålesund and two circular tours are suggested — one north, one south — which could easily be combined into a single holiday. On a clear day the air flight from Oslo is spectacular, crossing Norway's backbone of mountains at their highest. The airport is situated on the island of Vigra and a 12km (7

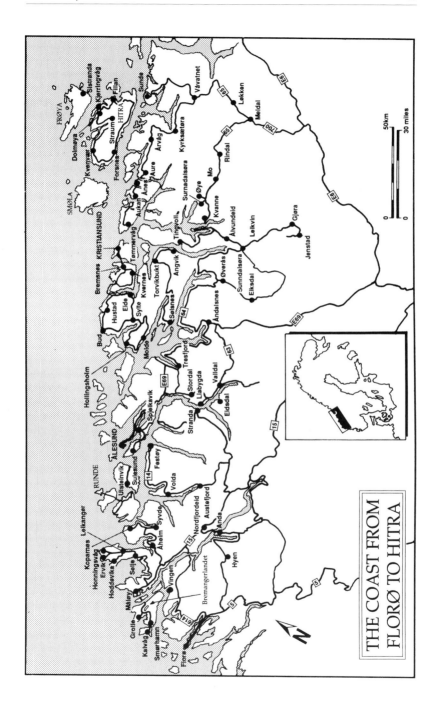

THE COAST FROM FLORØ TO HITRA

mile) network of tunnels and bridges links this with the other islands in the group and with Ålesund. As it is a toll road, it is best to explore these islands on the way to or from the airport. Each has its own attractions. Vigra has a sandy bathing beach and Valderøy a large cave where many prehistoric finds have been made. Giske's twelfth-century church is the only one in Norway to be made of marble. Its altarpiece is especially worth seeing. The most picturesque place is Alnes on Godøy with its harbour and lighthouse and another bathing beach beyond.

Ålesund itself is worth exploring for its architecture. Originally a wooden town, it suffered a devastating fire in 1904 which in the space of 16 hours destroyed 800 houses, rendered 10,000 people homeless, but only killed one. It was rebuilt in stone or brick in the currently popular art nouveau style with fancy mouldings on the façades and corner turrets. The best preserved streets are Kongensgata, Løvenvoldgata, and on the island beyond the eel sound (from which Ålesund derives its name), Apotekergata and Kirkegata. The *kirke* (church) on the latter street resulted from an architectural competition which attracted sixty-three entries. The pink and grey stone is particularly beautiful in sunshine after a shower. Inside it has stained glass windows and modern frescoes round the apse. The broad street beyond the church marks the divide (and firebreak) between the new town and the older wooden houses that escaped the 1904 fire. Nearby a rocky outcrop has been landscaped with grass and flowers and plenty of seats to provide a sunny look-out spot, complete with orientation table. A higher viewpoint is Mount Askla with its glass-domed cafeteria which can be reached by 424 steps up through the park — or by road, following the Fjellstua signs from the town centre.

There are several possible routes from Ålesund to Molde, the next important town up the coast. One could take the E69 most of the way but there are more interesting variations. First, on the way out of Ålesund on the E69, follow the Museer sign to the right for two museums and a church, prettily situated on the shore of the fjord. The Sunnmøre Museum is a collection of forty-one old houses, most turf-roofed, including two higgledy-piggledy farm complexes, and a boat section with thirty boats in covered halls. On the lake behind floats a replica of a Viking ship and a 1937 cutter that was used during World War II to ferry refugees to England. The Borgund Kaupanger concentrates on the medieval settlement that once existed here, with posts outside marking the pole-holes of long houses facing the shore. There are also the foundations of the original church. The present Borgund church contains a wealth of unpainted wood carving.

The view from Mount Askla

Beyond here one route to reach Molde is to fork right for Vølda, then left for Stranda. This leaves the E69 behind temporarily and also eventually the urban/industrial sprawl of Ålesund and Spjelkavik. Ignoring the ferry for Stranda, the road follows the Storfjord past a particularly pretty little port at Glomset to Valle. Rejoin the E69 just as far as Sjøholt, then go right on the 58 for Stordal. This is a scenic road blasted out of (and through) the rock face. At **Stordal** the octagonal old church (a medieval one rebuilt in 1789) was rose-painted inside by two travelling artisans in 1799. Their pictures of the saints, David and Goliath, and the sun and moon are crude and amusing. The cherubs and the wooden crucifix are considerably older. The turf-roofed farmhouse next door also dates from 1799. Unusually large for the period, it may well have housed several families at one time as the three bedroom areas are completely separate each with their own stairs. Returning north through the fjordside to the hilltop village of Dyrkorn, turn right for Vaksvikfjellet. Rising steeply out of the valley, this is a true mountain road that goes right over the hills, past old farms and summer cabins before dropping down beside a rocky river to **Tresfjord**, where the church is similarly octagonal to Stordal's. There is also a small *bygdetun* on the Øvstedal road. Tresfjord is on the E69 again and from here one can continue on it to Vikebukt or go left for Vestnes. Both have ferry connections to Molde, though the former is longer.

Molde is an interesting town with good shops and a pretty central section round the cathedral. As with so many Norwegian towns, most of Molde was destroyed during World War II, the church in the bombardment of 1940. The present cathedral was consecrated in 1957. Inside it is dark though the apse with its light blue Italian mosaics and symbolic cross is worth inspecting. The cross above the font has been in all three Molde churches and still shows the fire marks from the destruction of the first two. The best views of it are from the rose garden on top of the town hall. This and the rose girl statue down below are two of the reasons why Molde calls itself the town of roses, though they flourish in private gardens too. There is another open-air museum at the back of the town, a fisheries museum on the island of Hjertøya (reached by boat from the Torget quay) and the Varden viewpoint, for admiring the eighty-seven snow-capped peaks that line the far shore of the fjord.

From Molde to Kristiansund there are again several possible routes. For the fit with a good 3 hours to spare, the 67 between Sylte and Eide passes the footpath to the Trollkyrke (Troll's Church). The path is a 4km (2 mile) climb up a rocky hillside which in wet weather becomes the bed of a stream! There are also boggy areas and, being Norway, no plank bridges across them. The Norwegian answer is stout walking boots! At the top a metal ladder goes straight down into a tall cave. One can swing off the bottom of this onto rocks to penetrate the cave dryshod. Inside, tumbling down the far wall, a narrow waterfall lands in a white marble bowl in the rock. This is clearly visible by the light from the hole above but to explore deeper into the cave and passage system a torch is needed. Road number 67 then continues all the way to Kristiansund.

There are prettier routes to take though such as the coastal route which leaves Molde on the 662 for Aukra. Along the fjord shore the grass in the fields is amazingly green — due they say to long daylight hours in summer and therefore extra chlorophyll colouring, not to excess rain! Grass grows too on some of the buildings. It was the original way to roof farms, natural insulation that kept man, beast and stores warm in winter and cool in summer. Now it is reappearing on some modern houses. Once past the first ferry port (to Otrøy), the Atlantic comes into view, scattered with skerries and larger inhabited islands. **Hollingsholm**, to the left, is both ferry port for Aukra and marina. Beyond there turn left for Hoem for a circular coastal tour past **Vågøy** church. This stands above one of the many small harbours with just beyond, a 600th anniversary stone to Hermund, their first priest way back in 1336. As the road follows the fjord inland there is an original turf-roofed farmhouse, still lived in, shortly

Godøy near Ålesund, on the Norwegian coast (Chapter 3)

Rødven stave church (Chapter 3)

Fishermen's memorial near Høydal on Langøya, Vesterålen Islands (Chapter 4)

Fish drying racks beside the Prestfjord, Langøya, Vesterålen Islands (Chapter 4)

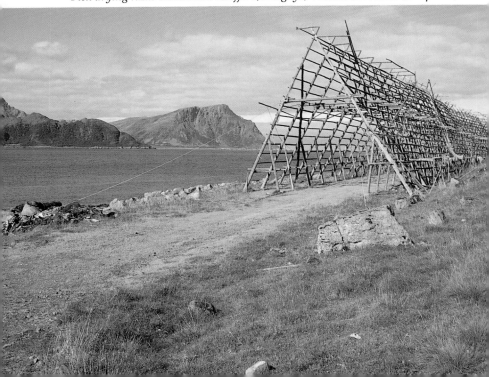

before joining the 67. Leave this again 5km (3 miles) later for Elnes-vågen and the coast road to Bud. This is a very pleasant stretch with farms, harbours and skerries beyond. **Bud** is a historic town, developing as a community from the Middle Ages. It is also of strategic importance; park at the picnic table and walk up the track opposite — the headland is riddled with subterranean passages and German gun posts with free access, at one's own risk. A torch would be useful here and also at the *Tilfluktrøm* or escape stairs further along the road. Being a headland, there are also good views from the top down over the town with its fish-drying racks and harbour.

Continuing along the road towards **Hustad**, the *Maleremm* signed to the right is a preserved cluster of turf-roofed farm buildings, unusual in that they are in their original site, not re-erected elsewhere as an open-air museum. The *Gravøyser* on the left are burial mounds built from the same stones as cover the beaches and therefore difficult to spot unless one is prepared for them. Past Hustad church follow Farstad and then the 663 for Vevang (the 67 from the Trollkyrke rejoins here), lead to the new Atlantic road (Atlantic-havsvegen) which bridges a series of skerries across to Averøy. The 8km (5 mile) road cost 105 million kroner to build so it is no wonder a toll is charged. **Stromsholmen**, beyond the first bridge, is a centre for scuba diving and **Håholmen**, towards the end, is a fishing village on an island, a traditional and protected community, a living museum with eighteenth-century buildings and equipment and the replicas of three Viking boats. It is only 3 minutes by boat from the parking place and overnight accommodation is available. The Møre and Romsdal tourist association in Kristiansund particularly recommend the *Atlantichavsvegen* in windy weather with the ocean whipping the breakers over the rocks! Once safely onto Averøy, follow the **Kvernes** signs round the southern shore of the island, for the stave church. Built into its present shape in the seventeenth century, the inside is painted, with a carved screen and pulpit separating the nave from the chancel. Note the choir stall at the rear with access only from outside. There is also a *bygdemuseum* further along the road and a marked trail from the Kirkevåghandel at Bremsnes through archaeological sites from the Stone Age to a cave in Bremneshatten and a 360° panorama. From Bremsnes the ferry crosses to **Kristiansund**.

This is a colourful town built across several islands. The oldest parts are on Innlandet where the wooden houses of the Gamlebyen cluster just above the shore. The oldest is the attractive Lossiusgården, a long white merchant house from 1780. On the hill above, the Bautaen is a monument with three cannon commemorat-

A view over Kristiansund

ing the repulse of an English attack in 1808. Good views can be had from there across to modern day Kristiansund. The equivalent viewpoint on the mainland is the lookout tower at one edge of the water park. This is a series of old reservoirs, starting with the Swan Lake just beyond the Kirkelandet Cathedral. One can walk either side of them to the high dam that holds them in, then down across Vuggaveien and out along paths on top of Brinchmann's down spouts — an ingenious system that collected water for the reservoirs. They wind along the wooded hillside until one reaches the straight track out to Klubba on the Atlantic coast. Follow this straight track back, into the churchyard, then right up into the water park again; the path to the left above the graves brings one round to the Varde. Originally a watch tower during the Napoleonic wars, the modern one is pretty rather than high and if it is closed, equally good views over town, shipping lanes and the distant Nordmøre mountains can be had from the rocky outcrop on which it stands. Back down in the town, the Kirkelandet Cathedral, 'Mountain Crystal in Roses' as its architect called it, is either elegantly aesthetic with its concrete lines and stained glass window tracing man's ascent from sin to Heaven. Or it could be seen as a monstrosity whose concrete pillars confuse the vision and obscure the message of the vast window. The oldest house in this part of Kristiansund is the courtyard complex, Christiegården, built over a period of 50 years from the late eighteenth century. There are also several museum areas including a complete barrel factory, old shipyard, fishing and fire brigade museums. An interesting half day excursion is to the island of Grip. Nowadays inhabited only in summer, it opens its fifteenth-century stave church and post office (with special postmark) to visitors.

The island-hopping route onwards to Hitra, involves several ferries. The first, from Seivika to Tømmervåg, threads its way through seagull-covered rocks and past isolated boat sheds. **Tømmervåg** is on Tustna, a delightful mountainous island, whose pine and birch woods provide perfect cover for some of Norway's largest herds of red deer. The ferry from Aukan follows the coast to Vinsternes on Ertvågøy, a similar though less mountainous island. The third ferry, a very basic model with no salon or superstructure apart from the captain's bridge, goes from Ånes to **Aure**, a pretty port backed by fields and farms. Follow the road towards Kyrksætøra past farms separated by rocks and trees and backed by mountains. On the Årvågsfjord, the coast is lined with inlets and boathouses and the barrenness of the opposite side, where the road is a scar along bare rock, contrasts with the continuing farms on this north-facing shore. When the road climbs out of the valley above Årvåg there are excellent views right back along the fjord. On reaching Kyrksætøra, turn left along the far shore for Holla. The road follows first the Hemne and then the Snillfjord, clinging to the cliffs where the two fjords meet. On leaving the coast it climbs through forests to almost clear the tree line before descending to 298m (977ft) to join the 714 for Hitra at Våvatnet. The next 50km (31 miles) have to be repeated, unfortunately, but the only alternative route to Hitra, by ferry from Aukan to Forsnes, only runs twice a day, at times convenient for the worker rather than the tourist. Still the 714 is a good quality road, winding past lakes and fjords to the ferry point at Sunde where, if one should miss the boat, the Utsiken Kro and Motell offers snacks on its terrace with a clear view over the fjord so that one can judge one's return to the car to a nicety.

Hitra, Norway's third largest island, is so amazingly rocky that most of its inhabitants live round the coast, leaving the forested and craggy interior to the red deer. Several hundred of these are culled every autumn and one can buy licences for this and for the wild fowl shoots. The roads follow the coast so that access to most of the 1,000 fishing lakes is on foot. Alternatively there is sea angling, diving to old wrecks, windsurfing and waterskiing on offer round the shore. To circumnavigate the island, take the unsurfaced 713 along the south coast first where occasional farms looking across to the mountains of Sør Trondelag intersperse the woods and rocks. Near

The southern coast of the island of Hitra

Forsnes, ridge behind ridge of bare rounded rocks prevent habitation. These turn into barren plateaux so that Kvenvær appears as a welcome oasis of greenery. From here the road runs east through forests to the farming valley of Straum. Turn left here for Melandsjø. Hestnes, a couple of kilometres off the road, used to be a whaling station but the quay is closed, the wharfhouse locked and the hoist idle. More interesting is the Hopsjøbrygga on the outskirts of Melandsjø. This old warehouse has been restored as a café and an old-fashioned stores, on the lines of the Jennestad Handelssted near Sortland. On meeting the 714 turn left over the Dolmensund bridge for Kjerringvåg, where a further ferry takes one to the outer island of Frøya. Attractions here include a rural museum and boat trips to the Froan islands where seals and cormorants breed; ask at Sistranda Culture Department in the Council Offices for both. Just before Kjerringvåg, the road left leads to **Dolmen By**, a delightful conglomeration of miniature houses based on the island including a model of Dolm eighteenth-century church that lies along the road; and also of the red wood church at **Fillan**, south down the 714. The rural fisheries museum at Fillan (in the library building) includes a 9m (30ft) long open boat, an *Åfjordsfyring*, that is traditional in the area. From here the ferry at Justenøya is only a short trip back down the 714.

Now begins the circle back to Ålesund on a more inland route. Follow the 714 almost to Orkanger. At the end of Gagnäsvatnet turn right for Fannremm and the 65 south down **Orkladalen**. A broad

Old farm buildings at the Meldal museum

farming valley, it has the long white farmhouses and old barns typical of this part of Norway. When Svorkmo is signed, cross the river for the Løkken road. The old Thamshavnbanen, electric railway, still runs, for tourists, between these two places. There is a turf-roofed station at **Svorkmo** and engines and carriages at **Løkken**. Other attractions here are tours of both the old and new mines, and the Bergverkmuseet devoted to stone-quarrying. For a lovely setting of old farm buildings on a steep hillside, continue south to the Meldal *bygdetun* where there is free access to the area out of season.

From here minor roads, surfaced in places, take one across to Rindal. Turn left for Stene first, passing through small farming communities to the east of the Orkla, then right for Å, right over a second bridge and left for Vålåsharet. This is a mountain road that climbs out of Orkladalen to Resvatnet where, with a backdrop of snow-streaked mountains, private cabins perch on all sides. Just beyond the lake, watch for the Vålåsharet Setergrend whose turf-roofed barns step across the hillside in rows. Descend from there through mountain farms to **Rindal** where there is another extensive open-air museum. From Rindal join the 65 for Surnadal but only until Dønnem is signed across the river. This minor road also follows the Surna towards the fjord but goes through more communities including Mo whose church is based on the Trinity, with three porches fronting three naves, and a triangular central tower. On rejoining the 65 at Øye, go left on the 670 for Sunndalsøra. Five kilometres (3 miles) further on, notice on the left the old Åsen farm, now a *bygdetun*, open on request. A more unusual attraction is the Svinvik arboretum, famous for its rhododendrons, signed to the left beyond Melhus. Return then to Kvanne for the ferry to Røkkum, where there are two possible routes to Åndalsnes.

The first goes south on the 16 for Sunndalsøra. On reaching **Ålvundeid**, turn left, past the small red octagonal church, for **Innerdalen**. This is one of the most beautiful Norwegian dales, heading towards the lovely peaks of the Trollheimen mountains. From the parking, a cart track leads 4km (2 miles) on to the tourist *hytte* (hut) from where there are longer trails through the mountains. **Sunndalsøra** is also surrounded by mountains but its ugly industrial waterfront is a blot on the fjordscape! However, a delightful diversion can be made from here along the Sunndal valley. Turn first into the Leikvin museum area. Buried in the small graveyard lie Lady Arbuthnott and her infant son. A Scottish lady, she fell in love with Sunndalen on her honeymoon, built the house Elverhøy for herself and lived here for more than 20 years. Elverhøy is not open to the public but the farmhouse that Lady Arbuthnott bought and gave to her friend, Mrs Cochrane, is. It contains much painted furniture including brides' chests, a chair and table made from water buffaloes' hide and horns, a nineteenth-century planetarium and much more. Nearby, the Philliphagen is a rhododendron garden originally planted by one of the Englishmen who came here for the salmon fishing. On the same site is one of Norway's largest burial grounds with some 200 graves from the fourth to the tenth centuries. Continue on the same side of the river, rejoining the 16 at Giking, for Gjøra. Turn right there for Hafsås and Åmotan. The road follows the turquoise-grey rapids of the river, past a monument to the navvies. Fork upwards at the cluster of brown walkers' signs for **Jenstad**. From the parking place, walk on to the *fossene* (waterfalls) signs and the red marked path that leads round the farmer's fields, past the view to the Reppdalsfossen, then down the hillside for the best views of Svøufossen. Here one is high above the Åmotan (meeting place), a deep gorge where four rivers cascade down the hillsides into one. It is an excellent area for walking with trails into the hills and down and across the rivers. On the opposite side of the valley one can see a road zig-zagging past Svøufossen. To reach this, return to the junction and turn left. The nearest point to the falls is at the information board but they are difficult to see from there. Beyond the log-built turf-roofed farms of **Svisdal**, with their overhead wires for hoisting hay into the barn roofs, follow the high valley to the fork for Vanshaugen. (The warn-

Lady Arbuthnott's hunting lodge at Alfheim

ing sign refers to winter snowfalls and affects the owners of the *hytte*, not the summer tourist!) The toll road (pay in the trust-the-motorist box), leads across the bridge, through a shallow ford and left for Alfheim, Lady Arbuthnott's picturesque hunting lodge, which is now let to parties by the Sunndalsøra tourist office. The other road, straight on at the Vanshaugen sign, leads into walking territory, with tracks for example through Grøvudalen to a summer farm some 2 hours away. The return to Sunndalsøra is by the reverse route.

From Sunndalsøra to Åndalsnes the obvious route is the 62 and then the 660, both good fjordside roads offering good fjordside views. For something different with spectacular climbing roads, try instead the loop across to Eiksdal. Take the 62 only to the Litledalen sign. This side road follows the clear glacial river to Dale where there is a warning sign on the condition of the mountain road — no rails; unsuitable for buses and trailers. As the road climbs up to Litledalselva lake, watch for the pine labels on bridges and water-falls. Beyond the lake, hairpins snake ever higher with breath-taking views to the valley below. One reaches some 900m (2,952ft) at the series of dammed lakes that provide the water for the Aura power plant. This high plateau is grey and bleak but soon the fishing lakes and *hytte* start and one curves past Aursjøn towards the snowier Lesja range. Beyond the dam, the road switchbacks high above the Aura valley before sweeping down the hillside (an improved road with guard rail) in a series of hairpins to Eiksdalen. The pretty village of **Eiksdal** with its tiny white church is a mere kilometre or two away from Reitan on the edge of the lake. The mountain road is 74km (46 miles) of concentrated driving, so that to board the ferry at Reitan for a leisurely hour's cruise was a relaxation. Unfortunately progress has arrived in the form of a new road blasted out past Vike to Øverås and the ferry is no more. Watch as you drive past the lake for Mardalsfossen, high above Marsdal hamlet. Europe's highest single drop waterfall at 297m (974ft), progress has reached that too in the form of hydro-electric power so that it only flows properly in July (a concession to all the Norwegians who chained themselves together to protest about its use.) It can also be reached by footpath from Reitan — allow $1^1/_2$ hours each way. From Øverås, drop down to join the 660 for Åndalsnes.

The alternate route from Rokkum to Åndalsnes turns right on the 16 for **Tingvoll** where there are several points of interest. On the outskirts the left turn signed Hindhammer leads to two Stone Age rock painting sites. The first, of salmon, is along a difficult and potentially dangerous path. The second route, signed Hellemalinger is easier, just 10 minutes each way, leading to a rock panel in the cliff painted in faded red with three or four large moose and deer. Along the far side of the fjord Tingvoll church is a stone structure from the twelfth century containing two Bibles and a service book from the sixteenth-century, altar, memorial and gallery from the seventeenth century; faded murals and lots of portraits. It is definitely a church well worth looking into! An old farm high on the hillside has been turned into an interesting museum with original furnishings and implements, two mills, a smithy and a schoolroom. Even if it is shut, there are excellent views from the site. From Tingvoll a ferry crosses to Angvik (signed Molde). Turn right here on the 666 for Batnfjord for a twisty fjordside road. In Torvikbukt, turn left for Heggen through wooded Torvikdalen, then right on the 665 with good mountain views. Left on the 62 and right for Røvik brings one through to the left side of the Fannefjord, to the 64 for Åndalsnes. As a route it is scenically varied; the roads are a mix of surfaced and unsurfaced.

From Sølsnes the ferry crosses to Åfarnes where the two routes run together to Åndalsnes. As one drives along the Rødvenfjord, **Rødven** church sits clearly on the other side. Much harder to spot is the smaller stave church beside it. To reach this, drive over the Straumen tide race (visible only at high tide) and back along the fjord. Used on special occasions like St Olav's day (29 July), and for services for tourists, the stave church is one of the oldest still standing — thanks to the large props supporting it! The key on the far side opens a strange tall panel to reveal carving around what was presumably once a door. All round the fjord between here and Åndalsnes there are toll roads leading up to walks, views and fishing. One needs plenty of coins as the tolls are of the 'pay into the envelope' variety with no change available. The quality of these roads varies considerably. For example, the one to Skogedalen is poor. It climbs up to 500m (1,640ft) with unsigned trails on into the dale and up the mountains. Alternatively, behind the town of Isfjorden, the signs to Dalsbyggda take one through the farming community of Dale to a toll road that is a good quality track through Erstadalen. This is an undeveloped dale with lots of birch providing cover for red deer and capercaillie. It is not a long road — only 2 to 3km (1 to 2 miles) — and one has a better chance of seeing the wildlife on foot! Either way there are waterfalls signposted from the end. Gluterfossen is 15 minutes away up a stony track — a far easier walk than to Saufonnfossen which deteriorates beyond the causeway to a muddy footpath climbing through trees. There is also a toll road up Vengedalen to the foot of Mount Romsdalhorn where there are numerous walks.

The mountains to the south of Åndalsnes are the famous **Trolltindene** with the Trollveggen, a diversion away at Horgheim on the E69. This vertical mountain wall provides some of the world's toughest climbs. It was also used for parachute jumping in the 1980s until the sport was banned after fatal accidents. To reach the next destination, Valldal, the Trolltindene have to be crossed. Unusually steep and peaked, they formed a barrier surmountable only by horses until 1936 when the famous Trollstigvegen was engineered up the mountainside. Climbing at 10 per cent over eleven hairpins, it crosses two waterfalls including the Stigfossen, cascading 180m (590ft) down the mountainside. To the right a line of white shows where the horse trail went. At the top there is a viewpoint, souvenir stalls complete with man-size wooden trolls, and a museum about the road in the café complex, for this is tourist territory and deserves to be. The highest point is 850m (2,788ft), not as high as the Litledalen/Eiksdal road but there is more snow on the mountains and the snowpoles tell their own tale. Watch for the Hesten glacier which appears humped behind the mountains to the right. Further down the river rushes through rocky gorges till it reaches Gudbrandsjuvet potholes where it foams beneath the road on its way to the Norddalsfjord.

There are several delightful expeditions to be made in this area. By turning left at Valldal, one drives along the Tåfjord, through a series of tunnels. The first place one reaches is **Fjørå** with its apple trees up

Fjørå on the Tåfjord

the hillside and a memorial to the people who died in the tidal wave of 1934. This was caused by an avalanche pouring rock into the fjord and killed families at Tåfjord too. Follow the Selboskar road up the hillside for tremendous views over the fjord. Continuing on, park just beyond the 4km (2 mile) tunnel and walk up to Muldalgård and the Muldalsfossen. The hikers' equivalent of the Trollstigen road, this zigzag track climbs 370m (1,214ft) in 2km (1 mile) but is in good condition and can be mounted in under the hour. Hot drinks and the local speciality of pancakes (*sveler*) with berry jam and sour cream are served at the top. The waterfall is a further 20 minutes away, through the farmyard and down the far side of the cliffs to a viewing platform that lets one see the full 200m (656ft) drop. Although utilised for hydro-electric power there is usually enough falling for one to imagine what the full flow used to look like. Allow 3 hours for the whole expedition including refreshments and return by the same route. If Muldalsfossen still flows, albeit in a lesser key, hydro-electric power has completely stopped the river that once flowed through Tåfjord. Follow the Rødalen signs to reach the towering Zakariasdam. One can walk across its dizzying height, see the old road and bridge and feel the cold air rising out of the gorge.

Returning by the same route to Valldal and on through the orchards of Linge, take the ferry to Eidsdal, where two similar excursions can be made. The first goes to the left towards Norddal, then right up the valley for Herdalsseter. Where Muldalgård is an isolated hillfarm, **Herdal** is a summer farm with thirty original huts clustered round the modern milking shed and cafeteria. It is a working farm with cows, sheep, ponies and 450 goats that also operates as a tourist attraction with cheese-making on Fridays, cabins for hire, fishing and mountain tours with local guides. The other excursion means taking the Geiranger road for 5km (3 miles) and then turning back right for **Kilsti**, a hill village giving magnificent views back over the fjord to Valldal, with Eidsdal in miniature down below. The energetic could leave their car at the Ytterdal camping site and walk.

Return over the ferry to Linge and follow the 58 on towards Ålesund. (From Liabygda this heads across the hills to Stordal with its painted church). Alternatively cross the ferry to Stranda and **Sykkylven** where there is a natural history museum with stuffed animals in realistic settings. To complete the circle to the north, cross the Aursnes-Magerholm ferry for Ålesund.

The circle to the south crosses the Solevåg-Festnøy ferry, or one could continue from Sykkylven direct to Festnøy by driving round the Sykkylvenfjord to Hundeidvik for the infrequent ferry across and so link the two loops into one whole. Either way, at Festnøy turn left immediately along the Hjørundfjord for **Standal**. This minor road passes through a succession of farming hamlets and over rushing rivers. From Standal a little ferry zigzags its way down the fjord to Sæbo, but the road climbs across the mountains to reach Follestadalen. Keep to the left side of the valley, then go left on the 65 and right for Øse. On reaching the 14 on the far coast, turn left for Volda. This area is littered with museums. The first is dedicated to Ivar Aasen, a dialectologist who 'invented' the modern Norwegian language. The second is to Sivert Aarflot who set up the first village printing press in Norway in the early nineteenth century. In **Volda** itself, the Sunnmøre cathedral has a huge mural for an altar piece and painted pillars and walls. There is a *bygdetun* too, along the hillside, complete with implements and vehicles and a boat section down by the shore. Beside the hospital, the horticultural society have planted a small show garden with shrubs, sculptures and a tiny watermill of the sort one can still find in the countryside.

Now follow the fjord south to **Austefjord** where purpose-built buildings contain a collection of model boats, everyday articles and implements for hunting, fishing and farming. Turn left there for Viddal and then right at Kalvatn for Nordfjordeid. This is fishing lake territory as it crosses plateaux up to 450m (1,476ft) above sea level, before dropping down to Europe's deepest lake, Hornindals-vatn. **Nordfjordeid** is to the right, a narrow town with old wooden houses and a rose painted church. There are also Viking burial mounds with excellent explanatory text and an army museum (Hær-museet) for a change! To reach the west coast again, this time at Florø, take the 14 across the Utfjord from Lote to **Anda** on the Gloppenfjord where distinctive tile-roofed boathouses cluster along the shore. None of them is big enough to house the *Holvikjekta* which is right at the sign in **Sandane** and immediately left. Built in 1881, this large trading vessel did the journey to Bergen three times every summer and spent every winter propped up as she now is in a boathouse. Also in Sandane the Nordfjord folk museum possesses an extensive collection of old buildings which are open for guided tours. In **Gimmestad**, the old church is well worth the trouble of ringing for the key at the yellow farmhouse just below it. It has painted walls and ceilings, carved pew ends and named seats, and numerous hat stands branching like antlers all along the men's side of the aisle. The altar has texts not paintings and instead of a boat there is a preserved catfish hanging from the ceiling! Further on at Rygg, the road has cut the old quay, where the best clusters of fishermen's huts stand, off from the sea.

Beyond Hyeneset, where the ferry used to run down the narrow fjord to Hyen, there is now a new road which intersperses tunnels with viewpoints. (It may improve communications but the ferry was more interesting.) Round the end of the fjord and heading across country beyond Hope one keeps company with a rushing river. After the bridge at Røyrvikgrend, the remains of a wooden pipe system run beside it. The road then climbs over an old stone-arched bridge, through wooded countryside to a series of lakes which grow pro-gressively bleaker until it joins the 5 for **Florø**. The last stretch to the town is particularly pleasant, crossing peninsulas and islands. On the outskirts, turn left for the Coastal Museum. The 500m (1,640ft) from the parking is along walkways and over bridges between rocky islets to reach the buildings on the shore. Their 200-year-old rowing boat is Norway's oldest vessel apart from the recovered Viking ships. Further fishing relics are to be found in the Kakebua café and a variety of boat trips are available. For example you can visit Kvinn for the medieval church with its beautiful wood carvings and the distinctive cleft on the west side of the island; the manor island of Svanøy with its unusual vegetation; or take thematic voyages to view birds, and seals.

From Florø one is reliant on ferries to circle back to Ålesund along the islands. An infrequent ferry service leaves Florø for **Smørhamn** on Bremangerlandet which is another of those rocky islands that sit off Norway's coast. The chief industry is fishing and there are a number of well-preserved wharfs, the largest at Kalvåg on Frøya, where the old-fashioned wharfhouses line the quays round the harbour. On the main island, the road left in Bremanger for Grotle passes a series of fishing hamlets with similar wharfhouses, some on special quays in deeper water, before reaching the largest sandy beach on the island, a full 2km (1 mile) long. At the far side of the island turn right for Berle and then Hunskår to reach first the harbour of Klubban from which boat trips leave every Sunday for the rock carvings at **Vingen**. This huge site of some 1,500 figures on the mainland coast has no road access — this trip is the only way of seeing them. Beyond Klubban the cliffs are the 860m (2,820ft) high plateau of Hornelen. At **Berle**, through the tunnel labelled Berleporten, a very modern church hides behind trees by the graveyard and, in a rocky hillock beyond, are the remains of a 1940s German fort and gun emplacements.

The ferry from Oldeide takes one to Måløy, entering the harbour under the graceful bridge that brings the 15 to this fair-sized town and port. Here on Vågsøy the beach at **Raudeberg** was voted Norway's most beautiful in 1988! Certainly it curves delightfully round a bay but the most interesting sights are on the Oppedal road, turning right at the base of the bridge. One reaches first Vågsvåg with old wharfhouses linked together on the quay. Then over the hill one drops down onto **Torskangerpollen**, a fishing hamlet huddled along the base of cliffs. Lastly, on the outskirts of **Oppedal**, the waves have worn away the rocks, leaving one, the Kannesteinen, like a wineglass on a slender leg.

Leave Vågsøy by the 15 for Stryn taking the 618 beyond the tunnel for Selje. This is a genuine coast road with views out to the Atlantic Ocean. The Selje peninsula is a delight at least to landlubbers. To sailors, the trip round the huge Stadlandet promontory has always caused problems, the Gulf Stream drift, submerged rocks, and the height of the cliffs between them setting up freak conditions and causing shipwreck. For this reason a ship tunnel is planned to cut across the base of the peninsula, opening to boat traffic in 1993. The island has a backbone of mountains rising to between 400 and 650m

(1,312 and 2,132ft) over which its roads hairpin giving views in all directions. The best are from Kjerringa, the 496m (1,627ft) high point that is also called Vestkapp. The westernmost point on the Norwegian mainland, it gives magnificent panoramic views from Hornelen on Bremangerlandet via the Ålfot glacier, the mountains of Olden and of Sunnmøre, to the coastal islands stretching towards Ålesund. A cairn by the parking reads, 'All the earth shall worship thee and shall sing unto thee; they shall sing to thy name'. A less happy note is struck by the remains of German fortifications. The Germans also bombed a coastal steamer in 1943, whose dead are remembered in St Svithun's chapel at **Ervik**. Also interesting is the road to Hoddevik from Leikanger which passes a large cross to Olav Tryggvason who made four counties Christian in AD997. Turn left in Drage for **Fure** on a narrow road that clings to shore and cliffs for 4km (2 miles) before reaching this delightful hamlet where the knot of farmhouses are surrounded by gay flowers. Those with a head for heights can walk further, on a narrow path high up the hillside to reach the tiny farmsteads of Ytre Fure. At **Hoddevik** itself the sandy beach is flanked by dunes. The main town of the peninsula is **Selje**, with rectory buildings from 1782, $^1/_2$km of sandy beach and the monastery ruins of St Sunniva on the island in the bay. In season, twice daily boat trips visit the ruins and the cave where this Irish princess was martyred. Alternatively one can see the ruins with their restored tower from Skarbo, or there are models and diagrams of it in the Selje hotel. Incidentally the latter serves a seafoods buffet where the hot and cold dishes are all fish and shellfish.

From Selje return to Eide for the road across the hill to Åheim. There are of course excellent views but watch too for the short stretch of the old king's highway zigzagging up dry stone walled bends to the left. At **Åheim**, there is a small museum of everyday objects and the little twelfth-century church of St Jetmund which commemorates the English Saint Edmund, whom the Vikings martyred in AD900. One can follow this road all the way to the ferry at Koparnes. Alternatively, strictly for the adventurous who like to 'climb every mountain', turn right in Sylte for Syltedalen. At the end of the dale a private road labelled 'driving at your own risk' climbs steeply up the mountain. It is better quality than some toll roads but narrow with no barriers between the road and the drop. There is a small lake at the top, then the similar descent to the dale the other side where a surfaced road leads out to Syvde and Koparnes back to the left. In kilometres, this route is scarcely further than the main road but it takes longer.

Take the ferry to Årvik, then follow the 61 to Gurskebotn and turn left there, signed Hangsbygda, but real destination the bird island of **Runde**. The road passes shipyards first, then circles the fjord along the populous south-facing shore. Beyond Gjerdsvika, the views are straight out to the Atlantic. Just into **Herøy** commune, watch for the series of burial mounds on the shore. From there Kjerringa is visible to the left and Fosnavåg straight ahead with, round the corner, the bridges leading to the outer islands. The Herøy Coastal Museum (Fyskmuseet) is to the left beyond the first bridge. Follow Fosnavåg and then Runde. There are old wharfhouses round the bay at Leine and more on Remøy, some built on rocky islets. Runde has three bird sanctuaries on its cliffs where 170,000 pairs of skua, cormorant, fulmar, puffin and others breed every year. There are boat trips from the harbour to view these from seawards or one may walk up the bird path beyond the tunnel. A stiff climb takes one past two tiny mills onto the higher slopes where streams and boggy ground make boots essential. Although there is no entry to the reserves during the breeding season (15 March to 31 August), marked paths lead to designated vantage points that are open all year. One should allow a good half day if doing the walk.

Return to Stokksund, then follow the Hareid signs across to Hareidlandet, turning into **Ulsteinvik**. Notice the church that was moved there in 1878. By following the Flø road, one passes its former site — the old graveyard at the original Ulstein. Now a turfy area surrounded by a dry stone wall, one of the few graves remaining is a large flat memorial to Kristoffer Rønneberg, proprietor and trades-man, who when he died aged 93 in 1824 was survived by 8 children, 50 grandchildren and 30 great grandchildren! Much older graves of the stone tumuli variety stand beside the road at Gåsneset while from Flø there are views back to Runde. On the far side of the island at **Hareid**, a 1911 Arctic vessel, the *Aarvak*, is moored next to the ferry point as a floating museum. There is also a small Arctic museum, Ishavsmuseet, with artefacts and photographs on the left at the end of Brandal. Beyond there, if one parks just past the last farm, a $1/_2$km walk onwards brings one to a scenario of German fortifications and gun emplacements from the last war. Back in Hareid, the ferry across to Sulesund is the last stage of this circle south. All that is left is to follow the signs back to Ålesund, to complete what is an interesting, varied, and mainly coastal, tour.

Further Information
— The Coast from Florø to Hitra —

Ålesund
Church
Open: June to August, 10am-2pm.
Closed Monday.

Ålesund Museum
Open: all year daily, 11am-3pm. Sunday 12noon-3pm.

Borgund Church
Open: June to August, Tuesday to Sunday 10am-2pm.

Borgund Kaupangen (Medieval Museum)
Open: mid-May to June, Sunday 12noon-3pm. Mid-June to end August, Monday to Friday 11am-3pm. Sunday 12noon-4pm.

Sunnmøre Museum
Open: late May to late June, Monday to Friday 11am-3pm. Saturday and Sunday 12noon-3pm. Late June to end August, Monday to Friday 11am-4pm, Saturday and Sunday 12noon-4pm.

Austefjord
Museum and Arsetøysamlinga
Open: mid-June to mid-August, Monday to Friday 10am-5pm. Saturday 2-5pm. Sunday 2-7pm.

Eid (Nordfjordeid)
Army Museum
Open: mid-June to mid-August, Tuesday to Thursday 2-5pm. Friday 2-8pm. Saturday 12noon-3pm. Sunday 2-6pm.

Florø
Coastal Museum
Open: mid-June to mid-August, Tuesday to Friday 12noon-6pm. Saturday and Sunday 12noon-3pm. Monday closed. Mid-August to mid-June, Monday to Friday 10am-2pm. Sunday 12noon-3pm. Saturday closed.

Boat trips to Kvinn
Tuesday, Thursday 10.15am; Svanøy Monday, Friday 10.15am;
Thematic Tours
Monday 5.30pm. 20 June to 20 August via tourist office.

Giske
Marble Church
Open: June to August, 11am-4pm.

Herdalsseter
Activities mid-June to mid-August.

Herøy
Coastal Museum
Open: mid-June to mid-August.

Hitra
Dolmen By Miniature Village
Open: June to August, daily 10am-8pm.

Rural Museum at Fillan
Open: June to August, Monday Tuesday, Wednesday 10am-4pm. Thursday 10am-6pm. Friday 10am-5pm. Saturday 10am-2pm. Sunday closed.

Kristiansund
Boat Trip to Grip
Mid-May to late August, Monday to Thursday 11am. Friday 11am and 5.30pm. Saturday 1.15pm. Sunday 11am and 4pm.

Kirkelandet Cathedral
Open: beginning May to end August 10am-7pm. Beginning September to end April 10am-2pm.

Vardetårnet
Open: mid-June to mid-August, Monday to Friday 11am-1pm. Saturday 4-6pm. Sunday 12noon-7pm.

Worldbrygga Museum Area
(workshops, boats)
Open: mid-June to early August, Monday to Friday 2-4pm. Sunday 1-4pm. Saturday closed.

Kvernes
Bygdemuseum
Open: June to August, Monday, Wednesday and Friday 2-4.30pm. Sunday 2-6pm.

Stave Church
Open: May to September, Sunday 1-6pm.

Leikvin
Kulturminne Park
Open: June to August daily 12noon-5pm.

Løkken
All mid-June to mid-August

Bergverkmuseet
Open: daily 12noon-4pm. Sunday 11am-4pm.

Gammelgruva (Old Mine)
Tours, daily 1pm, 2pm.

New Mine
Tours, Wednesday July, August 6pm. Saturday 12noon. Sunday 11am, 12.30pm, 2pm.

Thamshavnbanen
Tours, Wednesday 7.30pm. Sunday 12noon, 2pm, 3.15pm.

Molde
Cathedral
Open: 10am-3pm.

Fishing Museum
Open: June to mid-August, Monday to Saturday 10am-4pm. Sunday 12noon-4pm.

Romsdal Open-Air Museum
Open: beginning to mid-June and mid to end August daily, 10am-2pm. Sunday 12noon-3pm. Mid-June to mid-August daily, 10am-6pm. Sunday 12noon-6pm.

Rindal
Bygdemuseum
Open: mid-June to end August, Monday to Saturday 10am-4pm. Saturday and Sunday 12noon-4pm.

Sandane
Nordfjord Museum
Open: mid-June to beginning September daily 11am-4pm.

Selje
Monastery Ruins Boat Trips
June to August daily 10.30am and 2.30pm.

Stordal
Church and Bygdetun
Open: mid-June to end August daily 10am-3pm.

Sunndalsøra
Leikvin Museum Area
Open: June to August, Monday to Friday 12noon-5pm.

Surnadalsøra
Bygdetun
At Åsen Farm
☎ (073) 61 185 or (073) 61 133

Tingvoll
Bygdetun
Open: July daily 11am-4pm.

Church
Open: all year Tuesday to Friday 8.30am-3pm.

Tresfjord
Bygdetun
Open: mid-June to mid-August daily 11am-4pm.

Vingen
Rock Carvings
Boat trips from Klubban, Bremangerlandet late June to mid-August, Sunday 2.30pm.

Volda
Bygdetun
Open: mid-June to mid-August, Tues-

day, Wednesday, Thursday, Sunday
12noon-4pm. Boat section Friday, Saturday 12noon-4pm.

Tourist Information Centres

Ålesund
Ålesund Reiselivslag
Rådhuset
6025 Ålesund
☎ (071) 21202

Åndalsnes
PO Box 133
6301 Åndalsnes
☎ (072) 21622

Averøy
Averøy Reiselivslag
6550 Bremsnes
☎ (073) 11598

Florø
Florø Travel Association
PO Box 219
6901 Florø
☎ (057) 42010

Hareid
6060 Hareid
Open: June to August.
☎ (070) 93790

Herøy
Herøy and Runde
Reiselivslag
6096 Runde
☎ (070) 85905

Hitra
Central Tourist Information
Atlanten Reisebyrå
7240 Fillan
Hitra
☎ (074) 41470

Kristiansund
Kristiansund
    Reiselivslag
Kapt. Bødtkersgt 19
PO Box 401
6501 Kristiansund
☎ (073) 77211

Molde
Reiselivsforeningen
6400 Molde
Open: June to August.
☎ (072) 57133

Norddal
Norddal Reiselivslag
6210 Valldal
☎ (071) 57570

Nordfjordeid (Eid)
Eid Travel Association
PO Box 92
6770 Nordfjordeid
☎ (057) 61375

Sandane
Gloppen Travel Association
PO Box 223
6860 Sandane
☎ (057) 66100

Selje
Selje Travel Association
Selje kommune
6740 Selje
☎ (057) 56200

Stranda
Geiranger og Stranda
    Reiselivslag
6200 Stranda
☎ (071) 60044

Sunndalsøra
Sunndal Reiselivslag
6600 Sunndalsøra
☎ (073) 92552

Surnadal
Rindal and Surnadal
    Reiselivslag
6650 Surnadal
☎ (073) 61544

Ulstein
6065 Ulsteinvik
Open: June to August.
☎ (070) 93790

Vågøy
Vågøy Travel Association
c/o Kaptein Linge Hotel
6700 Måløy
☎ (057) 51800

Volda
Volda Reiselivslag
6100 Volda

4 • The Lofoten and Vesterålen Islands

The Lofoten islands are strung off the north-west coast of Norway, a strand not of pearls but of mountains, linked by bridges and a tunnel. The mountains that form their backbone, the Lofoten island wall, rise to between 500 and 1,000m, (1,640 and 3,280ft). They are some of the oldest in the world, worn by the Ice Age into fjords and narrow valleys, skerries and sandy beaches. Naturally, fishing has always been their main industry, fleets of up to 20,000 boats participating in the winter cod season, though less than half that number now take part. Every village has its harbour, surrounded by the traditional fishermen's cabins or *rorbu*. Originally built on the orders of King Øystein to house the men who came from all over Norway to join in the cod fishing, they are not only a picturesque part of the scenery. Balanced on their stilts round every harbour, they make simple and reasonably priced holiday homes, for tourism is now a major industry. Four airports with daily connections to Bodø, a car ferry service from here too, and the coastal steamer calling at Stamsund and Svolvær, all mean that the islands are accessible as never before. This does not mean that they are crowded: even in the height of the holiday season one can enjoy their attractions in peace. There are mountains for the climber, trails for the hiker and white sand beaches for the swimmer. However the sea is never very warm, despite the influence of the Gulf Stream Drift. Diving is a possibility with exploration of marine flora and fauna, and on land there are a wide variety of sightseeing and fishing trips available. Casting from the shore for cod, coalfish, haddock, catfish and tusk is free but for freshwater fishing a licence is required. Ice fishing is popular in winter and there is cross-country skiing available as well as a ski jump, and slalom slopes at Svolvær. Places to visit like museums are few and small but for the naturalist there are bird rocks and even a whale safari further north in Vesterålen. The main attraction of the islands lies in the small villages and the grandeur of the scenery, the peace and quiet miles off the beaten track.

The southernmost point one can drive to on the Lofotens is Å on

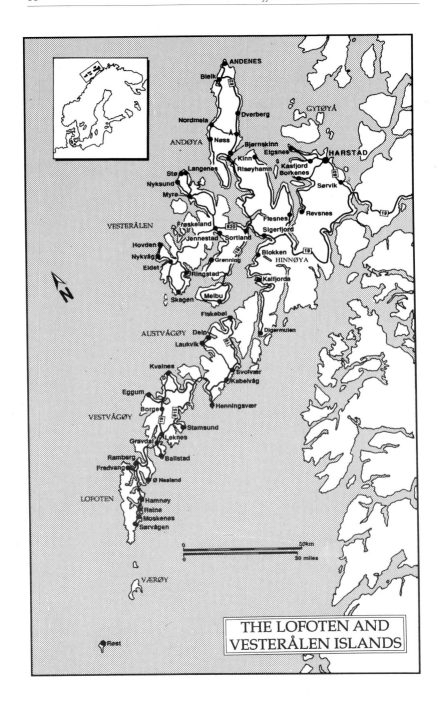

THE LOFOTEN AND
VESTERÅLEN ISLANDS

A Nordland boat at the Fishing Village Museum at Å

Moskenøy (*øy* means an island). Beyond here the famous Moskenes mælstrom tidal current lies across the route to the bird islands of Værøy and Røst. **Værøy** has auks, puffins, guillemots, kittiwakes, cormorants and the sea eagle which islanders used to trap with their bare hands from inside purpose-built hides. These can be seen via the hiking paths, along with the church, beach and deserted village beneath the main breeding cliffs, Mount Mostadfjell. **Røst** is the largest in an archipelago of small grassy islands. Apart from the birds found on Værøy, it also harbours eiderducks, the inhabitants providing them with shelters so that they can collect the down after hatching. These two islands are increasingly accessible with ferries now from Bodø, Moskenes, Reine and Å.

Å itself is a typical Lofoten fishing village, of which there are so many, unusual only in that much of it belongs to the Fishing Village Museum. The Ellingsen family have donated seven of the oldest buildings to the museum. Some like the smithy, bakery and boathouse are maintained as working environments, and they also own and let out a number of *rorbu*. Outside the main museum stand a line of the Nordland fishing boats with their upcurved prows. Larger boats provide a variety of trips. One can be a 'fisherman for a day', baiting, hauling, gutting, alongside a real fisherman in his boat; or go on an ocean safari to find sea eagles, cormorants and seal. You can also visit the far side of the island with its 3,000-year-old cave paintings. All trips last from 3 to 5 hours with a minimum of four adults.

Midnight sun trips, to watch it sink towards the sea only to rise again without setting, are also possible in season — from 25 May to 17 July.

Moving north from Å, **Tind** has unusually a line of mustard yellow *rorbu* and wharf buildings, their ledges lined with nesting gulls. (The common colour is of course Scandinavian red.) **Sørvågen** is much larger, with houses scattered round coast and lake until it almost joins **Moskenes**, built with its white church on the sheltered north side of a bay. Inland from here in an area of mountains and lakes there are a number of cairned or well-trodden footpaths. They vary in length and difficulty and should not be attempted without a proper mountain map, suitable clothes, boots, a rope and food. Always let someone know where you are going. These common-sense 'rules' apply to all paths in the Lofotens. With these warnings in mind, there are spectacular views to be had and experienced fell walkers should have no problems.

The road north to Reine and beyond is particularly pretty as it hugs the coast yet has sufficient soil to support a profusion of wild flowers. **Reine** itself lies to the right on a curving spur of land that juts into the bay so that, looking back from beyond, it seems built on an island. It is this perhaps that has earned it the title of the most beautiful spot in the whole of Norway (not just the Lofotens). Certainly its setting is delightful with peaked mountains encircling the bay and Reine lying like a jewel in the centre.

Beyond here the 19 bridges its way to **Hamnøy**. Here, where the road has been blasted out of the rock, there are seagulls nesting just above one's head as one drives through, their raucous cries rising above even engine noise! Travel 3km (2 miles) to find the small bronze plaque in the cliff wall that commemorates the opening of the Å to Svolvær road in 1963 by King Olav V. This southern end is much the same as it was then. Improvements in the Leknes area with the tunnel between Napp and Lilleidet opening in July 1990, have eliminated the last remaining ferry. From here the road follows the coast. The village one can see across the Kåkersundet just before the suspension bridge is **Sund** and it is well worth turning right for the 3km (2 miles) diversion down to it. There are two harbours here, both with their red *rorbu* perched on stilts, but at the second bay there is also a fishing museum and art smithy, famous for its cormorants. Notice on returning the paintings on the rock wall and also the grey house with the dated eighteenth-century weathervane.

North of Kåkern, the road leads along the side of the wider Selfjord. A new bridge crosses it to Fredvang where there is a wide sandy bay at Ytresand and 3km (2 mile) trails across to the outer edge of the islands. One can also drive round to Krystad and Selfjord for the longer trails to Kvalvika and to the sandy beaches of Horseid. East of here, back on the 19, at the innermost edge of the fjord, turn right for Nesland. This again is a no-through road but a pleasant one, though it does lose its tarred surface beyond Ytre Skelfjord. It follows the fjord to its southernmost tip then crosses to Ø **Nesland**, described in the brochures as a derelict fishing/farming hamlet. However in summer it does not look derelict. Ø Nesland is also the southern end of the Flakstad trail which leads across to Nusfjord and then to Napp via Stone Age caves at Storbåthallaren. To reach Nusfjord ($4^1/_2$ km, 3 miles away) by car one has to return to the 19 and head first through **Ramberg** with its beautiful curved beach and Flakstad with its eighteenth-century red wood church capped with an onion dome; then south again to the bottom of the Flakstadpollen. **Nusfjord** is signed to the right on a pretty road past Storvatnet. It is worth the long trip round. Listed by UNESCO as a preservation-worthy building environment, it has two bays of picturesquely-sited *rorbu* and an ex-fishing boat offering a variety of sea trips including sightseeing to the Stone Age caves and the midnight sun, as well as fishing.

The 19 heads north again through Kilan with its sandy beach to Vareid where the road to the left goes to **Vikten**. The Lofotens only glassblower works in a studio-workshop here, facing a white sand beach dotted with rocks. It is open all day, every day except Sunday. There is also handloom weaving next door. From Vareid the 19 heads for Napp and the new tunnel to the larger and more fertile island of Vestvågøy. This new stretch of road has changed the route towards Leknes but not beyond recognition. The red dragon-style church of **Gravdal** on its rocky hill is still a landmark over the coastal plain, where farming and fishing go hand in hand. A diversion past it leads along a well-populated peninsula to **Ballstad**, the port that brings in one of the largest catches during the fishing season. For the best view over the spread-out village, follow the Ballstadøy signs and climb the hill to the monument behind the wharfs.

A second diversion turns right at the start of Leknes for Stamsund. Bypassing **Fygle**, stop at the far end of the lake for the Vestvågøy Museum. The old schoolhouse contains among other things a classroom where the teacher slept as well as taught, and working looms which produce both woollen cloth and the rag rugs that are so typical of the area. Outside there is a boat, a whaling harpoon and a fishermen's hut. The next right (for Sennesvik and Mortsund) leads first past **Hol** church. Set off to the right, this white wood cruciform church from 1859 looks across the water to Fygle but the best views await on the road across to Sennesvik. Stop on the hairpin and admire the view back — it will make up for the poor quality of the unsurfaced road. At Sennesvik, go left again for Stamsund. This rejoins the 815 which is surfaced. The next right, for Steine, still surfaced and a pretty road round the fjord, also leads past numerous offshore skerries to **Stamsund**, the largest fishing village in the Lofotens and one of the two places where the coastal steamer calls. The houses spread themselves round the harbours and along the shore until they reach the large stone church that was built in 1937. A war memorial stands outside while inside there are stained glass pictures in the entrance and a relief of the Last Supper on the altar. From here one can either continue to Smorten or circle back to Leknes and the 19. The latter has the merit of excellent views backwards as one climbs to the Hagstua hotel and a wide panorama forwards as one descends towards Fygle.

Beyond Leknes the 19 passes through mechanised farmlands until it reaches **Borge**, where the 1986 church dominates the scene. Beautifully situated on a hill with extensive views all round, its modern white and maroon exterior is matched by the lovely woven altar hanging and the wooden Mary and Joseph in the entrance hall. Soon after the church turn left for Eggum for a diversion to the west coast. Though unsurfaced for most of the way, it is not a bad quality road and the scenery compensates. One passes the harbour first and then the brightly painted houses of **Eggum** itself. At the far end either park at the cattlegrid and walk to the round World War II German fort or drive on to the fort and walk beyond, as far as the headland. On a clear day the light is brilliant and the backdrop of mountains to the north spectacular. This is of course one of the best places on Vestvågøy for viewing the midnight sun. Another is Kvalnes, which can be reached by a westwards diversion a little further along the 19.

As one approaches Smorten, a very pointed peak appears to the left. This is **Hovel**, which is on **Gimsøya**, reached by turning left for Vinje beyond the bridge. The peak one passes first is 762m (2,499ft) high but then the area becomes flat with marshes, ponds and, on the road to Årstrand, peat bog which is still cut. Beyond steep-sided Hovel, there is a good sandy beach at Hov and views to the mountains to the north. On this side of the peninsula the land is fertile with fields and cattle and the small white church of **Gimsøysand** stands overlooking the water. Beyond the Gimsøysund bridge, **Henningsvær** deserves a visit. Turn right past the twin sandy beaches of Rorvik and follow this coastal road under towering peaks and rocky hillsides to the two bridges that now join Henningsvær to the main

Henningsvær, on Austvågøy, Lofoten Islands

island. The Nordland boat set as a monument on the first hill represents the livelihood of the picturesque port, with its long narrow harbour created by damming the sound. It used to be the gathering point for the largest fishing fleet of the season — so many in fact that one could walk across their decks from wharf to wharf. This is no longer possible but it is still very much a working port with wharfs and warehouses either side of the water.

Back on the 19, one passes through the Rorvik tunnel — the old road over the top is now closed — and so to **Kabelvåg** where the Lofoten Museum sits in an area awash with rosebay willowherb in summer. Here the main building has room settings and exhibitions on the history of the sea, a barn houses a fisheries museum and a boathouse holds three Nordland boats of varying sizes. The oldest remaining *rorbu*, dates from 1789 with a grass roof above its plain unpainted walls. Close by is the modern and imaginatively designed Lofoten Aquarium, which includes seals and a tankful of leaping fish in the waters of the fjord. The large cream and brown church at the far end of Kabelvåg is the Lofoten Cathedral.

The next town is **Svolvær**, a functional trade and administrative centre with a large harbour from which trips can be made to one of the most famous Norwegian fjords, the dramatically dark and narrow Trollfjord. The coastal steamer enters only if conditions are suitable on its run through from Stokmarknes. One way to reach the more northerly island group of the Vesterålen from here is to follow the 'Kaiser's Route' by ferry to Digermulen (Kaiser Wilhelm II spent several holidays there in the late nineteenth century) and along the beautiful Raftsundet to Kongselv where a second ferry to Kalfjorda is needed. This is the starting point for the mountain trail to Vesterålen's highest peak, **Møysalen**, which at 1,208m (3,962ft) gives views over the whole of the Lofoten/Vesterålen area and even into Sweden. However the trail is long (9 to 12 hours depending whether one takes the boat from Hennes mole) and involves hard climbing and a glacier. It should only be attempted by the very fit and with an experienced local guide arranged through a tourist office. The road north from here is particularly scenic beyond Blokken, situated on the first and largest of a series of bays. There is a rocky pass, mountains still with snow patched on them in July, and good views across to Sigerfjord and the Sortland bridge. The real problem with this route lies in the infrequency of the ferries and the difficulty of timing them as a complete journey. It is simpler to continue north on the 19. This emerges from a tunnel just before the airport turning to good views of the mountains ahead. The countryside here is very rocky with the odd cabin perched among the scrub. When the road follows the west shore of the narrow Austnesfjord, watch out for Sildpollen chapel down to the right on a tongue of land jutting into the fjord.

The next place is **Vestpollen** where fjord meets lake and the tide rushes under the flat bridge. Leave the 19 here, following the Laukvik sign to the left for a pleasant and varied diversion to the west coast. On its way across the island the road is flanked by hills and lakes, which flow in opposite directions to the sea. At the farming community of Straumnes turn left first for **Laukvik**. For the best views of the islands, sea and midnight sun, drive past the sailors' memorial and the harbour and onto the head of land beyond. Returning through Laukvik, pause at **Straumnes** church. The word *Fred* above the door means peace. Certainly the simple interior is tranquil with its pastel paints and round stained glass altar window of the Lamb of God. Although this road is only signed to Delp, it continues beyond the hamlet to cross the Grunnførfjord by causeway. A well-surfaced road so far, it is reduced to hard-packed mud beyond but is still worth pursuing. It passes **Hadselsand** with church and school adjoining and graveyard overlooking the sea; an area of dunes at the mouth of the Murfjord; a wrecked fishing boat and sandy beaches, before coming round to meet the 19 for the ferry crossing at Fiskebøl.

This is the end of the Lofotens. The Vesterålen islands start where the ferry docks at Melbu. Although they have similar mountains and are a northwards continuation of the same chain of islands, the differences are immediately apparent. The narrowness of the Lofoten islands, all backbone and little shore, is lost even where the actual islands are no wider. Here the farming plains are broader and the islands spread side by side with fjords between. Thus the *rorbu* of the Lofotens, with their harbours directly on the ocean, disappear and instead smaller boats tuck themselves into the shore beside the farmers' fields. That is not to say that fishing is not a major industry. About half the population are in employment connected with the fisheries. Travel round the area is easy with bridges linking the five main islands and a ferry-free route out to Narvik in the north. There are also airports at Andenes and Stokmarknes; three points of call for the coastal steamer and a rapidly developing express boat network.

To return to **Melbu**, a tree-lined street leads from the harbour to Melbu manor, which is now part of the Vesterålen Museum. More is in the basement of the meeting centre opposite and there is also a culture trail from the manor with information boards on the farm and the development of the port. This leads on to the 18km (11 mile) Melbu-Stokmarknes culture trail with similar boards on nature and the surroundings all the way.

Again, instead of following the 19, why not head left out of Melbu for Haug and Dragnes? The road is unfortunately not signposted but it is the only road leaving town in that direction. As with the previous diversion, it forms a loop with the 19, round opposite sides of, in this case, Hadseløy. Interestingly the two roads make a complete circle of 42.395km (just over 26 miles), the exact distance of the marathon, so perhaps it is not surprising that such a race is held here every August. The Dragnes road crosses a coastal plain at the foot of the mountains giving views initially back to the Lofotens, then onwards towards Bø. The two roads meet again in Stokmarknes for the bridges across to Langøya but first go south just a few kilometres to the octagonal church at **Hadsel**. Built in 1824, it contains a triptych from 1520 and sixteenth-century portraits in the gallery. This stretch of road also gives good views of the gracefully curving bridge that one must cross to continue north.

Descending from the bridge onto **Langøya** turn immediately left for Eidsfjord, another alternative to the 19 and one which passes through exceptionally varied terrain. It follows the sound first between the two islands. Where the road approaches the Fleines peninsula, watch out for the Eidsfjord painted stone. It is a large rock by the roadside, with an upright surface painted around 1920 by Konrad Johnson with scenes representing safety at sea and restored in 1986 by Melbu artist Bengt Ellingsen. The road then follows the Eidsfjord

The Eidsfjord stone near Fleines, Langøya

to the little white church at **Gronning**, with a monument impossibly situated on the hill behind. The further one goes along the fjord, the rockier the terrain becomes, and on a dull day, the more brooding the mountains over the deep dark water — though of course it only takes sunshine to add sparkle to the scene! The surface disappears from the road, in sympathy with the increasing ruggedness but fails to return when habitations increase near the inner end. The white sheds and quay on a shallow promontory to the left are the remains of Sild-pollen's herring fishing industry — killed not by competition but by lack of shoals. Beyond, at Oshaugen, one is back to farmland in a well-watered valley. One can cut back across the island here for Sortland or continue on, viewing Sildpollen from the fjordward side, to **Holmstad** where the 1969 inner Eidsfjord church sits imposingly on a hill, looking down the length of the fjord towards the open sea. By continuing on to Frøskeland and turning right there for Sortland on the 820 one can visit **Jennestad** Handelssted. Once a trading centre for this part of the world, the shop has been restored with old-fashioned goods of which sweets are for sale via the early cash register. There is also an art gallery, work and repair shops and a guided tour in English available.

If one turns left in Frøskeland, taking the 821 for Myre, there are interesting excursions in this part of Langøya. One travels along Steinlandsfjorden first to **Myre** itself where the local museum and the 1978 church are both to be found off the road opposite the tourist office. Head north then on the road for Sto and left for Nyksund. Unsurfaced beyond Høydal, the road passes a fishermen's memorial and picnic table overlooking the mouth of the Prestfjord before clinging precariously to the cliffs on its way to this deserted fishing village. Once the second largest in Vesterålen, **Nyksund's** last inhabitant moved out in 1977 after spending 3 years alone there. A repair project by young people from Germany, Denmark and Norway, which has restored some of the wharf-front buildings has run into financial difficulties and the Norwegians have now taken over responsibility for the site. A trail leads across the headland to the still-working fishing village of **Sto** but to reach it by car one must return practically to Myre and turn left over causeways and flat coastal plains with views to Andøya. **Langenes** fourteenth-century church, on the right by the shore, is also worth looking at. One can leave the peninsula by a different route by turning left beyond Myre for Alsvåg on the east coast and Lia on the Lifjord.

The western part of Langøya is the district of Bø. The 820 takes one here, passing first **Straumsjøen** where craft souvenirs including jewellery from local hand-polished stones are for sale at Krambua; then Fjærvoll and Gimstad with their dunes and sandy beaches. There are good views from here across to the Lofoten mountains. Bø Bygdemuseum is at Vinjesjøen which is signed right from Vinje. It includes a police office, a fishermen's cabin complete with figures and plaster fish made by the local schoolchildren, and items in the house. There are a few signs in quaint English and the curator offers additional comments. The next village to the right is **Skagen** where Jens Eriksen lived. In 1912 he constructed the now universal triangular fish-drying rack for preserving coalfish without the blowflies laying their eggs (and therefore their maggots) on it. Round the corner at Bø the 1824 church contains medieval figures but is only open to visitors twice a week. One passes then through a succession of villages, all facing across to the mountains of Hadseløya. Round the corner again and one is looking across to **Ringstad** where the tiny waterfront has been refurbished for holiday lets. To complete the circle back to the 820, follow the Skåbrekka signs. Worth diverting to while in this area is the Nykvåg/Hovden peninsula. Turn left for Eidet, past Malnes church, and along the right side of the Åsanfjord. Pause at the top of the hill beyond Sandvika for good views of the rocks off the coast and of the open sea in both directions. **Nykvåg** is best known for its bird cliffs where thousands of seagulls nest on every scrap of ledge. This is an active fishing village with a number of boats anchored in the harbour. So too is **Hovden** where a stretch

Prestfjord from Høydal, Langøya

of dunes separates two sandy beaches, facing one east and one west. There is no alternative route back but the scenery is well worth watching in both directions!

Andøya, the most northerly of the Vesterålen is the least visited of a chain of islands that even at the height of the season are deserted. Yet at Andenes, on the northernmost tip, is the most unusual attraction. The access road is the 82 across the bridge from Sortland. Otherwise one can arrive by coastal steamer at Risøyhamn in the south or fly into Andenes itself. The 82 follows the coast of Hinnøya through comparatively gentle fjord and mountain scenery. At **Dragnes**, where the old ferry used to operate, there is a handicrafts workshop and salesroom. Now a new bridge, high-arched to accommodate the coastal steamer, leads across to Risøyhamn. From here it is possible to circumnavigate Andøya. (The bus tour from Andenes takes $3^{1}/_{2}$ hours.) Leave the 82 beyond the town, following the signs for Skjoldehamn. The first church one passes, at **Bjørnskinn**, has medieval altar carvings though it dates from the nineteenth century. The road down to the southern tip of the island gives views across to the mountains of Langøya. Beyond Skjoldehamn there are deserted white sand beaches and floriferous verges in shades of purple and mauve, yellow and white. The odd turf-roofed hut remains dotted along the shore. Soon after the road from Risøyhamn comes across, study the area to the right closely; it is just possible to spot prehistoric housemounds standing small and green above the peat!

North of Nøss the mountains rear closer to the sea and the road squeezes beneath them. Watch for a large rockface towering above the road to the left. This is the **Bukkekirka**, which is used for outdoor religious services in the summer. You can identify it by the three crosses. **Nordmela** is prettily situated round the northern curve of a sandy bay backed by jagged peaks. There is a well-preserved turf-roofed sea-house by the lighthouse and a pleasant stroll to be had along the harbour wall beyond. Take binoculars to study the terns, gulls, oystercatchers and maybe gannets too. There is a road across the island here to Å. Passing a series of lakes, it is a more interesting route than the alternative cross road to Dverberg. This west coast route passes between the sea and Skogvall lake on its way to Stave with its sandy beaches. It then moves inland before dropping down with a pretty view over the island in Bleikvatnet, with its castle house. **Bleik** itself is worth exploring for the architecture of its houses both old and new. It also has the longest sandy beach in Norway and the bird rock Bleiksøya, where puffins, cormorants, kittiwakes, razorbills and other seabirds nest in colonies. Boat trips to view the birds are arranged by the Andenes tourist office.

The road to Andenes passes fishheads still dangling on the drying racks in July; dunes that past gales have swept halfway up the mountain sides and the widest variety of flora in the islands. On the outskirts of **Andenes** one passes the Andøya Rocket Range which investigates, among other things, the Northern Lights. There is more to do in Andenes than in the rest of Andøya put together. Clustered together at one end of the harbour are the Polar Museum, with artefacts from Amundsen's expedition as well as from the local men who spent seasons trapping on Spitzbergen; the deep red lighthouse built in 1859 which one can climb up for the views and the Whale Centre which shares a former fishing plant with the tourist office. This is not only an information centre about whaling and whales; it is also a research centre that runs a unique and fascinating attraction — the whale safari — as a means of funding its work. The trip starts with a researcher in the whale centre explaining among other things the sperm whale's echo system that is probably used to stun its prey and showing slides of local whale and bird life. Then one boards the 23m (75ft) long ex-whaler *Kromholt* — with a second boat in use if demand requires — under its third generation whaler captain. As a reminder of the past, the harpoon gun is still in place on the prow but these are photo safaris that not only give tourists slides that will be talking points for years but also allow the researchers to measure and identify the sperm whales through their pictures. Ideally, having

The octagonal church at Dverberg

spotted one blowing on the surface, the boat drifts silently closer and closer delaying the moment when the browsing whale takes fright and dives, displaying its tail flukes that are the researchers' chief means of identification. Over 90 per cent of the trips do locate whales and there is the bonus of puffins, fulmar and guillemots and perhaps smaller whales to be seen. It is a popular trip and worth booking in advance via the tourist office. In bad weather it will be postponed — not only for the tourists' comfort but also because the whales themselves will be less in evidence. The safari is a full day's outing.

Back on dry land to complete the circuit of the island follow the 82 along the east coast, admiring the mountains of Senja to the left. The Ramsåfallet is a nature trail over the **Ramså** dunes. It is about $1^1/_2$ km (1 mile) long but feels more due to the soft conditions underfoot. There are information boards about the dunes and fossils in the area. **Dverberg** octagonal church is also worth a visit — telephone in advance to book a guided tour.

Hinnøya is the last island in the Vesterålen group, and also the largest in Norway. It can be reached from the outer islands via the Sortland bridge or from the mainland by the 19 off the E6 north of Narvik. There are also ferries and express boats into Lødingen and Harstad. Hinnøya has more spectacular scenery than the outer islands — the mountains are higher, the fjords reminiscent of their more famous counterparts further south. There are also a lot of dead end roads, like those to Kinn and Røykenes to the north of the

Hognfjord or out to Øksneshamn from Kanstad in the south. From Sortland, follow the 19 along the Sigerfjord, past the road to Kalfjorda and Digermulen described earlier. A few kilometres further on, the 850 provides a viable alternative for reaching Harstad. It is a much shorter route than using the 19 and 83 but involves a car ferry from Flesnes to Revsnes. The tourist information kiosk just before the junction has timetables and if the queue should prove too long, Flesnes is only 11km (7 miles) out of the way. The route is scenically pleasant beyond the ferry with views across the fjord and to Kvæøya with its striped farm fields facing south. To see the most of this northeastern corner, turn right at Straumen for Sørvik and Storfjorda. This good quality road goes up through the mountains with plenty of parking places near the lakes. Storvatnet is the largest of these, set against a backdrop of snow-streaked mountains. On descending the other side, at **Sørvik**, there is a local museum comprising furnished red farmhouse and a collection of turf-roofed huts. Unfortunately it only opens Sunday evenings.

From here left on the 83 brings one to **Harstad**, with a good viewpoint at Stangnes on the right at the start of the town. Alternatively climb to the 1958 church, standing high above the town. Much more interesting though, on the **Trondenes** peninsula, is the most northerly stone church in Norway. Built in the thirteenth century, it has been restored as nearly as possible to that period with frescoes, decorations, a carved altar screen, iron door and three medieval triptychs. The most interesting of these is the high altar with carvings of the Holy Family including seven women and their children. An attraction of a totally different type is the Trondenes gun (or Adolf Cannon) set up to protect Narvik's iron ore industry by the Germans in World War II. It is inside a modern Norwegian army base so guided tours must be booked through the tourist office and a military policeman accompanies all visitors. They are well worth the effort and the price. Identical to the Channel gun used against Britain, the one shown here is still in working order. It was capable of firing Adolf shells over 50km (31 miles). The guide demonstrates various working parts. Although fully automatic, everything could be performed manually, including ramming in the shot with a rod requiring 20 men to lift it! All this information and much more comes from the English-speaking guides.

Beyond Harstad the northern tip of the island can be circled. Take the 850 back across to the Kvæfjord. Beyond Borkenes the scenery is excellent with views across the fjords over a long stretch of road but the most spectacular are on the road from Kasfjord to Elgsnes. It is the best mountain road in the whole of Vesterålen with views in both directions from its hairpin bends. Just before Elgsnes, the Hans Egedes memorial chapel stands, where there are evening services every Friday in July at 10pm. Hans Egedes was a missionary from Greenland who carried out evangelical work here in the eighteenth century and is remembered also in street names in Harstad and by a statue outside the Harstad church. There are three further memorial stones in the area of the chapel. On the way back to Harstad turn left for Stornes on the ferry road, for the old trading station of Røkenes Gård. Licensed as an inn since 1777 it is now a guesthouse and restaurant where one can enjoy a meal.

These then are the Lofoten and Vesterålen islands, accessible but quiet, even at the height of the tourist season, an area for a leisurely scenic holiday well off the beaten track!

Further Information
— The Lofoten and Vesterålen Islands —

Places of interest are all only open June, July, August.

LOFOTEN ISLANDS
Å
Fishing Village Museum
Open: daily 10am-6pm.

Fygle
Vestvågøy Museum
Open: Monday to Friday 11am-2pm. Saturday and Sunday 12noon-3pm.

Kabelvåg
Lofoten Aquarium
Open: daily 10am-6pm.

Lofoten Museum
Open: daily 10am-9pm.

Sund
Fishery Museum and Art Smithy
Open: daily 10am-5pm. Sunday 12-5pm.

VESTERÅLEN ISLANDS
Andenes
Lighthouse and Polar Museum
Open: Monday to Friday 10am-1pm, 3-6pm. Sat and Sun 11am-2pm, 3-6pm.

Whale Centre
Open: daily 8am-8pm.

Bø
Church
Open: Tuesday and Friday 12noon-2pm or via tourist office.

Dverberg
Church
☎ 46189

Hadsel
Church
Open: Monday to Friday 10am-4pm.

Harstad
Trondenes Church
Open: Monday to Friday 9am-2pm.

Saturday 9am-12noon. Also Tuesday and Thursday 6-8pm. Sunday 5-7pm.

Jennestad
Handlessted
Open: Tuesday to Friday 11.30am-9pm. Saturday and Sunday 2-6pm.

Melbu
Vesterålen Museum
Open: mid-June to mid-August, Monday to Friday 9am-3pm. Saturday and Sunday 11am-3pm.

Sørvik
Local Museum
Open: Sunday 5-7pm.

Vinjesjøen
Bø Bygdemuseum
Open: mid-June to mid-August Tuesday and Thursday 12noon-3pm. Wednesday 12noon-6pm. Sunday 3-6pm.

Tourist Information Centres

LOFOTEN
Svolvær ☎ 71 053
Stamsund ☎ 89 394
There are summer bureaux in most tourist areas.

VESTERÅLEN
Andøya
Hvalsenterst
8480 Andenes
Open: beginning June to end August. Monday to Friday 8am-8pm. Saturday 10am-2pm. Sunday 8am-6pm.
☎ 088 42611

Bø
Ryggedal-tunnel
Open: Monday to Friday 10am-6pm. Saturday and Sunday 10am-4pm.
☎ 090-14559

Hadsel
Gammel Bræcks Bakeri
8450 Stokmarknes
Open: Monday to Friday 10am-8pm. Sat 10am-6pm. Sun 12noon-6pm
☎ 52600

Fiskebøl RV19
Hadsel
Open: end June to late August, Monday to Friday 10am-6pm. Saturday and Sunday closed.

Harstad
Torvet 7
PO Box 447
N-9400 Harstad
☎ 082-63 235

Øksnes
Rådhuset
8430 Myre

Open: 18 June to 18 August, Monday to Friday 10am-8pm. Saturday 12noon-4pm. Sunday 2-4pm.
☎ 34444

Sortland
Bykonteret
8400 Sortland
Open: 18 June to 20 August, Monday to Friday 10am-7pm. Saturday 10am-2pm. Sunday closed.
☎ 23494

Langvassdalen RV19
Open: 26 June to 18 August daily 10am-6pm.

5 • The Arctic Circle Tour

This is the ultimate Scandinavian holiday, a 2,100km (1,302 mile) tour beyond the Arctic Circle encompassing the northern territories of Finland, Norway and Sweden, and the more nebulous area of Lapland. Here one finds the Lapps themselves and their reindeer, the midnight sun and the most northerly point in Europe, the North Cape. The scenery is varied from the endless forests of Finland; to the rocky tundra, treeless and boggy, of the central plateaux; the fjords, islands and mountains of the Norwegian coast and the Swedish lakes and rushing rivers. The climate is very similar to an English summer. The only snow is on the peaks of the Lyngen Alps and even the Arctic Ocean, warmed by the Gulf Stream, is no colder than the Atlantic.

The Lapps, or Same in their own language, are traditionally nomadic, herding their reindeer in winter across the tundra, regardless of national frontiers. Nowadays, however, many families live in villages, the herdsmen alone continuing the annual trek. Some are fully integrated with their Scandinavian neighbours but there is also a strong movement to preserve their traditional culture and crafts. The tourist sees this in the wayside souvenir camps where the short stocky Lapps dress up in their traditional winter garb, the deep blue hat, tunic and trousers with gay red and yellow trims and the reindeer-skin boots with their turned-up toes. Here too in a series of utilitarian plastic-wrapped stalls, they sell their bags and purses, skins, knives and slippers and the inevitable antlers. They still have wigwam-shaped tents but also small caravans and pick-up trucks. Far from romantic, these settlements undoubtedly supplement the Lapp family income.

The reindeer roam wild in the summer. Dun brown with heavy antlers, they merge into the trees beside the Finnish roads, or speckle the high plateaux of Norway. Used to man, they do not run away but rather turn their backs just as the photographer clicks the shutter! If surprised after dark, they run straight at cars — injuries to the reindeer must be reported to the nearest police chief. Some are now kept on farms, particularly in Finland, where they provide a tourist

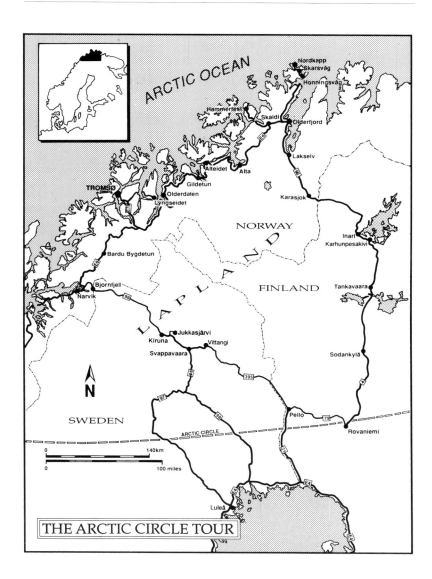

THE ARCTIC CIRCLE TOUR

attraction as well as venison.

Travelling in this northern area is made more enjoyable by the phenomenon of the midnight sun. At the North Cape it does not set between 14 May and 29 July. Further south the period is shorter so that on the Arctic Circle itself only Midsummer's Day has continuous light; but even if the sun does set, the nights are incredibly bright. Far from disappearing around the world, it seems to hide just below the horizon, tinting the clouds lemon against the clear blue sky. This continuous daylight infects the people with endless energy. The grass is vividly green, not from the rainfall but from increased chlorophyll, and grows so fast that two hay crops are possible in one short season. Similarly plants that elsewhere follow each other over a period of months, here bloom in rapid succession. It is wonderful compensation for the winter months of darkness when the only relief is the Aurora Borealis or Northern Lights. These can illuminate the sky for hours at a time with lightning-like shafts of green, white, red and yellow. It is not yet fully understood by the scientists who have special observatories, as at Tromsø for studying it.

The chief activities in these northern areas are outdoor pursuits. Fishing is by permit in specified waters including rivers and lakes in Finland and Sweden and deep sea fishing in the Norwegian fjords (details from local tourist offices). There are water-bus and sight-seeing boat trips, or canoeing, or rubber-rafting down the fast-flowing rivers from Karasjok and Jukkasjarvi. Some rivers also provide gold and one can pan for it at Tankavaara and Karasjok.

Another activity is hiking with marked trails that double in winter as cross-country ski tracks. For the expert, longer trails are available with overnight huts but the Finns warn against hiking alone in the interior. Always tell someone where you are going and when you can be expected. Remember too that wilderness plant and animal life is protected, including predators like wolves and bears.

Some activities are only available in certain places. Reindeer-driving, for instance, a crash course culminating in a reindeer-driving licence, is a Finnish speciality found at reindeer farms near Rovaniemi, Sodankyla and Inari. The Lyngen Alps give good mountaineering and also glacier tours. Hang-gliding is a speciality of Narvik and Tromsø where the nearby mountains provide the necessary thermals. Perhaps the widest range of activities, either for a few hours or as a week's holiday, can be found at Karasjok.

Not surprisingly, in winter Narvik and Tromsø also provide the best Alpine skiing but slalom courses and ski jumps are also available at Rovaniemi and Karasjok. Nordic or cross-country skiing exists everywhere and most major towns have kilometres of well-lit track. The Finnish towns also offer reindeer or snowmobile safaris. Rovaniemi in particular is establishing itself as a centre for Christmas-in-Lapland holidays, including Santa Claus in person and a range of activities from visiting a genuine Lapp village to ice golf.

The whole of the Arctic area is accessible by internal flights from

Oslo, Stockholm or Helsinki but this means hiring a car which is expensive. One excellent route for taking one's own car is from Harwich to Hamburg, where an 80km (50 mile) drive takes one to Travemunde on the north German coast. From here gigantic Baltic liners float one effortlessly to Helsinki. They provide not only on board entertainment but also a magnificent *smorgåsbord* or cold table, complete with English booklet telling how to tackle it, from breathing in both sight and scent, to sampling every course in the correct order and in moderation. A day in Helsinki is a bonus and then the motorail to Rovaniemi deposits one practically on the Arctic Circle, with almost no driving. The Finnish car sleepers are efficient, the compartments compactly furnished including washing facilities and pots of drinking water. Their only drawback is that the one small buffet section provides only snacks and is crowded. It is better to eat in the excellent station restaurants beforehand and afterwards.

This tour starts at **Rovaniemi** (though Narvik in Norway or Kiruna in Sweden are valid alternatives). Rovaniemi is a market town on the confluence of the Kemijoki and Ounasjoki rivers, with a good shopping centre and a complicated road system. There are museums, a minigolf and an excellent summer bobsleigh run on the Ounasvaara 'mountain'. Reindeer farms in the vicinity offer reindeer driving licences (book through the City Tourist Office).

Six kilometres (4 miles) north, on the 4 or Arctic Road, one crosses the Arctic Circle, the Napapiiri, marked by several roadside signs. Here too is the Santa Claus Village which is open to the public. Here one will find the world's most northerly glassworks, the blowers operating behind a clear glass screen; a hall full of Lapp souvenirs and an indoor street of specialist craft shops. Santa Claus's office which deals with world-wide Christmas mail and a Post Office using a special Arctic Circle postmark is also here. Santa Claus himself may well be there too, slapping 'Santa lives in Finland' stickers on young and old alike. For the children there is the House of the Hundred Elves; for the adults, look out for the arrows on the reception area floor pointing to the North Pole.

The road all the way to the Norwegian border is the 4. Well-surfaced and straight, it runs through the conifer forests of northern Finland. Pine and spruce abound, though there are silver birch too and glimpses of water through the trees. Borders of purple willow-herb add a splash of colour but scenically it can only be described as dull. It is also deserted, though one does find the occasional Russian juggernaut powering its way to or from Russia, which is never more than 200km (124 miles) away to the east.

*Statue of a Lapp and
reindeer at Sodankylä*

Sodankylä makes a useful overnight stop in an area where towns
are few. It has wide, straight streets and blockish buildings but do not
miss the powerful Lapp and reindeer statue. Behind it lies the new
church and to the left a signposted footpath leads to the old one
through a wood of ancient trees and graves bright with flowers. It is
the oldest surviving church in Finnish Lapland. Timber-built in 1689,
its planks and shingles are unpainted and weathered to the same
silver-grey as the birch tree that towers above the porch.

Travelling north again, watch out for a wooden walkway on the
left, opposite a parking place. It leads across marshes to a viewing
platform over the nearby lake. The next stop is the **Tankavaara** gold
village. Finland, like Australia and America had its nineteenth-
century gold rushes, equally frenetic and equally short-lived. Today
only a handful of professional 'wilderness men' remain, prospecting
on their own in the lonely wastes of the north. At Tankavaara the
museum reconstructs that period and one can also pan for gold in the
river under professional guidance.

Beyond the small township of Ivalo with its boarding schools for
the children of the migrant Lapps, the scenery changes. The forests
are interspersed with tundra plateaux sporting enormous blocks of
granite. One of these is the fascinating 'Bear's Cave' rock at **Karhun-
pesakivi** which is always open. Reached by another plank route up
a wooded hillside, it balances among trees, a huge hollow boulder

with two scrambling entrance routes into a cosy cave interior with boil holes in its roof. These are 'devil's bowls' gouged out by swirling stones in the rocky beds of rivers which means the boulder, tumbled here at the end of the Ice Age, came to rest upside down!

There are glimpses here through the trees of Lake Inari the third largest lake in Finland though it does not look it, scattered as it is with some 3,000 islands. One is an ancient Lapp sacrificial spot which local boat trips visit. The village of **Inari**, standing at its westernmost point, has an excellent Lapp open-air museum. Besides well-labelled village sites there is an interesting display of the ingenious traps used to catch predators such as wolverine, fox and bear.

From Inari to the border is a further 96km (60 miles) of barren landscape. There the 4 becomes the 96 to **Karasjok** in the Norwegian county of Finnmark. A small modern town — in common with all other towns in Finnmark it was destroyed by the Germans in 1944 — it makes another sensible overnight stop. A pleasant after-dinner stroll takes one down to the river. Beyond the suspension bridge stands the oldest original church left in Finnmark, pristine with its white-washed walls and red-washed roof. Dating from 1807, it was used as school, hospital and supply base during the re-building of Karasjok. There is a new church too, square with a pyramid roof and central tower dating from 1974.

From Karasjok to the North Cape is an easy morning's journey. The scenery softens as one drops towards Lakselv so that the 70°N sign is surrounded by trees and it is hard to realise that this same parallel bisects Greenland and runs along the north coast of Siberia. That Finnmark is so much more pleasant is due to the warming influence of the Gulf Stream Drift that keeps the harbours ice-free all year round and gives Norway a plethora of 'most northerly' places.

At **Lakselv** one reaches the foot of the Porshanger Fjord. Norway's widest, it is not spectacularly steep and rocky like those on the west coast but offers instead a shoreline, tide-marked by seaweed, speckled with occasional groups of fishing boats. Follow the fjord here on the 6 and the 95 for the North Cape, the farthest point of the island of Magerøy, reached by ferry from Kåfjord. Do not leave the crossing too late as the evening boats become crowded with tourists arriving for the midnight sun. The ferry docks at **Honningsvåg**, a simple fishing port that has geared itself up to the North Cape tourist trade. The new North Cape House contains high quality souvenirs on the ground floor, while above, the museum deals mainly with the year-round fishing industry. There are also hotels and guesthouses.

Originally visitors arrived at the foot of the North Cape cliffs by

The ferry to Honningsvåg

boat. In 1929 a quay was built there and 8 years later, steps up to the plateau. These were removed after the road was built in 1956. When one drives north on it now in summer, curving past a strategically situated Lapp souvenir settlement, then twisting and climbing up to 312m (1,023ft), it is hard to believe that the road is only open from about 20 May to 1 October. The landscape is green with grass and moss; the white hill ahead is covered not with snow but chalk, which is what its name, Duken, means. The island itself is a long-standing nature reserve, the numerous reindeer summer residents who have swum the Magerøysund at its narrowest point to breed here. Beyond Duken, follow the signpost to **Skarsvåg**, the most northerly fishing village in the world. It huddles picturesquely round a small bay, but the old-fashioned fish-drying racks are no longer so much in evidence now that Honningsvåg boasts a large fish factory.

From here it is only a few kilometres to the 307m (1,007ft) high table of slate rising perpendicular from the Arctic Ocean that is the North Cape (Nordkapp). Bleak, grey, exposed to the elements, not prepossessing at all, it is the most northerly point, at 71°10′21″, that one can reach in Europe. Discovered and named in 1553 by Englishman Richard Chancellor who was seeking a north-east passage to China but instead made it by sled to Ivan the Terrible's Moscow, it has been a place of pilgrimage ever since. In 1664 Francesco Negri wrote of it, 'Here the world ends... '. He and Chancellor, Louis Philippe of France and the King of Siam are all commemorated in a series of dioramas in the modern complex built above and into the rock. A 2-day parking ticket gives one access to all the facilities, including an excellent 5-screen video show. There are souvenirs to buy, postcards to send with a special postmark, monuments and statues both inside and out. One can even join the Royal North Cape Club with their own exclusive range of souvenirs. The only problem is whether one will actually see the sun here at midnight. Climactically the odds are against it. The coldness of the sea and the height of the rock combine to produce hanging cloud — but it will still be daylight at midnight for those commemorative photographs of the skeletal globe that multi-national tourists take here. It is the one crowded spot of this whole tour but also the one that can best be boasted about back home.

There is only one way to go from Nordkapp and that is south, retracing one's steps as far as Olderfjord, where one turns right on the 6 towards Alta. First visit Hammerfest, the most northerly town in the world. Follow the 94 right at Skaidi to Repparfjord. At Kvalsund, Norway's longest suspension bridge (at 714.5m, 2,344ft), and naturally the world's most northerly, takes the road across to the island of Kvaløy. Here it follows the south and east coast closely with good views of glaciers on neighbouring Seiland. Near at hand one can study the Norwegian farm economy with its handkerchief-sized fields set between the sea and the rocky hillside where the grass is scythed by hand and slung over wire fences to dry into hay.

One comes on **Hammerfest** suddenly — one last turn round the coast and there is the triangular-shaped church at the start of the town, an unmistakeable landmark. Built in 1961, with a separate bell-tower, its simple interior is dominated by the huge stained glass window in the west end. The reason for its newness and the austere appearance of much of the town, is the same as at Karasjok — the total destruction of the town by the Germans in 1944. It is an event commemorated in Latin on the wall of the Roman Catholic Church, on a stark plaque that contrasts with the colourful George and the Dragon mosaic beside it. Here only the sexton's cottage beside the graveyard was left and even that is gone now. The town was also destroyed in 1890, by fire, and during re-building became the first town in Europe to have electric street lights!

For good views over the town climb the zig-zag footpath from just above the green oasis that is the Ole Olsen Plass up to the Varde on Salen hill. A solid square tower, scaleable by a 'fireman's ladder', it was re-built with contributions from the Germans after they had used the original for building gun-sites. Looking down, the town, whose name means 'rope-fastening for boats in the mountain

Church at Hammerfest

slopes', is strung round both sides of what is one of the best ice-free harbours in northern waters. Five thousand ships a year call here not only to trade but also for the boatyards, oil and chandlers that supply their every need. The Meridian monument, on the far side of the bay commemorates a joint Russian/Swedish/Norwegian attempt to determine the exact size and shape of the earth. To see the midnight sun follow the road to its furthest point at the fishing village of Forsøl. Hammerfest enjoys permanent daylight from 17 May to 28 July and total darkness from 22 November to 21 January.

One must now retrace one's steps to Skaidi, to pick up the 6 once again, for Alta, across the flat uplands of the reindeer and tundra moss, its trees stunted by the barren soil. The road reaches a high point of 380m (1,246ft) at Sennalandet before dropping eventually to the gentle shores of the Alta fjord.

Alta is a sprawling town that has over the years spread across four original villages from Middebakken to the old Dutch port of Bossekop. A former whaling station, it is now more important for slate quarrying. Its biggest tourist attraction is the extensive rock carving site just beyond the town at Hjemmeluft which is open daily during the season. Designated a World Heritage Site by UNESCO in

1985, there are over 2,500 figures carved into the large flat rocks. Dating from between 6,200 and 2,500 years ago they depict people, animals, boats, fish.

Beyond Alta the 6 follows the coast past the viewpoint at Isnestoften and along the narrow Langfjord. Across the county border into Troms there is a worthwhile diversion from just before Alteidet. Take the side road to Jøkelfjord for a good view across the water to the Jøkelfjord glacier which calves into the sea several times each summer. Further on, from the new bridge at Sørstraumen one can see the tide eddying in strong circles below and there are magnificent views beyond of the Kvænangstiden, rising straight up from the sea.

The road climbs up to a high point of 402m (1,319ft), with a long-established Lapp encampment on the way and, commanding a spectacular view over fjords and islands, the picturesque Gildetun Inn. It still sports the traditional grass roof, the original Scandinavian insulation system, and has even built its new motel cabins to match. Years ago most roofs were constructed this way, with a board edging to retain the earth that was packed onto the gently sloping roof. Sprouting grass, wild flowers and even small bushes kept the houses warm in winter and cool in summer and if local yarns are to be believed, could also be used to pasture the goat, who while cropping it to a suitable length was being fed for free! The Gildetun has always been used as their 'local' by the Lapps from the nearby settlement and the 'signpost' outside, a hollow tree with three arms, indicates Lappish places like Kiruna and Ivalo.

Although the mountains here are impressive, some of them reaching 1,100m (3,608ft) high, they pale beside the glacier-capped Lyngen Alps that run from 1,400m (4,592ft) and more straight down into the sea. They are mountain peaks, just as the true Alps are, and attract many rock climbers while the fjord provides good deep sea fishing with shrimps as their local speciality. When one reaches the end of the main range, there are two possible routes to Tromsø.

The main road follows the Kåfjord. At Lokvoll, the Manndalen Domestic Arts and Crafts Society runs craft demonstrations in its shop. Look out too for the native Lyng or Nordland horse which is bred locally. At Olderbakken, the 6 is joined by the E78 and from Nordkjosbotn that is the road to follow to Tromsø. The alternative route leaves by ferry from Olderdalen. It takes half the time provided the queue is not beyond the marked places on the road. The ferry crosses to Lyngseidet where one follows the 91 to Svensby. It is surprising to find the far side of the Alps spreading in a green agricultural skirt, with fields large enough to support tractors. The next ferry crosses to the tiny port of Breivikeidet, where the 91 follows the valley of the Breivikelve down to Fagernes on the E78. From here Tromsø is some 25km (15$^1/_2$ miles) to the right.

There is a tourist information office with a carpark just as one approaches the town and it is worth stopping to study the view. To the left is Tromsø, with its university and northern lights observatory, sprawling along Tromsøya island. Ahead is the graceful 1km ($^1/_2$ mile) long bridge connecting Tromsø to the mainland, which won a prize for concrete architecture in the 1960s. Visible near its mainland end, in the suburb of Tromsdalen, is the Arctic Cathedral. Built in 1965, it is a series of glass triangles, symbolising an iceberg. Slabby in effect in summer, when lit through the winter dark, it is awe-inspiring. Inside it contains the largest stained glass painting in Europe. Also visible to the right is the cable car, operating every half hour until roughly sunset, that climbs 420m (1,378ft) up Storsteinen. It is signposted off the E78 beside the Arctic Cathedral which is fortunate as Tromsdal is a warren of traffic restrictions — 'No cars or motorcycles' alternates with 'buses and taxis only'! The view from the top of Storsteinen is good, revealing the smaller but similar Sandnessund bridge connecting Tromsø to the islands beyond, plus the fjords and islands one expects to see. There is also a Lapp tent at the top with souvenirs but the restaurant is a burnt out shell.

Tromsø itself is a large town that, while earning its living from the fish industry, also boasts the most northerly brewery and most northerly university in the world. The latter houses a good museum with lifelike displays geared to attracting children's interest in the zoology and botany sections, and detailed exhibitions on the Lapps. The separately housed aquarium is minute. There is a brand new planetarium, and a polar museum. A statue in the town commemorates Arctic explorer Roald Amundsen who with Nansen, among others, set off from Tromsø on polar expeditions, giving it the nickname, 'gateway to the north'. In the early 1920s it was also nicknamed the 'Paris of the north' in tribute to its fashionable ladies. Today it is the best northern town for shopping, night life and live entertainment. Because Tromsø was never devastated as Finnmark was (their only war action was the bombing of the *Tirpitz*) there are several streets of old wooden houses as well as two wooden churches, the original cathedral and the old Tromsøya church, twice transferred and now behind the main town at Elverhøy.

There is also an alternative route south from Tromsø following the 862 across the Sandnes bridge, then left along the edge of Kvaløy island with its tiny hamlets strung along the shores. This is rural

Norway with the grass drying on its fences while the next crop springs bright green beneath. The older buildings are typical Scandinavian deep red with white windows and corner planks. There are fishing nets hung to dry too and occasionally fish, giving the impression of an older way of life. From Larseng take the ferry to Vikran for the 858 back to Storsteinnes and the E6.

Further on the Malselv waterfall and salmon ladder are worth a visit. A circular diversion can be made from Olsborg, left on the 854 through Moen to Rundhaug and back right on the 87. The falls, dropping some 20m (66ft) across a wide river, are reached from the Malselv Turistcentre.The salmon ladder is one of Europe's longest and twists and turns beside the rather muddy path, protected by a high mesh fence from poachers and photographers alike.

Also interesting, some 10km (6 miles) beyond Bardu is the **Bardu Bygdetun** or District Museum, a series of farm buildings furnished in period. Try climbing the steep stairs to see where people slept and investigate the WC hut. It is a double loo of the type one still finds on Scandinavian picnic sites. Some of the buildings now house historic weapons and an exhibition about Norway's past wars.

As the E6 approaches Fossbakken, watch out for the view along Spandal to Lavangen. There are similar excellent views from the tourist station near Gratangen. The road then drops down to Bjervik on the Ofotfjord which it follows, crossing Norway's biggest suspension bridge at Rombak, before reaching **Narvik**. The oldest artefact here is a large carved reindeer overlooking the pleasure harbour. Dating from only 1000BC it is a line portrait as opposed to the Alta stick drawings, to which it provides an interesting contrast. In the more recent past, many people will associate Narvik with the bitter battles of 1940 which are commemorated in the excellent Red Cross War Museum. Outside in the market square stands the Statue of Liberation, a mother with her child on her shoulder. Other statues are Trygve Thorsen's *Playing Children* dancing half-naked on a bronze plinth and Josef Marck's *Little Peter* sitting outside the library. More significant for the town is *The Navvy* in Guldbrandson's Park. Originally a fishing village, Narvik was developed deliberately as an outlet port for Swedish iron ore from Kiruna, as the nearest Swedish port (at Luleå on the gulf of Bothnia) ices up in winter. The connecting railway was driven through the intervening wilderness by the navvies and with its opening, in 1902, the town grew around the marshalling yards and harbour facilities.

One can best see the effect of the iron ore industry on the town from the top of the cable car which, like the one at Tromsø, runs every half hour until sunset. It takes 13 minutes for the 1km ($^1/_2$ mile) long journey above the new Alpine ski run. The view from the top is extensive, not only of Narvik itself with its massive marshalling yards and the iron ore vessels still working late at night, but also seawards, on a clear day, as far as the Lofoten mountain range.

Narvik is as far south as this tour goes. From there one must recross the suspension bridge at Rombak to pick up the new Nord-Kalotten highway. Although the railway was constructed at the turn of the century, the 98 is the first road link across this bleak and unpopulated area of Lapland. Since the road's opening in 1984, the Norwegians have moved in with their weekend cabins on the banks of the lakes. The area near Bjornfjell, where the railway has provided access for years, is strewn with them, perched, with matching loo huts, wherever the rock is flat enough to build. It is a Norwegian ideal, the wooden *hytte* in the wilderness for a weekend's isolated fishing. Crossing the border it is a surprise to find the Swedish countryside totally deserted, apart from the bright red station buildings, identical to those at Bjornfjell. Deserted but well-labelled — blue signs name every river that tumbles under the road to the large lakes and when civilisation appears in the form of carparks with toilets for all, including the disabled, there are blue signposts for walks and ruck-sacked hikers setting off.

Being new, the 98 is a good fast road and **Kiruna**, the Swedish iron ore town, is only half a day's drive away. Try to arrive by lunchtime as the very interesting tour of the mine has to be booked at the tourist office. This takes one inside the largest underground mine in the world. An English-speaking guide reels off facts and figures; a video explains the workings; giant machines give live demonstrations of drilling and clearing methods; and one is even invited to remove iron ore pellets as souvenirs. The top of the slag heap gives views over the town and it is possible to pick out the town hall, with its extraordinary clock tower of open iron work, which was awarded a prize as Sweden's most beautiful public building in 1964. An interesting mural on the main mine building shows Kiruna past (a genuine Lapp district of reindeer farming and fishing), present (with the mining) and future (dominated by spacecraft). High quality examples of Lapp crafts, including silverware, can be bought in the town and the Lapp church is a landmark worth visiting. Constructed from bright brick-red timber, it is shaped like a typical Lappish hut. The altarpiece, with its grove of trees, is a reminder of how interwoven Lappish Christianity is with older pagan beliefs.

The small church at **Jukkasjärvi** (signposted a few kilometres

Deserted fishing village of Nyksund, Langøya, Vesterålen Islands (Chapter 4)

The midnight sun at the North Cape (Chapter 5)

The Kvænangstiden rising up from the sea, Arctic Norway (Chapter 5)

The bridge linking Tromsø with the mainland, Arctic Norway (Chapter 5)

beyond Kiruna) has an even more interesting, modern three-panelled altar painting by the artist Bror Hjort. Dominating the altar wall, it features Lapp people as well as a central Christ. A marriage here is said to ensure a loving and fruitful union! One is now near to completing the circuit back to Rovaniemi but the route is complicated for, although termed the Nord-Kalotten highway, or sometimes the Arctic road, right through from Narvik to Rovaniemi it is, apart from the new section, a combination of previously existing roads. Thus at Svappavaara one goes left onto the 395 for the border at Pello and from there takes the 83 to Sinettä and the 79 for the last 20km (12 miles). Beyond the Finnish border, watch out for a well-signposted 'Ice Age Sight'. In the middle of nowhere, it has an English description at the start and a wooden walkway plus waymarked path up a hillside leading one to a valley of glacial rocks.

Back at Rovaniemi one has completed the circuit, though if driving one's own car the return route doesn't have to be identical. For example, one could leave the train at Tampere and drive through southern Finland to Turku where an overnight liner crosses to Stockholm, giving one a taste not only of the Swedish capital but also of the countryside before finally embarking for home from Gothenburg. Alternatively from Kiruna one could follow the 98 south through Svappavaara to reach Luleå, through the Swedish Lappland area from where Swedish motorail goes direct to Malmö. For the adventurous motorist the possibilities are endless!

Further Information
— The Arctic Circle Tour —

Alta
Hjemmeluft Rock Carvings
Open: daily, 1 June to 31 August.

Bardu
Bygdetun (District Museum)
Open: daily in season at 11am.

Honningsvåg
North Cape Museum
Open: mid-June to mid-August, Monday to Saturday 11am-3pm and 6-8pm. Sunday 6-8pm. Rest of year, Monday to Friday 11am-3pm.

Inari
Sami Museum
Open: beginning June to -mid-August 8am-10pm.
Early to late August, 8am-8pm.
Beginning to mid- September 9am-3.30pm.

Kiruna
LKAB Mine
Visits have to be booked at the tourist office on the same day.

Narvik
Red Cross War Museum
Open: daily in season 10am-10pm.
Sight-seeing bus tours, 10.30am daily
in season from railway station.

North Cape (Nordkapp)
Complex open: daily in season, from
10am; attractions open from 12noon
till past midnight.

Rovaniemi
Arctic Circle Glass
Open: daily June to August 8am-9pm.
August to September 9am-8pm.

Santa Claus Village
Open: beginning July to end August
9am-8pm. July 8am-9pm. Beginning
September to end May 9am-5pm.

Tankavaara
Gold Museum
Open: beginning June to mid-August
9am-6pm. Mid-August to end September
10am-5pm. Rest of year, 10am-4pm.

Tromsø
Arctic Cathedral
Open: Monday to Saturday 10am-5pm.
Sunday 11am-12noon and 1-5pm.

Cable Car
Daily 10am-5pm. June to August also
11.30pm-12.30am when sunny.

Polar Museum
Open: daily in season, 11am-5pm.

Tromsø Museum
Open: beginning June to end August
daily 9am-6pm. Beginning September
to end May, weekdays 8.30am-
3.30pm. Saturday 12noon-3pm. Sunday 11am-4pm.

Tourist Information Centres

FINLAND
Ivalo
(for the Inari area)
Arctic Travels
99800 Ivalo

Rovaniemi
City Tourist Office
Aallonkatu 2C
96200 Rovaniemi

Sodankylä
Sodankylän Matkailu oy
Jäämerentie 9
PL60
99601
Sodankylä

NORWAY
Alta
Alta Tourist Office
9500 Alta
Open: 15 June to 15 Au-
gust only.

Hammerfest
Hammerfest Tourist
Office
9600 Hammerfest

Karasjok
Karasjok Feriesenter A/S
PO box 45
9730 Karasjok

Narvik
Narvik Reiselivslag
PO box 318
8501 Narvik

North Cape
(Nordkapp)
Nordkapp Reiselivslag
PO Box 34
9751 Honningsvåg

Tromsø
Tromsø Tourist Office
Box 312
9000 Tromsø

SWEDEN
Kiruna
Kiruna Turistbyrå
Hjalmar Lundbohms-
vägen 42
981 85 Kiruna

6 • North Jutland

Introduction to Denmark

Denmark is the prettiest of the Scandinavian countries. Here the mountains of Norway, the forests and lakes of Sweden and Finland, are muted into a rolling, pastoral landscape, a patchwork of fields and farms, hills, woods and water. Half-timbered houses abound, their thatch held in place along the ridge with crossed wooden staves. Many are surrounded by trees to provide protection from winds and also, in byegone days, to draw lightning away from roofs and dampness from walls. White-washed, red-roofed churches, with Romanesque stepped gables, stand sentinel in brightly ordered graveyards. A certain number of them retain their medieval frescoes, in glorious profusion over walls and roof vaults and nearly all contain a votive ship hanging above the aisle, a reminder of the fishing and trading connections that exist throughout this sea-ringed and islanded country.

For centuries Denmark has been the most prosperous of the Scandinavian countries and this is reflected in the profusion of manor houses, built in a wide variety of architectural styles from the genuine or pseudo castle to the solid four-square house. Many open their gardens, grounds or woods free of charge to the public. The notice headed *Til publikum* grants this access, normally during daylight hours, provided one follows countryside rules like not lighting fires or disturbing wildlife. One should keep to the paths or tracks and respect the no entry signs that protect the privacy of the residents.

The oldest residents of Denmark were prehistoric people and they have left barrows and cromlechs and passage graves (*jættestue*) by the score, particularly in the south. Many of the latter are open to visitors but one needs to be supple or short as the entrance passages usually involve bending double for some 2m (7ft) before reaching the main chamber and even there it is generally impossible to stand upright. They are usually very dark too and a torch would be useful.

For the active, Denmark is ideal for walking and cycling, with long

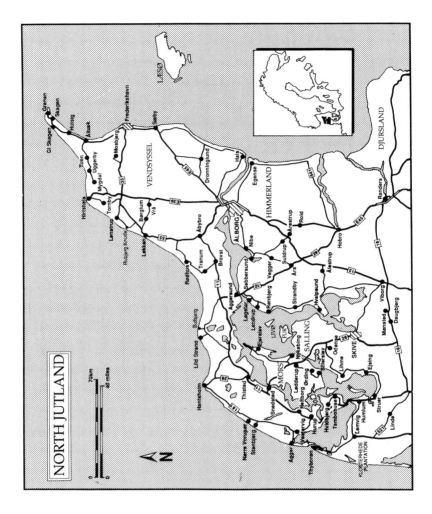

distance trails and cycle hire available for the latter. The long coastline is well-provided with clean, sandy and safe beaches from many
of which one can also windsurf, and with marinas for yachting
tourists. Angling is possible both offshore and in the lakes as is
birdwatching at the protected reserves. For the less active, there are
museums to suit all tastes from district history to art and specialist
vehicles, not to mention preserved farms, mansions that open their
rooms to the public and some very interesting gardens. The high
season is mid-June to mid-August but many are open for longer and
it is the only Scandinavian country that can realistically be visited as

early as Easter and as late as mid-October, for not only is the weather reasonable then but many attractions open especially in the school spring and autumn holidays. Communications are very easy with good main roads and an abundance of surfaced country lanes linking the villages. Inter-island connections are by ferry or bridge and driving is on the right.

North Jutland

North Jutland is not so 'pretty' as other parts of Denmark. There is less thatch despite reeds harvested by the lakes in spring. Instead, the houses, hidden behind their wind shield of hunchbacked trees, are roofed with tiles. The wind that bends the trees also blows the sand. What makes beautiful white beaches destroys farmland. The worst years were at the end of the eighteenth century when churches and parishes were abandoned or moved away from the coast as violent storms threw shoals of sand over the land forming today's dunes and heaths. Since then, control has been achieved by planting dune grasses and fir trees to hold the sand in place and only at the northernmost tip can one still see deserts, white mini-Saharas where nature has failed to take a hold. Further south the plantations are now recreation areas with walks and lakes. Pamphlets are available on the largest giving marked trails which, even if not in English, contain diagrams of the walks.

The 'pointed hat' of North Jutland is nowadays an island. In the 1800s the sea broke through into the Limfjord above Thyborøn. This gives two shores, only kilometres apart. The eastern shore onto the Limfjord is gentler with farmland. The Limfjord itself is a large stretch of water, extending in Bredninges and Vigs from Thyborøn in the west to Hals in the east, south to Struer and north towards Åbybro. From the south fingers of land reach into it and its islands are all of them worth visiting, from Mors, the 'Pearl of the Limfjord', to tiny Livø and Venø, neither more than a few kilometres in length.

North Jutland as an area extends from the tip at Skagen as far south as Mariager, Hobro and Viborg, but for this chapter a southernmost semi-circle is drawn from Rold Skov in the east to the Klosterhede State Forest in the west, omitting the largest towns (Ålborg and Frederikshavn) altogether. There is plenty to do in each but neither is 'off the beaten track'.

General activities within this area include seaside holidays with acres of white sand beaches, ideal for wind-surfing on the North Sea coast. It is safe bathing all except a few areas, such as south of

Hantsholm and round the tip at Grenen. Bathing is also possible in parts of the Limfjord, particularly between Løgstør and Hvalpsund. Angling is a Danish national pastime and here one has the sea, fjord, lakes and rivers at one's disposal. Sailing and rowing boats can be hired in a number of towns, as can bicycles. North Jutland, in common with the rest of Denmark, is geared to the cyclist, with special cycle tracks, including up the west coast from Bulbjerg to Skagen. It is excellent walking (or jogging) country too, with numerous waymarked trails and open access (provided one obeys simple forestry and environmental rules about fires and protecting the flora and fauna) to practically all their woods and forests.

To reach North Jutland from Esbjerg, the main North Sea ferry port, take the 12 to Varde, then either the 11 all the way to the Oddesund or the 181 coast road to Thyborøn. For the purpose of this chapter, the area will be considered clockwise from here. Arriving on the 11, the 'almost island' of land surrounding Hvidbjerg is worth exploring. **Tambohuse**, to the right after crossing the Oddesund bridge, has an interesting story attached to it. An ex-army drummer (or *Tambour*) settled here in 1830 and, after saving an old woman from drowning, was given royal permission to run a ferry service to Jegindø. Later, for trapping a gang of criminals, the king let him establish a ferry inn, the Tambohus Kro, which still today commands a beautiful view across the fjord to the island and church. The ferry has gone and now one crosses a dam to see the grey frescoes in the church and admire the view back to the village. Between Tambohuse and Hvidbjerg, the Hellige Kilde a clear spring, bubbling through sand, is only a short walk from the parking place.

It is impossible to tour Denmark today without noticing their three-armed windmills. There are several fields of them in the Oddesund area, and at **Sønder Ydby**'s alternative energy station just beyond the next narrow neck of land, every shape and size of wind machine whirr in close juxtaposition. Passing from the ultra-modern to the prehistoric there are fifty round barrows at nearby **Ydby Hede**, a heath giving views over the Skibsted fjord. Take the coast road from there through Doverodde to the Næssund ferry, for the island of Mors. Other access routes to this pleasantly undulating island include ferry across the Feggesund or bridge across the Sallingsund or from Vilsund Vest.

The 26 traverses Mors but the many side roads offer better scenery. The main cliffs of Hanklit and Feggeklit, and the highest point at Salgerhøj, are all along the north-west coast. Made of moler, which the Danes call white clay, the cliffs are full of fossils. Amateurs can

According to legend, Hamlet killed his wicked step-father here at Feggeklit

find samples for themselves or visit Wagner Toft's vast collection in his geological and archaeological museum. There is also a moler museum on the way to Feggesund. **Feggeklit** is a 25m (82ft) high wedge of cliff stranded between two parts of the Limfjord, with a monument commemorating the local legend that it was here that Hamlet killed his wicked step-father Kong Fegge.

An interesting by-road leads from Feggeklit left to Ejerslev and left again along the Strandvængen or coast road to Jørsby and back round to Sønder Dräby. In the south, one can similarly take the minor road from Nykøbing along the **Sallingsund**, stopping first at the spectacular Jesperhus Blomsterpark with its massed displays of colourful bedding plants. Next door, but much more peaceful, is the Legindbjerge Plantage with two $2^{1}/_{2}$km (2 mile) marked trails. The hilly yellow route gives good views over the Sallingsund. The coastal drive, through Ording, Sillerslev and Vester Assels, peaks near Tissinghus with the run along the shore of Glamstrup Vig to Glamstrup manor where there is an open-air museum. There are also two tractor museums, the Baks Museum of Agricultural Machinery on the 26 at **Solbjerg** and the Morsø Tractor Museum signed from **Outrup**. **Lødderup** on the outskirts of Nykøbing has a bottle museum and in **Nykøbing Mors** itself there is a historical museum in the Dueholm Monastery, a foundry museum and a Bible garden at the Kirsten Bogcafé with huge frescoes on the background walls.

Returning to the mainland, just north of Næssund, at **Heltborg**, the

The restored windmill at Heltborg

mill has been restored including all the machinery inside and 3,000 new shingles on the outside. If the mill is not open you can get the key from the cottage opposite. Just up the main road the **Lindhøj** passage grave is a large two chamber grave, accessible provided one can bend double! Candles are provided.

West of here, just beyond Hurup, Ashøje is, at 93m (305ft), the highest point around and the tower on top improves the view. At **Vestervig**, the largest village church in the north has what must be the longest tomb in its graveyard. According to legend, Liden Kirsten, half-sister of Valdemar the Great, had a love affair with Prince Buris. Valdemar, disapproving, forced her to dance to death, then tortured the prince and chained him to the church wall where he could just reach her grave. He was buried with her and brides still put flowers on the grave. On a mound nearby an Iron Age village has been excavated and the monastery mill restored.

On the way to Agger one passes a memorial stone in memory of a seventeenth-century battle by local peasants against invading Swedish troops. The Danes are very fond of memorial stones — perhaps it is a throwback to the days when men carved their own runic stones. **Agger** is a small town at the north end of the narrow road up from the Thyborøn ferry. Here the North Sea and fresh water lakes are only 5 minutes apart. One can hear the North Sea rollers while bird-watching over Agger and Flade Søs — or catch pike and perch in the latter before angling for flatfish, cod or mackerel in the former. The lane between Flade Sø and Ørum Sø leads to a gravelled road to Lodbjerg lighthouse (*fyr*) with views from the top and marked trails in the woods. Similar trails also pass tiny Lodbjerg church. Alternatively, for walks by a river, try Morup Mølle.

Returning to the fjord coast, the road through Skyum to Vilsund Vest passes **Skyum Bjerge**, a hilly area with narrow valleys running down to the shore. Less pretty is the large parking/picnic spot by the Vilsund/Stenbjerg road, a kilometre short of **Snedsted**, but two paths behind it lead into the Elsted Bible Garden which is open throughout the year. Here a maze of paths lead to clearings and hollows lined with Bible texts and decorated with pebbles, shells and paint. Beside **Stenbjerg**, where the road meets the dunes, a 'street' of old toolhouses, sheds and winch houses has been preserved. An interesting information board flanks the old lifeboat house which is now a museum of winchhouse tackle and rescue materials. Nearby **Nørre Vorupør** which is much more commercialised has an excellent aquarium, small in size, but possessing many different fish.

Divert next to **Tvorup**, whose parish was devastated by sand drift in the storms of 1794. The grassy remains of the old church are signed 'Kirkeruin' back to the left on a sharp corner. To return to the 181, pass through Vang and the Nystrup plantation where there is a golf course. The area between here and Hantsholm is the Hansted state reserve, a vast bird sanctuary of dunes, lakes and swamps, with no access at all during the breeding season from 15 April to 15 July. Thereafter its kilometres of paths are available to walkers and birdwatchers alike. **Hantsholm** itself should be visited if only for its museums. The town was fortified by the Germans and one of their bunkers has been turned into a museum. The most interesting feature is probably the size of the gun emplacement. Alternatively, at the lighthouse complex, displays range from lifeboats and local history to geology and birdlife, and there are fine views from the top of the working lighthouse.

Further along the North Sea coast are the neighbouring places of Lild Strand and Bulbjerg. At **Lild Strand**, as yet unspoilt by the outcrops of holiday homes found elsewhere, sizeable power-driven boats are winched onto the beach, for commercial fishing still takes place here. **Bulbjerg**, a 40m (131ft) high outcrop of limestone cliffs is a nature reserve with marked paths. Unfortunately the only connection is a footpath. By car one has to trek down no through roads.

Heading south, the ship-shaped **Højstrup** Viking burial place is situated between Frøstrup and Vesløs on the medieval shore of the Limfjord. Near the present shore at Øsløs the church hill gives good views over the water. The 11 now follows a causeway between the fjord and the **Bygholm Vejle**, one of northern Europe's largest and richest bird sanctuaries. There is a parking place with information half way along the causeway. South again at **Aggersborg**, behind the church, are the very faint outlines of a Viking fortress. If, despite the diagrammatic information board, one's imagination still fails to see beyond the crops, there is a good view towards Løgstør.

Beyond Aggersund in the area around Brovst, several interesting excursions can be made. About 2km (1 mile) south of Lerup church, **Janum Kjøt** is signed. Jutland's largest erratic boulder, left behind by the Ice Age, it measures some 6m (20ft) long by 2m (7ft) high. The very pretty Fosdalen is signed on the road past the church. Park where the surfaced road stops and enjoy a walk along a dale filled with murmuring water and birdsong, lilies of the valley and honeysuckle. The gravelled road continues to rejoin a surfaced road and one can circle round towards **Tranum**. Follow a parking sign into the Tranum Plantage for maybe $^1/_2$km to find a steep pine staircase leading to a viewing tower on the highest point. On a clear day this gives views to both coasts. There are also several manors which, in a comparatively manor-less part of Denmark, are worth driving past. Kokkedal is a beautiful moated house, now a hotel/restaurant. Nearby Skovsgård is a huge manor (privately owned), while Bratskov, in **Brovst** itself, is now a community centre housing the local tourist office. The most picturesquely sited is Oxholm manor with the old monastery church of Øland beside it. Beyond Oxholm, the Vejlen Ulvedby is a dammed area with extensive bird life.

The northern area beyond Åbybro and Hammer Bakker is shaped like a pixie hat, its point at **Grenen** facing due east. This is the area where the effects of sand drift are most noticeable on the North Sea coast. The southern part from Rødhus Klit to Løkken is summerhouse land with acres of hard flat beaches. Only a few kilometres to the north however, at **Rubjerg**, one encounters first the few lumps and graves remaining from the old church and then the purposeless lighthouse at **Rubjerg Knude**. Backed by mountainous dunes that are visible as a landmark many kilometres away it is hidden from the

Fishing boats on the steep beach at Lønstrup

sea! On a windy day in dry weather, the sand penetrates eyes, nose, teeth — everywhere. The lighthouse buildings now contain a museum cataloguing the effects of sand drift along the coast. Just further north, **Maarup** church still stands, an anchor outside it from the English frigate *Crescent* which sank offshore in 1808. Two hundred and forty sailors from the ship lie buried in common graves in the churchyard. For most purposes, the church has been replaced by the new one at **Lønstrup**, a small town at the north end of a stretch of cliffs. Originally a fishing hamlet, boats are still winched up the extraordinarily steep northern beach.

Inland of this stretch of coastline, **Vrå** church (between Bronderslev and Hjørring) has frescoes round the chancel vaulting and eight medallions in the nave, telling the story of Easter week. East of there beyond Børglum Mill the finely decorated chapel of **Børglum** Kloster can be visited. Inland of Lønstrup, the Klangshøj burial mound beside Vennebjerg church is an excellent viewpoint. More extensive views can be obtained north of Hjørring from Hellehøj and from Tornby Bjerg. Both have picnic spots and **Tornby** church contains runic inscriptions which were originally translated as '(Thorsten) had much joy of Johanne here in the morning.' To the locals' relief it was later realised that Johanne was the music for the psalms! Nearby **Asdal** church has a rare peasant gravestone near the porch which begins, 'Here lies my poor wife.' For the medieval enthusiast, one can also walk from the church, past Asdal manor and

Skagen harbour

round its farm buildings to see the original castle mound.

The ferry port of **Hirtshals** to the north boasts a North Sea aquarium and museum. The byroad east through Lilleheden and Uggerby Klitplantages is a pleasant route, with tracks through the trees that invite exploration but few parking places. At **Uggerby** one can canoe on the broad Uggerby Å down to the sea. Alternatively, take Bottevej left off the 597 beyond Uggerby and follow the signs for Uggerby Å. A 10-minute walk from the parking leads to both river-mouth and sea. More interesting walks can be had at Tversted Plantage. Follow the signs to Tversted Søerne for paths through woods and round lakes; also two viewing towers for the energetic climber. Beyond **Tuen**, there is an eagle sanctuary where you can see the feeding of the eagles and the breeding of rare and shy species.

This brings one to the northern tip of Jutland with its extensive sand damage. The **Råbjerg Mile**, a name that has no connotation of distance but means a desert of drifting sand, is like the Sahara in miniature with dazzling hills of soft white sand. **Sandmilen** is a similar area, with a cycle track across it and lies to the right of the 40 between Hulsig and the tower of the abandoned St Lawrence Church. Smothered in the storms of 1794-5, just the tower has been left standing as a landmark for sailors.

On this tip of land there are two towns, Gammel Skagen, now called Højen and Skagen, both of them distinguished by yellow houses whose red-tiled roofs are edged in white. **Skagen** boasts a

Grenen, where Skaggerak meets Kattegat

replica of the original 'lighthouse' (a fire bucket on a pole) and five museums. One of these is the house in which the painter, poet and writer, Holger Drachmann, spent his last days. He is buried in a mock passage grave in the northernmost end of the dunes. At **Grenen** the last sandy tongue of Jutland curls eastward into the seas. Here Skaggerak meets Kattegat, a fact revealed by the long line of breakers beyond the point where the two tides overlap. These indicate the dangerous currents beneath the surface and, though you can stand with one foot in each sea, the local tourist board warn against going more than 1m (3ft) into the water to do so. It is a brisk 20-minute walk to the point. Alternatively there is a tractor bus from the carpark at the Grenen café and sculpture museum.

Heading south now, the plantation behind Albæk contains interesting but long trails across to **Gårdbogård**, the most northerly manor in Denmark. Park opposite the FDM camping site on the 40. Walks can also be undertaken at the Museum of Landscape and Agriculture between Vogn and Mosbjerg. Marked footpaths lead from the exhibitions at Højen farmhouse through a landscape dotted with tumuli to the working smallholding at **Bjørnager**. This is well organised and complete with animals as it would have been in 1914. The road south from Vogn to Tolme is picturesque with walks in Tolme Skov and a nature trail from the high point of Bålhøje. Left and right across the 35 into Kastigvej also gives access to marked trails.

One is now in the area of **Frederikshavn** where two attractions west of the town deserve a mention. Cloostarnet is a modern viewing tower. Bangsbo manor, a museum for 50 years includes handicrafts from human hair, objects from the World War II and a Viking-style ship in the stables. There is also a collection of a thousand stones, from fonts to milestones. A pleasant route to Sæby from here is to leave the E45 by Øksnebjergvej, left into Rugtvedvej, right into Gadholtvej, then left and left again into Langtvedvej. Because this route follows the old coastal slopes it gives good views, and has the added advantage of bringing one directly to Nellemann's Have, situated on a sharp bend just before one reaches Bolmindevej. Here there are orchards, the Paradise apple trees planted in rings, a lake, woods and gardens to explore. The garden is open daily, sunrise to sunset. Bolmindevej then leads straight to Sæbygård Skov where there are walks either side of the river. **Sæby** itself has pleasant old houses on Ågade and an alternative walk would be a circle from the church along Ågade and back by the river and harbour.

Inland to the south-west, just off the Ålborg road, stands the beautiful moated manor of **Voergård**. Part medieval fortress, part Renaissance castle, it houses a rare collection of French art and royal treasures, inherited when the last count married a French widow. **Dronninglund** manor to the south is now a conference and exhibition centre but the adjoining chapel repays visiting. Its frescoes depict bible characters as knights on horseback fighting each other. Not only can one walk in the grounds but this is the southern end of the Jutland Ridge (Jyske Ås) along which a trail/cycle path has been established running for some 20 to 30km (12 to 18 miles). One need not walk the whole distance. There are parking places at intervals. For instance, at Pajhede Skov at the northern end, unsurfaced roads lead to a centre called 'Lunken' where there are nature trails.

South of Dronninglund to the ferry crossing at Hals and south again from Egense, the coastal landscape is flat and uninteresting. The next area worth exploring is Rebild and Rold Skov. **Rebild** is Denmark's only National Park, given to the state in 1912 by Danish Americans, who congregate there on 4 July to celebrate Independence Day. It consists of surprisingly steep and high hills, woods, ravines, springs and lakes. There are many places of interest to find, such as the Trolls' Wood with its twisted trees, also a viewing tower and two sink holes. The yellow trail from Rold Storkro or Rebildhus visits most of these but is long and hilly. An interesting shorter route is from the second parking past Rebildhus in the direction of the Stovring to Rold road. The path goes right to Ravnkilde (Raven Spring) where the water bubbles delta-like from the hillside, then

Bird sculpture in the square at Sæby

climbs steeply behind the spring to emerge from the beechwoods onto a heatherclad hilltop giving excellent views over the Lindenborg valley. Follow the yellow dots to complete the circuit, rejoining the main road at the first parking. The forests also contain wildlife from red deer to red squirrels, badgers and the occasional wild boar, plus birds of prey and waterfowl, not to mention unusual flora.

Other places of interest in the Rebild area are the lakes of Madum Sø and Store Sø which have very clear water; the Jutland Arboretum, identifiable by its Japanese-style entrance, with 125 varieties of trees and Blåkilde, Blue Spring, signed beside the 519 south of the arboretum. This deserves its name, bubbling up bright blue in an ordinary-coloured pond, at the rate of 150 litres per second. South-west of here, at **Rold**, there is a Circus Museum with furnished caravan, wooden big top and mementoes of the Miehe family who ran a circus here in the early part of the twentieth century. South-east is **Willestrup** manor where a Baroque garden dating around 1750 has been re-established with tulips in May, followed by roses in the summer.

North-east of Rebild National Park there is an interesting route through Årestrup. Follow the Oplev sign but turn left along Rødemøllevej through the old estate and deer farm of Røde Mølle, rejoining the original road near Ersted. **Årestrup** church is pleasantly situated above a pond. In its churchyard a neat line of well-tended graves commemorates Commonwealth airmen shot down in World War II. The propeller from their plane is preserved, in Torstedlund forest where they crashed, but it is poorly signed and a long walk as driving is forbidden within the forest. Albæk manor to the north is a fine example in an area that contains comparatively few and at nearby Suldrup there is a passage grave in the middle of the village.

Moving north to the fjord coast, **Nibe** is a pleasant old-fashioned town. The area to the west around Halkær Bredning is attractive. The road runs first alongside the long distance foot or cycle trail that follows the old railway track all the way to Års. Cross the Sebbersund and fork left past Sebberkloster. This minor road gives excellent views. At Storbæk, a square east and south can be made. This crosses the long distance trail near both Halkær and Vegger, where it is following the river and makes a pleasant easy walk. Returning north from Ejdrup there are good views over the Bredning and a picnic area beside one of the lakes that make up Storbæk Hedder.

West again, the port of **Løgstør** lies on the Limfjord, backed by a canal running to nearby Londrup Strand. The canalkeeper's house has been turned into a museum and the canal bank has a good footpath. The coast road gives excellent views all the way down to Rønbjerg Huse, where the ferry for Livø departs from 1 April to 30 September. This uninhabited island with a grocer's, café, toilet and campsite has no roads and no wheeled vehicles except bicycles.

South again at **Vitskøl** Monastery the medieval herb garden is arranged in sheltered hexagonal areas, each labelled with a sculpted cross-section of the human body showing the organs the herbs will heal. For flowers that will interest the enthusiast there is an orchid nursery at **Strandby**. South of **Hvalpsund**, the Hessel museum of agriculture is one of the best of its genre. The farmhouse is furnished in period and the barns equipped but what makes it superior is the quality of its labelling; the English texts bring the scenes to life. The minor roads north from here are interesting with good views in the Lovns area and colourful gardens at Gammel Ullits. They are private but two specialist gardens lie not too far away. At Års there is one devoted to fuschias and **Ålestrup** boasts the Jutland Rose Garden and also a cycle museum.

Beyond Viborg there are two museums of a creepier nature. Based in limestone caves, both are inhabited by bats. **Mønsted** contains a permanent exhibition about them while **Daugbjerg** holds 'bat evenings' in August with them flying around! If that is too spine-chilling, try the **Stubbergård** Klosterruin instead. Between Mogenstrup and Sevel watch for the large parking sign on the right labelled 'Stubbergård Sø — Klosterruin — Natursti'. The unsurfaced road takes about 1km ($^1/_2$ mile) to reach the parking. From here a sandy

Lighthouse at Rubjerg Knude, North Jutland, hidden by sand dunes (Chapter 6)

Voergård Renaissance castle in North Jutland (Chapter 6)

Ærøskøbing on the island of Ærø to the south of Funen, Denmark (Chapter 7)

Hesselagergård manor house, Funen, Denmark (Chapter 7)

track leads on to the ruins, but do not expect an abbey with stone arches open to the sky. From a distance this resembles a brick-built barn, for the nuns' refectory and cooking rooms that are all that remain of the Benedictine convent have been thatched over to protect them from the weather. It is a scenic walk though and inside the ruins look more religious than from afar. This walk is just south of the very well-known Hjerl Hede Open-Air Museum which is an outstanding example of its kind and should not be missed.

Here one is at the base of the fat thumb of land that thrusts up into the Limfjord between Struer and Skive. The 'nail' at the top is the island of **Fur**, reached by ferry from Branden. Though not a large island it is scenically interesting and worth a half or full day excursion. One attraction is the Fur Museum at **Madsted**. It is full of fossils, for the northern hills are once again made of moler. To see these follow the signs to Rødsten and Bette Jens Hyw. On top of the hills a gravelled road leads to a wide parking place. Bette Jens Hyw is the primitive watch tower to the right — good views can also be obtained from the tumuli by the parking and from the road to the beach. Stop on the way down and follow the path to Rødsten, a large red rock outcrop. Similar red rock can be seen in the cliffs along the beach. There are waymarked walks both along the cliffs and in the hills, or one can reach a different stretch of shore by following the signs to Langstedhuller. The only blots on the Fur landscape are the scars of the quarries that supply the thriving moler industry.

Further south the main attraction is **Spøttrup** medieval castle, standing red and strong within its green grass ramparts. Behind it, the medicinal herb garden is one of Europe's largest. To the north **Hjerk Nor** is a pretty lake set just in from the fjord. There are also four interesting churches in the area. **Odense** has very clear frescoes all over the nave, the Bible stories easily recognisable and the inscriptions in Latin. More frescoes decorate the chancel of **Lihme** church, where shouting devils have holes for mouths. There are curious stone figures outside too, high up on the chancel walls. North of Vinderup the village church of **Ejsing** has a wealth of painted woodwork, pews, pulpit, a screen and monuments on the walls. There are also excellent frescoes. Lastly, **Sahl** church, east of Vinderup, has one of only three golden altars in Denmark. Dating back to around 1200 it is probably the work of a master craftsman from Ribe.

From Vinderup the 513 leads west to Struer. The area between here and the North Sea coast could also be visited at the start of the holiday. Just north of Struer, **Kilen** inlet was formed during the Ice Age and is now a preserved area with walks from various parking places round it. Just north again, a road runs east to **Kleppen** where the ferry leaves for one last Limfjord island. This is **Venø**, with Denmark's smallest parish church. It is an excellent island for exploring on foot, having less than 10km (6 miles) of roads but twice as many tracks. Ask Struer tourist bureau for their leaflet of walks.

South of Lemvig between the two main access roads of the 11 and the 181 where this tour began, lies Denmark's largest state forest, the 67sq km (26sq miles) of Klosterhede Crown Forest. Gravelled roads run through it, the main one from Rom to Linde being the Gammel Landevej. There are twenty-three parking places, twelve of them serving the twenty-five marked trails within the area. These vary from $1^1/_2$km to 7km (1 to 4 miles) in length, some suitable for cycles, all clearly and plentifully waymarked in coloured paints. To give just one example, the white and green trail from Møllesøen is a $2^1/_2$km (2 mile) circuit through varied forest, traversing gullies and climbing hills clad in white heather, on a combination of paths and gravelled roads. The Struer tourist bureau can provide a Danish map pamphlet with English translation for all the walks.

Further Information
— North Jutland —

Ålestrup
Danish Cycle Museum
10 Borgergade
Open: beginning May to beginning November daily 10am-6pm.

Jutland Rose Garden
Open: late June to late September daily 9am-8pm.

Års
Fuschia Garden
89 Sdr Boulevard
Open: mid-May to mid-September daily except Monday, 10am-6pm.

Børglum
Kloster
Open: late June to mid-August daily 10am-6pm.

Brovst
Bratskov Manor
8 Fredensdal
Brovst
Open: Monday to Friday 10am-4pm, beginning June to end August, also Saturday and Sunday 9am-12noon.

Daugbjerg
Limestone Mines
15 Dybdalsvej
Open: mid-April to end May and mid-August to mid-September, Tuesday to Sunday 12noon-4pm. Beginning June to end June daily 10am-4pm. 1 July to mid-August daily 10am-5pm.

Frederikshavn
Bangsbo Museum
Dr Margrethsvej
Open: beginning April to end
October daily 10am-5pm. Winter
closed Monday.

Cloos Tower
Bronderslevvej
Open: Easter 10am-6pm. Beginning
May to mid-June Monday to
Friday 1-6pm. Saturday and Sunday 10am-6pm. Mid-June to mid-August daily 10am-6pm. Mid-August to end August daily 1-6pm.

Hantsholm
Bunker and Lighthouse Museums
Open: beginning June to end
August daily 10am-5pm. Beginning February to end May, Monday to Friday 9am-4pm. Saturday and Sunday 11am-4pm. 1 September to end November, Monday to Friday 9am-4pm.

Hirtshals
Aquarium and North Sea Museum
Willemoesvej
Open: late June to beginning September daily 9am-7pm. Rest of year, Monday to Friday 9am-4pm. Saturday and Sunday 10am-5pm.

Hvalpsund
Hessel Manor House
40 Hesselvej
Open: beginning April to end October daily 10am-5.30pm.

Lødderup
Bottle Museum
52 Harrehøjvej
Lødderup
Open: late June to early August daily 10-11am and 2-5pm or ☎ 97 72 18 34 for appointment.

Løgstør
Limfjord Museum
40 Kanalvejen
Open: Easter, then beginning May to mid-June and beginning September to end October, Saturday 2-5pm, Sunday 10am-5pm. Mid-June to end August daily 10am-5pm.

Madsted (Fur Island)
Fur Museum
28 Nederby
Open: beginning April to late June and beginning September to end October, daily 1-4pm. Late June to end August daily 10am-5pm.

Mønsted
Limestone Mines, Museum of Bats and Limeworks
10 Kalkværksvej
Open: mid-April to late May, early August to mid-September, Tuesday to Sunday 1-4pm. Late June to early August daily 10am-5pm.

Mosbjerg
Højen Museum of Agriculture/ Vendsyssel Historical Museum
613 Jerupvej
Open: daily 10am-4pm.

Nørre Vorupør
North Sea Aquarium
Vesterhavsgade
Open: May and mid-September to beginning November, Saturday and Sunday 10am-4pm. Beginning June to mid-September daily 10am-4pm, extended beginning July to mid-August from 10am-8pm.

Nykøbing Mors
Bible Garden
8 Ågade
Nykøbing Mors
Open: late May to beginning October daily 2-5pm.

Jesperhus Blomsterpark
Legindvej
Nykøbing Mors
Open: mid-May to late October, 9am-6pm except beginning July to beginning August 9am-9pm.

Morsland Historical Museum
Dueholm Kloster
Nykøbing Mors
Open: daily 10am-4pm. July daily 10am-7pm.

Outrup
Morsø Tractor Museum
49 Kjeldgårdsvej
Outrup
Open: mid- May to mid- August daily 10am-5pm.

Rold
Circus Museum
1 Østerled
Open: beginning March to end October daily 10am-4pm.

Rubjerg Knude
Museum of Sand Drift and Natural History
Rubjerg Fyrvej
Lønstrup
Open: end April to end October daily 10am-4pm. Late June to early August daily 9am-9pm.

Skagen
Drachmann's House
21 Hans Baghsvej
Skagen
Open: beginning June to mid-September daily 10am-5pm.

Solbjerg
Baks Museum of Agriculture
1 Rebslagervej
Solbjerg
Open: Monday to Friday 8am-6pm. Saturday and Sunday 8am-7pm.

Spøttrup
Castle
Open: beginning April to end April, Sunday and holidays, 11am-5pm. 1 April to 31 August daily 10am-6pm. September daily 10am-5pm. Gardens open all year.

Stenbjerg
Winch House Collection
Open: beginning July to beginning August 2-4pm.

Strandby
Orchid Nursery
63 Løgstørvej
Open: beginning May to end August, Tuesday to Saturday 9am-5pm.

Tuen
Eagle Sanctuary
107 Skagensveg
Open: Easter 3pm; May, Wednesday 10am; June, Wednesday 10am. Saturday and Sunday 5pm; July, Tuesday to Sunday 5pm; August, Wednesday and Thursday 10am, Friday to Sunday 5pm; September, Wednesday 10am, Saturday 3pm.

Vinderup
Hjerl Hede Open-Air Museum
Open: beginning April to end October 9am-5pm. Late June to early August 9am-7pm. Includes working exhibitions 1-5pm.

Vitskøl
Monastery Garden
475 Viborgvej
Open: mid-June to beginning September daily 10am-7pm.

Voergård
Castle
Flauenskjold
Open: Easter, May to August, Saturday 2-5pm. Sunday and holidays

10am-5pm. Mid-June to mid-August
daily 2-5pm. Sunday 10am-5pm.

Willestrup
Baroque Garden
Willestrupvej
Arden

Open: beginning May to end August
daily 11am-6pm. Beginning September to beginning October, Saturday
and Sunday 11am-6pm.

Tourist Information Centres

Ålborg
8 Østerå
DK-9000 Ålborg
☎ 98 12 60 22

Ålbæk
1 Stationsvej
DK-9982 Ålbæk
☎ 98 48 81 50

Blokhus
17 Ålborgsvej
DK-9492 Blokhus
☎ 98 24 85 11

Brovst
Bratskov
8 Fredensdal
DK-9460 Brovst
☎ (98) 23 21 88

Fjerritslev
1 Østergåde
DK-9690 Fjerritslev
☎ 98 21 16 55

Frederikshavn
1 Brotorvet
DK-9900
Frederikshavn
☎ 98 42 32 66

Hals
Torvet
DK-9370 Hals
☎ 98 25 14 33

Hjørring
5 Åkseltorv
DK-9800 Hjørring
☎ 98 92 02 32

Løgstør
2A Sønderport
DK-9670 Løgstør
☎ 98 67 20 10

Løkken
6 Vrenstedvej
DK-9480 Løkken
☎ 98 99 10 09

Lønstrup
90 Strandvejen
Lønstrup
DK-9800 Hjørring
☎ 98 96 02 22

Nykøbing Mors
4 Havnen
DK-7900 Nykøbing Mors
☎ 97 72 04 88

Rebild-Skørping
1 Jyllandsgade
Torvet
DK-9520 Skørping
☎ 98 39 22 22

Skagen
18 Sct
Laurentiivej
DK-9990 Skagen
☎ 98 44 13 77

Skive and District
7 Østerbro
DK-7800 Skive
☎ 97 52 32 66

Struer
Rådhuspladsen
DK-7600 Struer
☎ 97 85 07 95

Støvring
86 Hobrovej
DK-9530 Støvring
☎ 98 37 33 55

Sydthy
2 Jernbanegade
DK-7760 Hurup Thy
☎ 97 95 22 00

Thisted
6 Store Torv
PO Box 210
DK-7700 Thisted
☎ 97 92 14 24

Tversted
10 Østervej
Tversted
DK-9881 Bindslev
☎ 98 93 11 26

Viborg
5 Nytorv
DK-8800 Viborg
☎ 86 62 16 17X

7 • Funen and the Islands to the South

Funen is probably the most attractive of the Danish islands. Her most famous son, the fairy tale author Hans Christian Andersen, who was born in the main town of Odense, called it 'the garden of Denmark' and it lives up to that name. The undulating countryside blooms with rich farmland, orchards and woods, which in spring are carpeted with anenomes and celandine. The villages blossom with colourful gardens and cottages whose roofs are thatched with reeds harvested from the many lakes. The churches, pristine in their white paint and red tiled roofs, stand proud amid the well ordered graveyards. The manor houses, in a rich variety of styles and colours, invite photography. Many open their grounds to the public all year and several now deal in antiques, beautifully displayed in appropriate settings.

Antiques and artware are offered for sale in the towns too, often in the older streets that cluster together near the local museum, church and pedestrian shopping area. Many of the towns are on the coast with port facilities, ferry or fishing harbours, and marinas for the many yachtsmen from Germany and Scandinavia who arrive under their own power. Sail or motorboat hire is possible and fishing from cutters, though one can also fish from any stretch of the 1,000km (620 miles) of coastline without permit or by licence in the Odense river. Windsurfing is available on all shores with the sheltered west and south best for beginners, speed surfers preferring the more exposed east and north. The waters all round are comparatively calm and shallow, ideally suited for children. The tourist board produces a map each year indicating the best beaches and the hygiene rating of the water.

Other activities include cycling for which the Danish countryside is so suited with hire available in several towns including Lohals on Langeland and Marstal on Ærø. These are the two largest islands to the south. Langeland is, as its name says, long and also comparatively flat, ideal for both bicycles and the prairie wagons which can be hired from Bagenkop as well as from Skårup on Funen. Ærø has

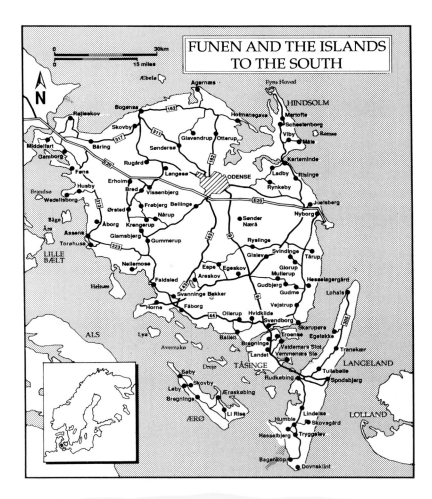

more varied scenery and the old world charm of an island where the sea has successfully kept modernisation at bay. Riding holidays are available via the Marstal tourist office. If one prefers golf, just turn up at any of the four golf courses, at Svendborg, Glamsbjerg, Odense or Nyborg, with a valid membership card from a recognised club.

Odense is the main town with innumerable attractions in its own right but being very much on the beaten track, it is omitted from this chapter. Similarly the larger towns are only touched on, concentration being placed instead on coasts and hinterland and the islands of Ærø, Langeland, Tåsinge and Thurø. Funen lies between Jutland and Zealand. It is only $2^1/_2$ hours from Kiel in Germany to Bagenkop at the southern end of Langeland. The motorway from Copenhagen takes slightly longer, though that journey will speed up once the Store Bælt connections are built. Alternatively one can arrive from the North Sea ferry port of Esbjerg, a mere 2 hours drive away along main roads. This brings one to the north-west point of Funen and the much-neglected town of Middelfart. Most people shoot past on the motorway on their way to Odense or Copenhagen, but it is the proper place at which to start a trip down the west coast of Funen.

To reach **Middelfart** one must take the 161 and cross the Lillebælt, arriving on the wooded point of the Middelfart peninsula. Park at Hindsgavl for a good circular walk signed in blue. It begins at the far exit to the house garden from the car park and traverses a pleasant belt of trees. At the asphalt road, follow the track signed Mindelunden (a memorial grove to British airmen) straight down and out to the coast path. Here the blue marks continue left, past a campsite and into the woods behind. There are views across to Kolding before dropping down a ravine to the meadow with the old castle mound. Beyond it a gate leads back into Hindsgavl grounds. The circuit, with its varied scenery, takes $1^1/_2$ hours. The red trail through Teglgård woods, opposite the Karoline cafeteria, takes half the time.

Leaving Middelfart on the 313, fork right for **Gamborg**. Here they have recreated a village meeting place by the village hall. The area beyond at Svinø is a bird reserve. Keep as near the coast as possible, through Ronæs to **Føns**, which boasts Funen's oldest church. A possible diversion here is onto the Fønskov peninsula. Beyond the huge half-timbered barns of Sparretorn manor, one can walk in the woods. There are good views across the water in both directions but not much point in driving beyond the end of the surfaced road.

Continuing south one approaches the **Wedellsborg** estate whose grounds are open all year. Nearby, **Husby** church contains a grand collection of Wedellsborg sarcophagi but a memorial stone of a different sort sits beside the road just before the 1689 gatehouse. It is to a weaver who was once employed on the estate. Follow the parking sign through the next gate and down to the farm. The park gives good views of the manor. Emtekær is a pretty village and leads one through to Sondager and the main road south. By turning right again to Åborg and left into Mariendalsvej, **Assens** can be approached along the coast directly into the older part of the town. Park at the harbour and explore. The statue there is to Peder Willemoes, a local naval hero from the Napoleonic Wars against England, who fought against Nelson in the Battle of Copenhagen. His birthplace on Østergade (straight up from the harbour) is now a museum and there are several other good houses in the same street. It is worth looking through doorways and alleys into the courtyards behind.

Leaving Assens directly southwards, the coast road leads to the village of Torøhuse, then round past **Sønderby Klint** to the 'Seven Gardens', just inland of Åkrog Bugt. Here a comparatively small area has been turned into a plantsman's paradise with some 700 different varieties, many of them labelled. Seven different national styles of garden are represented. Set in one of the warmest corners of Funen the gardens are relatively frost-free. They are also mature, having been created over 25 years ago as a botanical garden.

Some 2km (1 mile) further on is the manor of **Hagenskov** which is not open to the public. Approach it via Slot Allee past the mound where a four-winged fortress once stood. The present manor, through which one drives, was built in 1776. Turn back right and right again for the Helnæs peninsula and one passes the eye-catching bright red gatehouse to the estate, backed by the longest oak avenue in Denmark. The road passes Flenstofte farm and crosses a causeway to reach Helnæs. Park at the top of the hill for good views in all directions. The village is pleasant and there are woods and beaches.

Back on the mainland follow the coastline as closely as possible. **Løgimose** manor is quite attractive (one can drive down and look through the courtyard at it) and the next village, **Nellemose**, has a quantity of eighteenth-century thatched houses. On the Fåborg road, Faldsled also has thatched homesteads and the oldest chartered inn in the area. Along the road at **Millinge**, one finds the Funen Toy Museum. Three crowded rooms house a wide variety of old toys and there is a working train layout in the shed.

Before entering Fåborg, explore Horneland, to the west. **Horne** church is described as the only round church on Funen but this is a misnomer in that only the central portion is round, and that is traversed by a long nave. On a clear day the road to Bjerne Mark and Dyreborg gives good views to the island of Bjørnø and across the Fåborg Fjord while, just off the main road, the Hvedholm Plejehjem is a must. A rest home in a former manor, its lovely grounds, with lake and flowers and a gentle hill, are open to the public every day.

Fåborg is dominated by its bell tower. It is the only part remaining from the first church which was built here and is open in summer for the views. It contains Funen's largest carillon, playing hymns four times a day. The oldest streets in the town are those clustered at its foot. Kaleko Mill on the outskirts is an old watermill, now converted to a museum. By circling round on the same road, through Diernæs, to reach Holstenhus manor. Park at the obelisk on Alleen and walk

The town of Svendborg from the bridge leading to the island of Tåsinge

into the grounds, where you are allowed to go close to the house.

Heading south to Åstrup, the turning windmill sails are an eye-catching advertisement for an enterprising shop. Keeping south the road leads through Nakkebølle Sanatorium, now a centre for refugees, round the bay to Fjællebroen and Ballen, and so along the coast into Svendborg. Aternatively, join the 44 and fork left in **Ollerup** for the manors of Nielstrup and Hvidkilde which are not open to the public. Between the two lies the old watermill of Utre Mølle, unfortunately, like so many others, no longer sporting its wheel. Hvidkilde is a huge manor with farms and barns right beside the road, the red and white half-timbered buildings kinder on the eye than the faded white mansion itself.

Svendborg, a thriving commercial port, marks the end of the west coast route. Here there are various museums, recreation areas such as the waterfront at Christiansminde, and trips on the preserved steamboat, the *M/S Helge*. It is worth parking beneath the graceful bridge that makes Svendborg the gateway to the islands. Take the last exit on the 9 before crossing it and circle left. Stairs lead up onto the bridge and it gives excellent views down on the shoreline. There are similarly good views at the far side down onto **Tåsinge**.

This island, used by the 9 as a stepping stone on its route to Langeland, deserves fuller exploration. A kilometre or two ahead in the village of **Bregninge** (Tåsinge) stands a church with a look-out tower. Already on the highest point of the island, a whole 72m (236ft) above sea level, on a clear day the view encompasses some 20 islands, 63 churches and 15 manors. The Tåsinge Skippers home and folklore museum is just below the church.

To the south at **Landet**, the churchyard contains the graves of two English airmen, along with their broken propeller, lying south-east of the big oak. Even larger and Denmark's oldest the Ambrosius Oak stands beside the road to Valdemars Slot just beyond a pair of thatched yellow cottages. But before visiting the castle, Vemmenæsvej along the shore of Lunkebugten is probably the prettiest road on the island and there is a glassblower at work at number 10 on the outskirts of Vemmenæs.

Valdemars Slot is a red brick mansion with picturesque white and yellow outbuildings. Large sections of the house are open to the public as well as several different restaurants and a naval museum in a barn. Beyond Valdemar the road curls round to the old-fashioned 'town' of **Troense**. The oldest houses, belonging to the ships' masters 200 years ago, are in Grønnegade and Badstuen which lead inland from either side of the Hotel Troense. There are splendid views across to neighbouring Thurø from the hotel terrace.

Thurø is a much smaller island, connected to Svendborg by a dam. Horseshoe-shaped, it has orchards and pleasant woods and good bathing beaches at Thurø Rev and Smørmosen. The latter also possesses an imaginative concrete mini-golf that will amuse as well as frustrate. The prettiest spot is perhaps the churchyard, descending in terraces to the Skårupøre Sound and giving fine views across to Bjornemøse manor.

From Tåsinge, the next bridge leads across to **Langeland**. Although its highest point is a mere 41m (134ft) it is neither flat nor uninteresting. The farmland rolls and the scenery is diversified by the many deciduous woods. There are orchards and flowering trees in the gardens, a variety of well-preserved windmills, thatched houses with an edging of tiles and a number of privately owned manor houses. The most famous of these is **Tranekær** castle, a solid structure made monstrous by its bright red paint. To explore the grounds, turn towards Botofte and park there. The prettiest views are from the path that circles the lake. This is open year round to visitors and is well-provided with picnic tables. The parking further along the main road is for the Galaxy Sculpture. Centred around a large boulder that was excavated locally, the galaxy group are carved with symbols and words whose meanings are explained on the board nearby. Tranekær village has well-preserved houses including eleven built to replace the thirty that were destroyed by fire in

Tranekær Castle

1875. A galleried Dutch mill is open also and contains all its working equipment, plus a history of windpower in the adjoining building.

Further north, **Egeløkke** manor opens its grounds on Sundays and public holidays. Again there is a lake walk giving views of the classical white mansion on its hill, before entering the woods. A third manor, **Skovsgård**, in the south houses a carriage museum with imaginatively arranged horse-drawn vehicles including a wedding couple in their bridal carriage. A different museum for those who like stuffed animals' heads, is at 49 Hovvej at **Lohals**. Tom Knudsen's Safari Museum displays his trophies from big game hunts.

To appreciate the scenery fully, one should leave the through road and try some of the lanes. For example north of Tullebølle, turn into the village of Frellesvig and take Pæregårdsvej out. This leads through deciduous woods. It does lose its surface for a while but it is a pretty route. Look out for the long barrow where the tar starts again. Ravnebjergvej, Krybskyttevej, Åsøvej and Langesøvej bring one round past Koresbølle manor to Tranekær Mill. An interesting alternative route leads behind Tranekær Castle to Botofte and into Bukkeskovvej. In the woods there is a signed Viking double passage grave which, being roofless, is ideal for those who have always wanted to see inside one but have been unable to negotiate the low entrance passages. Stengadevej continues the route and one can follow by-roads all the way across road 9 to Pederstrup.

Langeland has a rich harvest of barrows, graves and cromlechs.

The longest barrow is near **Humble**. Park at the church and read the direction board. The walk, right through Tingbjergsgård farm, takes a good 10 minutes; the reward is a 55m (180ft) long barrow with most of its seventy-seven edge stones in place. The King Humble to whom it is attributed is a local myth. Another famous landmark is the Hulbjerg passage grave on the minor road south of Bagenkop, but many more simply dot the fields.

In the far south **Dovnsklint** makes a pleasant stop. The cliffs are of moler rising from a shingle beach. There is also a walk to Keldsnør through woods white with anemones in spring and redolent of honeysuckle in early summer. The path gives excellent views across the lake to the lighthouse. Alternatively the bar between sea and lake can be reached along the beach. There is a bird sanctuary with walks on the same stretch of road and another at Tryggelev Nør, north of Bagenkop. To reach this, take Vestervej and Vesteregnsvej north from the ferry port. Beyond the sanctuary take Kinderbøllevej and Nørrebøllevej to Hesselbjerg. Continue north through Helsped and past Vestergård church to Kædby Havet, then right past Bogøgård to Lindelse. This is a pretty route throughout with good views over the sea now and then.

One last island to the south is a must. It is delightfully old-fashioned **Ærø**, hilly enough to give good views, off-the-beaten-track enough not to get crowded. It is reached by any of three ferry crossings; from Fåborg to Søby in the north; from Svendborg to Ærøskøbing in the centre or from Rudkøbing on Langeland to Marstal in the south. All these ferries should be booked if travelling in peak Danish holiday periods (mid-June to mid-August) or on the last boat of the day. Tickets are valid for any route so that one can arrive at one end of the island and leave at the other. The following tour does precisely that, beginning at Marstal and leaving from Søby.

Marstal is a ferry port with narrow streets of old-fashioned houses leading up from the sea. 'Minors Hjem' in Teglgade has been turned into a museum home and in Prinsensgade several large buildings now house the very comprehensive Jens Hansens Maritime Museum. Here are model ships and ships in bottles, objects from abroad brought home by Danish sailors, captain's logs and even a section on local life rather than the sea. One of the very few English notices tells of the Royal Navy's failure to capture Marstal in the early nineteenth century. The large church contains no less than six votive ships and also an altar painting of Christ stilling the storm where the witnesses are all based on well-known local inhabitants.

From Marstal go north to **Ommel**, a large village with a fair

The Lindsbjerg prehistoric graves

sprinkling of half-timbered thatched houses. The road north from the village leads along a tongue of land, Ommelshoved, giving views and a beach at the end. A circle east from Ommel takes in Kragnæs where there is a well-signed passage grave that it is possible to enter.

Cross the island now to the coast at Drejet, where a dyke protects the reclaimed land of **Gråsten Nor**. There are walks here from the parking places along the road. Follow the Lindsbjerg signs, first right along the shore, then inland with signposted prehistoric graves on the hill to the right. Circle now round the south coast to **Rise Mark**. Every village on Ærø has a lane leading to its 'mark'. This one has good bathing beaches and dunes. Beyond here at **Store Rise** the massive twelfth-century church contains a triptych illustrating the Passion of Christ. Another long barrow is signposted from the church. Going right to Dunkær and left up Møllevej brings one through to **Lille Rise** where, just north of the village, is a picnic place with panoramic views towards Funen. Similar views can be seen from the road north towards Ærøskøbing.

A gem of a preserved town, **Ærøskøbing** dates from the 1680s, the oldest house being Kjøbinghus in Søndergade though two others in the same street are also dated in the late 1600s. The shop just beyond the Kjøbinghus has a plaque saying that King Frederik V stayed here on the 23 and 24 June 1750. Gyden, Vestergade and Smedegade are all streets of eighteenth-century houses. Look at the doors. Many of them are finely carved. The Bottleship Museum in Smedegade is very interesting as much for the bottles the ships are in as for the models themselves. There are also some fine wood carvings on display. The Ærø Museum and Hammerichs Hus are both in Brøgade. Number 24 Nørregade is unusual in that it is brick built between the half-timbering and every square of bricks forms a different pattern. Look out too for the viewing mirrors placed so that inhabitants could see what was going on in the street outside.

Drive out of Ærøskøbing past the preserved town mill and south to **Olde**. This village has some good examples of thatched houses with colourful gardens. Beyond the village to the north there is another picnic place with good views and also a stone commemorating 200 years of Danish crown rule. Immediately beyond the picnic place, fork left through **Tranderup**, a long village boasting several *gårds* or large farmhouses. For something different fork left at the end of Tranderup for **Voderup Klint**. The unusual cliffs, created at the end of the Ice Age, step downwards in broad grass-covered terraces to a shingle beach.

Picking up the main road again at Vindebølle, turn left through **Bregninge** which is Denmark's second longest village. The church has very delicate frescoes, dated 1513 over a devil's head. The elaborate altarpiece dates from 1530 but the pulpit is seventeenth century. Opposite the church the lane is signposted to Ærø's highest point, Synneshøj but sadly the 68m (223ft) high spot itself is not marked. Continue to **Skovby**, past an old mill and along a road with sea views to both sides. It is a pretty village as is **Leby** on the other side of the main road. The road signed Lebymark also gives good views and comes past the thatched mill at Vitsø. If instead of this, one stays on the main route to Søby, Vestermølle, standing proudly on the hillside on the right, is much better preserved. There is also another thatched mill on the far outskirts of Søby and the lane beyond here runs to the northernmost point of the island at Næbbet. If one is staying on the island overnight, then a good nature ramble is to follow the beach from Søby to Næbbet. If not, although it would be possible to cover everything mentioned here within the $5^1/_2$ hours that ferries allow on the island, it would be more comfortable to concentrate on one's individual preference within it. Peace not rush is the essence of the island of Ærø.

There remains the interior and north of Funen excluding the main town of Odense, which will be described in an anti-clockwise direction. The northern area of Funen is the least interesting scenically being generally flatter and less wooded but there are still places to visit and enjoy. **Hofmansgave**, for instance, on the Odense fjord, has

Hofmansgave

pretty gardens which are open all year. There are beds of colourful flowers along the side wall of the house and also beside the small Museum of Sketches. Individual trees are labelled and there are walks through rocks and woods out to the sea. Just to the north at Enebærodde, it is possible to park and walk either along the shore or on the long peninsula that stretches out to the Gabet. An information board shows possible circular walks here, bird-watching all the time on marsh and sea. The coast at Flyvsandet and Agernæs has the only dune beaches on Funen. Further west, the island of **Æbelø** is connected to the mainland by Ebbevej. The causeway is only visible at low tide and it is a curious sight to see the white road marker posts marching across the water.

Bogense is a small market town on this northern shore. The oldest streets are in a rectangle formed by Adelgade, Annagade and Torvet. Here are several large half-timbered merchants' buildings — notice the painted woodwork of Den Gammel Købmandsgård on Østergade and the nineteenth-century terraced houses in Torvet. The large church has a spire covered in 27,000 oak shingles. Watch out too for the copy of the Brussels little boy fountain in a garden on the corner. Just outside the town is the rather plain brick manor of Gyldensten and south of it the far prettier Sandagergård. Park at the church for good views. Both estates' woods are open to the public though not with the usual *'Til publikum'* notice. South of Bogense at **Skovby** a different attraction is the Kuntsgården, a permanent exhibition/salesroom of arts and crafts by Danish entrepreneurs ranging from knickknacks to high class paintings and glassware.

Before turning inland, one last stretch of this northern coast deserves a mention. From Båring on the 317 drive north on the minor roads through Båring Mark and Vejlby Fed to Røjleskov. Although this is summerhouse land, it is worth visiting. The road is hilly enough to give good views across the water, even if on the last stretch they are to the factories of Fredericia. Take the turning to Røjleklint for a parking with toilets and a circular walk that is part cliff and part shell-covered beach. There is also a signed viewpoint on the cliffs.

Returning now to the rest of the north above the motorway, the scenery becomes more interesting as soon as one leaves the coastal plain. There are several attractions in the Søndersø area. North-east of the town at **Glavendrup**, there is a burial site edged with stones set in the shape of a ship. At the prow stands the largest, carved with Denmark's longest runic inscription. Dallund manor has a 45 minute walk round its lake which includes not only good views of the mansion from the far side but also allows one to pass close beneath the house itself. **Søndersø** church is also well worth a visit. Entrance is through a magnificent door with a wrought iron inscription nailed to it. Inside there is a modern painted altar, flanked by two old tombs, one medieval and one from the 1580s with a lady dressed in 'Tudor' style. But it is the frescoes which attract the eye. Painted in 1525, they are unusually three-dimensional with hills and castles in the background and the faces, particularly the men, look lifelike. There are three dogs too, representing faith, hope and charity. Even the outside of the church is unusual with its granite ashlar brickwork alternating with white-painted munk stones to give a striped appearance.

South of Søndersø there is a picnic spot at **Trærskov Mølle** and one can see where the waterwheel once stood. South again at Langesø, the house is private but there are places to park and walks both in the woods and round the long narrow lake which ends at a red brick chapel. West of here, at Rugård there are good views of the lovely manor house and the deer that are farmed here. Deer are also kept just south of the motorway at **Erholm** manor. There is a pleasant 20 minute walk round the lake, past deer enclosures, through the wood and back by the house. They also sell Romanian wines on Saturdays!

One has now reached the **Vissenbjerg** area which caters particularly for 'animal' lovers. There is the Funen Aquarium, signed off the 161 at the 20.4km mark between Vissenbjerg and Gribsvad as well as from several other places, which includes a small aviary outside. In Vissenbjerg itself, close to the church, the terrarium contains north-

ern Europe's largest collection of reptiles, including vividly coloured
frogs as well as lizards, crocodiles and snakes, a few animals and
birds and some enormous bats. The hill behind the terrarium gives
good views. The minor road south and west to Bred passes through
an area of ponds, birds and nature trails. From the parking signed
Afgrundet there is a way down into a ravine.

The area southwards, between Bred and Glamsbjerg also contains
various places of interest. Due south at **Frøbjerg**, the Bavnehøj is
Funen's highest point. The climb is enlivened by various memorial
stones and at the nearby Mindelunden Funen's dead from World
War II are remembered on a sculpted monument. West at **Ørsted**, on
the road towards Glamsbjerg, nine American fliers who were shot
down on 20 February 1944 are commemorated and there is a runic
picture stone in the church porch. South-east of here lies **Krengerup**
manor where the road passes through the courtyard. The woods
contain marked trails of various lengths, the most interesting being
the shortest, red route, a 30-minute circuit through woods, past a
folly with a view to the house, and then past the house itself. There
is also a golf course at the southern end of the woods. Beyond Nårup
at 50 Skovvej there is a popular bird park. The church at **Bellinge**, on
the southern outskirts of Odense, has unusual frescoes. St George,
slaying the legendary dragon, is being applauded by kings and
queens, including one with a pet lamb on a lead.

South of Glamsbjerg at **Gummerup** a yellow and white thatched
farm has been turned into the West Funen Farm Museum. It is similar
in style and scope to the one at Hessel in North Jutland but unfortunately not labelled in English. Nearby **Voldtofte** is an interesting
village with many half-timbered properties. The small town of
Brobyværk also has thatched houses, including an old watermill, its
wheel still in place over the Odense Å. It was used in the seventeenth
century for the manufacture of arms thus giving the town its name
of Broby works. The mill is no longer used despite the machinery
being still in place and its thatched buildings have recently been
converted into apartments. Surprisingly perhaps, the Odense Å is
here flowing northwards, as are all the rivers to the north of the
Funen Alps — the hills that lie in the south-west of the island. Their
waters rise in lakes like Sobø, set prettily amongst woods.

A much larger lake is Areskov Sø, a state bird reserve, which can
be approached either by the minor road past Areskov manor or from
the Svanninge Bakker woods. These cover the Sollerup Skov, from
where there are trails through to the lake as well as the Svanninge
hills nearer Fåborg. Other lakes of interest in the area are firstly

Norresø, with a 6km (4 mile) trail from the parking on Brændegårdsvej. It circumnavigates the lake through woods where one may well glimpse deer. If 6km (4 miles) is too energetic, at nearby Brændegård Sø, one can sit in one's car in the parking opposite the manor farm and watch a protected colony of cormorants.

Set in the middle of this area is the very large manor of Brahetrolleborg. It is a useful landmark from which to begin the search for **Tingskov Have**, a nurseryman's personal garden containing 1,200 different flowers. Its postal address is Espe but that is merely misleading! Take the minor road north from Brahetrollesborg to Haagerup. Turn right at the very end of Haagerup village, then fork left at the Tingskov sign and left again at the sign in the first wood. Alternatively, driving south through Espe, turn right along Lydinge Møllevej, right again signed Tingskov, and right again along the continuation of Tingskovvej. The garden is at number 17 on the right, down a track through the woods. The garden is not the nursery plots but the massed beds of herbaceous plants behind the house itself.

Much easier to find and much more popular is the nearby tourist attraction of **Egeskov** castle. With its state apartments and access to the attics, veteran vehicles museum, and varied gardens including one devoted solely to fuchsias it is probably Funen's best known stately home. Nearby Egeskov Mill is also open for arts and crafts sales and for workshops.

Egeskov is close to Kværndrup through which the 9 runs from Odense to Svendborg. There are a number of interesting places between here and the east coast. Starting on the outskirts of Svendborg, the coast road east past Bjørnemose manor to Skårupøre, then left and right along Ulkens Dal gives good views across to the northern end of Langeland. Passing through Øster Åby to Vejstrup, the watermill is visible down below the road on the left. **Gudme** church has frescoes including an unusual cuboid frieze along the bottom metre of the walls and flowers above the altar. At **Gudbjerg** church, look for the tombstone to a blacksmith, identifiable by the hammer and pincers engraved on it. Nearby **Mullerup** Castle is one of those now selling antiques. Alternatively, the manor of **Hesselagergård** is worth driving past. There is no parking within 500m (550yd) but there are good views from the road and it is possible to walk round provided one circles behind the farm buildings. Not far to the north is the **Damestenen**, Denmark's largest erratic boulder. According to legend, it was thrown here by a giantess from Langeland aiming at Svindinge church steeple. The legend also says that it continued growing where it landed until it was partly excavated! Now it has stopped, one can stand on top and try to spot the giantess on Langeland. On the way to Svindinge, to look at its steeple (a rarity in Denmark which is what so enraged the giantess) one can stop at **Glorup** manor for a 45-minute walk round its park which is decorated with classical statues.

Glorup comes within the section of East Funen running up to Nyborg on the coast and down to Ringe in the centre. It is an area containing the usual mixture of churches and manors, walks and ancient monuments that makes Funen so varied. **Gislev** church, on the Lykkesholm road, has dark frescoes on the chancel walls but for something more modern try the Nazareth church located at the southern end of Ryslinge. Outwardly it is a typical white painted Danish church but the interior decoration is a feast of every type of craft. There is stained glass, wrought ironwork, frescoes, woodcarvings, a stone picture and a modern painting at the altar, let alone decorated pews and balconies and a barrel roof.

Lykkesholm manor to the north of Gislev is a three-winged yellow-painted house fronted by the free-standing 'Odense Gate' that is all that remains of former farm buildings. There is no parking at the manor but there are walks at the far end of the lake along Magelundsvej. This lane brings one through to the 323 and a small conglomeration of prehistoric remains.

Lindeskovdyssen at about 150m (165yd) long, flanked by 130 stones, is Denmark's longest barrow. The walk shown on the information board by the barrow takes 30 minutes and is not particularly interesting. Visit the other graves in the wood and return the same way. North of here at **Ravnholt** stands a sixteenth-century manor approached from Ryslinge along a chestnut avenue. Park at the eagle entrance and walk down the drive and round the French-style park with its several lakes and good views of the house. A 3km (2 mile) elm avenue leads on to the smaller manor of Hellerup, which belongs to the same estate. North-west from here at **Sønder Nærå**, the church has early frescoes cut across by later roof vaults. The Møllehøj signed beyond the church is a tree-rimmed hill.

Returning to the east coast, south of Nyborg, the Kongshøj Å sports several factory-style watermills, notably the Kongshøj Mølle nearest the coast. Just north of here at **Tårup**, number 1 Brandgaden is a smallish village garden that is open to the public. It lies behind the Hjornegården Kunsthandværk barns at the junction with Tårup Byvej. Much larger are the manor grounds at **Holckenhavn**, open just twice a week to the public. The road from here crosses a causeway into **Nyborg**. At present a ferry port for Zealand, the Store Bælt bridges and tunnels will replace this aspect within a few years. The exhibition centre on the Knudshoved peninsula has models and diagrams on the project including two programmed screens with English commentary. North of Nyborg on the Skabohuse road, there are extensive gardens behind the huge concrete buildings labelled 1-14 Strandvængt. A centre for retarded children, the grounds which are open all year include not only gardens in and out and on top of the buildings themselves but also animals and birds and access to the seashore. Just up the road at Skabohuse the town suddenly vanishes into a country lane with thatched homesteads. Another manor park open to the public throughout the year is at nearby Juelsberg.

The area north of here towards Kerteminde is rather flat. The manor of **Risinge** on the coast road is most unusual. Huge in size, it is dominated by a square red-roofed tower, which, along with the entire manor, is half-timbered in black and white. There are even half-timbered duck houses on the water in front! There is no access but it is just possible to stop for photographs on this busy main road. Inland, beyond Skovsbo manor, which hides behind a barrier of trees, a crucifix stands in the fields, raised perhaps by a sixteenth-century mistress of the manor in gratitude for a miraculous cure. This road leads into **Rynkeby** where the Hardenberg chapel within the church contains most unusual frescoes. Painted at the request of Eric Hardenberg (of Skovsbo), an enthusiastic convert to Lutheranism, they portray an angel orchestra conducted by Christ himself in the role not only of crucified man but also of Lord of Heaven and earth.

An unusual museum lies north of **Ladby**. First, on the junction where the museum is signed, notice the roof of the corner house. Rather weathered by time but certainly visible, there is a pattern cut in the thatch. The road stops at a cottage from where the path leads across a field to a barrow for the museum is inside. Electrically lit and air-conditioned, it is the Ladby ship burial. However what one sees is not the ship as it rotted centuries ago. What is left is its clear imprint in the soil. Plank marks and nail holes are all clearly visible and excellently explained in English.

The road into **Kerteminde** from here skirts the edge of the Kertinge Nør. To the right, between this and the 165, lie the woods of Lundsgård manor, where there are circular walks of various lengths returning along the shore. North of the bridge, the main street is Langegade with many old houses, the best one housing the town museum. A combined ticket gives entrance also to the Johannes Larsen Museum and the Swan Mill. Larsen was a Danish painter and his home has been restored and furnished as it would have been in about 1900. His paintings adorn the walls and his wildlife frescoes still decorate the dining room. There is a garden too and an exhibition of other artists' work. The mill next door, named for the swan on its roof, contains complete machinery and, unusually, one is allowed right up to the cap.

North of Kerteminde the long peninsula of **Hindsholm** stretches its three fingers into the sea. The coast road leads out past Hverringe manor to the pretty villages of **Måle** and Viby. The former has a wealth of half-timbering in a dull red. Måle Bakker, just north of the village, is at 36m (118ft) the highest point on the headland, giving views across to the island of **Romsø**, a nature paradise. The chestnut trees on the island were planted especially for the deer who are remarkably tame. Access, in summer only, is by twice weekly boat from Kerteminde. **Viby** has a restored mill, thatched houses and a church with an unusual tower and chapel and fresco paintings inside. The coast road north to Digerbanke gives good views. At **Snave** the Marhøj passage grave is unusually large. Situated halfway up the burial mound, the entrance passage leads into a chamber in which average-sized people can actually stand upright.

The last long stretch of road leads up to the curving finger of **Fyns Hoved**. There are parking places and walks both at the end of the surfaced road and of the gravelled road to the right. From the latter a circuit of the headland takes about an hour over cliffs. It is also possible to drive out to Langø Hoved. South of there one has the choice of the coast road (for views) or driving past impressive **Scheelenborg** manor. Lastly the road out on the 'thumb' leads through Midskov to Lodshuse which neatly completes the circuit of Funen, for from there one can see across the narrow Gabet to Enebærodde, the long tongue of land beyond Hofmansgave where this tour began.

Further Information
— Funen and the Islands to the South —

ÆRO

Ærøskøbing
Æro Museum
Brøgade
Open: beginning June to beginning
October daily 10am-4pm. Thursdays
2-6pm.

Bottleship Museum
Smedegade 22
Open: all year daily 10am-4pm.

Hammerichs Hus
Gyden
Open: beginning June to beginning
September, Tuesday to Sunday 1-
3pm. Thursday 6-8pm. Late June to
early August also daily 10am-
12noon.

Marstal
Jens Hansens Maritime Museum
Prinsensgade 1
Open: daily beginning April to mid-
June and mid-August to end October,
10am-4pm. Mid-June to mid-August,
9am-5pm. Also 7.30-10pm in July.

FUNEN

Assens
Willemoesgården
Østergade 36
Open: Easter and beginning June to
end August, Tuesday to Sunday
10.30am-12noon and 2-5pm. Begin-
ning May to end May, Saturday,
Sunday 10.30am-12noon and 2-5pm.

Egeskov
*Castle Gardens, Veteran and Vintage
Museum*
Open: daily beginning May to end
September 10am-5pm. Beginning
June to end August grounds and
museum 9am-6pm.

Erholm
Manor
Open: beginning May to end December. Admission to grounds daily
9am-5pm. Wine cellar (for Romanian
wines) Saturday 12noon-3pm.

Espe
Tingskov Have
Open: daily beginning April to
beginning November 9am-6pm.

Fåborg
Belfry
Tårngade
Open: mid-June to mid-September,
Monday to Friday 10am-12noon and
2-4pm. Saturday 10am-12noon.

Kaleko Mill
Prices Havevej
Open: daily mid-May to mid-Sep-
tember, 10.30am-4.30pm.

Glorup
Manor
Admission to grounds all year 10am-
6pm.

Gummerup
West Funen Farm Museum
Klaregade 23
Gummerup
Open: Tuesday to Sunday, beginning
April to end September 10am-5pm.

Hofmansgave
Museum of Sketches
Open: daily mid-May to mid-October
9am-4.30pm.

Holckenhavn
Manor
Grounds open: Tuesday and Satur-
day 2-6pm.

Kerteminde
Cultural and Fishing Museum
Farvergården, Langegade 8
Open: daily, beginning March to end
October 10am-4pm.
Ticket also valid for

*Johannes Larsen Museum and Swan
Mill*
Møllebakken
Open: Tuesday to Sunday, late
March to end May and beginning
September to end October, 10am-
4pm. Beginning June to end August,
10am-5pm.

Knudshoved (Ferry Port)
Exhibition Centre of the Great Belt Link
Open: Tuesday to Sunday 12noon-
7pm.

Ladby
Ship Museum
Vikingevej 123 Ladby
Open: Tuesday to Sunday, beginning
May to end September 10am-6pm.
Beginning October to end April
10am-3pm.

Millinge
Funen Toy Museum
Assensvej 279
Millinge
Open: daily beginning April to end
August, 9am-6pm. Beginning Sep-
tember to end October, 10am-4pm.

Skovby
Kunstgården
Ømosevej
(art/handicraft exhibition/sales)
Open: Tuesday to Sunday 11am-5pm.

Sønderby Klint
Seven Gardens
Å Strandvej 62
Å Strand
Open: daily mid-April to beginning
November, 10am-5pm.

Svendborg
M/S Helge. Round trips on veteran
ship. Five trips a day beginning June
to late August.

Vissenbjerg
Funen's Aquarium
Open: beginning January to end
March daily 10am-7pm. Beginning
April to end October daily 9am-4pm.

Terrarium
Kirkehelle 5
Open: beginning May to end Septem-
ber daily 9am-6pm. Beginning
October to end April 9am-4pm.

LANGELAND

Egeløkke
Manor
Admission to grounds Sunday and
holidays, 9am-6pm.

Skovsgård Manor
Carriage Museum
Kågårdsvej
Lindelse
Open: early May to end September,
Monday to Friday 10am-5pm, Sun-
day 1-5pm.

Lohals
Tom Knudsens Safari Museum
Hovvej 49
Lohals
Open: June, Saturday and Sunday 3-
5pm. Beginning July to end August,
Tuesday, Thursday, Saturday 3-5pm.
Sunday 10am-12noon and 3-5pm.

Tranekær
Castle Mill
Open: mid-May to end September,
Monday to Friday 10am-5pm. Sun-
day 1-4pm. Beginning July to end
July also Monday to Friday 7-9pm.

TÅSINGE

Bregninge
Skippers' Home and Folklore Museum
Open: mid-May to late June 10am-3.30pm. Late June to mid-August 10am-6pm. Mid-August to late August 10am-4pm.

Valdemars
Mansion Museum
Open: Easter to end April and beginning to end October, Saturday, Sunday and holidays 10am-5pm. Beginning May to end September daily 10am-5pm.

Tourist Information Centres

Ærøskøbing
Torvet
DK-5970 Ærøskøbing
☎ 62 52 13 00

Kerteminde
Strandgade 5a
DK-5300 Kerteminde
☎ 65 32 11 21

Nyborg
Torvet 9
DK-5800 Nyborg
☎ 65 31 02 80

Assens
Østergade 57
DK-5610 Assens
☎ 64 71 20 31

Langeland
Torvet 5
DK-5900 Rudkøbing
☎ 62 51 35 05

Odense
City Hall
DK-5000 Odense
☎ 66 12 75 20

Bogense
Adelgade 28
DK-5400 Bogense
☎ 64 81 20 44

Marstal
Kirkestræde 29
DK-5960 Marstal
☎ 62 53 19 60

Otterup
Jernbanegade 39
DK-5450 Otterup
☎ 64 82 32 00

Fåborg
Havnegade 2
DK-5600 Fåborg
☎ 62 61 07 07

Middelfart
Havnegade 10
DK-5500 Middelfart
☎ 64 41 17 88

Svendborg
Møllergade 20
DK-5700 Svendborg
☎ 62 21 09 80

Glamsbjerg
Nørregade 2
DK-5620 Glamsbjerg
☎ 64 72 33 99

Mid-Funen
Algade 42
DK-5750 Ringe
☎ 62 62 23 23

**Tommerup,
Vissenbjerg, Årup**
Bredgade 26
DK-5560 Årup
☎ 64 43 11 50

8 • Storstrøm County

Storstrøm County is a roughly heart-shaped area encompassing South Zealand and the islands of Møn, Falster and Lolland. The scenery is varied, ranging from rolling farmland in the north to flat reclaimed fields in the south-west. Most of the farms are built court-yard style — house adjoining barns round a square. The older ones are thatched, romantic to look at but not necessarily practical to maintain. It is expensive to produce straw for thatching as it has to be reaped and stooked in the old-fashioned way. Reed-thatch lasts longer but despite plenty of reeds round the lakes, it is now cheaper to import them from Hungary and Poland.

All the many manors possess tracts of woodland, many of which are open to the public — wherever there is a notice headed *'Til publikum'* in fact. They are normally deserted and it is possible to walk for kilometres in perfect peace. They harbour man-sized anthills among the firs, red squirrels amid the beechmast and prehistoric graves for the finding. Many are also near the coast, which ranges from sand dunes and bathing beaches with EEC approved clean water to the flinty shore footing the white cliffs of Møn. Nor is it necessary to swim with the masses in the resort areas of eastern Falster — every village has its *strand* with soft deserted sand and invitingly clear water. The only peril are the jellyfish. Much of the coast (and the lakes too) abounds in bird life, with protected reserves and occasionally observation points.

For the enthusiast, cycling, horse-riding, tennis and water sports are available, from windsurfing on the sea to canoeing on the Suså. Yachting into one of the many marinas, angling both offshore and fishing tours, splash-cats from the sandy beaches, all are possibilities. Only golfers will find their options limited, to two courses, one near Næstved and the other on Falster.

As Storstrøm County is naturally fragmented, the following chapter has been divided into tours of individual areas. A multiplicity of deserted country lanes link the sights so the ones suggested here pass

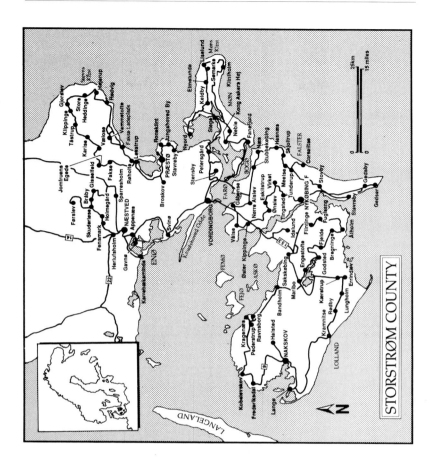

through particularly pretty villages or past interesting sights and viewpoints. None are intended as day tours as there is too much to do and see in every area to accomplish within a normal holiday day!

Route 1. The North-East from Fakse to Stevns Klint

Fakse is a modest town with interesting memorials to its past and an industrial present based on brewing and chalk quarrying. The impressive brick church (key from the white house beyond the churchyard), contains frescoes of St John the Baptist in the tower vaulting, also St George slaying a very small dragon; a motif which is repeated on a pew end in the chancel. The wooden figures beside the altar date from around 1500 while the interesting carved pulpit dates from the early seventeenth century.

Progressing through the town centre, one passes the magnificent fountain statues to the mythological horses of the night (Hrimfakse) and day (Skinfakse) which may have given the town its name. More prosaically it comes from the old Danish word *fax* meaning a stand of trees! Beyond here at the Faxe Brewery, there are guided tours every hour during the Danish school holidays. The tour is excellent, with slide shows of the history of Faxe beer and of the bottling process plus a visit to both the original brewing machines and the modern bottling department where the empties are washed, filled, capped, labelled and crated ready for sale. It ends with a sampling of Faxe beers and fizzy drinks.

One can also visit the chalk quarry, a little further on the right, to look for fossils at one's own risk. The quarry museum opposite contains a very good collection of these. At the end of town, the blue and white cottage on the corner is the oldest preserved village school in Denmark and there are plans to turn it into a museum. Returning through Fakse, a memorial stone on the right commemorates the town's most famous man, former Viking warrior, Rollo, who founded a dynasty in northern France, and was a forebear of the famous Duke William of Normandy who conquered England in 1066!

Opposite where this road leaves the town is Blåbæk's mill. Admission is via the mill farm beyond. This road leads past Rosendal manor to the prettily thatched villages of Vallebo, Strandhoved (Lille), Elmue and St Elmue, to **Røholte** on the 209. The limestone and brick church sports a block with a curious projection on the wall beside the porch. In the Middle Ages people who failed to attend church had to hold the projection in their mouth during the 3 hour services.

Return from here towards **Fakse Ladeplads**. Shortly before the town, troll hills or ancient burial mounds (Troldhøj) are signposted down a track to the right. The near end of this little town is summer-house land (holiday homes), for the beaches and bathing are good but it is also a working port, shipping corn and chalk from the Fakse quarry, all round the world. Leave by the minor road that follows the coast and then turns north for **Vemmetofte** Kloster. Park beyond the farm for a walk in the grounds of this former monastery. There are more walks signed in blue and yellow through the woods or along the coast from Vemmetofte Strand (leaflet available from the camping office).

Rødvig, a working port and marina on the Baltic coast, is well-signed from here. Its preserved flint oven on the quay is a good landmark, and at the ships' engines museum in Havnevej the staff will start an engine or two on request. The 261 north leads past the restored mill at Lille Hedinge. Turn right at the church to reach **Højerup** village close to the chalk cliffs of **Stevns Klint**. Neither as high nor as white as the more famous cliffs on Møn they are equally prone to crumble, as can be seen from the old church. According to legend it moves itself a 'cock's step' inland every Christmas night to avoid falling into the sea but by 1928 this was not enough. One can still see parts of the chancel on the beach below! The story of the old church can be seen on the pew ends of the new. The Stevns museum is comprehensive and interesting, with prehistoric tools, workshops and costumes and a changing display of ships in bottles. The fisherman's cottage next to the old church is furnished in simple nineteenth-century style.

North-east from here is **Store-Heddinge**, with northern Europe's only octagonal medieval church. The interior has been over-restored but outside stands the largest weeping beech in northern Europe and, near it, in the church wall, the head of a monk who was put to death for opposing the local landowner over the siting of his private graveyard. Now wind through Sigerslev and Holtug to the manor of **Gjorslev**, where the 50-acre garden, containing rare trees and lakes laid out in the English style, is open to the public. From there, join the 261 at Klippinge and head towards Køge. After a kilometre or two, a high wire fence with a reptile sign on it signals the Stevns Vivarium. This is an interesting collection of snakes, lizards, crocodiles and turtles. The building smells of its occupants but there is a treat in store when the enthusiast owner lifts out lizards and boas for the visitors to stroke!

Return through Klippinge and Klippinge Bjerge heading for **Tåstrup**. Another treat awaits here. At Tåstrupvej 31 'Trine's House' has been preserved, a dark little labourer's cottage furnished in early twentieth-century style. There is also a barn full of old implements and farm machines some of which have been used in Danish films. Circling back towards Fakse, there is a fortress church at **Karise** built to withstand attacks by the Wends. Further on turn right through the pretty thatched villages of Værlose, Tokkerup and Atterup, to the manor church of **Ør Egede**. Opposite the half-timbered building north of the church is an enormous oak, its circumference measuring $6^1/_2$m (21ft). The road past the manor of Jomfruens Egede leads to Lystrup. There is a clear view of this tiny manor (exterior dimensions a mere 25m by 12m, 82ft by 39ft) before one joins the 154 to return to Fakse.

Route 2. North and East from Næstved

Næstved is a sprawling town at the head of the Karrebæk fjord. It retains many medieval buildings the most interesting of which can be seen on a short walk from the tourist office. Opposite, on the corner of Riddergade is the Apostleshus with its carvings of the Apostles flanking the windows. St Marten's Church, with a unique altarpiece, is at the top of Riddergade. Through the shops of Torvestræde to Axeltorv and left between the buildings, brings one to St Peter's Church. Here are also Denmark's oldest town hall, in red brick with gable end and Denmark's oldest terraced houses which now contain a museum of silver, glass and ceramics. From here complete the square back to the tourist office diverting down Kompagnihuset for the medieval guildhall. For more country walks, there are tracks on both sides of the Suså for 2 to 3km (1 to 2 miles), from the canoeing centre to Herlufsholm. Once a monastery, then a grammar school for noblemen's sons, this is now one of the largest boarding schools in the country, its many buildings a conglomeration of architectural styles and materials. Alternatively, Herlufsholm Allé, off the 22, goes to the school and, beyond the narrow bridge, to the sports complex. Just north of Næstved at **Fensmark** is the Holmegård Glasværk. Guided tours need pre-arranging otherwise one is free to wander into the hand-blowing department to watch the crafting of the molten glass and a corner of the factory where 1.8 million bottles and jars are made every day! From here, follow the signposts for Haslev to Skuderløse. A diversion can be made from there, through Teestrup to **Førslev**, which boasts the oldest country store in Denmark. It has been in business since 1858 when it was set up with government help. A working shop, serving the people of Førslev, it still uses the old-fashioned balance scales, till and coffee grinder. In season the adjoining rooms become a period coffee shop with home made cakes. Alternatively continue to **Bråby** which has interesting thatched houses, a typical white-washed church and an imaginative children's play area. An avenue of beech trees leads from here to the Gisselfeld estate — parking and entrance to the left. **Gisselfeld** is a moated, red brick manor whose park was landscaped by the English gardener Milner. The most interesting part lies beyond the road. There one can circle the large lake, past the weeping beech where Hans Christian Andersen perhaps found the inspiration for *The Ugly Duckling*; across the little wooden bridge at the centre of the hour-glass lakes and round to the museum in the old watchman's house. It contains an interesting collection of nineteenth-century artefacts arranged in room settings. The carp dam

The guildhall at Næstved, the oldest in Denmark

leads to the bamboo avenue to complete the tour. Unusual plants can be bought from the greenhouses.

The Gisselfeld estate also covers **Hesede Skov** (wood). Heading south for Vester Egede, turn right at the sign for the Villa Galina, which is a popular restaurant. About $1^{1}/_{2}$km (1 mile) beyond the villa, park on the right. The forest track leads down to the **Paradise Garden**. Once a nursery supplying rare plants to botanical gardens, only an overgrown arboretum is left behind the red house. The main trees are still labelled and the paths are clear enough for walking but the whole has a sad air of neglect. Beyond the garden, follow the signs for Svenskekløften the Swedish ravine. Named for Swedish soldiers who camped there in 1660, it lies to the right of the forest track along the grassy path that is in earshot of the water. This skirts the ravine to the far end — return through the pine forest on the opposite bank. Allow a good hour for the whole walk. The through road from the parking brings one back onto the 54. The carriage museum at **Sparresholm**, with horse-carriages dating back to the eighteenth century, is signposted off if one turns left. From there one can return to Næstved cross-country via Sørup and Kalby.

Route 3. South Through Præstø

This route begins on the 209 Fakse/Præstø road, just south of Røholte (see earlier), where it reaches the Præstø fjord. At the far end of Leestrup Strand, turn right opposite the camping into Leestrup-skovvej and park. Ten minutes walk along the right hand forestry track and right again at the first 'crossroads' brings one to the rag oak, a huge tree decorated with ties and scarves and torn pieces of cloth, in remembrance of a medieval cure effected by crawling naked through the branches and leaving a rag behind in thanks!

Further south follow the fork to **Broskov**, signed 'Oldtidsvej', for a walk on a grassy track leading to two ancient roads; one from the Iron Age paved with large boulders and a medieval one superimposed across its route. The site has a good information board in English. Head now for **Præstø** and fork left at the sign for Thorvaldsen's sculpture museum. Housed in the cavalry building at Nysø, the collection consists of statues, reliefs and sketches made in the last 5 years of his life. In July the surrounding manor park is open to visitors. Præstø is also home to Denmark's oldest working pottery on the 265 Næstved road. The loft contains a museum of Kähler earthenware but downstairs teapots and dishes, mugs and piggybanks are still being made by traditional methods — the only concession to modernity being the conversion of the kilns from wood-fired to electricity in 1966. One can watch whatever process is in progress and of course, buy the finished articles.

In cobbled Grønnegade, the typical terraced house at number 14 has been converted into a museum of dolls and dollshouses. Called 'The Little Town' this runs through the attics in street settings. Most are Danish but one of the oldest is an English butcher's shop dating from around 1843. There are also several hundred dolls and downstairs there is an excellent shop for doll and dollshouse enthusiasts. The Dansk Brandværnshist Orisk Museum (Fire Service Museum) next to the bus station includes a photograph collection of Adelgade through the years, showing its development into the modern shopping street of today. Outside on the real Adelgade look for the inscribed paving stones. An ingenious way of raising money to extend the pavement in the 1960s, amid ordinary citizens they include Queen Margrethe (then Crown Princess) and Prince Henrik.

Several excursions can be made south of the town. The bird sanctuary at **Maderne** can be reached via Lundegård, Ambæk and Roneklint. The small earthworks at the end of the road gives views over Præstofjord and to the Feddet peninsula opposite — another birdspotters' paradise. From here follow the signs to Jungshoved By and Stavreby. All the villages on this head of land contain good thatched properties and pretty gardens but **Stavreby** has more than most. From here there are views across to Nyord and Møn, both within easy reach from Kalvehave to the south.

Route 4. The West Coast from Karrebæksminde to Vordingborg

Karrebæksminde, which was once a fishing village, still retains its original street and working fish harbour beyond the green bridge. Today it is a holiday resort with clean dune beaches, camp-sites, holiday homes and a large marina. It is best visited outside the Danish holiday season as is the marshy island of Enø beyond, with its rich bird life.

Across the shallow water from Enø lies the manor and flower park of Gavnø but it can only be reached by driving round the Karrebæk fjord and through Næstved. As the signed road from the 22 approaches the edge of the fjord, turn back into Abbednæs Bygade and park. The original village of **Appenæs**, containing a wealth of thatched eighteenth- and nineteenth-century houses, lies just along this road. **Gavnø** itself is one of Denmark's show places. The yellow and white manor is picturesquely situated beyond the water and its grounds sport beds of bulbs, summer flowers and roses in season. There is a butterfly house, a private chapel, a fine collection of paintings and a Falck museum with fire and rescue service vehicles.

Beyond Gavnø one drives through the prettily thatched villages of Vejlø and Svenstrup, rejoining the 22 at Vester Egesborg, to cross the end of the Dybsø fjord, with its viewing point for the birdlife. Take the first right and head for **Svinø** whose church has a garden of

The lifting bridge at Karrebæksminde

remembrance for allied airmen and inside, a delightful *Lord's Prayer* in lace. Svinø Strand has a fishing beach where one can see the fast current that runs through the narrow entrance to the fjord. Return via Sallerupgård and Sallerup to the 22.

The second right from here leads onto the long tongue of land called **Knudshoved Odde**. There is a restored passage grave at the first parking but its entrance is low — strictly for crawlers and children. From here walking through the ancient woods beyond, it would take a day's expedition to explore to the furthest point. Alternatively on a weekday between 7am and 6pm drive the 2km (1 mile) on to park at Knudskovgård. From there a sandy track leads through undulating farmland to the tip where there is a causeway to the 'island' beyond. Here there is a bison reserve where one can walk right in and find them which is easier than finding the rare fire-bellied toad in the small ponds and presumably safer than meeting the native black viper!

Head next past Rosenfelt manor to **Vordingborg**, arriving at its northernmost corner, where at 6 Broværket there is a glass workshop with both handblowing and glass cutting. The main street of the town, Algade, leads to the green spaces round the ruined castle. The Goose Tower, the only one of eight fortified towers remaining from King Valdemar Atterdag's fourteenth-century fortress is open for views. Nearby a wing of Prince Jorgen's seventeenth-century home houses the museum of South Zealand with collections from ancient times to the present century, including a dollshouse replica of 'Sara's House' in Riddergade. The botanical garden opposite the museum is based on her herb garden. Down the hill a deep meadow shelters sika deer and peacocks while back at the Goose Tower parking, the toilets are housed in what was once the town hall, then court and lock-up!

From Vordingborg take the minor road through Nyråd towards the east coast and Kalvehave, bridging the E4 motorway to the manor of Stensbygård and Stensby village. Note the apple trees growing here, introduced into the area by the Prince Jorgen. **Petersværft** on the coast, now a peaceful backwater with fishing, walks in the estate woods, and views to the Møn bridge, was a shipyard and naval base during the war against England in 1807. Across the 59, after Langebæk, Petersgård Allé (between white gateposts) leads through an avenue past the white and red manor house. The road on round to (Gammel) Kalvehave also gives views to the Møn bridge and from there Møn itself is the next obvious destination.

Route 5. The Island of Møn

The only direct bridge from South Zealand to Møn crosses from Kalvehave to Koster giving good views along the South Zealand coast and back to Kalvehave but there is nowhere to stop for photographs. The road leads to **Stege**, the island's main town with a working harbour and busy streets. The oldest houses are round the church and the most interesting, in the main square. Stege also boasts medieval ramparts, one preserved town gate and the Møn Museum in the cream-coloured merchant's house next door.

Take the minor road north from Stege to **Ulvshale** where both reeds and seaweed are harvested. The woods to the right on the Nyord road are 'ancient woods' in Danish terminology, meaning natural undisturbed areas with rank vegetation and tangled trees. An information board at the parking by the Nyord bridge shows sites for bird-watching. One is from the old entrenchment to the right (a relic of the Napoleonic wars against England) while another is from the observation tower in trees beyond the bridge. The flat salt meadows that cover most of Nyord are the breeding ground for many water birds. **Nyord** itself is a traffic-free fishing village. Park on the outskirts and explore. One shop remains, with enamel signboards still outside, and eels are landed at the harbour. The church is nineteenth-century octagonal, built because the vicar of Stege thought the locals were becoming ungodly, with nowhere to worship nearer than the town and successfully petitioned King Christian VIII for a church of their own. In gratitude, there are portraits of both king and queen above the door.

Several roads lead back to **Keldby** where the church is beautifully decorated with frescoes, the earliest mutilated by later extensions to the church but one can still recognise the stories they tell. One showing a king and queen probably illustrates the wedding of King Valdemar Atterdag to Queen Helvig in 1340. The much more colourful and lively scenes in the roof vaults belong to the 'Elmelunde workshop' of the late fifteenth century and are repeated, on a larger scale in **Elmelunde**'s own church along the road. The Bible stories are set in medieval times, with farm workers as peasants with their sickles and Herod's men as knights in armour. Between the two churches, the road signed Keldbylille brings one to a viewpoint over the lake of Stege Nor. Called Lillehøj it is actually a round barrow, and there is a long barrow in Elmelunde graveyard.

For a more interesting prehistoric site, leave the 287 at Børre for Ålebæk, then right for **Sømarke**. Sømarkedysse is a round dolmen with an enormous capstone, strikingly situated beside the road. The

The prehistoric burial chamber of Sømarke

smaller passage capstone is inscribed with nearly 200 cup-marks, the sacred magic fertility signs of the Bronze Age inhabitants. This eastern end of the island is tourist territory with the tiny thatched château of **Liselund** deservedly popular. Built by Antoine de la Calmette as a summer residence, the house is only open for specified guided tours. The English-style park is well worth exploring. Once much larger, a landslide in 1905 took 110 acres down into the sea, for the land is part of the chalk cliffs of Møn which also regularly erode away. One can drive from Liselund straight into the Klint area, with its acres of beechwoods flanking the spectacular cliffs. Park first at the red cottage just before the Hotel Hunosøgård and follow the track opposite. The steep chalk path to the right leads to the top of Aborrebjerg, at 143m (469ft) the highest point on Møn. There are several other parking places, the most popular being the furthest at **Store Klint**. Here there is a small museum of fossil finds from the cliffs. There are walks in both directions for a total of 8km (5 miles), giving tantalising glimpses through the trees of white cliffs, blue Baltic and passing boats. Three sets of 400 or more steep steps lead down to the beach where, depending on the tide, one can circle back, looking for fossils and even amber if there has been a recent storm from the east.

Continuing towards Busene and Klintholm, there are harbours at the end of every no through road. The road cross country from Busemarke to Rabymagle is hilly with possible views to Germany on a clear day. Just before reaching **Keldbylille**, the preserved courtyard *museumsgården* (farmhouse) is signed to the left. Look for the goose-pen bench in the kitchen and the original cooking area inside the chimney. The garden and pond are also part of the museum. The prettiest route from here is via Tåstrup to Svensmarke on the shores of Stege Nor. Picking up the 287 at Neble, drive through Damsholte and immediately right into Marienborgvej. **Marienborg** was the permanent home of the Calmette who built Liselund. He landscaped the park here too, though the site is much flatter and even built himself a mock barrow. To find the real thing, continue through St Lind and Borren to **Kong Askers Høj**. This is a well-preserved passage grave from the late Stone Age, hidden inside the grassy mound of a barrow. It is well-worth visiting if only because adults can negotiate the entrance passage bent double. Take a torch though as it is pitch dark inside and impossible to realise the size of the burial chamber without one. At **Røddinge** Klekkende Høj hides a double passage grave with very low entrances.

Now go south across the main road to **Fanefjord**, an imposing white-washed church overlooking Grønsund. Inside is another feast of frescoes. The altar and pulpit are high Renaissance from the seventeenth century. Beyond the church, towards Hårbølle, is the longest long barrow in Denmark, Grønsalen, stretching for 100m (110yd) away from the road. Tree-sheltered and edged with 145 huge stones, it is a fitting burial place for, as tradition says, Queen Fane and her husband Chief Grøn Jæger.

One has now reached the end of the rolling island of Møn with its thatch and cliffs and white-washed churches. An alternative route out is the causeway to neighbouring Bogø, and then to the eye-catching Farø bridge and the motorway. The parking area provides somewhere to eat and also the best view of this unusual bridge.

Route 6. Falster

Falster is a much larger island than Møn but neither as hilly nor as thatched; it does still have much to offer. This tour begins at Nykøbing in the east, where road 9 crosses from Lolland but one could also arrive on the old E4 from Guldborg or from the north over the Storstrøm or Farø bridges. There is even a passenger and cycle ferry from Bogø to Stubbekøbing.

Nykøbing F is the largest town on the island. Its most famous building is the Czarens Hus which was named after Peter the Great's visit in 1716. Today it houses the Falster Minder Museum. The abbey church originally belonged to the Grey Friars. The family tree of the Mecklenburgs dominates its chancel wall and outside there is a small

The church at Nørre
Alslev

medicinal herb garden containing some 300 plants grouped for what they heal. The town also possesses a good shopping centre, a zoological garden and a water tower, for views.

Leaving the town northwards on the old road, turn right just before a wood and head through Øverup to **Tingsted** whose pink brick church has decorated pew ends, a pulpit and altar from the High Renaissance and frescoes. Now follow the Horreby then Falkerslev signs through Hannenov Skov towards **Virket**, which means 'earthworks'. These cross the fairway of Falster's only golf course and form the cliff wall of Virket Sø. Circle past Skørringe and Ovstrup to **Eskilstrup** for the huge Tractor Museum. Occupying all three floors of a disused factory, it contains several hundred tractors from all over the world. Cross the E64 into **Ønslev**, watching out for the old Møllehus on the right just before the shops. This is a low thatched cottage and worth studying for all the carvings and artefacts around it. Follow Stadager church signs from here past yellow and white Vennerslund manor with its matching cottages. The

One of the reed-walled and thatched houses in Hesnæs

church matches too but is locked. **Øster Kippinge** church though is open. It contains carved and painted pulpit and altar, a rood screen and within the chancel a private pew decorated with the seven virtues. All are High Renaissance in style while the chancel walls have fourteenth-century frescoes. Beyond there, at **Vålse**, the pink church is also open and the village gardens are colourful.

Turn east now across the two main roads to **Gåbense**, an ex-fishing village on the Storstrøm sound. The tiny thatched cottage at the end of the harbour is the old ferry house. South of here lies **Nørre Alslev** whose church is again decorated with frescoes. From here the 293 leads direct to **Stubbekøbing**. The picturesque main street runs parallel to the shore with its working harbour, ferry to Bogø, marina, and views to Bogø, Møn and Fanefjord church. Stubbekøbing also has the largest radio and motorcycle museum in northern Europe.

Drive east from here past pretty cottages at Øre and the manor at Næsgård to the northern edge of **Korselitse** woods. Planted between 1805 and 1973 and stretching for 15 to 20km (9 to 12 miles) along the coast, they are open to the public with marked trails (yellow, blue and red) in the area surrounding **Hesnæs**. This is the most unusual village in the whole of Storstrøm county, for not only are the roofs thatched, but the house walls are made of reed too, held in place with rows of laths. Through Skjoltrup at Halskov Vænge one can take a different type of walk. Follow the 'Fortedsminderskov' signs to the parking and the forest track to the Naturmuseet with its visual display of life in a Bronze Age village. A trail then leads through an ancient landscape of round tumuli, long barrows and dolmen back to the car park. The walk takes less than 45 minutes. The road beyond the site leads to the sea with further walks along the tree-lined coast.

Another short diversion left passes through **Tunderup** village, along the coast and back past Corselitze (sic) manor whose park with eighteenth century gardens is open. Various roads from here head towards the southernmost tip of Falster, the most obvious one being that running behind Marielyst but this is the pleasure beach area, miles of soft sand, clean blue sea, chalet houses amid the trees and tripper-style shops and cafés — an area to avoid unless one is looking for a crowded beach or the Familieland Falster pleasure park, on the road across to Marrebæk. Instead travel across country to **Stovby** where the restored stump mill is open certain days of the week. The E64 then leads south to **Gedser** with ferry connections to Travemünde and Warnemünde in Germany. There is a geological museum in the town or one can go up the lighthouse. Signposted 'Fyret' it stands on the steep clay cliffs of Denmark's most southerly point.

Inland of Gedser, **Gedsby** is an old-fashioned village best explored on foot. Admire the pond, typical of many Falster villages, and look for the monument in the churchyard showing the flood level in 1872. A stroll through the interconnecting lanes will reveal a host of attractive cottages. Then take the old road north through Skelby and Stavreby to Marrebæk and the E64 back to Nykøbing.

Route 7. Lolland

The largest of the islands by far is Lolland with its flat fields and large farms. It would take a stay of several days to do it justice though, for convenience sake, **Maribo** is here suggested as a starting point with possible routes east and west. Maribo spreads round the northern edge of the Søndersø. Based originally round a Birgittiner convent, the impressive three-naved cathedral was the monastery church. The oldest streets are those behind it, leading to the main square with its imposing white town hall.

The eastern tour leaves Maribo on the Nysted road as far as the church at **Engestofte** which contains an interesting memorial to Lady Monica Wichfeld. Related to the manor family, she was born in London but lived in Denmark during World War II and was arrested by the Germans in 1944, dying in prison the following year. There are other memorials to the family both inside the church and in the graveyard. The thatched red house opposite was once the manor hospital. The lane to the right from the church leads between two wooded lakes. Beyond the woods turn left and left again at Godsted Manor. After 1km ($^1/_2$ mile), park beside the wood. Clear paths lead to the forty-five Bronze Age tombs among the trees!

Now drive through Fjelde and along Rykkerupvej. Park just before the far end of the forest and follow the forest road for 500m (550yd). Turn back right onto another forest road and watch carefully after a mere 50m (55yd) for a narrow path to the left. This leads, within 50m (55yd) again, to a very impressive passage grave — one which is well worth finding. From Rykkerup turn right for **Døllefjelde**. On Bregningevej 19 there is a bird park. Beyond Grønnegade turn left for Kettinge where there is a mill open during Danish holidays and a church with frescoes covering its ceiling. From an earlier period than the Master of Elmelunde, their colours are dull in comparison but they have interesting features. Look in particular for the birds and the unicorn on the chancel arch.

Ålholm Castle, on the outskirts of Nysted, lies directly south from here. An interesting and popular tourist attraction, the castle contains a magnificent dinner service in the dining room, a steam bath in the cellars, a wax figure of King Christoffer II in the dungeon and a royal bed that gives a whole new meaning to the word king-sized. A short drive away is Europe's biggest car museum, containing over 200 cars, plus a model railway and a wood-burning engine that takes passengers to the lake and back three times a day.

Pass through Nysted to Frejlev and **Frejlev Skov**. These woods contain graves and long barrows, including Kong Grøns Høj. The main track leads to the coast and the sun stone — a tall rock with a pointing finger which will at certain times cast a shadow over the shaped round stone inside the stone circle. Map leaflets are available from the Lolland tourist offices. North of here the 297 goes to **Fuglsang**, a manor retreat with interesting gardens and named trees. Turn left now for **Flintinge** and Flintinge Byskov, watching out for the prehistoric graves in the fields. For the best one, with an adult-sized entrance and light enough to see inside without a torch, turn right at the T-junction and left past the first farm down a tarred track labelled 'Fuglsang Skovdistrict'. Park at the thatched farm and follow the sandy track left past the barn to two *jættestue* (passage graves). The second of the two graves is the most impressive.

Now head left on the 9 and right along Idalundvej for **Majbølle**'s newly restored mill. From here the 153 leads into the town of **Sakskøbing**. The tourist office provides an English pamphlet for a town walk. The two most interesting buildings are the water tower, with its smiling face, and the Kong C's Café which stands on the site

Søholt Manor

of the house from which King Christoffer II was taken a prisoner to Ålholm. Also of interest are the modern fountain sculpture, *Girl With An Umbrella* and the bronze *Sugarbeet Girls* remembering the Polish workers of 90 years ago. From here the 153 leads back to Maribo.

The western tour leaves Maribo on the 153 towards Rødby, stopping first at the Frilandsmuseum in **Maribo**. This collection of old buildings includes a school, a smithy and a house with reed walls like the ones at Hesnæs. From here circle the south side of the Søndersø to Søholt Manor for views across the lake to Maribo, of the waterfowl and of the manor itself. The manor park is open (via the far lodge) but it consists mainly of alleys between high hedges which exclude any views! South from here through Fuglse and across the 297 brings one to a gem of a moated manor house (not open) at **Kærstrup**. Many Danish manors are hidden behind trees or huge farms but this one is in full view on its island beside the road. Pass through Errindlev, an attractive village with a large pond, onto the Rødby road for **Lungholm**, with a wolf park and museum, and a riding centre.

The next stop is **Rødby** with its amber museum and workshop where one can try amber-grinding and the memorial in Nørregade to the 1872 floods. Nowadays Rødby is 5km (3 miles) from the sea. The Rødby fjord was drained to create the pancake flat farmland that one crosses on the minor road to Kramnitse, whose pumping station still keeps it dry. The whole of this south-west coast from the Hyllekrog peninsula beyond Rødbyhavn through to Langø near

Nakskov is dune beaches restrained by dykes along which one can walk. Kramnitse and Hummingen beyond are summerhouse land (holiday homes) and, after one has joined the main road from Gloslunde to Langø, every left turn leads to a different 'strand'.

At Næsby, circle left to **Kappel** which has an old mill and a good-looking white church with a memorial to Allied airmen in the churchyard. Turn left into Vesternæsvej where at number 56 Peter Hansens Have is an imaginative garden with twisting narrow paths, water feature, herbaceous beds, shrubs and roses. There is also a rock garden behind the house. Beyond the Albuen camping a sandbar provides a 3km (2 miles) walk to the bird island of Albuen. It can also be reached, as a half day round trip, by mailboat from Nakskov! Divert next to the fishing harbour of Langø for views of the various islands in the fjord. Nakskov itself presents an industrial front from this angle; the real town has much more to offer!

The road from Langø arrives at the harbour end of **Nakskov**, with parking along the harbour's edge. The narrow streets and alleys leading to the main square are flanked by old yellow and black houses. The church contains a Swedish cannonball in the chancel — look for the hole it made in the arch over the altar! The lake beside the harbour is a bird reserve, fed by the Halsted Å and an excursion can be made along Maribovej to **Halsted** where the Klosterpark is open daily and the estate houses are all painted orangey-red.

Alternatively from Nakskov follow the signs for Tars crossing over the 9 to the old road at Sandby. Head for Frederiksdal manor, near the west coast, for walks to a delightful Chinese pavilion. From here head towards **Købelevskov**, taking Oddevej right before reaching the wood. At number 16 the Købelevhavn is a rather cramped Japanese garden, containing a tea house and bridge as well as many statues. There are various routes from here to **Pederstrup** for the Reventlow park with walks round the lake and the museum to CDF Reventlow, the Danish statesman who amongst other reforms, set the peasants free. Not far to the north is the well-signed Kong Svends Høj. This is Denmark's largest passage grave and easy to enter and light enough without a torch.

Now follow the 289 to **Kragenæs**, the ferry port for Femø and Fejø. Beyond, the hilly area of Ravnsby Bakke contains a selection of well-signed sights. The passage grave at **Glentehøj** is easy to enter but a torch would help inside; Ravnsborg has the embankments of a thirteenth-century fortress. The round barrow, **Bavnehøj** is Lolland's highest point and stands a whole 30m (98ft) high, giving views of the Lolland Alps. Birket church, its medieval bell-tower on one of the two barrows in the churchyard, completes the sights of the area. The 289 leads on to **Bandholm**, the end of the museum railway from Maribo and the ferry port for Askø. The oldest houses are on the street leading to the harbour. The popular Knuthenborg Safari Park is signposted from here. The exit to Maglemer leads back to Maribo.

Further Information
— Storstrøm County —

Ålholm
Automobile Museum
Ålholm Parkvej 7
4480 Nysted
Open: mid-April to end June and beginning September to mid-October, Saturday, Sunday and holidays, 10am-6pm. Beginning June to beginning September daily 10am-6pm.

Castle
4880 Nysted
Open: beginning June to beginning September daily 11am-6pm.

Bandholm
Knuthenborg Safari Park
4930 Maribo
Open: daily beginning May to mid-September 9am-6pm.

Eskilstrup
Lolland-Falster Tractor Museum
Nørregade 17-19
4863 Eskilstrup
Open: mid-May to mid-June and mid-August to mid-September, Monday to Thursday 10am-4pm. Friday, Saturday and Sunday 1-4pm. Mid-June to mid-August daily 10am-4pm.

Fakse
Faxe Brewery
☎ 53 71 37 000
Open: Danish school holidays, Monday to Thursday guided tours at 9am,
10am, 11am, 1pm, 2pm and 3pm. Friday 9am, 10am and 11am only. Other times phone to book. Closed Saturday and Sunday.

Geology/Culture/History Museum
Torvegade 29
4640 Fakse
Open: January to end April and September to mid-November, Thursday 2-4pm. Beginning May to end August, Tuesday to Friday 2-4pm. Saturday 10-11am.

Gavnø
Gavnø Park and Manor
4700 Næstved
Open: beginning June to end August daily 10am-4pm.

Gedser
Gedser Lighthouse
Gedser Odde
4874 Gedser
Open: beginning April to beginning October daily 10am to lighting-up time.

Gisselfeld
Kloster and Park
4690 Haslev
Open: Palm Sunday to beginning May 10am-4pm, Saturday and Sunday 10am-5.30pm. Beginning June to mid-August 10am-7pm. Mid- to end August 10am-5.30pm. Beginning September to beginning October 10am-4pm.

Kappel
Peter Hansens Have
Vesternæsvej 56
Vesternæs
4900 Nakskov
Open: beginning May to beginning
November daily 10am-5pm.

Keldbylille
Museumsgården
Skullebjergvej 15
Keldbylille
Møn
4780 Stege
Open: beginning January to end April
and beginning November to end December 10am-4pm. Beginning May to
beginning November daily except
Monday, 10am-6pm.

Kettinge
Bregninge Birdpark
Bregningevej 19
4892 Kettinge
Open: mid-May to mid-September
daily 10am-7pm. Saturday and Sunday to end October, 10am till sunset.

Kettinge Mølle
Grønnegadevej
4892 Kettinge
Open: late June to early August, Tuesday 2-5pm.

Købelevskov
Købelevhaven
Kurt Rasmussen
Oddevej 116 Købelev
4900 Nakskov
Open: beginning April to end June
daily 12noon-7pm. Saturday and Sunday 10am-6pm. Beginning July to end
August daily 10am-7pm. Saturday
and Sunday 10am-6pm. Beginning
September to late October daily
12noon-6pm. Saturday and Sunday
10am-5pm.

Klippinge
Stevns Vivarium
Bjælkerupvej 160
Open: daily 9am-5pm.

Liselund
Mini Château and Park
Open: all year. Grounds 10am-5pm.
Château by guided tour.

Lungholm
Wolfmuseum
Rødbyvej 20
4970 Rødby
Open: beginning June to end October
daily 10am-5pm.

Majbølle
Mølle
4862 Guldborg
Open: beginning June to end August
daily 1-5pm.

Maribo
Frilandsmuseet
Meinkesvej
4930 Maribo
Open: beginning May to end September daily 10am-5pm.

Næstved
Holmegård Glasværk
Glasværksvej
Fensmark
4700 Næstved
Open: Monday to Thursday 9.30am-
12noon and 12.30-1pm. Friday 9am-
12noon summer weekends, holidays
11am-3pm. Closed for 3 weeks in July.

Museum
Open: Tuesday to Sunday 10am-4pm,
June, July and August

Nykøbing F
Falsters Minder Museum
Færgestræde
4800 Nykøbing F
Open: beginning January to end April
and mid-September to end December

daily except Monday, 2-4pm. Beginning May to mid-September, Tuesday to Saturday 10am-4pm. Sunday 2-4pm.

Watertower
Hollands Gård
4800 Nykøbing F
Open: mid-June to mid-September daily 11am-4pm. Saturday 10am-12noon.

Pederstrup
Reventlow Museum
Pederstrup
4943 Torrig L
Open: beginning May to end August, Tuesday to Sunday 12noon-5pm. Beginning September to end October, Tuesday to Sunday 1-4pm.

Præstø
Dansk Brandværnshistorisk Museum
Havnevej 4
4720 Præsto
Open: beginning May to late June, Saturday and Sunday 10am-12noon and 2-4pm. Late June to early August daily 10am-12noon and 2-4pm. Early August to mid-October, Saturday and Sunday 10am-12noon.

Det Gamle Pottemageri
Røde-led
4720 Præstø
Open: daily till 5pm. Saturday, Sunday and holidays till 4pm.

Dollshouses Collection
Grønnegade 14
4720 Præstø
Open: beginning June to end August, 11am-4pm.

Thorvaldsen's Collection
Nysøvej 5
4720 Præstø
Open: beginning May to late June and beginning to mid-August, Wednesday and Saturday 2-5pm. Sunday 11am-5pm. Late June to early August daily 2-5pm. Sunday 11am-5pm.

Rødby
Jack-Stone (Amber Museum)
Østergade 5
4970 Rødby
Open: all year Monday to Friday 10am-12.30pm and 2-6pm. Saturday 9am-12noon.

Rødvig
Rødvig Ships Engines Museum
Havnevej 7
Open: beginning June to end August daily 10am-12noon and 2.30-5pm.

Stege
Møn Museum
Storegade 75
Open: all year daily except Monday, 10am-4pm.

Stevns
Museum
Højerup Klint
4660 Store-Heddinge
Open: beginning May to end September daily except Monday, 1-5pm. Every day in July.

Stovby
Stovby Mølle
Stovbyvej
4873 Væggersøse
Open: beginning April to beginning September, Tuesday and Thursday 1-3pm. Mid-June to mid-August, Saturday and Sunday 10am-12noon.

Stubbekøbing
Radio and Motorcycle Museum
Nykøbingvej 54
4850 Stubbekøbing
Open: Late March to end May and beginning to end September. Saturday, Sunday and holidays 10am-5pm. Beginning June to end August daily 10am-5pm.

Tåstrup
Trines Hus
Tåstrupvej 31
Druebjerggård
Open: all year 10am-8pm.

Vordingborg
Bjornskunstglas
Broværket 6
Open: Monday to Saturday 10am-5pm. Sunday 11am-4pm.

Goose Tower
Ruinterrænet
4760 Vordingborg

Open: Easter and October holiday 12noon-4pm. Mid-May to mid-June and mid-August to mid-September daily 1-5pm.

Sydsjællands Museum
Ruinterrænet
4760 Vordingborg
Open: beginning April to end May and beginning September to end October daily except beginning June to end August daily 10am-4pm. Beginning November to end December daily except Monday, 1-4pm.

Tourist Information Centres

OPEN ALL YEAR
Fakse Kystens
Hovedgaden 33
4654 Fakse Ladeplads
☎ 53 71 60 34

Langebæek
c/o H.P. Mathieson
Østervej 1
4771 Kalvehave
☎ 53 78 84 78

Maribo
Rådhuset
Torvet
4930 Maribo
☎ 53 88 04 96

Møn
Storegade 5
4780 Stege
☎ 55 81 44 11

Næstved
Købmagergade 20
4700 Næstved
☎ 53 72 11 22

Nakskov
Axeltorv 6
4900 Nakskov
☎ 53 92 21 72

Nykøbing F (Falster)
Østergågade 2
4800 Nykøbing F
☎ 53 85 13 03

Nysted
Adelgade 65
4880 Nysted
☎ 53 87 19 85

Præstø
Erhvervshuset
Adelgade 91
4720 Præstø
☎ 53 79 11 90

Rødby og Omegn
Willersgård
Vestergade 1
4970 Rødby
☎ 54 60 21 10

Sakskøbing
☎ 53 89 56 30

Stevns
Algade 32
4660 Store-Heddinge
☎ 53 70 64 64

Vordingborg
Glambæksvej 3
4760 Vordingborg
☎ 53 77 02 17

SUMMER OFFICES
Gedser
Langgade 61
4874 Gedser
☎ 53 87 90 41
Open: end May to 1 August.

Karrebæksminde
Alleen 36
4736 Karrebæksminde
☎ 53 74 21 50
Open: mid-June to mid-August.

Stubbekøbing
Havnegade 9
4850 Stubbekøbing
☎ 53 84 13 04
Open: end May to 1 August.

9 • South-East Sweden

Introduction to Sweden

Sweden is the largest of the Scandinavian countries and the most varied in scenery, economy and climate. The south rivals Denmark with its prosperous farming while the north is, like Finland, covered with commercial forestry. The western border with Norway lies in the backbone of mountains that separates the two; the north and eastern borders in the tundra plateaux where the Lapps and their reindeer roam freely. Large lakes and broad rivers provide variety in the scenery and the seaboard, indented and islanded, is 2,500km (1,550 miles) long.

The towns are connected by a network of fast main roads with a top speed limit of 110kph (68mph) on motorways. Speeding leads to on the spot fines on a sliding scale according to one's ability to pay. Refusal to state one's job only leads to a higher fine! In Sweden drive on the right-hand side of the road. On wide roads, the Swedes drive down the centre lanes, only moving in to the narrower edge lane (in reality the hard shoulder) when someone wants to overtake them. Traffic is only a problem in the larger towns. Elsewhere roads are comparatively deserted. In country areas the minor roads are often not surfaced, being of hard-packed mud or gravelled instead. Many of the routes given here use these for one cannot go off the beaten track without doing so. While most are well-maintained it is wise to allow more travelling time than for surfaced roads. The main hazards are the wildlife, elk in the south and reindeer in the north, which cross roads at whim, particularly at dawn or dusk, and can cause serious damage to vehicles and their occupants. All such accidents must be reported to the police.

The Swedes are very proud of their national heritage and their past is preserved in a variety of ways. Barrows and ship burials, power stations and pitch valleys, old cemeteries and frescoed churches, all are maintained, signposted and labelled. The larger mining centres have their trips underground to old workings and their mine museums. In the countryside there are *kulturminne* or cultural trails round

Denmark's oldest country store at Førslev, South Zealand (Chapter 8)

Fanefjord church on the island of Møn, Storstrøm County (Chapter 8)

A thatched cottage at Halstedkloster, Lolland, Storstrøm County (Chapter 8)

Near the start of Skatelov nature trail, Småland, South-East Sweden (Chapter 9)

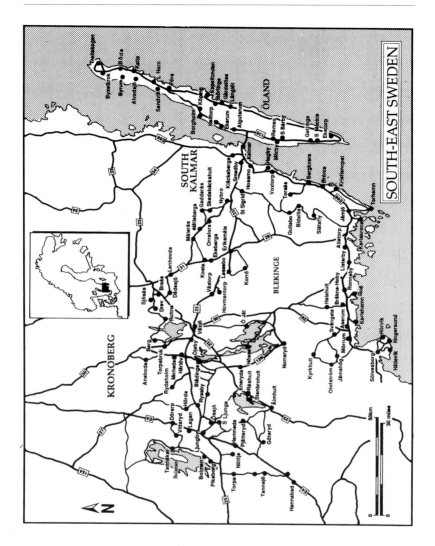

all manner of old industrial sites. As their attractions are mainly ruins there is normally open access to them at any time. Their former way of life is preserved with restored mills and homesteads, the smallest open for any passerby to look inside. At local *hembygdsgårds* or *gammelgårds* one can wander round the site peering through windows at any time but the house and outbuildings are only opened on Sunday afternoons from late June to early August. The largest, proper open-air museums, run full summer seasons often with craft displays and special events on site. In the appropriate provinces Lapp and Finnish sites are also preserved and on display.

The traditional Swedish farm is built of deep red wood trimmed in white and where the soil is poor farmers still maintain the old-fashioned hay meadows that bloom so delightfully in June and July before they are harvested with a scythe. The countryside is governed by Sweden's Right of Public Access which confers both freedoms and responsibilities. The freedoms are to walk, jog, cycle, ride or ski anywhere except in private gardens or enclosures round a house; to camp for a day or two on non-agricultural land, preferably with the owner's permission; to swim, row, sail, canoe and cruise in and on private waters. The responsibilities are to show respect for the local inhabitants' privacy and peace; not to cause damage by fires or leaving gates open or by disturbing the plant and animal life. Rare plants are protected; no growing trees or tree products can be removed; hunting and taking birds' eggs are banned. There are also limits to access to sanctuaries during the breeding season. Fishing with a rod is allowed anywhere along the coast but fishing with nets and with rods in most lakes and rivers requires a licence from the local tourist office. Cars are not allowed on private roads that are signed *enskild väg* or have prohibitory traffic signs. This Right of Public Access means that the whole gamut of outdoor pursuits are available all over Sweden to the sensible tourist.

Most National Parks have hiking trails, overnight huts, toilet and barbecue facilities, bridges over awkward rivers and board walks across bogs for Sweden is a civilised country in everything, even in catering for the outdoor enthusiast. The smaller nature reserves are similarly well provided. Lakes and rivers have in addition licence machines and wind shelters as well as well-stocked waters for the fishermen. They also have mosquitoes and a strong repellent as well as an anti-histamine cream is a must. Canoeists are catered for too with long distance trails through some lake and river systems.

South-East Sweden

This area comprises the coastal province of Blekinge, southern Kalmar with the island of Öland, and the Småland province of Kronoberg. Blekinge is long and narrow descending in three steps to the shore. The uppermost is rock with thin poor soil that supports only conifers. The middle step has broad-leaved woodland, the native oaks bearing enormous leaves, the forest floor carpeted with anemones in spring. Farming is carried out wherever the soil is deep enough, mainly in valleys leading down to the third, the coastal step.

Even here the fields are small and boulder-strewn and the houses perch on rocky outcrops. In early summer the verges near the villages bloom with wild lupins in pinks and cream and mauve. Blekinge has kilometres of rocky coastline, stretching from Solvesborg in the west to Kristianopel in the east but it is elusive. There is no true coast road and glimpses of the sea can be tantalisingly rare. Harbours are often down no-through roads and the routes across the islands south of Karlskrona pass through military restricted areas where foreigners are not allowed.

Öland, despite being an island, has a similarly elusive coastline. There are too many trees and fields between the roads and the shore. The chief feature of Öland is its windmills, which were used to grind the farmers' grain in the eighteenth and nineteenth centuries. They are mainly stubble mills just large enough for each farmer's needs though some larger ones remain, often converted to restaurants. There are also prehistoric remains from grave mounds (*grävfalt*) to forts, bathing beaches, nature reserves, bird sanctuaries and areas of holiday homes, for Öland is a Swedish holiday island. Its second largest industry, after farming, is tourism. For that reason it is advisable to visit it in the first three weeks of June before the Swedes themselves go on holiday in force. It is, besides, a very good time to visit this whole area as the meadows are full of flowers before the hay making and most attractions open only for June, July and August.

The flowering meadows are also a feature of Kronoberg province. They surround the red wood farms that create oases in the endless forests, for the soil is poor and stony and conifers grow more easily than crops. Yet they are themselves a crop, harvested for paper or posts or telegraph poles or for more of the wooden houses — though it was not just availability that made the Smålanders build their homes of it centuries ago. Wooden houses are moveable where stone ones are not and this made sense in an area where farming was only marginally profitable and employment of labourers uncertain. Most farms are collections of dark red buildings trimmed in white, with two or three barns and usually at least two houses which are sometimes yellow instead. Porches have decorative fretted friezes and maybe a balcony above. Fields have been created by clearing the ground of stones, building them into the distinctive Småland walls, two sides deliberately raised but the centre filled haphazardly. Where the boulders are too large to move, there the flowering meadows grow, grazed by cattle or dotted with trees. The latter have the widest variety of flowers. All are mown with the scythe, no mechanical instrument being suitable for the terrain. The general poverty of the land is also the reason for the paucity of large manor houses. Even those marked on the map are often little larger than the best farms.

The other main feature of Kronoberg province is its lakes. They are just as elusive as the coastlines, frequently only a narrow belt of trees away but just as invisible as if they were not there at all. But there they undoubtedly are, particularly in the area round Växjö, with their birdlife, water lilies, fish, bathing places and canoe routes. Many of the twenty-six state nature reserves in the province border onto lakes as well as extending through mixed woodlands. An English brochure of these is available from tourist offices, as are lists of glassworks (*glasbruk*) and their opening hours, for Kronoberg is also part of the 'Kingdom of Glass' with large factories in the major towns. In general glass-blowing can be seen from 9am to 3pm. A special treat at some glassworks, in July and August, is a *hyttsill* evening, eating herrings cooked in the cooling pipe of the furnace, followed by the Småland delicacy of curd cake. This is a re-enactment of the days when the glassworks were a social centre for local people, the furnaces providing free warmth as well as fuel for simple cookery.

Another feature of the whole area is the homestead museum (*hembygdspark*) with one or more old buildings maintained by the local historical society. Usually the area is unlocked so that one can wander amongst the buildings but they are only open for viewing inside on summer Sunday afternoons when demonstrations or events are organised. Tiny preserved cabins or mills in the depths of the countryside are often permanently unlocked. Access to the churches is similarly varied but the most interesting are usually open in daylight hours during the summer. In Kronoberg these are those medieval churches that were not destroyed when the nineteenth-century population explosion led to the building of larger replacements. In southern Kalmar where the present boundary with Blekinge was for centuries the border between Sweden and Denmark, there are three-storeyed medieval defence churches, built to serve the double purpose of place of worship and fort against marauding Danish armies.

Most activities in this area are outdoor ones. There are marked trails varying from half hour circles in the nature reserves to long distance paths like the Blekingeleden wandering for 240km (149 miles) through the province's countryside and the 96km (60 mile) circular emigrant trail through the area made famous by author Vilhelm Moberg in his novels about the Swedish emigrations of the last century. Some areas also have culture trails (*kulturminne*) round the ruins of their industrial past, from broken-down mills to tar ovens and pitch valleys. There are also long distance bicycle routes like the 120km (74 mile) trail round Lake Åsnen and prepared canoe routes like the one starting in Lake Bolmen and following the River Lagan out to the sea. There are official bathing places in many of the lakes as well as bathing beaches round the various coasts. Bicycles, canoes and other boats can be hired and there are facilities for tennis and some golf courses in the area too.

The main road system throughout the area is excellent but dull. The side roads which wind through the countryside instead of cutting straight through the forests are much more interesting but they may not be surfaced. Often they are hard-packed mud which is a perfectly driveable surface up to the speed limit of 70kph (43mph). The smaller ones are single track with passing loops. Forest roads always go through to the place signed on blue at the start, with turnings off to individual settlements signed on yellow.

The through road along the south coast is the E66 from Malmö but there are plenty of more than adequate alternatives. To begin at the west of **Blekinge**, the chief town on the coast is **Sölvesborg**. The oldest building there is medieval St Nicholas Church with frescoes of the Virgin Mary's life round the chancel vaulting. The carved crucifix is also medieval but the altar and pulpit date from Sölvesborg's early seventeenth-century prosperity. There are more frescoes in the porch and also a sixth-century rune stone.

Beyond Sölvesborg a fat tongue of land stretches into the Baltic. This is Listerland with white sand bathing beaches, a fishing museum at **Hällevik** and a puppet maker at **Nogersund** on the right of the entry road. Almost immediately afterwards Kryddträdgården is signed left, then right along Garnvågen. Set behind an ordinary little house this is a well-tended herb garden with beautiful wooden signboards giving Swedish and Latin names and medicinal uses of the plants. From the harbour a half day trip goes to the island of **Hanö** which has one of northern Europe's tallest lighthouses and also an English cemetery from the days during the Napoleonic Wars when Hanö harboured an English fleet. Along the road between Nogersund and Hörvik (another fishing village with a traditional Blekinge smoke-house for the smoking of fish) Strandvallar is signed to the right. An unmade road leads through forest to a parking place by the Listerhuvud nature reserve. Here 'Litorinavallen' leads straight down to the original coastline, now a broad ledge with a path along it. To reach the present-day coast, go 40m (44yd) right from the information board, then left down a narrower track. This brings one out of the woods opposite Hanö. The well-marked Listerhuvud trail

Lake Orlunden from Valhall

is more interesting, leading past deep bowls in the woods and across the *strandvallar*, or glacial slopes, but giving no real views, apart from a glimpse of Hanö to the right. One must return the same way.

The other main town in the west of Blekinge is **Olofström**, some 30km (19 miles) north of Sölvesborg by the minor road through Kylinge and Jamshog. One reaches Halens nature reserve first, with marked paths such as the 5km (3 mile) Holjeleden from the first parking. Just beyond the third parking Djurvilan is a pets' cemetery in a forest clearing, with bright flowers on the mini-graves and a pump in the woods for water. Alternatively one can circle lake Halen by car. Follow Nebbeboda signs to the north-west of Olofström, turning immediately round the top of the lake onto a dirt road. Boggeboda såg kvarn, a restored watermill, complete with timber sawing equipment and grain grinding, is a short walk through the woods from the sign. There are several views of the lake and also the highest point in this area at Boafallsbacke. By turning right at Alltidhult one can also penetrate into the Harasjömåla Kronopark with its dozen or so fishing lakes. One licence covers them all.

The best view in the area is over Lake Orlunden to the east of Olofström. Follow the Akeholm road taking the forest road to Valhall just before the lake. This rocky outcrop gives the views down over the water, islands, and wooded hillsides that are so often lacking in Sweden. Another forest road to try is that signed north of Olofström to Snöfleboda. It passes through a mixture of pine and broadleaved woodland and past farms, leading eventually to the Vishult/Kyrkhult road. At **Slagenås**, to the right, the Galax tourist centre has woodland gardens with statues and pools, open to the public, on the steep slopes down to the lake. **Kyrkhult** has one of the more interesting modern churches, with three-dimensional paintings of the saints on its walls.

Beyond Kyrkhult the 126 leads south down the Mörrum valley whose river is famous for its salmon. In **Mörrum** itself one can fish by permit and also see how the fish were once netted and observe them in the Salmon Aquarium. There is also a homestead museum on the Svängsta road into Mörrum and another at nearby Asarum.

South of here, **Karlshamn** is the next town on the coast, with museums and in summer boat trips to the fort on Frisholmen island. Called Karlshamn Castle, it was built in 1675 when the Danes declared war on Sweden with the intention of regaining their lost province of Blekinge. Beyond the rose gardens at the end of the town, Väggavägen leads out to Vägga with its smokehouses and to the island of Yttervägga where Svaneviksvägen gives good views over the marinas on 'Swan Lake'.

Another excursion to the north can be made from here. Leave Karlshamn for Boddestorp, across the E66 for Hällaryd, then north to **Halahult**. Here the Offerlund signed to the left is a sacrificial altar just a short walk away through a lightly wooded gorge. **Nottastugan**, signed 5km (3 miles) further north, is a homestead museum which runs a programme of entertainments every Sunday afternoon in summer. The return route south, on the mud road signed Åryd, is prettier. It goes round rocks, past lakes and through settlements before broadening to tarmac in a farming valley. Pass under the E66 to the old road, virtually traffic-free and of a good quality, which runs parallel to the E66 from Hallaryd to **Bräkne-Hoby** and beyond. An unusual natural phenomenon at Bräkne-Hoby are 'giants' pots' or boil holes. Turn left towards the church, then right on the bend immediately in front of the Lanthushållskolan. This lane leads to the edge of the woods and about $1/_2$km beyond is the 'Jättegrytorna'.

To the right of where one went under the E66 is **Guö** whose inn commands a good view of Guöviken. One of the best attractions of the area is nearby **Eriksberg** Game Reserve. Here in over 2,000 acres five species of deer, pure-bred European bison, mouflon sheep and wild boar live in a totally natural state. For this reason, the Swedish Right of Public Access is waived here and admission is only by guided tour in tractor-drawn tailor-made wagons or by pre-booked coach. The farm is now used for scientific research into the animals'

Vieryd at the head of an estuary

habits and for the breeding of rare geese. Rare red waterlilies flower here too on the lake. There is no guarantee that any animals will be seen, for they are free to roam but you would be very unlucky not to.

Beyond Åryd going east, take the coast road towards Ronneby. Jarnavik is the ferry port for **Tjärö**, an island with bathing beaches, trails and bird life which is a designated nature reserve. The walk from the parking just before Jarnavik harbour leads to a rocky promontory that gives excellent views over the islands and waterways. It is part of the 'Blekingeleden' long distance trail and there are further marked paths beyond the bay. Back and right for Saxemara brings one to Vieryd, at the head of a very pretty estuary. Beyond Saxemara one passes the Risanäs School Museum in the original school which opened in 1854.

Ronneby is a pleasant town. The old centre with its narrow cobbled streets of wooden houses in pastel hues is on the hill around Heliga Kors church. Here too is Möllebackagårdens cultural heritage museum. To the south lies the old spa of Ronneby Brunn, today

Sweden's largest conference and recreation area with many of the nineteenth-century buildings and gardens preserved. A good varied walk, taking about an hour, follows the 'Blekinge Naturum' signs into the gardens, past the nature centre to the pool with the waterfall tumbling down the cliff. Follow the water to the right past Brunn's Hall and the rose garden to the far end of the rhododendrons, then enter the woods for the 'Japanstradgård'. One passes a pergola garden first, full of climbing plants on pillars. The Japanese garden is very simple, gravel and greenery not water and colour. Continue to the lake to pick up the white nature trail through the woods to the left of the grillhouse. After some 10 minutes a viewpoint and a Bronze Age cairn (*gravröse*) are signed to the right. This overlooks the starting point of the walk — look for the word 'Fred' (Peace) written in the plants down below. The nature trail brings one back down to the pools and so to the start. From the spa the road continues beside the river to the harbour. For a different attraction leave town on the 30 for Karlshamn and follow the 'Blekingestugan' signs to the right just before the railway bridge. This is a café, serving hot waffles with jam and cream. In peak season it is quite busy but in May and early June, or again September it is an oasis of fragrant tranquillity.

An interesting circular route beyond Ronneby takes one south first to Göholm, then up to Listerby and across the E66 to Johannishus and its good-looking castle (not open to the public). The next stage is all dirt roads following first Mölleryd and then Tolseboda signs, past a series of lakes where no motor boats are allowed to reach the Sänneshults Nature Reserve. After walking here, pick up the major road to circle back to Kallinge. As one leaves the town, 'Djupadals-klyftan' is signed to the right. Park just before the bridge to the factory. Unfortunately the latter has diverted most of the water that once flowed through this ravine but for a circular walk, take the trail up behind the board and fork right into the ravine to pick up the red marks. Just beyond the next information board, follow the blue arrow up and back. This leads onto the cliffs for an excellent view of the Cascades Paper Mill! Returning to the main road, Ronneby is just across the E66.

Head next towards Karlskrona but take the Alletorp exit from the E66 and turn under the main road. Follow the signs to **Skarva** and park at the farm. The track past the farm buildings leads to a yellow and white manor which is private but one can admire its classical Greek portico, the bell tower and the temple, all of which are made of wood. The circular walk descends through an anemone wood to the shore, turns right to the jetty, and returns through the woods.

Karlskrona itself is traditionally a royal naval base. This is reflected in the imaginative marine museum — look for the 300 years of shipbuilding exhibition and the submarine periscope that goes through the roof to give views of the harbour! A World War II minesweeper anchored off Kungsbron is also open for viewing from the engine rooms to the crowsnest. Karlskrona is built across a series of islands (some of the best views are from Saltö with marinas and shipyards in between and sight-seeing boats touring the waters in summer). An alternative attraction is the collection of twenty-two buildings in Värmöparken which open every day in the summer season and are therefore more accessible than the smaller Sunday-only homestead museums.

Beyond Karlskrona the first road south that is open to tourists (because of the military restrictions) goes from Jämjö to Torhamn. It passes nature reserves at Hallarum and Steneryd. Very soon afterwards Hällristning is signed to the left. These are Bronze Age rock carvings just 300m (330yd) away through the woods. **Torhamn**'s late nineteenth-century church has some splendid modern decorations. The fishing and farming altar painting and the wood and glass font are both worth studying. The harbour is much older with its line of fishermen's huts. Beyond, Cape Torhamn is a bird sanctuary where birds are ringed and observed. From here the road heads north through dunes and heath, farmland and a succession of villages to the settlement of **Kristianopel**. Founded in 1600 by Christian IV of Denmark as his northernmost outpost against Sweden, the old defence walls still exist and one can walk their 1km ($^1/_2$ mile) length. There are also the remains of an old bastion on the minor road leading north. The Danish-style church, also built by Christian IV, contains a carved pew bearing his monogram and a 1624 altar backed by painted trees on which hang three royal crowns. The 1645 frontier is a few kilometres up the road at Broms, on the line of a tiny river. It is marked by the 'Fredstenen', commemorating the peace between the two countries. Nearby are the remains of a fourteenth-century stronghold from their wars.

Crossing the old Danish/Swedish frontier means crossing from Blekinge into Kalmar. The Kalmar Sound pathway begins there at the border. This long distance coastal trail passes through **Bergkvara** with its fishing museum at the south end of the harbour, past the old Viking stronghold at Påbonäs and Djurvik with its old fishing harbour, to Fulvik and the Örarevet nature reserve with its many birds. Inland in this southern area, there are homestead museums at Bergkvara, Söderåkra, Gullabo and Torsås. One interesting route is

The fortifications at Kristianopel

to leave Torsås on the road signed Flyveryd and then Bjorsebo, to the typical eighteenth/nineteenth-century village of **Oxlehall** with its small wooden houses built around two or three farms. Here the road loses its surface and winds through forest. Turn right in Slätafly for Skärgol, past Inglasjön lake, with its bathing place and waterlilies. Beyond Hällasjön lake turn left into **Hällasjön** village to admire its large farmhouses with beautiful carved friezes round the porches. Return and continue to join the 511 in Stromsberg and head right for Bidalite. Now follow the 504 left towards Gullabo but in Juansbo go left again for **Hästmahult**. Here, sitting low beside the road, is a tiny grass-roofed crofter's cottage which one may walk into. Beyond Gullabo, a circle right, signed first Paryd and then Söderåkra brings one through N Gullabo to a small restored red watermill right beside the road. From there one can continue through Söderåkra to Djursvik and along the minor roads signed Gunnarstorp and Fulvik to the nature reserve at Örarevet.

Between here and Kalmar there are several interesting churches, often with free-standing wooden belfries. **Halltorp** church is very solidly built of stone; **Voxtorp**'s has a round centre section; **Hagby**'s is massively round; **Hossmo**'s is very tall and thin. Just beyond Kalmar, **Kläckeberga** has a three-storey medieval defence church which was used against Danish attacks as late as 1611. Today one enters at the middle storey into the nave and the defence level has been replaced by a barrel ceiling painted in 1766. To understand how

The Karlevistenen rune stone on the island of Öland

these defence churches work visit Kalla old church on Öland.

Kalmar is the gateway to **Öland**, Sweden's second largest island and its smallest province. Road number 137 crosses Europe's longest bridge at 4 miles (6km) on the way. This has increased the number of tourists and holiday homes and the overcrowding of the main attractions but in early or late season it has much to offer and scenically, with its windmills and farming, it makes a pleasant change from the endless forests of the mainland.

The windmills are the first sight that strikes one on arrival. A group of three dominates the skyline just to the right at Björnhovda including the island's largest stubble mill. Most are much smaller, just large enough to grind one farmer's grain. If one turns south first, there is a good alternative to the 136 in the road from Färjestaden to Mörbylänga. Just past the Eriksöre signs, 'Karlevistenen', signed to the right, is the island's oldest rune stone, telling the story of a Danish sea hero buried there. The island has a surfeit of ancient remains; for example, just south of Resmo (whose church has faded frescoes) Mysinge Hög is a large Bronze Age burial mound in a field of graves, and south again, just beyond Sonder Bårby, the earthworks of Bårbyborg hill fort still stand.

The central area of southern Öland is a barren plateau called the Stora Alvaret. The soil is thin and drainage poor, ideal for unusual alpine plants including unique rockroses and wormwood. There are roads across it from Resmo, S Bårby and further south, S Möckleby.

Before one reaches the latter, **Gettinge** is a photogenic burial site with the standing stones of ship burials backed by a typical windmill. There are good views of the coast further south and the inlets near Grönhögen are lined with flowers. Soon afterwards one passes through Karl X Gustav's wall. Built in the 1650s to keep the deer to the southern tip of the island, it marches straight across from coast to coast, pierced only by the two roads. There are more birds than deer here nowadays for this is the Ottenby nature reserve with a bird station for watching migratory birds by the Långe Jan lighthouse, which is open for views across to Kristianopel on the mainland.

Heading north up the eastern coast, the **Eketorp** fortified village is a prime tourist sight, containing a reconstructed Iron Age settlement. At present it seems too brash and new, the ruins of Gråborg and Ismantorpsborg being preferable. Stop first at **Gräsgård** harbour (signed from Gammalsby). A small working harbour on the rocky coast, it faces across the Baltic towards Poland. North towards Segerstad one passes 200 graves and a rune stone beside the road. North again and Hulterstad is a typical Öland village with farms lining the street.

If the south of the island is rather barren, the north (beyond the level of Kalmar) is more fertile, both in its farmland and its mixed deciduous woods. A mass of roads criss-cross the central area between here and Borgholm where the most interesting remains are found. For example, **Gråborg**, west from N Möckleby, has ring walls and an arched entrance like Eketorp's before they rebuilt it. Here there are also the ruins of St Knut's chapel from the twelfth century, flowering hay meadows and a signed walk. A similar ruined fort but with nine gates and the foundations of 88 buildings inside lies in woods at Ismantorp east from Långlöt. Further on, towards Högsrum, two limestone blocks beside the road are called Woden's Teeth and 1km ($^1/_2$ mile) to the north Noah's Ark is a stone burial ship.

The area around **Långlöt** contains several places of interest. To the south just beyond Lerkaka five windmills stand in a row on the old sea wall. This is proof that here, as at Listerhuvud in Blekinge, the land has risen over past centuries. Today the sea is out of sight several kilometres away. Opposite the mills stands a rune stone with dragons' heads among the inscription. A kilometre or two north, watch right for the *folkeslundastenen*, a beautifully rounded erratic boulder, balanced on smaller stones. Långlöt has an excellent farm museum at Himmelsberga with English explanations in each house, including the tiny one to which the farmer and his wife retired in old age. Långlöt's church is one of only two on the island to retain its medi-

The weathered cliffs at Rauker on the island of Öland

eval tower top and original graveyard, but **Gärdelösa** church is more interesting with its unrestored frescoes, massive altarpiece and dragons' heads over the lych gates. Continue north through **Störlinge** — its seven windmills on the old sea wall are not as good as those at Långlöt — to Bredsätra for a diversion to **Kappellunden**. There stands a thirteenth-century limestone cross near the ruins of St Brita's chapel.

Just beyond **Föra**, whose church sports a massive tower reminiscent of a Norman keep and where the island narrows to a long finger, the east road joins the 136. Continuing north a very different attraction at L Horn are the *lövänger* or forest meadows where the flowers bloom amid the trees. Fork right next in **Kalla** (signed Kallahamn) for the old church. This is a very high medieval church and its gutted interior allows the guide to point out the marks in the walls where earlier floors ran so that in times of danger the women and children had a low-ceilinged area to themselves directly below the fighting men who were shooting down on the enemy from the highest level. North beyond Hagaby, **Högby** retains two rows of tiny red church houses down the lane beyond the church. Very like the church stables that remain in Kronoberg, they were used by people who had to travel a distance to services. They are the only ones left on Öland.

The far north of the island is sandier than elsewhere. Böda bay has sandy beaches and the Böda Crown Estate is duneland planted with conifers. Turning right at Melby one can circle via Grankulla and back to Byxelkrok. **Trollskogen** on the right hand claw of land at the top has a fascinating $4^1/_2$km (3 miles) red-marked trail. Follow Storstigen first and then Trollskovstigen.

Once the Trolls' wood is reached there are excellent pictorial signboards ranging from legends about trolls to interesting facts about Swedish fortifications with dummy guns to fool the Danish invaders, to a Finnish boat wrecked on the Baltic coast in 1927. The going varies from narrow and twisty through trees gnarled with ivy, to rough or stony underfoot, to excellent track. Crossing to the west coast, watch out for Neptune's Fields, named by famous botanist Linné (a native of nearby Kronoberg province) for the blue-flowered Viper's Bugloss that grows out of the stony beach.

Travelling south now, turn right at the beginning of Böda for Byrum then follow the **Rauker** sign for an unusual stretch of coastline. Westerly gales have exposed the stratified rocks and worn them into stacks along the shore. From here a genuine coast road goes to Alvedsjö Bodar. Out at sea the silhouetted island is **Blå Jungfrun** (Blue Maiden), an uninhabited but protected granite rock with caves, mixed woods, an ancient stone 'labyrinth' and a colony of hares that reached the island via the ice one winter in the early 1950s. Visitors can reach Blå Jungfrun either from Byxelkrok or from Oskarshamn in Kalmar province for a day trip — overnight camping is forbidden! The road passes one corner of the Horn Crown nature reserve with its 500 species of plants, including orchids and 170 varieties of birds. Beyond the lighthouse it reaches the old turf-roofed fishing huts and tiny wharf of Alvedsjö Bodar. Unfortunately the through road stops there and you have to go inland (passing alternate access to the Horn Crown Reserve) to Högby and road 136.

The coast can be reached again south of Kalla. Turn right for Grytehamn, then left along the coast to the tiny hamlet of **Jordhamn** where the skeleton mill on the shore was once used for stone-breaking. At **Sandvik**, a huge Dutch mill has been restored as museum and restaurant. Unfortunately the rest of the coast 'road' is suitable only for walkers which restricts one to the rather uninteresting 136 to **Köping** where to the left of the road one finds Öland's largest Bronze Age cairn, *Blå rör*. Beyond lies **Borgholm**, the largest 'town' on Öland. It has several tourist attractions, the most obvious being the castle ruins south of the town. The most attractive is the Italian-style park round Solliden royal summer castle.

Continuing south, an unusual natural feature is the oak grove at **Halltorp** on the Ekerum road where the massive oaks are riddled by the rare buck beetle. All insects and flowers in the reserve are pro-

The church and wooden bell tower at Halltorp

tected. Various walks are signed and one has the option of returning along the coast. In this area the 136 is pleasanter, with a plethora of windmills both by the road and in miniature inhouse gardens. South of Glömminge at **Algutsrum** there are permanent eighteenth-century market stalls, shuttered wooden lock-ups, in the open space in front of the church where markets are still held in the summer.

From here it is but a kilometre or two back to the 155 arches of Öland's bridge across to **Kalmar**. One sees little of the town from this route but it is worth exploring for its sixteenth-century castle, and the nearby Krusenstiernska Gården, its ramparts, old houses and the preserved remains of a royal battleship in the town's museum.

North of Kalmar the island of **Skäggenäs** which is signed right from Rockneby, has a host of small wooden houses set among trees. **Revsudden** on the far shore still retains its old red fishermen's sheds somewhat incongruously backing the modern marina. But one is really travelling west from Kalmar into the 'Kingdom of Glass' as a dozen or more glassworks lie in the area between Kalmar and Växjö. Most allow visitors to watch the glassblowing and many also have glass museums and shops. However there is more to this area than glass! For example in **Nybro** walk into the Störa Hotellet to see the 1968 mural in the council chamber on the first floor. Covering an entire wall, it depicts nineteenth-century life in the town using local people as models. On the western outskirts, at Madesjö, church stables have been preserved. One hundred years ago, these extended

The general store at Ölme in Värmland, Sweden (Chapter 10)

A preserved iron-smelting furnace, Borgvik in Värmland, Sweden (Chapter 10)

Polhemsgården at Stjärnsund in Dalarna, Sweden (Chapter 11)

Vuollerim church in Swedish Lappland (Chapter 12)

on seven of the eight sides of the roads to the church for a total of 700m (770yd). Most were gradually destroyed, some even being used to fire the glassworks, until just one block remains, converted into an excellent homestead museum, with English commentary and notes, rooms and workshops and even a tiny old-fashioned shop.

Head then across the 31 on the minor road signed Flerokopp, then Gadderås. At **Skedebäckshult** the village has well-preserved fields. At the start of Gadderås turn left for Orrefors and then north on the 31 to **Hälleberga** where there is a well-preserved area of old red wood buildings, including stables and vicarage round the very modern church. The road through Gullaskruv returns one to the 31 just south of **Målerås** where splendid glass sculptures of wildlife are produced. Unfortunately only the shop is open, not the factory. An interesting way to cut cross country from there to Kosta is to take the unsigned road (with the speed limit) just beyond the Målerås turning. It does lead through a military area but if that is shut (and do obey the signs as it is used for target practice) take Ringvatn to the left to reach Ekeberga, just south of Kosta.

The area south from here is very interesting. At **Eriksmåla** there is the Smålands game and fish museum along with an aquarium and market place nearby. The stalls are similar, though not so good as, those at Algutsrum. The dirt road south to Bökevara (Skruvvägen) passes farms with beautifully carved porches and flowering meadows on its way to Skruv. Beyond here, the crossroads at Åkerby is a landmark in emigrant literature and is duly marked with a monument. Just north of Åkerby, **Ljuder** also possesses church stables and a homestead museum. Alternatively, straight on at the crossroads brings one to **Älmeboda** where the original church stands ruined in the old graveyard overlooked by the wooden belltower and a memorial stone to the plague of 1711. From here follow the 31 north and turn right (signed Bymiljo) for the handicrafts village of **Korrö**. Part museum and workshops, partly private, it has also two mills, a tannery and river running through. The longest trail in the adjoining nature reserve takes about an hour through meadows, woods and alongside the river. Further on at **Linneryd** more market stalls stand on the left and a church with church stables overlooks a small lake. The area has been prettily laid out with a walk, seats and wild lupins. North again at **Ingelstad** there is a large burial mound from the sixth and seventh century with a carved round stone on top and other graves in the surrounding grass.

To return to road 25 and Lessebo, there is a twisty switchback of a road from Linneryd that traverses forests and passes through the pretty village of Ugnanäs. **Lessebo** possesses a mill for producing paper by hand, a double row of old red cottages on the green opposite, where a paper maypole is erected each year, a homestead museum and a 7km (4 mile) culture trail signed off the road to Kosta. This passes old houses, charcoal and tar pits and the typical Småland stone walls. Further north on the 25, at **Strömbergshyttan** there is a glass-painting studio where one can have a go and also a doll museum. At **Västorp**, beyond Hovmantorp there is an ox museum. Here oxen are used in the traditional way and one can ride in an oxcart past the widest stone wall in Småland.

This brings you almost to Växjö which is an excellent centre from which to explore the lake district that lies to both north and south. For this last section several circular routes, starting from Växjö, are suggested. First, westwards taking the 25 towards Ljungby. Just north of the road at **Lekaryd** the Kronoberg Agricultural Museum in the old Hjärtenholm farm has comprehensive collections illustrating farm work for men and women in the past in a series of recreated scenes. About 6km (4 miles) later turn left for Blädingeås on a well-signposted mud road through forest, farms and villages. Turn right at the crossroads for Mörhult to the old main road that runs straight through the forests towards Ljungby. Two or three kilometres (1 or 2 miles) to the right at **Tutaryd** the seventeenth-century church and its matching belltower are clad in red shingles. Inside the altar and pulpit are both ornate and the gallery is painted typically with the apostles and Jesus Christ. There are also two royal documents from Gustav III on the walls. Returning the same way, the small nature reserve at **Prästboda** has easy and quite short trails. Across the old main road, lies another reserve at Bräkentorpsåsen by the red house on the northern edge of the lake. The 'Finnstuga' signed further on is a leisure area with bathing and jogging tracks. At Össjö turn left on the 124 to **Tjurkö**. At the far end of the village one can drive down a track to a restored mill which is open.

From Tjurkö turn north for **Agnshult**. This is a typical village with stony flowering meadows separated by Småland walls. At the T-junction turn right into Lammakulla, then left in the pretty village of Trekanten for **Målaskog**, where the nature reserve has whispering woodlands alive with small animals and birds. The marked trails are hilly but only 1 to 2km ($^1/_2$ to 1 mile) long. In Målaskog turn right at the parking, past the old station and the timberyard, to follow the Jordskulan signs along the disused railway embankment to the lake. Here a path through the woods leads to a preserved cabin showing how the poor lived in nineteenth-century Sweden. It is open and

A Swedish wooden house near Tjurkö

worth a visit but there is no room to park and it is $1^1/_2$ km (1 mile) from the village. Beyond Målaskog turn left for Ryssby and cross the 25 for the long village of **Hörda**. Here, beyond the crossroads in the centre, the farmers have created not walls but round cairns with the stones so painstakingly removed from the fields to provide more arable land for the rapidly growing nineteenth-century population.

From Hörda cut east for **Rydaholm**, where on road 27 north of the town, there is an imaginative car, music and toy museum which will interest even the non-enthusiast. Across country from here, is the small town of **Moheda**, its rather plain church (with faded frescoes) prettily situated on the river, with walks on either bank. Beyond the church there are both wagon and homestead museums. To the south east of the town all the roads round lake Furen are pleasant. At **Grännaforsa** there is a *kulturmine* of ruins in the trees round the fast-flowing river. At **Härlöv** the church, prettily situated on the far side of the lake, contains a wealth of interior decoration from faded frescoes to large Biblical medallions on the ceiling, and an elaborate pulpit and altar, the latter surrounding a stained glass window. The return to Växjö is via Nöbbele and Öjaby.

For a circle to the north, return to Moheda then north to Torpsbruk, where one turns left for Klasentorp and right on the mud road for Vitteryd. The destination is actually **Aneboda** where a stork colony has been reintroduced. Turn right round the top of the lake (signed Växjö), then right and left across the 30 for Bjursjö, and right to Lädja.

Watch out for **Hultaklint** signed to the left. This high and rocky viewpoint is well worth finding. Beyond the farm of Hult the road becomes a cart-track but follow it on to the parking. From here it is a scrambling 15-minute walk to the viewpoint and the same on again to Singoallas grotto, which resembles a passage grave formed by nature instead of man. Beyond Lädja turn left in **Berg** and watch for the belltower where the original Tolg church stood. Turn right in Tolg past a series of sluices where the river joins the lake, to reach the Nykulla watch tower, which also gives views over the area. Returning to Tolg, follow the signs for Braås, to **Drev**'s tiny old church which has good frescoes, including the apostles, a tree of life and a painted gallery. In Braås, turn left along the lake for **Sjösås**. As one leaves the town there is a homestead museum on the left. The old church opposite also has a painted porch and ceiling, a gallery with the saints and wooden altar figures. Nature trails in the Sjösås reserve begin from the carpark beside it. To visit a third church, return through Braås and turn left for Eke, past a field full of round barrows, and left again for Lenhovda, across the 23, turning into **Dädesjö** when it is signed. The unique thirteenth-century ceiling frescoes are in excellent condition, having been preserved in the hay loft when the old church was used as a barn after the new one was built. They were restored in the 1940s and glow in the specially fitted lighting. To return to Växjö, head back through Eke to Rottne and so down through Stojby to rejoin the 23 just north of the town.

A similar length loop can be made southwards to Lake Åsnen. Leave Växjö on the minor road past Teleborg castle and the water tower with its famous echo, heading through Tävelsås to **Ö Jät** whose church is a tiny medieval gem with a painted wooden porch, side room and ceiling, and a typical apostles' gallery. Beyond the bottom of the lake at **Urshult** a candle factory can be visited, and a diversion away on the 120 at **Norraryd** a mechanical music museum. Returning to Urshult, fork left north of the town for **Lunnabacken** and Sånnahult. The former is a homestead museum with good views over Lake Åsnen. Just beyond lie the Korrebo orchards and experimental gardens with alpines, herbaceous plants and roses. One can walk through from there to the beaches of Kärrasand on the shore of the lake, though this is very crowded at weekends and in the Swedish holiday season. This road northwards passes through orchards and then from island to island across the middle of the lake. At Hössö turn left for **Bjurkärr** nature reserve. Like many of the smaller islands in the lake, this is a bird sanctuary with restricted access to some areas in the breeding season, but one can always walk the shore ring about

3km (2 miles) and the shorter blue trail is suitable for wheelchairs.

Heading north again, turn left at the start of Vrankunge to cross the Skatelovsfjorden and right to **Skatelov** itself. Here at the start of the town the local homestead park holds different events every summer Sunday. Park at the old graveyard for a nature trail along the cart-track beyond and Iron Age circles to the left from the farm. To return to Växjö turn right here on the 23 passing first **Huseby Bruk** manor museum and then, shortly before Växjö going left to Berkvara for the ruined four-storey fortress-house on the shores of the lake.

In the west of Kronoberg province two particular areas are of interest. For the first, begin at **Ljungby**, between the 25 and the E4, where the old centre has been restored to the early nineteenth century with inn and district courthouse, a tannery and two houses, forming a homestead museum that is open daily in the tourist season. The old main road leads north from there parallel to the E4 to **Lagan** where there is a run-of-the-mill car museum in the exhibition centre. North again at **Dörarp** the medieval church has frescoes and carved figures. Go west from there to Vittaryd, then north for 1km ($^1/_2$ mile) to find a prehistoric *trelleborg* on the right of the road. Similar to the one on Blå Jungfrun, it is a spiral of stones for which the information board gives a variety of possible interpretations. Return to Vittaryd and follow the signs for Bolmso as the road twists and turns through farms and forests.

Bolmso is the island in the middle of Lake Bolmen, a name meaning 'very big'. Certainly it has space for yachts and windsurfers as well as canoeists; its many islands offer sanctuary to a variety of birds; and 116 species of fish. Following the east shore of the lake, one comes beyond Angelstad to the old railway town of **Bolmen**. The station buildings and yard are relics only but one can walk along the old track to Piksborg, past the mound of a short-lived fifteenth-century castle from the wars against Denmark, and over the railway bridge to the big beech wood of Norrnäsudde. Alternatively, one can drive to Piksborg and walk from there. Due south of Piksborg, the town of Torpa offers a 30km (19 miles) veteran bus tour 3 days a week in peak season. The loop can be completed from there via Nöttja, Hamneda and S Ljunga back to Ljungby. To explore further south, take the very straight road from Nöttja to Hinneryd and head for Tannsjö. This is a hilly and interesting route; watch for the unusual garden on the right with life-size models of people and animals. Beyond Markaryd a series of lakes lead to Köphult in the very south western corner of Kronoberg. The **Hannabadsåsen** nature reserve, with a short marked trail and plenty of paths, lies between the lakes

— signed from both Åmot on the 117 and from the E4.

The last area of interest lies around Lake Möckeln. Starting at **Eneryda**, where there is a glassworks, take the minor road through Liatorp to **Diö** where the Höö nature reserve is signed with its marked trails through flowering meadows or along the shore of the lake. The botanist, Carl von Linné, who first recorded the country's flowers was born just south of Diö at **Råshult** where his house and herb garden have been restored. A statue of him stands at nearby Stenbrohult among the trees by the church and church stables. Continue south into Almhult and north again towards Pjätteryd. Two kilometres (1 mile) out of town, a 7km (4 miles) culture trail is signed to the left, which circles past religious, agricultural and industrial remains. Soon afterwards, turn right for Runnersköp and Möcklehult. Shortly before the former, running away to the left from a passing loop is an exceedingly wide stone wall. There are good views of the lake from the road and just beyond the bridge to Möcklehall, a flax workers' hut has been preserved down below the road. In Möcklehult turn left for Oshult where a very long stone-arched bridge flanks the modern one. The next place is **Pjätteryd** with a homestead museum on the Hamneda road. Head south again for Svinaberga and Traryd, then left for **Gustavsfors** rapids and ruined settlement which includes papermill and manor house, and for Bäckaholm for the fishing. A $4^1/_2$ km (3 mile) circular walk can be made from the Bäckaholm parking via both Gustavsfors and the smaller Frederiksfors, or one can drive down to each separately. Turning right soon after the Frederiksfors road, one can drive through forests towards Askenäs and then left for **Göteryd** where a tiny homestead museum sports English labels. From there the 120 leads back to Almhult and the 23 to Eneryda.

Although presented as separate circuits, a glance at a map will show how nearly related these routes are, not merely as adjacent east to west in Kronoberg but also north to south. Norraryd, for example, some 20km (12 miles) north of Kyrkhult in Blekinge. The whole area, too, is easy to reach. From the north from Stockholm, drive straight down the E4 and E66 to Mönsterås and Kalmar. The latter road also gives access to Blekinge from Malmö and the E6 is a good fast route south from Gothenburg, with the 25 connecting across to Ljungby. Gothenburg, Helsingborg and Malmö all have ferry links to Denmark, and the latter to Germany as well, making the area accessible from many directions.

Further Information
— South-East Sweden —

Blå Jungfrun
Boat from Byxelkrok high season only 10am, return 3.45pm.

Borgholm
Castle Ruins
Open: early May to end August daily 10am-6pm.

Solliden Palace Gardens
Open: June to August daily 11am-5pm. Last entry 4pm.

Eketorp
Fortified Village
Open: daily beginning May to mid-June, 9am-5pm. Mid-June to mid-August, 9am-6pm. Mid-August to end September 9am-5pm.

Eriksberg
Game Reserve
Åryd exit from E66
Open: beginning June to end August. Guided tours at 12noon, 2pm, 4pm and 6pm.

Eriksmåla
Smålands Game and Fish Museum and Aquarium
Open: beginning May to mid-June and mid-August to end August daily 12noon-5pm. Mid-June to mid-August daily 10am-6pm. Otherwise Saturday and Sunday 12noon-5pm.

Hällevik
Fishing Museum
Open: June to July, Tuesday to Thursday 10am-5pm. Saturday and Sunday 2-5pm. Otherwise Saturday 1-4pm.

Huseby Bruk
Farm Labourers Museum
Open: June, Saturday and Sunday, beginning July to mid-August daily 11am-5pm.

Manor
Guided tours June to August
☎ (0470) 52097

Kalla
Old Church
Open: mid-May to end August daily 10am-5pm.

Kalmar
Castle
Open: beginning May to mid-June and mid-August to end September, Monday to Saturday 10am-4pm, Sunday 1-4pm. Mid-June to mid-August, Monday to Saturday 10am-6pm, Sunday 1-5pm.

Läns Museum (includes Royal battleship *Kronan*)
Open: mi-June to mid-August, Monday to Saturday 10am-4pm. Sunday 1-5pm. Otherwise Tuesday to Friday 10am-4pm. Saturday and Sunday 1-4pm.

Krusenstjernska Gården
Open: beginning June to mid-September daily.
Gardens 10am-5pm. *Museum* 1-5pm.

Karlskrona
Marine Museum
Open: daily 12noon-4pm. July 12noon-8pm.

Minesweeper Bremon
Open: June to mid-September daily 12noon-4pm.

Värmöparken
Krutviken
Open: beginning June to end August
daily 10am-6pm.

Korrö
Handicrafts Village and Museums
South of Linneryd
Open: beginning May to September
daily 9am-8pm.

Lagan
Car Museum
In industrial exhibition centre
Open: daily 10am-6pm.

Långlöt
Himmelsberga (Farm Museum)
Open: beginning May to end August
daily 10am-6pm.

Lekaryd
Kronoberg Museum of Agriculture
Open: mid-May to beginning
September, Monday to Friday
9am-5pm. Saturday 11am-3pm.
Sunday 1-5pm.

Lessebo
Handmade Paper Mill
Open: mid-June to mid-August,
Monday to Friday 8am-3pm.
Guided tours in English 9.30am,
10.30am, 1pm and 2.15pm.

Ljungby
Gamla Torg (Old Market) Museum
Open: mid-June to mid-August
daily 12noon-4pm.

Lunnabacken
Homestead Museum
Open: June to August, Sunday 3-
6pm. Daily 3-6pm in high season.

Mörrum
Salmon Aquarium
Open: daily beginning April to end
September.

Nogersund
Kryddträdgården
Open: beginning June to end August
daily 9am-10pm.

Lottas Dockmakeri (Puppet Maker)
Open: Tuesday to Thursday 1-5pm.
Sunday 10am-1pm.

Norraryd
Trasthes Mechanical Music Museum
Open: July, August, Sunday 1-5pm.

Nybro
Madesjö Church Stables
Open: June to August daily 2-6pm.

Råshult
Linnés House and Herb Garden
North of Almhult
Open: mid-April to mid-October,
Tuesday to Sunday 9am-6pm.

Ronneby
Blekinge Naturum
Open: June to August daily 11am-6pm.

Blekingestugan
Open: beginning May to end September daily 11am-8pm.

Möllebackagårdens Cultural Heritage Museum
Open: beginning June to end Au-
gust, Tuesday to Sunday 11am-6pm.

Risanäs School Museum
Open: June to August, Tuesday to
Sunday 12noon-6pm.

Rydaholm
Motor and Toy Museum
Open: May to October, Sundays.
June to August daily 10am-6pm.

Sandvik
Mill Museum
Open: late April to end August daily
12noon-8pm, except mid-June to
mid-August daily 10am-10pm.

Slagenås
Galax Tourist Centre Gardens
Open: mid-May to mid-September
daily 11am-7pm.

Strömbergshyttan
Alice Bergmans Museum of Dolls
Open: beginning June to August
daily 11am-5pm.

Lindblom Glasspainting Studio
Open: Monday to Friday 8am-
3.30pm.

Urshult
Candle Factory
Open: daily 10am-6pm.

Västorp
Ox Museum
Open: beginning May to end
August, Saturday 10am-4pm,
Sunday 1-5pm. Plus, early June to
end August, Monday to Friday
10am-6pm.

Tourist Information Centres

BLEKINGE
Karlshamn
Drottninggatan 54
S-374 81 Karlshamn
☎ (0454) 81203

Karlskrona
Södra Smedjegatan 6
S-371 83 Karlskrona
☎ (0455) 83490

Ronneby
Söderbro
S-372 25 Ronneby
☎ (0457) 17650

Sölvesborg
Turistbyrån
Blekingeporten
Skånevägen 30
S-294 01 Sölvesborg
☎ (0456) 10088

KALMAR COUNTY
Kalmar
Larmgatan 6
S-391 20 Kalmar
☎ (0480) 15350

ÖLAND
Öland
Box 115
S-387 00 Borgholm
☎ (0485) 12340

SMÅLAND
All June to August
    except Växjö
Älmhult
Stortorget
S-343 00 Älmhult
☎ (0476) 12160

Alvesta
Allbogatan 3
Folkets Hus
S-342 00 Alvesta
☎ (0472) 12260

Bergkvara
Storgatan 1
S-385 02 Bergkvara
☎ (0486) 20437

Kosta
Kosta Glasbruk
S-360 50 Lessebo
☎ (0478) 50706

Ljungby
Ljungby Gamla Torg
S-341 26 Ljungby
☎ (0372) 13404

Nybro
Sveaplan
S-382 00 Nybro
☎ (0481) 45087

Strömbergshyttan
By road 25
S-360 51 Hovmantorp
☎ (0478) 11731

Tingsryd
Dackegatan 14
S-362 01 Tingsryd
☎ (0477) 44164

Växjö
Kronobergsgatan 8
S-351 12 Växjö
☎ (0470) 41410

10 • Värmland

Värmland is a central province of Sweden bordering on the north shore of Lake Vänern. In shape it is roughly triangular, its western boundary defined and redefined over the centuries by conflicts with Danish-owned neighbour, Norway. Yet in the Middle Ages its religious links with Norway were strong. Their eleventh-century king, Olof, having converted to Christianity on a visit to Normandy, fled to Sweden when he was overthrown. He began his bid to regain his throne by making his way north along the Klarälven valley. Killed in battle, miracles happened at his grave and he was canonised. For the next four centuries Swedish pilgrims followed his route to his grave at *Nidaros* (modern Trondheim) arriving by 28 July for the week long St Olof's mass during which they hoped for cure of their ills and sins. The traffic was only stopped when in 1544 Gustav Vasa forbade it. To this day the road that follows the Klarälven is called the Pilgrims' Way and those churches dedicated to St Olof or with medieval statues of him are reminders of the role he played.

Scenically Värmland is a province of lakes and rivers, excellent fishing and canoeing territory, with waters warm enough for swimming in the summer. There are rich farmlands in the south and rocks and pine forests in the north. Prehistoric man has left his mark with cairns, barrows and hill forts and so have the Finnish immigrants with their forest farms in the west. The mineral workings in the east linger as water-filled mines and ruined buildings. The province is rich in flowers, with hay meadows, colourful verges, reserves of rarer species, berries on hills and fungi in forests. Waterfowl are plentiful; beavers thrive in the rivers and elk roam the forests. The largest nature reserve is Glaskogen, easily accessible from the E18 Oslo-Stockholm road. This is the obvious entry route from either direction, or from Gothenberg the 45 leads to Säffle, just to the south.

First then a scenic, cultural and wriggly route from the Norwegian border (the E18) to Säffle, then on across the south of the region to Karlskoga, the entry point from Stockholm. Immediately on entering Sweden go left towards **Öster Vallskog**. After some 6km (4 miles),

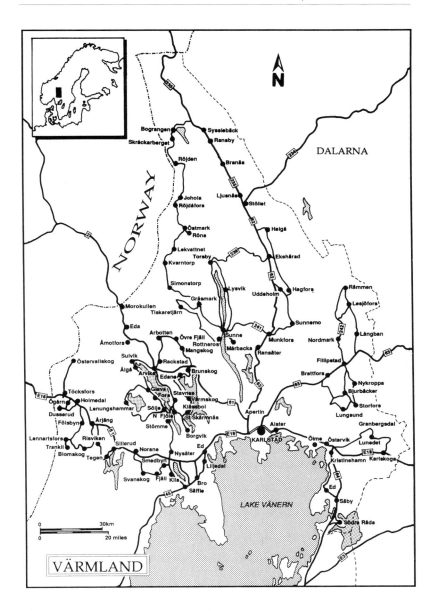

VÄRMLAND

high above flowering hillsides and overlooking a quiet lake, lies the Gamla Kyrkplatsen (Old Churchyard). Park at the old parish store-house and admire the beautifully maintained wrought iron crosses. A stone in the neighbouring garden commemorates King Charles

The Dalsland canal at Lennartsfors

XII's visit during the Great Northern War. Return to **Töcksfors** where this churchyard too has a line of these old crosses. Take the road opposite now for **V Fägelvik**, past Mangsgården, the home of author and evangelist Frank Mangs. Turn left for Holmedal past the church sitting as so many do on its own peninsula and over the bridge with its long views of Lake Foxen. Left again to **Dusserud** takes one to Ögårn farm where almost everything is as it was when first built. The storehouses stand on stilts to protect them from predators and inside the house tar crosses protect the inhabitants from evil. Continue to the E18, then right for **Holmedal** where the Karl XII *stuga* (cottage) near the church was occupied variously between 1710 and 1712 by him.

Pick up the E18 again as far as the **Fölsbyn** turning. Here the *fornborg* is an Iron Age hill fort well-depicted on the board at the top. Continue to **Lennartsfors**, an old mill community, now of more interest to leisure mariners lying as it does at the head of three locks taking the Dalsland canal down to Lake Lelång. **Trankil** church (red-shingled eighteenth century) a few kilometres further on is also beautifully situated beside the lake, but the real route returns round Lelång, first towards Gustavsfors and then across to Blomskog. Two to three kilometres (1 to 2 miles) further on, **Källtegen** is a village of original wooden buildings. It has two claims to fame. Firstly that 661 people emigrated from here to America between 1869 and 1929 and secondly, the Borgås dry stone man. Turn right at the village noticeboards and right again past a farm to the small parking for the steep path that leads up to where he stands surveying Lake Västra Silan. Possibly erected during the seventeenth century as a fake sentinel to keep marauders away, he is an imposing and amusing figure.

Go north next on the 172 towards **Årjäng**. The old railway one crosses is now used by holiday trolley traffic — enquiries to Årjäng information bureau. Circle right round the top of the lake for Sillegårdsed and right again for Risviken for a beautiful lakeside run. About 2km (1 mile) beyond the Tokil turning, park and walk along the track for some 10 minutes to **Tegen**, an old farmstead with traditional flowering meadows that include rare species. Continue then for some kilometres on this forest road to a T-junction labelled 'Udden 2'. Go left here to Signebyn and park at the second Gravfelt (barrow) sign. There is bathing from a sandy beach and on the hill one can walk through Sillerud's old graveyard to the Iron and Viking Age barrows on the peninsula beyond — a reflection on how often Christianity adopted pagan sites. Soon after turn right for Bäcken to reach the E18 again. Follow this now through the pretty boating area of Norane, then turn back right for Halland and Svanskog. Just before reaching Svanskog there is an excellent bathing place on the lake. **Svanskog**'s red-shingled church is set in a delightful area beside the water. Return now up the larger road and right for Pellerud, cutting cross country via Fjäll (and left again at the arrowed bend) through Flatebyn to **Smedbyn** where the Von Echstedtska Manor is just round to the right. This beautiful eighteenth-century house was nearly sent to Stockholm in 1939 for firewood. When you step inside you will see what a crime this would have been. In the entrance hall painted Grenadiers stand guard and pastoral pictures deck the side walls. The drawing room has Biblical scenes all round, painted on a linen/cotton mix that is fastened to the wooden walls. The other rooms are less elaborate and not all are yet restored. The count's own room shows how these Rococo paintings were later covered with wallpaper. Don't miss the toilet pavilion outside. A real 'throne' room that seats five adults and two children, its octagonal roof shows the count and one of his wives similarly seated with attendants attending!

Continue through to join the road for Säffle pausing only at **Kila** church for the viewpoint over Harefjorden. Säffle makes a good entry point to Värmland if coming from Gothenberg but the town has little to offer the tourist. Take the 45 here towards Karlstadt. In Bro turn right for **Liljedal** and right again for the *kulturminne*.

(Budaparken signed beyond is a nature area with walks and bathing.) The *kulturminne* is the site of Liljedal's glassworks that were once Sweden's largest bottle factory, blowing 13 million bottles a year and exporting them all over the world. The *hembygdsgård* has a short English tape about this and an exhibition of the bottles and of glassblowing. Beyond the bridge, **Ed** church has an eighteenth-century chandelier made there and a cabinet of glass as well as four beautiful tree of life iron crosses in the vestibule. Now join the E18 which is a good fast road round the top of Lake Vänern in an area where there is no sensible alternative. **Karlstad** is worth diverting to for the twelve-arched stone bridge that is the longest in Sweden and also Värmland's Museum and art gallery. On the island beneath, **Hammarö** church contains medieval frescoes in the vestry behind the elaborate eighteenth-century altar.

Continuing towards Kristinehamn, **Alster** Manor was the birthplace of poet Gustav Fröding. A red house on the same site contains exhibits relating to emigration to America — unfortunately with very little English text. Nearer to Kristinehamn, the **Ölme** Divershandel (General Store) is a country shop preserved as it would have been at the turn of the century, selling everything from china to sweets, toys to old postcards and ringing up the sales through its silvery cash register. **Östervik**'s chapel, in nineteenth-century English style and recently renovated, is worth looking into before one reaches **Kristinehamn**.

This pleasantly flowery town developed at the river crossing into Lake Vänern. Having suffered several disastrous fires over the years, very little old remains — just some houses in Trädgårdsgatan. It concentrates on the modern with the curious water art sculpture in the railway park and the Picasso 'totem pole', southwards on the coast, which is the largest existing work of this kind by Picasso. The runic stone standing beside the 64 Mariestad road at Järsberg is of course much older. Take the next right through Hult for a cultural diversion. This southern tip of Värmland is littered with grave mounds, cairns and stone rings, proof of early man's occupancy of the area. Eighteenth-century man's more civilised existence is well-illustrated at **Säby** (left at Ed, right on the 64). Värmlands Säby was built in 1771, and contains only twelve rooms. However they are large and beautifully decorated with cloth wall paintings rescued from the attics by the present owners. Only the Chinese panels in one of the parlours were still in position. There is Chinese porcelain on display too in rooms heated once by the elaborate decorated stoves. More recently a maze has been created in the gardens in the shape of

*Picasso's statue at
Kristinehamn*

a falcon's egg in honour of the Falkenberg family who now own the estate. More paintings are to be found in **Södra Råda** old church which is reached south on the 64 and left. Its walls are completely covered with frescoes. The best are the 1323 series in the chancel. Those in the nave are cruder but they all add up to a visual feast that one is lucky to find today especially here where the villagers were going to demolish the church when they built their new one in the 1850s — fortunately the State stepped in and bought this tiny gem.

Return to Kristinehamn on the 64 and cross the E18 for Bjurtjärn on a loop round to Karlskoga. At Kväggeshyttan there are iron foundry remains by a small river; later good views as one crosses the Bergslag canal. This can be explored better when one turns right for Karlskoga and stops at the Lunedet canal park which has been developed for leisure with reopened shop and smithy, nature trails and canoeing. Continuing, go left for Löka then right for **Granbergsdal**. Where Kväggeshyttan was ruined, this has the genuine article — a tall brick building housing an immense blast furnace. Here pig iron was made for 283 years. Good English texts explain the processes.

In **Karlskoga**, to the south, the Gråbo Museum displays workmens' cottages from three different periods, with appropriate furnishings and by contrast, their rural branch shows country life in the eighteenth century, but what most people visit Karlskoga to see is Alfred Nobel's home at **Björkborn**. He lived here for the last 2 years of his highly productive life in the course of which he took out patents on an incredible 355 inventions before leaving almost his entire 33 million kroner fortune to found the Nobel Peace Prize. You can see his house, study, books and most interesting, his laboratory. While in Karlskoga the church is also worthwhile with its medieval paintings once again in the vestry behind the altar.

At Karlskoga southern Värmland has been crossed from west to east. Karlskoga is not only in the easternmost portion of Värmland but also the westernmost part of the Bergslagen mining area where old pits and industrial ruins abound. One can sample these on a tour from **Filipstad**, the centre of the mineral area. Here there is an interesting museum in a mill that should be visited first as it explains the old mining methods. The sight of a deep pit half filled with water is more meaningful when one can visualise hoists and long ladders running over and under the rock walls. There are also displays on forestry methods and important local industries like Wasabröd which is the biggest crispbread factory in the world. There are a number of interesting statues in Filipstad (do not miss the top-hatted man on the park bench) and a mausoleum in the cemetery to her most famous son, John Ericsson, who invented the propeller and the armoured ship *Monitor* that participated in the American Civil War.

Leave Filipstad on the 246 north, past Storbro restored smelting house, for **Nordmark** where the *hembygdsgård* possesses a gun forge. Just east on the Rämmen road there are well signed remains from the local mines — shaft towers, an old truck, fenced pits and a lock-up, though none are as old as the first recorded date for a mine here — in a royal decree of 1413. A restored waterwheel is just up the road. Continue then to Sandsjön where one can either cut across to Lesjöfors or continue right up to **Rämmen**. Rämens Herrgård (note the old Finnish spelling of the name) is a beautiful yellow manor complex containing a memorial room to poet and bishop Tegner. Look up at the chimney pots — iron castles, they are reminders that this too was a mining area. Drive on past the beautifully situated church (on a promontory into the lake) before returning to **Lesjöfors** on the 242. Here one can hire trolleys to travel the old railway to Vansbro and visit the industrial museum. Further south, **Långban**

The mining museum at Långban

has a mining area similar to Nordmark's but more plentiful, with guided tours, a nature path, a mineral exhibition and the house where John Ericsson was born. South again, the **Högsbergsfältet** nature reserve also has trails past pits and ruins and one can maybe find garnets in the old *skarn* mounds. Beware of any unfenced pits as they are much deeper than they look. Soon after there is a lookout tower at **Storhöjden**, open when the café is.

South of Filipstad and from **Nykroppa** there is a 3km (2 mile) silver trail up to Hornkullen's silver mines where gold panning can be tried and there is an eagle owl breeding centre. Continue to Storfors and out on the Lungsund road. Where it splits, **Bjurbäcker** to the north has an area of industrial remains and some interesting wrought ironwork on the eighteenth-century bridge. Circling round the lake here one also passes two locks on the Bergslag canal. Alternately, from Lungsund one can follow the old Prästvägen road to Lindås that twists up and down hills in very unmodernised fashion. On the way it passes smithy ruins at **Ackkärr** and an old mill at **Kvarned**, both off to the left. From either direction take the Brattforshyttan road across to the 63. On the edge of **Brattfors** this passes a restored blast furnace and one end of the Lungsälvsravinerna nature trail. The Lungälven is one of the local rivers renowned for beaver activity but one is more likely to spot their works than the animals themselves. From here Filipstad is just 10km (6 miles) up the road.

The central area of Värmland lies around the vertical axis of its

Restored blast furnace at Brattforshyttan

triangle, the 62 or Pilgrims' Way mentioned earlier. It follows the Klarälven river from Karlstad on Lake Vänern through Munkfors, Ekshärad, Stöllet, and Sysslebäck to cross the border at the top of the Höljesjön but to drive straight up and through is to miss all the places of interest on either side. At the southern end there is perhaps only **Apertin** Manor that is worth a visit. It stands near the bottom of Lake Nedre Fryken, some 14km (9 miles) north of Karlstad. Now a hotel, there are guided tours of the house in season but the park is open all day with a variety of marked paths, ponds and ravines. However, once one reaches the level of Sunnemo, Ransäter and Rottneros, a whole area of interest opens out.

Sunnemo is an old iron-working village. The *hembygdsgård*, Gubbkroken, (Old Men's Corner) is where the iron ore drivers used to rest. Part of the main house is now used by local ladies making rugs and textiles on old-fashioned looms. Opposite, Hyttdalen contains both ruins and restored elements like the waterwheel that drives a shingle machine for making wooden roof 'tiles', all set beside an old 'road' that follows the river gently down to the lake. West of here, **Munkfors** has a much more impressive site to offer. Gamla Bruk is the older part of what is still a works area for which the much dammed river provides the power. The guided tour includes a film with English commentary on the old works, an open hearth foundry for casting iron, a small fire engine museum and a walk to the remaining waterfall. North of Sunnemo, **Hagfors** is also connected with industry with its Railway Museum in an old engine shed. The collection includes engines, trolleys, railcars and rolling stock as well as two signal boxes. The *hembygdsgård* is a workers' home from 1850. Even elegant **Uddeholm** manor (7km, 4 miles west) where one can wander in the park, was built from the proceeds of the ironworks. The Uddeholm company still exists today making high quality steel for precision tools. Hagfors church on the other hand contains a notable modern interpretation of the pilgrimage story that brings one away from the working Bergslag to the more cultured life that existed round the river and lakes just to the west. An extensive view over these can be obtained from the unusual lookout tower on Vårmullsåsen which is worth the 5km (3 mile) drive to reach it.

Not many kilometres south of Munkfors, **Ransäter** boasts a variety of museums. The *hembygdsgård* contains displays on forestry, agriculture, iron processing, and village life, with models in realistic scenarios. Prime Minister Tage Erlander's boyhood home is another gem. His father was the village schoolmaster and the ground floor is the school, with woodwork room and classroom — admire the unique arithmetical chart and various mathematical devices. The family lived upstairs in four interconnecting rooms with pull-out beds and furniture made by the schoolteacher himself. Lastly there is Geijersgården, the childhood home of both Erik Geijer and F. A. Dahlgren, two scholars and poets. The house is a manor and reflects a more elegant style of living so that in these three differing museums one can compare the quality of life of all levels of Swedish society. Ransäter also boasts a lookout tower, a 3km (2 mile) drive from the sign and then a 10 minute walk from the wooden board. The reward is a fine view over the village and the Klarälven valley.

West of here at the head of Lake Mellan Fryken lie **Mårbacka**, **Sunne** and **Rottneros**, all connected with authoress and Nobel prize-winner, Selma Lagerlöf. The first was her home and she used both Sundbergsgård in Sunne and Rottneros Park in her most famous book, the *Story of Gösta Berling*. Mårbacka and Sundbergsgård are only open by guided tours. At Rottneros Park it is the grounds that are the attraction not the house. This park is unique. Developed after World War II, its 98 acres contain a series of separate gardens designed round statues, both modern Swedish and classical copies. Particularly colourful are the herb, flower and rose gardens. Recent additions are lynx and wolves in enclosures with viewing platforms, a minizoo and a terrarium — and do not miss the toilet pavilion, next to the manor, complete with adult and child 'thrones' in vivid blue. Just north of here, the Friendship Monument with its winged eagle is unmistakeable. Raised to both Swedish emigrants to America and Finnish immigrants into Sweden, it dominates the skyline above the Sunne golf course. While in the area, the Sunne *hembygdsgård* has a country shop, school museum and courthouse.

North of Sunne one can drive on either side of Lake Övre Fryken. On the west bank one passes **Tossebergsklätten** with a steep road up to its viewing tower. On the east, at **Lysvik** local people grumbled in the eighteenth century at the cost of erecting their new church, both in taxes and in labour. It is worth looking into for its windows and ceiling paintings though both are twentieth-century renovations. At the head of the lake, **Torsby** has an extensive *hembygdsgård*; twenty odd buildings on a headland overlooking the water including a school, smithy, mill and a small traction engine. From here **Ekshärad** is some 35km (22 miles) to the east. This village possesses one of the most interesting church sites in the whole of Sweden. The graveyard contains 320 wrought iron crosses, most of the tree of life variety with musical leaves, probably introduced by the Walloons who worked in the area's iron industry. A descendant carries on this work in the smithy to the present day. The seventeenth-century church is also a treasure house, the south porch containing priceless textiles from as far back as the thirteenth century. Apart from those on display, there are more in the drawers beneath. Beyond the road one finds the church stables that are used as handicraft stalls in the summer and an extensive *hembygdsgård* with unique Dalecarlian wall paintings — unique in Värmland that is as they are usually only found in Dalarna. Do not miss the symbolic totem pole either, that represents elements of provincial life from the Finnish house at the top through elk, beaver and wolf, the Värmland emblem, to mythical figures.

Now for a loop round the north. Cross the Klarälven here and turn left. One cannot really say 'along its eastern bank' because from here to Sysslebäck it meanders lazily, leaving oxbow lakes in its wake, with so little current at times that the logs adrift in it seem hardly to move. At Halgå on this minor road there are marked trails along the delta and to the small Brannafallet waterfall. Rejoin the 62 then for **Stöllet** where the Norra Ny church contains interesting medieval wood sculptures. Cross the river here and follow the minor road. The *hembygdsgård* in **Ljusnäs** is a small farm that was occupied until the 1940s. Continue on this side of the river for **Branäs** where a ski centre has recently been built. This benefits the summer tourist as the gondola lift to the 567m (1,860ft) hill operates then too. There are long views of the silvery Klarälven. Down below Dalby church stands out, its 62m (203ft) tower the highest wooden one in Sweden. Branäs runs a full summer programme too. Here one can build a timber raft (under expert instruction) and float downriver for a week; one can fish, canoe, cycle, play golf and go on a beaver safari. Introduced from Norway in 1922, there are now several thousand of these protected creatures and evidence of their building activities is fairly common but to spot the animals themselves is much more difficult, hence the safaris with local guides. Recross the river to **Ransby** for the Dalby *hembygdsgård*. The monument here is to Willgodt Theophil Odhner who constructed the first prototype of modern calculators.

At **Sysslebäck** the valley of the Klarälven narrows; there are rapids on the river and the farmlands cease. This is a good point at which to circle south again, going left for Bograngen. This leads to the Finns-koga area where in the seventeenth and eighteenth centuries Finnish immigrants settled both in northern Värmland and in adjacent Norway — so many of them that in 1821 a Finnish student tried to create a Finnish county straddling the border. A number of these farms have been preserved. The most northerly, at **Skråckarberget**, is called Tomta. It is unusual in having a double farmhouse. From here one can continue to **Falltorp** (keep right at every junction) which is on the Norwegian border. Go left here for an oddity at **Röjden** — the *korset* is a cross in the ground where nothing grows. Go right next for Röjdåfors. **Johola** is another Finnish farm, once famous for its cheese. Now martins nest under the eaves. At **Röjdåfors**, just to the right of the junction is a large restored watermill. It was used by farmers from both Norway and Sweden — so many that at peak harvest time they had to queue and even sleep overnight in the mill cottage.

The road now leads down to Östmark and **Röna** where the *hembygdsgård* contains some unusual attractions. It has a tiny water-mill down by the Rönälven and its own copper mine in a deep red hollow. South of Östmark and **Lekvattnet** there are two more Finn-ish farms. Ritimäki, a kilometre walk up the mountainside from Lomstorp is the most original. The main building contains just the large smokehouse and a little kitchen. This is a typical Finnish house. The beams are blackened where the smoke collected — it could be let out through the roof when necessary. The amazing thing is that the house was used like this — smoke oven, no water, no electricity — until 1964! Kvarntorp, on the other hand, while maintaining the Finnish tradition of scattered buildings for different purposes, has been modernised. It contains china racks and photographs in its

Lake Kymmen at Simonstorp

'Swedish' room, bearing witness that these were richer Finnish settlers who could afford a better life style. Continue through to
Simonstorp for something entirely different. The Vardshuset
Tvället (across the end of the lake and right) keeps wild boars in two
runs just beyond the hotel. The road south from here to Gräsmark is
unusually scenic, running right alongside Lake Kymmen.

Gräsmark church has a splendid eighteenth-century ceiling with
scenes of angels over the body of the church and hell at one side of
what is now the organ loft. From here you can travel south on either
side of Lake Rottnen and there are nature reserves whichever way
you choose to go. Following Charlottenberg, the second sign to
Tiskaretjärn takes one to a marked walk round a farm still worked
by old methods with haymaking by scythe or horse mower and
breeding of rare Swedish redpoll cattle. Further on, **Kalvhöjden**
reserve is best visited in spring or early summer for its herbs and
orchids. The road continues alongside Borrsjön to emerge onto the
road to Rottneros. Following Sunne from Gräsmark instead,
Gettjänsklätten reserve, right beside the road, boasts a 1km ($^1/_2$ mile)
path that rises steeply to its 214m (702ft) summit for views of Lake
Rottnen through the trees. This reserve also has orchids and many
leguminous plants. Whichever way you travel, you arrive at the top
of Lake Mellan-Fryken and Sunne/Rottneros.

This leaves just the western area to explore between Gräsmark and
the E18 and Arvika makes a good centre for doing just this. For

example, one could explore the area between Glasfjorden and Värmeln from here. **Klässbol** has a linen weaving mill that can be visited where damask is produced as well as huckaback. The next place south is **Stavnäs** with a pretty jetty area and a church set high above the lake. **N Fjöle** is worth turning into for its eighteenth-century village street winding picturesquely between farms. Further south **Borgvik** has an industrial museum with well-preserved ruins round the river and an excellent church with a heaven and hell ceiling painted in 1745 by Michael Carowsky in which Christ is standing on a rainbow. Take the L. Skärmnäs road from here past **St Skärmnäs** Kapell. The small house is a soldier's home from the Grums division of Värmland's regiment and the monument is to their 'knights'. Further north at **Värmskog** the church contains a rock carving of the head of a griffin dating back to AD900, which has now been adopted as Värmskog's coat of arms. In the churchyard, the larger of the two white vaults is a winter grave where bodies were stored until the ground softened enough in spring for graves to be dug. The 7m (23ft) high wooden cross marks the site of two former churches. Ericssons *Minnesgård* signed from here is the birthplace of the developer of the Swedish telephone system and contains a telephone museum. Halla and Nytomta in the Rombotten area are two other tiny local museums. By cutting across through Edane one can reach **Brunskog** where the much larger *hembygdsgård* is brought to life in the last full week in July with the local people in period costume carrying out trades and crafts in traditional ways. There is a 100-year-old store, a nightly stage coach departure, paper making in the first Värmland paper mill and lots of other authentic sights and sounds during the 9 day festival. From Brunskog, right and left for Åmot takes one along what the local tourist bureau calls 'the most beautiful road in Sweden'. Certainly it is pleasantly undulating with good views of small valleys and of Lake Mangen. In Manskog go left and right towards Treskog, then follow the Övre Fjäll road across to Arbotten. Left at the lake brings one down to Lake Racken. The Perserud road gives the best view of this and takes one through Rackstad, from where the colony of artists inspired by Christian Eriksson at the turn of the century took their name. If one crosses the main road from here, one drops into **Arvika** past Eriksson's studio, Oppstuhage, which is a museum to his work.

While in Arvika, the Trefaldighetskyrkan also contains work by members of the Rackstad colony. The Sågudden *hembygdsgård*, spreads round the end of the lake. Its old farmhouse has over 5,000 objects from bygone days and in summer old crafts are plied in some of the cottages. There is a church boat, a soldier's cottage and even a windmill, which is unusual for Värmland. The path past the small herd of fallow deer leads out to a bird tower overlooking two stretches of water. On the edge of town, higher views of the locality can be obtained from the steeply laddered viewtower.

A different loop could take you north-west of Arvika right up to the Norwegian border, to **Morokulien** peace province, a tiny demilitarised area owned by the peace organisations of Sweden and Norway. It is dominated by the 1914 monument commemorating 100 years of peace between the two countries. This is the only place in the world where two different countries' stamps can be put on one postcard. The statue of the white elk represents the only herd of these in the world. They are a protected species and live at Valfjället. South at **Eda** near Lake Bysjön, Eda Skans is a fort restored to its 1808-9 condition. It contains three cannon but otherwise looks amazingly unwarlike with its low ramparts and flourishing flowers. Pass through Åmotfors on the Sulvik road to find an unusual 'church' at **Hälla**. A path into the woods from the sign leads to a huge overhanging slab under which a wooden cross and benches have been set, for services are occasionally held here in summer. The return to Arvika can be made through Norserud if one wants a watery route with several large manors.

This leaves the west side of Glasfjorden. Beyond Jössefors on the Sulvik road, the Bergsklätt nature reserve offers walks. The Klätten Utsikt signs give a 2km (1 mile) round route up to several viewpoints with Bronze Age cairns. Similar cairns are signed in various locations on this route, along with barrows, hill forts and other prehistoric remains. South of Sulvik, **Älgå** offers remains of a later type. Here the Nailsmithy has been restored, complete with waterpower from the rushing river. At its peak it produced 28,000 nails a week from each nailhammer, or one every 7 seconds. Most of these were exported to England via the wharf where a storehouse still stands. A footpath leads through the various areas. South again at **Glava**, the church has a beautifully painted ceiling of the heaven and hell variety though unusually it includes God the Father as well as Christ. The line across the middle divides life from death, good from evil. It is surrounded by medallions of Biblical scenes. Altar, pulpit and pictorial altar rails are also eighteenth century but there are interesting medieval artefacts as well. Medieval ironwork is rare but Glava possesses both a seven-branched candelabra on the altar and a Viking boat shaped candlestick in front of a thirteenth-century Madonna.

From Glava one can detour into the Glaskogen nature reserve, a wilderness area with lakes, beaver, elk and marked paths that are meant for the hiker rather than the casual tourist. If one goes in to **Lenungshammar** (on a road that continues through to join the E18) and turns left to the information boards there, by following the Sölje signs one reaches a $3^1/_2$km (2 mile) route round Lake Rämmingen. This road then brings one back to Glasfjorden at **Sölje** where one can walk past the manor to the steamboat jetty and round to a glass museum. To the north of here at **Fors** a monument marks the site of the medieval Glava church where pilgrims worshipped on this route to Nidaros. To the south at **Stömne**, an old hill fort on the Nordtorp road gives good views over Glasfjorden. One can also reach it on a 3km (2 mile) path from the nature reserve by Stömne manor (not open to the public). Also at Stömne, Högsäter and Nysäter, there are barrows built along a Viking shipping route. Close by at **Nysäter** a double row of eighteenth-century market booths, log-built and turf-roofed, have been restored and open for business on special occasions in the summer. Here one is not very far north of the west-east coast route, the E18 above Säffle, where this chapter started.

Further Information

— Värmland —

Älgå
Nailsmithy
Open: late June to mid-August, daily 2-5pm.

Alster
Manor
Open: early May to mid-September daily 11am-6pm.

Apertin
Manor
Open: mid-June to mid-August. Guided tour daily 2pm.
Park open: May to September, daily 8am-8pm.

Arvika
Oppstuhage
Open: June to August, Tuesday to Sunday 12noon-5pm.

Sågudden Hembygdsgård
Open: mid-June to mid-August daily 1-6pm.

Borgvik
Bruksmuseum
Open: mid-June to mid-August daily 12noon-6pm.

Branäs
Gondola Lift
Open: June to August daily 10am-3pm.

Dalby
Hembygdsgård
Open: June to late August, Sunday 12noon-6pm.

Dusserud
Ögårn
Open: mid-June to mid-August daily 1-5pm.

Ekshärad
Church
Open: June to August, Monday to Saturday 8am-9pm. Sunday 11am-9pm.

Church Stables
Handicrafts open: July daily 11am-5pm.

Filipstad
Kvarnen Museum
Open: June to August, Tuesday, Wednesday, Friday, 10am-12noon and 1-4pm. Thursday 1-6pm. Saturday 12noon-4pm.

Granbergsdalstorp
Ironworks
Open: July to mid-August daily 10am-6pm.

Hagfors
Railway Museum
Open: early June to July, daily 12.30-5pm. August, September, Saturday 11am-3pm.

Karlskoga
Alfred Nobel Museum
Open: June to August daily 1-5pm.

Gråbo Museum
Open: June to August daily 1-5pm.

Karlstad
Värmlands Museum
Open: June to August, Monday to Friday 11am-6pm. Saturday and Sunday 12noon-4pm. September, Tuesday to Sunday 12noon-4pm. Wednesday 12noon-8pm.

Klässbol
Linen Weaving Factory
Open: May to September, Monday to Friday 8am-4pm. Saturday 10am-3pm.

Långban
Mining Village
Open: early June to late August. Guided tours daily 9.30am-1pm and 2-6pm.

Lekvattnet
Kvarntorps Finngård
Open: June to August, Tuesday to Sunday 11am-5pm.

Ritimäki Finngård
Open: July, Sunday 12noon-5pm.

Liljedal
Hembygsgård
Open: mid-June to mid-August, daily 10am-2pm.

Mårbacka
Selma Lagerlöf's Home
Open: May to end August. Guided tours daily 9am-6pm.

Munkfors
Gamla Bruk Museum
Open: June to August daily 10am-6pm.

Nykroppa
Hornkullens Silver Mine
Open: late May to mid-September. Guided tours 11am-5pm.

Ölme
Divershandel
Open: late June to end August, Monday to Friday 12noon-6pm. Saturday 10am-1pm. Sunday 1-5pm.

Ransäter
Erlandergården
Open: May to August daily 9.30am-5.30pm.

Geijersgården
Open: mid-May to mid-September. Guided tours daily 9am-1pm and 2-6pm.

Hembygdsgård
Open: mid-June to mid-August daily 10am-4pm.

Röna
Torntorps Hembygdsgård
Open: late June to mid-August daily 11am-7pm.

Rottneros
Park
Open: May to August daily 9am-6pm.

Säby
Värmlands Säby
Open: mid-June to end August, daily 11am-5pm.

Skråckarberget
Tomta Hembygdsgård
Open: July, Sunday 2-6pm.

Smedbyn
Von Echstedtska Manor
Open: mid-May to end August, daily 11am-6pm.

Södra Råda
Church
Open: May to August daily 10am-1pm, 1.30-5pm.

Sunne
Hembygdsgård
Open: June to August daily 6-8pm.

Sundbergsgård
Open: late June to end July, Tuesday to Sunday. Guided tours 1-6pm.

Sunnemo
Hembygdsgård
Open: late June to early August, Thursday to Sunday, 2-5pm.

Torsby
Hembygdsgård
Open: early June to mid-August, daily 12noon-8pm.

Tossebergsklätten
Tower
Open: June to August daily 9am-6pm.

Värmskog
Minnesgård
Open: June to mid-August daily 3-6pm.

Tourist Information Centres

Årjäng
Torget
67200 Ärjäng
☎ (0573) 14136

Arvika
Stadsparken
67132 Arvika
☎ (0570) 13560

Filipstad
68201 Filipstad
☎ (0590) 11560

Hagfors
68301 Hagfors
☎ (0563) 11515

Karlskoga
Katrinedalsgatan 2
69183 Karlskoga
☎ (0586) 61474

Karlstad/Hammarö
Tingvallagatan 1D
65184 Karlstad
☎ (054) 195901

Kristinehamn
Västerlånggatan 22
68131 Kristinehamn
☎ (0550) 88187

Morokulien
67044 Morokulien
☎ (0571) 23370

Munkfors
68400 Munkfors
☎ (0563) 51138

Sunne
68600 Sunne
☎ (0565) 13530

Sysslebäck
68060 Sysslebäck
☎ (0564) 10373

Torsby
68500 Torsby
☎ (0560) 10550

11 • Dalarna

Dalarna is the area of Sweden just north of Värmland. Like Värmland it has a central river running through — the Öster and Väster branches uniting at Djurmo to flow south as the broad, smooth Dalälven. The 'Copper Route', is the central road from Falun, at its heart, across the Norwegian border to Røros. Not that this has been a road for long. It was only completed in the 1960s, the earlier cross-border trading traffic taking advantage of the winter-frozen rivers instead. There is also a central lake, Siljan, formed by a meteorite 360,000,000 years ago. Since then the Ice Ages have affected land patterns with the result that old shorelines are visible as ridges above the existing water level. Men in their village homes passed the winter evenings here whittling wooden horses which were painted and sold in the spring to augment the family income. Colours and patterns became traditional so that Leksand horses were yellow, Rättvik ones grey, and those from Mora, bright red. Today, the bright red Mora horse is the main souvenir of the area. Equally traditional, and preserved in many of the *hembygdsgårds* are the Dalecarlian wall paintings. It was the custom to paint furniture but in the late eighteenth century peasant artists started painting the walls of houses too. They were usually sickly young men, not strong enough for normal farm work, who earned their living as itinerant 'decorators' and often died young. The scenes they painted are mainly Biblical with the variation of an unhappy love story. The figures wear contemporary costumes and the scenes are decked with flowers and leaf designs known as *kibbutz* or gourds.

Scenically Dalarna offers a wide variety from broad farming plains, through the inevitable forests, to skiing mountains in the north up to 1,200m (3,936ft) high. The 6,000 lakes, not to mention the rivers in between, provide canoeists and anglers with a choice of scenario and of catch. There is a cycle trail round Lake Siljan and hiking routes of all degrees of difficulty from circular walks in nature reserves to tough trails in the Töfsingdalen National Park. Wildlife includes elk, beaver and bears, with a real chance of seeing bears in

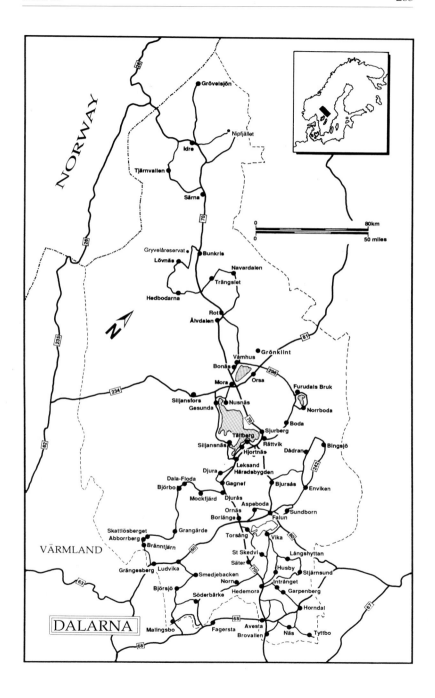

*The 43ft (13m) high
Dala horse at Avesta*

the largest bear park in Europe. On the cultural side there are music festivals and a variety of museums and for the sportsman, no less than ten 18-hole golf courses. Road access is easiest from Stockholm — only 162km (100 miles) to Avesta in the south-eastern corner — but perfectly possible from Gothenberg as well. Both Borlänge and Mora have direct flight connections with Stockholm.

The 70 Mora road is the fast route into Dalarna from Stockholm. It is appropriate that soon after it crosses the boundary, the world's largest Dala horse should greet one by the roadside. Thirteen metres (43ft) in height and of traditionally decorated orangey-red equine art, it is true in every respect except that it is not carved from wood but cast in iron and concrete. It is the gateway to the first Dalarna town, **Avesta**, which developed as a copper mining community from the 1630s in the area now called Gamla Byn. Lundgren's house has the date 1656 carved in a log in the gateway and there are others almost as old to be found in this wooden backwater. Here too is the Mint Museum, for most of Sweden's copper coins were minted in Avesta between 1644 and 1831. It includes coins from as far back as the Viking era but its prize exhibit is the world's largest coin, a 1644

10-daler piece weighing 19.7kg. Also of interest is the Visentpark where for 50 years a herd of European bison has been maintained. There is a viewing platform over the nearest paddocks. One can also admire Dodafallet, the 'Dead Falls' where 6,000 years ago the river changed its course. This is explained pictorially at the end of the path. South Dalarna offers scope for a series of circular tours. This first one is based on Avesta, starting behind the Dala horse. Cross under the 70 from here and circle right, through Grytnäs and Folkärna (both with *hembygdsgårds*) to **Brovallen** for the Erik Larsgården. Two up-stairs rooms in the main house have Dalecarlian paintings on mainly Biblical themes, though one is entitled in translation *I Ride My Horse Pretty Good*! Coffee and cakes are served here; the smaller buildings sell all kinds of handicrafts. Return and follow the By signs to **Strandmora** where the *klint* is signed to the right. It involves a 15-minute walk from the end of the track up onto a rocky outcrop for views over Lake Bäsingen. Cross the water at **Näs** where the old hydro-electric power station has been turned into a museum. There is a salmon hatchery on the same site which provides 2kg fish for the rapids area at Tyttbo. On the way there, pause in **By** for the *hembygdsgård* whose 1700 house has a painted porch and best room. **Tyttbo** itself is a diversion off the round route — a fishing milieu created especially by the Swedish State Power Board, with a variety of fish to be caught, permits for sale, parking places and facilities and even boats to take one to the far side. The circular route continues north to Hornedal, then west across the 68 for **Garpenberg** with its *hembygdsgård* and church opposite each other. The latter is decorated in Art Nouveau style with its organ set behind the altar. Sweden's last remaining mining chapel is on the way out. Very plain indeed, it contains no altar, just a pulpit, for it was used not for communion but simply for prayers for the miners' safety. Another mining relic is the 25m (82ft) tower at Intrånget (key at number 18 opposite) which gives wide views over the surrounding countryside.

The through road continues to join the 270 for Hedemora but there is another loop that should certainly be undertaken at some point and could easily be put in here. Called the Husby Ring, it involves some 75km (46 miles) extra. Before reaching the 270, go right for Brovall, through several farms beside the river, then right again for Kloster. This takes one round the ring in the anti-clockwise and least popular direction. One passes a nature trail at **Flinsberget** and a birdtower overlooking Lake Flinesjön before reaching **Kloster** itself where there are scanty remains of the northernmost Catholic monas-tery in Sweden. Later a gunpowder factory existed here and this is commemorated both in the two remaining storage houses and in the Bruksmuseum where an interesting touch is the monk in one window. Go left past inventor Laval's workshop (by the pools and waterfall), across a wilderness road to Stjärnsund. There are several information points on the way and a geological trail at Högsta kustlinjen. **Stjärnsund** was the home of another inventor, Christopher Polhem, who established the world's first manufacturing works here. He invented pumps to keep the mines dry and is also the father of the grandfather clock. These inventions are commemorated in Polhemsgården Museum. Now follow the signs to **Silfhyttea**, a lovely spot with streams and bridges, a lock between two lakes and scattered picnic tables. **Långshyttan** is the next stop; an ironworking town with various preserved 'machines' in the park by the Brukshotell. The hotel holds the key for the Modellkammeren, which explains through models the processes of the iron industry in different ages. Leave on the Arkhyttan road but continue straight through Myckelby to circle along the Dalälven to **Husby**. The *Torkhus for Säd* that one passes was a drying house for corn — look inside at the stovehouse with its drying roof. At Husby church cross the river past the manor for Hedemora.

Hedemora is the oldest Dalarna town, founded in 1446. Its church, which is older still, contains medieval wood sculptures. Its *hembygdsgård*, beautifully situated on the shores of Lake Hovran, is one of the oldest in Sweden, having been inaugurated in 1915 and its theatre barn is the oldest of its type. Now restored to its 1800s charm, there are still occasional performances given there. From Hedemora one can either return to Avesta on the 70 (past signs to two birdwatching towers on Lake Hovran) or take the same road north to Säter for a further loop from here.

Säter is a small wooden town with several museums, a peaceful enclave past which motorists rush on road 70. The Car Museum has a good array of motorbikes and cars, some of the earliest being right-hand drive, for Sweden was the last continental country to change to driving on the right. In the same building the Biograf Museum records early developments of photography and films. The *hembygdsgård*, has twenty-three buildings including the seventeenth-century home of the mint master, with Renaissance frescoes, a school museum, a smithy complete with weapons and armour and a dairymaid's quarters from a mountain farm. On the opposite side of road 70 is the entrance to Säterdalen, a 7km (4 mile) stretch of ravines and rushing streams through which paths have been laid.

For a circle north and east of Säter, take the 70 as far as the St Skedvi exit and go first to **Rösåsen**. A 650m (710yd) walk leads to this ever-open tower, with sliding windows from which to photograph the 360° views. The largest lake in sight is Lake Runn, which this route will eventually almost circumnavigate. Continue and go left for **Torsång**, a place set amid channels of water. The small Motor Museum is on one side, the *hembygdsgård* in the middle, and the church on the other. This is the oldest church in Dalarna but its interior is dominated by the 1912 stained glass window above the altar. The carved and painted pulpit dates from 1624. Perhaps the oddest feature are the figures in the roof of the side chapel where the original altar now hangs. Outside on the west gable, look for the standing man, traditionally interpreted as Thor, God of Thunder, but more probably an early saint.

Continue to Borlänge entering past Stora Tuna church. Just beyond, Frostbrunnsdalen is a nature reserve with a marked trail in a ravine where the waters have traditionally been drunk as a cure. **Borlänge** is a modern industrial town so perhaps it is fitting that it should possess an ultramodern Museum of the Future. Pick up the English leaflet at the entrance as the only labelling is in Swedish; it will help make sense of the unusual exhibits. For those who prefer older things, Borlänge also has a traditional *gammelgården*.

Leave on the 60 for **Ornäs** where Ornässtugan is one of many places in this part of Dalarna connected with Gustav Vasa. In 1520 he fled from the Danish king, Christian XII, through the area. Here he was hidden in this wonderful old guesthouse. The guided tour shows a model of the farmhand who helped him escape, the privy through which he was lowered to the ground and the undergarment he wore to stop his armour chafing. It tells tales not only of the king's history but also of eating habits at ancient banquets. For a church with a difference, north at **Aspeboda**, a new one has been created round elements of the old. Amid all the modern imagery of the pillars and the stained glass windows, the painted Renaissance ceiling from the old church has been retained as has the old vestry in the shape of a new porch. From here, proceed to **Falun** which has been a coppermining centre for 1,000 years. The old mine has been re-opened for visitors and experienced guides lead one through galleries at the 60m (197ft) level with displays of old equipment and there is even a *son et lumière* show in the cave known as the 'General Peace'. One also sees the red ochre which becomes the Falun red paint that coats all the oldest buildings. The Stora Museum nearby illustrates the history of copper mining through models and machinery, while the Dalarnas Museum is the definitive museum on local culture.

The view from Carl Larsson's house

From here one could complete the circle of Lake Runn back to Säter or undertake this more northerly loop first. Take the Sundborn road out, stopping first at the **Sveden** estate where Carl Linné, the famous botanist, was married in the guest cottage. The main room inside is painted in the Dalecarlian manner. In **Sundborn** itself the home of painter Carl Larsson is open as is the nearby Stora Hyttnäs manor, a home unaltered from the turn of the century. Both are by guided tours only. Further north at **Svardsjö** the church has complicated grey frescoes from about 1500. Opposite the *hembygdsgård* there is a nature trail area and signs point to Isala lada, a barn where Gustav Vasa hid in 1520.

Continue north to Enviken on a delightful road that leads along a ridge between stretches of water. The old church in **Enviksbyn**, constructed without permission in the seventeenth century, is of plain painted wood, with unyielding rough hewn benches, a home-built church for the local population. Heated only by the huge iron stove, it proved untenable in winter and has now been replaced by the new church in Enviken. Now join the 294 for a trip to the best Dala painted house of them all. On the way, Väckelberget has a $1^{1}/_{2}$km (1 mile) nature trail to the top. At **Bingsjö**, one of the greatest Dalecarlian painters, Winter Carl Hansson, spent 3 years painting the inside walls of the summer house at Danielsgården. (In this sense, summer house means the house that was lived in during the summer months as opposed to the winter house that was presumably better

Painting of the Ages of Man *at Danielsgården, Bingsjö*

heated). Admire the *Ages of Man* in the kitchen and lie on the floor of the living room to view Elijah in his chariot of fire taken by the whirlwind into heaven. Other artists decorated the main building and there are later Dala paintings on the gallery of the church. The return trip south from here via Dådran is a long and slightly complicated run through mainly empty countryside. Just before Dådran there is a summer pasture farm at Pråstbodarna that is worth a visit in June or July before the meadows are cut. To work through to Bjursäs, go right at the start of Marnäs; left at the first fork; left at the T-junction where Finnbo is signed right. **Bjursäs** is worth visiting for the Dössberget complex high on the hill overlooking the Rogsjön. The cottage here has a painted room and interesting touches like the unpainted Dala horse. The unpainted grandfather clock between the wall beds in the farmhouse is still keeping accurate time. There is also a carriage museum in a purpose-built barn.

To complete the ring to Säter, take the 80 past Falun, then the Hedemora road. Gamla Staberg is an old settlement laid out to a pattern 'like Versailles'. Do not miss **Vika** church, to the right. The interior is completely covered in sixteenth-century frescoes. The unknown master who painted them has added individual touches like the faces on the ceiling and in some of the 'roses' in the border. There are also numerous medieval wood sculptures and a magnificent eighteenth-century chandelier that has been ingeniously electrified. Just past the church one can walk through the Gramångs Udde nature reserve. Continue towards Torsång, then left to **Rankhyttan** where the king's barn (*kungsladen*) was also used by Gustav Vasa in his flight! This is part of a collection of historic buildings signed as the Skovsvårdsgård. Pick up the Hedemora road again but then follow **St Skedvi**. Here the church has sixteenth-century Dutch-style murals in the roof arches. The peacock in the chancel could hardly be earlier as such Eastern birds were unknown until the Portuguese found a way to India. Also strange is the clock above the altar ticking loudly into the silence of the church. Return to Säter from here.

Now for a wriggly route through the remains of Dalarna's mining past that will eventually take one to Ludvika. Many of these roads are unsurfaced, through forested countryside: remember that side roads are signed — the through route often is not. Take the 70 south to **Vikmanshyttan** where there is a small Industrial Museum. The road south from here goes all the way to Söderbärke. On the way stop at **Norr** where the old mining village is very well maintained. Buildings are named (in Swedish) and dated, some going back to the mid-seventeenth century when Hans Steffers became chief bellowsmaker and later mayor of Hedemora. The industry died early this century because of the very bad roads. **Söderbärke** church is beautifully sited by Lake Bärken. It was built in the eighteenth century over the existing church without interrupting the schedule of services! Its interior has been restored to its original colours making it bright, light and rich with its gold-painted statues and ornamentation on pulpit and altar. Return to the **Hemshyttan** road for this old mining village is worth finding. The centre round the pond is delightful with the laundry house over the water and several two-storeyed miners' homes nearby. The name dates back to the fourteenth century when a miner called Hemming lived here. Continue through towards **Fagersta**, taking the Ulfsbo road to the right for picnic areas by the Semla locks on the Strömsholmen canal.

In theory it is possible to cut through from here to the 65 but it is safer to circle the edge of Fagersta on the 68 following the Ludvika signs. On the 65, **Tunkarlsbo**, right straight after the sign, is built along a stream with laundry houses beside the water. At the bottom the old road hugs the lake. Take the next left back onto the 65, then left for Malingsbo to reach the Domain reserve, 50,000 hectares of state forest, lakes and streams set aside for walking, canoeing, fishing and bathing. Many of these activities are signed. For example, there is a nature trail just before Gärdsjöbo. The next left takes you along the northern shore of the lake — remember that you do not want Bisen! Keep right at the fork and right at the crossroads. There are more nature trails along here and a sandy beach. On meeting the surfaced road, go right for **Malingsbo** where the industrial remains are signed Ekomuseum for this is part of the area called Bergslagen where all remains are given that name. Malingsbo octagonal church was originally the chapel to the local ironworks. There is a set of matching red-painted buildings nearby and the manor has a seed store with fifty-seven airholes in each side. Continue back along the south shore of the lake. To the left, **Skräddertorp** has picnic places by a small waterfall dropping a total of 32m (105ft). As one drives on remember that the woods are inhabited by elk, roedeer, capercaillie and blackcock and that the present Swedish king hunts elk here every autumn. In **Björsjö**, go right for the Tombogruvor, an area of old mines. Do not miss the small wooden sign that eventually points the way in. The track is driveable to the 'loop' at the end. From here a 10-minute walk across and into the woods leads to a circular tour of the mines. The most impressive is the one at this very point, number 8. It is called the Ice Mine because the ice in the cave does not melt until August. It is a dark, dripping, eerie place. Take the 65 left once the road gets through to it. At the start of **Smedjebacken**, Flatenbergshytta is a restored smelting house. The mineral art exhibition is a collection of unusual crystals and mineral rocks from around the world and there is an imposing statue of a miner where one rejoins the 65. A little further on, Flogbergetsgruva is an old mining area similar to that at Tombogruvor but more accessible.

One has now reached **Ludvika**, a mining town that grew out of Gustav Vasa's need for iron for weapons — he founded a crown mill here in 1555. Its heyday was the eighteenth-century but by the end of the nineteenth century the mines were closing down. One can obtain a very good idea though of the old atmosphere from the *gammelgård* where a period mine has been reconstructed, complete with waterwheel, winding house, and miner's home. The mining remains continue on the 60 to Grängesberg. Klenshyttan is a very impressive restored blast furnace — it is an immense way down to the stream at its base from the 'hall' beside it. **Grängesberg** itself developed much more recently because of the high phosphate content of its local ore, which British investors developed, along with the railway to Oxelösund. The old loco sheds are now a museum whose prize exhibit is the world's only steam turbine engine. Englishman Sir Ernest Cassel gave 250,000 Swedish kroner for the benefit of his workers. One can still see the huge stone house with its concert hall and the model homes that he built, each containing four separate apartments. One of these, near the railway station, is now a museum.

Grängesberg is on the edge of the area called Finnmark where at the beginning of the seventeenth century, Charles IX allowed Finnish immigrants to settle. They preferred hilly country, hunting, fishing and establishing short term farms by burning the forest. One can travel via two such settlements on the way north to Lake Siljan. Leave Grängesberg on Finnmarksvägen past Fjällberget skiing area. Keep to the north of the lake and follow the **Bränntjärn** signs for Bränntjärnstorpet, a tiny settlement of one cottage and two sheds, 5 minutes walk through the forest from the parking. Everything is homemade — the log-roofed buildings and all their contents; wooden utensils, furniture and even cutlery — and nothing is painted Falun red. It is all naturally weathered. Return and continue to **Abborrberg**, an old village with a tiny rural shop, open just three times a week. Go right at the end of the village to pick up the 245 towards Fredriksberg to find the other Finnish settlement at **Skattlösberget** (the Vattsten signed on the way was supposed to have healing powers). Called *gammelgård*, this is a much larger holding. There are only two tiny cottages but the outbuildings include a threshing barn, sauna, and charcoal stack, for the Finns also did smallscale ironworking. A hilly path beyond the parking leads to the secluded cottage where poet Dan Andersson once lived.

Go north now on the 245 for Grangärde. This is a lovely run past marshes with good bird life and round Lake Bysjön. The Vastansjö side has old villages set in arable land and backed by forested hills. From the main road one can go beside the lake into **Grangärde**, the old regional capital. Continuing north, the road runs along a ridge between lakes with picnic places and fishing to Björbo. Go left there on the 71 for about 2km (1 mile) to **Fänforsen** where one can shoot the rapids on the Västerdalälven by rubber raft. Returning past Björbo the road is lined with huge old farms, built courtyard style with painted porches, all facing the river, which one follows now to **Dala Floda**. Here, from the church, one can drive across the longest wooden suspension bridge in Sweden, left past the *hembygdsgård*, to a foot suspension bridge over rapids. This minor road continues through to Mockfjärd (keep right of Wålstedts textiles and take the 70 limit road). In the tiny village of **Björka**, park and follow the path to Trolldalen nature reserve. This is a canyon-shaped valley containing mixed trees and meadows with abundant bird and animal life and unusual flora. Various walks are possible. Soon afterwards head to **Djurås** where Ålmötet, to the right off the 71 behind the hospital, is a peaceful promontory overlooking the confluence of the east and west Dalälven rivers.

The pontoon bridge at Östjärna

From here cross the 71 for Östjärna to approach Gagnef over the pontoon bridge. Once there were at least eleven of these but now only two are left — the other is at the northern edge of Gagnef at Österfors. The river has removed the rest! In **Gagnef** the Minnestuga is a worthwhile *hembygdsgård* with twenty buildings, wall paintings, and a collection of national costumes. Beyond the Österfors turning, go left for Djura, past Leksands-Gråda village set on a knoll above fields of corn. All the villages here follow the same traditional pattern with crowded log farms interspersed with newer houses. By contrast **Djura**'s *hembygdsgård* beyond the chapel is an unpainted wood farm. Continue towards Leksand and then Häradsbygden to join the 70. This road passes the Rastplats Leksand where a church boat has been preserved. Originally used by villagers round Lake Siljan to travel to church, in recent years new ones have been built for the sport of church boat racing. The 70 takes one past Leksand. Immediately past the golf course, one can drive to the café at the top of Asleden (about 5km, 3 miles) for long views over Lake Siljan. Fräsgården *hembygdsgård* on the right of the 70, at Ytterboda is a farm preserved on its original site, again with exhibitions of local costumes. You can continue on this road to **Norr Lindberg** where Bosse Kristenson creates yellow Leksand Dala horses in his small workshop. From here wriggle down, across the 70 to Tällberg on the very corner of **Lake Siljan**.

Siljan is the sixth largest lake in Sweden. One can drive right round

it though the roads themselves afford few views. One needs to climb
to one of the *bergets* or hills for that. You can also cycle the 310km (192
mile) circular Siljansleden (and hire bicycles to do so) or take lake
cruises from several different points. Here two routes are suggested,
the first a circle north of Siljan, based on Rättvik; later a loop round
the south to Mora.

Rättvik is situated round the eastern end of the lake. For this
reason it is best to climb Vidablick, the lookout tower, in the morning
when the sun shines across to the opposite shore. Below one can see
Langbrygga, the 625m (690yd) pier that one must walk to join a lake
cruise here. Beyond that stands the white church with its eighteenth-
century painted galleries. It is surrounded by some ninety church
stables, some huddled some along the shore and some near a small
mill. They are grey unpainted wood as is the *gammelgård* with its
Dala-painted and furnished houses and its parish costumes. This is
just along the **Sjurberg** road where soon after one finds Gudmunds
Träslöjd where grey Rättvik horses are handmade. This road continues to rejoin the 70 at **Vikarbyn**, opposite the road to Karl Tofäsens
fäbodar (mountain dairy farm) where one can buy homemade butter
and cheese. There are several similar signed off this route, all welcoming visitors to their high pastures and old-fashioned farms.
Continue through now to **Nusnäs** where in Nils Olssons factory one
can watch the most popular Dala horse being produced in red, blue
or black. At **Färnäs**, where there are Dala horses on their midsummer
pole, a smaller factory is in operation.

Rejoin the 70 briefly but go right for Orsa and right again for
Bergkarlås. This route rises high above Orsasjön and there are good
views of Lake Siljan as you drop down again through Sundbäck to
reach **Orsa**. From here a very special expedition can be undertaken.
Signed from the centre of town Björnpark, Europe's largest bear
park, is 15km (9 miles) up into the hills. At **Grönklitt** the park has
been created in an area where wild bears live so that the animals
inhabit their native terrain with trees and rocks to climb, pond,
wetland and forest divided into three enclosures. There are two
viewing platforms built out over the enclosures but take binoculars
as the bears do not necessarily congregate close by. Return the same
way but bypass Orsa heading towards Sveg for a trip to two water
features. Go right when Tallhed airport is signed, then follow
Helvetesfallet and Storstupet. **Helvetesfallet**, 11km (7 miles) up the
road despite what the sign says, is an impressive chute of water with
old log-floating contrivances among the rocks. It is 10 minutes walk
down from the parking. **Storstupet** is a log-floating channel with a

railway bridge high above the gorge. Rejoin the 296. Another *fäbodar* is signed off in Mässbacken and then at **Skattungsbyn** there is an old village shop, still fitted out with some of its original equipment though it is really a *slöjd* (handicraft shop) nowadays.

Continue to **Furudal** where one can loop round Oresjön. Furudal Bruk — a slightly larger loop — has a beautiful manor overlooking old workmen's houses. Signed off here too is Äteråsens *fäbodar*. Continue down the east side of the lake for Norrboda *gammelstan*. The preserved farms here are almost unique. They are original seventeenth-century closed courtyard farms, with the size of rooms limited by the length of log that could be handled. There is only one other site left like this in all Sweden. The Fångstgrop signed opposite is a pit for trapping elk set above the road in a group of pines. Rejoin the Rättvik road and continue to **Boda** whose *gammelgård* only opens on Mondays and Fridays for special events. Shortly afterwards, follow the Styggforsen signs round past the church. This is an excellently-constructed short walk over and past a geologically interesting waterfall. Read the information board opposite the reconstructed mill first. From Boda, Rättvik is not far down the road.

For the southern route divert from the main Rättvik-Leksand road into **Tällberg**. This is a quiet place of old hotels and wooden buildings. On the highest hill, the artist Gustaf Ankarcrona's home, Holen, is now a *hembygdsgård*. Follow the coast road to **Hjortnäs** where the unique museum has dioramas of historical scenes peopled with tin figures. On the way into **Leksand** one passes the Sommarland Park with its Scandinavian-style attractions (much simpler amusements than you find in the large theme parks in Germany or England). Of interest to English visitors is Hildasholm, the house that Queen Victoria's private physician gave to his English wife. It is beautifully furnished but only open by guided tour. The Culture House is also very good with its comprehensive collections of Dalecarlian paintings, costumes, textiles, and slideshow of the area.

Leave Leksand on the **Siljansnäs** road. Here Bjorkberget Naturum combines a tower giving a 360° panorama over the Siljan ring with an interesting nature museum. You can make the birds sing and study the animals that you might see in the surrounding reserve, while the bee display is fascinating with its wild bees coming in from outside and its glass-sided hive. Further on the restored twin mill at **Mångbro**, of the type once jointly owned by farmers for the corn harvest, sits in its own peaceful dell. The next place, **Gesunda**, is overtopped by Gesundaberget, scene of winter sports, with a cabin lift to the top in the summer season too. On the lower slopes,

Tomteland is Sweden's claim to being the home of Santa Claus, with workshops, games and a minizoo as well as Santa and his gnomes. From here one can continue to join the Malung-Mora road where, by a diversion of some 7km (4 miles) towards Malung, one can visit the **Siljansfors** Forestry Museum with its trail round displays of logging equipment and living quarters from the past up to the 1950s. Alternatively one can cross from Gesunda to **Sollerön** where the largest Viking burial ground in Sweden lies beyond the *hembygdsgård*. One can walk through the area admiring the bird life and the views before continuing to **Mora**.

Anders Zorn, one of Sweden's best known artists, lived here. His home, Zorngården, kept untouched since the death of his wife in 1942, is open as is the Zorn Museum with both his own works and those he collected. There is also a Zorn *hembygdsgård* whose large collection of buildings includes a twin mill, sauna, and watchmaker's workshop. The other name to occur in Mora is Vasa, for from here in 1522, Gustav Vasa fled to Sälen on skis. Since 1922, the 400th anniversary of this feat, the Vasaloppet crosscountry ski race has been held here every year. A statue glorifies the skiers and the Vasa Monument commemorates the king. From Mora take the **Våmhus** road north through Bonäs, Sweden's longest village, for the Sivarsbacken *hembygdsgård*. They specialise in displays of two local crafts here. Men weave baskets of split pinewood — appropriately, as the name Våmhus denotes this very type of basket. Women produce jewellery from human hair. It takes fourteen hairs each 30cm long to produce one thread and these are then 'plaited' in a movement reminiscent of lacemaking to produce a circular braid that is imperishable. Would-be customers provide the hair.

To continue north into both wilderness and skiing country, leave Våmhus on the **Rot** road. Where this joins the 70 just north of Älvdalen, Rot Skans *hembygdsgård* is built inside the ruins of an entrenchment raised in 1677 against possible attack from Norway. **Älvdalen** itself is famous as the home of porphyry, a hard stone that can be ground and polished for making ornamental vases and jewellery. Porphyry manor hotel has a recostructed grindery and there is also a museum containing many of the larger items that used to be made. As a side line it has exhibitions of accordions and guitars and on bog iron too. The oldest timber building in Sweden is also in Älvdalen, the former tithe barn next to the church.

The aim now is to reach Idre in the far north of Dalarna but rather than drive straight up the 70, here are various loops to points of interest that can be undertaken on the way. First, for a trip into the

The old church at Särna

wilderness, return to Rot and take the Sveg road for **Navardalen**. This summer café is in elk and bear country on the shores of a lake with fishing, bathing and the possibility of a sauna afterwards. There is a path to it from the parking, through the wood and round the shore of the lake. Continue through the military exercise area and left for Trängslet dam, the largest of its type in Sweden. Cross the top and descend through the military camp to the 70. Go left, then first right for **Hedbodarna**. This is a mountain dairy farm which one can visit (contact Älvdalen tourist information centre). Continue to **Lövnäs** which is set amid lakes, and go right for Älvdalen. Before meeting the 70 go left for the Gryvelåreservat. This is state forestry land and there are boards on modern forestry methods along the way. Park at the information 'centre' for a variety of walks. Myrstigen, the bog path, is an excellent cultural trail that takes about 45 minutes on a good part-boarded path. One passes reconstructions of charcoal burning, tar making, an early bog iron furnace with working waterwheel, haymakers' and foresters' quarters, and evidence of beavers and woodpeckers, all with diagrams and English explanations. For the more energetic there are also 3 and 6km (2 and 4 mile) walks. Continue through and rejoin the 70. About 2km (1 mile) south at **Bunkris**, the *brandtorn*, built round a gigantic pine, gives 360° views with the skiing mountains clearly visible to the north. This is a diversion which could be left out on the northwards trip if one intends to return south on the 70.

Särna, to the north, once belonged to Norway. A stone by the old church commemorates the bloodless conquest of the area for Sweden in 1644. This church is interesting in its own right. The pulpit was made by the vicar who lies buried in the centre aisle. Originally the walls had simple painted designs but the parish council in 1843 covered them with white-washed boards decorated with the apostles. When the church was renovated in 1953 a section of this was removed revealing the original patterns. A mini-lookout tower at **Mickeltemplet** lies 3km (2 miles) south of here on the 297 which again could be left to the return journey if desired.

North of Särna on the 70 the new forestry museum has a $1^1/_2$km (1 mile) trail past a variety of log-working buildings. One has a display of old and new equipment while another demonstrates life in a workmen's hut. Down by the lake there is a trapper's cottage, a boatshed and a new winchraft for transporting timber on small lakes. The next left leads to **Njupeskär**, at 94m (308ft) Sweden's highest waterfall. It is a 2km (1 mile) walk on a well-constructed path from the parking. Continue towards Norway to **Tjärnvallen** where a 1.7km (1 mile) nature trail leads past the Fulubågen rapids, a 400m (1,312ft) stretch of eight waterfalls and rapids dropping some 80m (262ft). The next right takes one across to the 70 again, with **Idre** back to the right. The scenery on this last stretch is good, including views to the Norwegian mountains. For even more extensive views, go up to **Nipfjället** from Idre, to the end of the Trollvägen, on the highest road in Sweden and climb the hill at the end. From Idre one can also reach Lake Grövelsjön on the borders of Norway, from where a hiking trail leads to the top of the highest Dalarna peak (1,204m, 3,949ft), Mount Storvätteshogna. A shorter walk goes to the old mountain pastures of Valdelsbygget and there is a mountain chapel in Storsätern. This is as far away as one can get from the civilised life of south Dalarna. Beyond here lies Norway. This is of course an illogical place at which to end a description of Dalarna but by returning south on the 70 and putting the earlier loops together in a different order the independent tourist can produce his or her own individual route. Alternatively, if you have the time, you could return through Värmland.

Further Information
— Dalarna —

Älvdalen
Porphyry Museum
Open: May to late June and early August to end September. Tuesday to Friday 12noon-5pm. Saturday and Sunday 1-5pm. Late June to early August, Monday to Friday 12noon-5pm. Saturday and Sunday 1-5pm.

Avesta
Mint Museum
Open: early June to mid-August, Tuesday, Wednesday, Friday, Saturday 10am-12noon.

Visentpark
Open: May to September daily 7am-3.30pm.

Bingsjö
Danielsgården
Open: June to mid-August, Wednesday to Saturday 11am-5pm. Sunday 12.30-5pm.
Key at next farm.

Bjursäs
Dössberget Hembygdsgård
Open: mid-June to end July daily 12noon-6pm.

Borlänge
Gammelgården
Open: June to August daily 12noon-6pm.

Museum of the Future
Open: May to September, Monday to Wednesday, and Friday 10am-5pm. Thursday 10am-9pm. Saturday and Sunday 12noon-5pm.

Brovallen
Erik Larsgården
Open: mid-May to end August, Monday to Saturday 10am-6pm. Sunday 1-6pm.

By
Hembygdsgård
Open: June to August, Tuesday to Sunday 1-5pm.

Dala Floda
Hembygdsgård
Open: late June to early August, Monday to Friday 10am-4pm.

Djura
Hembygdsgård
Open: July, Wednesday 2-4pm.

Falun
Dalarnas Museum
Open: May to August, Monday to Thursday 10am-6pm. Friday to Sunday 12noon-5pm.

Falu Gruva Copper Mine and Stora Museum
Open: May to August daily 10am-4.30pm.

Furudal
Ärteräsens Fäbodar
Open: early June to mid-August, daily 10am-6pm.

Gagnef
Minnestuga
Open: July, Saturday and Sunday 1-4pm.

Garpenberg
Hembygdsgård
Open: late June to early August daily 12noon-4pm.

Gesunda
Cable Car
Late June to early August daily, 11am-6pm.

Tomteland
Open: mid-June to mid-August daily
10am-6pm.

Grängesberg
Miner's Cottage
Open: mid-June to early August daily,
3-5pm.

Railway Museum
Open: June to August daily, 10am-6pm.

Grönklitt
Björnpark (Bear Park)
Open: May to mid-June and mid-August to end September daily, 10am-3pm. Mid-June to mid-August daily,
10am-6pm.

Hedemora
Hembygdsgård
Open: early June to mid-August, Monday to Friday 11am-2pm. Saturday and Sunday 12noon-7pm.

Hjortnäs
Tin Figure Museum
Open: mid-June to mid-August daily
10am-4pm.

Kloster
Bruksmuseum
Open: mid-June to early August daily,
1-5pm. Early August to early September, Saturday and Sunday 1-5pm.

Långshyttan
Modellkammeren
Open: May to September, Tuesday to Friday 2-6pm, Saturday 10am-1pm. Key at Brukshotell.

Leksand
Culture House
Open: May to mid-June and mid-August to end September, Tuesday to Friday 11am-4pm, Saturday 11am-2pm, Sunday 2-4pm. Mid-June to mid-August, Monday to Friday 11am-5pm, Saturday and Sunday 1-4pm.

Sommarland Park
Open: late May to early June and early August to mid-August daily 10am-5pm. Early June to late June daily 10am-6pm. Late June to early August daily 10am-7pm.

Mora
Vasa Monument
Open: early June to mid-August, Monday to Saturday 12noon-6pm. Sunday 1-6pm.

Zorn Hembygdsgård
Open: June to late August daily 10am-5pm.

Zorn Manor
Open: May to September, Monday to Saturday 10am-5pm. Sunday 11am-5pm.

Zorn Museum
Open: May to September, Monday to Wednesday, Friday, Saturday 9am-5pm. Thursday 9am-8pm. Sunday 11am-5pm.

Näs
Power Station and Fish Farm
Open: mid-June to mid-August daily
12noon-3pm.

Norrboda
Gammelstan
Open: mid-June to early August daily
12noon-5pm.

Norr Lindberg
Kristensons Horse Workshop
Open: June to August, Monday to Friday 9am-6pm. Saturday 9am-12noon.

Nusnäs
Nils Olssons Dala Horse Factory
Open: June to late August, Monday to Friday 8am-6pm. Saturday and Sunday 9am-6pm.

Ornäs
Ornässtugan
Open: June to August, Monday to Saturday 10am-6pm. Sunday 1-5pm.

Rättvik

Gammelgård
Open: mid-June to mid-August, Monday to Saturday 11am-6pm. Sunday 12noon-6pm.

Vidablick
Open: early June to early August daily 10am-11pm. Early August to mid-September daily 11am-6pm.

Rot

Rot Skans Hembygdsgård
Open: late June to early August, Monday to Friday 8am-4pm. Saturday and Sunday 12noon-4pm.

Särna

Forestry Museum
Open: June to August daily 12noon-5pm.

Säter

Biograf Museum
Open: June to August daily 12noon-5pm.

Car Museum
Open: June to August daily 10am-6pm.

Hembygdsgård
Open: mid-June to mid-August, Tuesday to Sunday 1-5pm.

Siljansfors

Forestry Museum
Open: June to August, Monday to Friday 9am-5pm. Saturday and Sunday 12noon-5pm.

Siljansnäs

Bjorkberget Naturum
Open: early June to end August daily 11am-6pm.

Sjurberg

Gudmunds Horse Workshops
Open: May to September, Monday to Saturday 10am-6pm.

Skattlösberget

Finn Gammelgård
Open: mid-May to mid-September, Sunday 1-3pm.

Luosa Cottage (Dan Andersson)
Open: mid-May to end August daily 11am-5pm.

Skattungsbyn

Country Shop
Open: mid-June to mid-August, Monday to Saturday 10am-6pm. Sunday 1-6pm.

Smedjebacken

Flatenbergs Smelting House and Flogbergets Iron Mine
Open: mid-June to mid-July daily 10am-6pm.

Stjärnsund

Polhemsgård Museum
Open: mid-June to early August daily 12noon-5pm. Early August to early September, Saturday and Sunday 12noon-5pm.

Sundborn

Carl Larssonsgården
Open: May to September, Monday to Saturday 10am-5pm. Sunday 1-5pm.

Stora Hyttnäs
Open: June to August, Tuesday to Sunday 10am-4pm.

Sveden

Linnés Wedding Cottage
Open: mid-June to end July, Thursday to Tuesday, 12noon-4pm.

Tällberg

Holens Gammelgård
Open: mid-June to mid-August, Monday to Saturday 12noon-5pm. Sunday 1-5pm.

Torsång
Motor Museum
Open: May to late June and early August to early September, Saturday and Sunday 12noon-6pm. Late June to early August daily 12noon-6pm.

Våmhus
Sivarsbacken Hembygdsgård
Open: late June to late August, Monday to Saturday 12noon-6pm. Sunday 1-6pm.

Vikarbyn
Karl Töfåsens Fäbodar
Open: early June to mid-August daily 10am-6pm.

Vikmanshyttan
Industrial Museum
Open: June to August, Saturday and Sunday 2-5pm.

Ytterboda
Fräsgården
Open: mid-June to mid-August, Monday to Saturday 12noon-5pm. Sunday 1-5pm.

Tourist Information Centres

Älvdalen
Dalgatan
S-79600 Älvdalen
☎ (251) 80290

Avesta
S-77481 Avesta
☎ (226) 85001

Borlänge
Borganäsvägen 25
S-78131 Borlänge
☎ (243) 74597

Falun
Stora Torget
S-79183 Falun
☎ (23) 83637

Gagnef
Box 1
S-78041 Gagnef
☎ (241) 15150

Hedemora
Box 201
S-77600 Hedemora
☎ (225) 10100

Idre
Box 83
S-79091 Idre
☎ (253) 20710

Leksand
Box 52
S-79322 Leksand
☎ (247) 10840

Ludvika
Sporthallen
S-77182 Ludvika
☎ (240) 86050

Mora
Ångbatskajan
S-79200 Mora
☎ (250) 26550

Orsa
Centralgatan 3
S-79400
☎ (250) 52163

Rättvik
Box 21
S-79500 Rättvik
☎ (248) 30670

Särna
Särnavägen 6
S-79090 Särna
☎ (253) 10205

Säter
Box 56
S-78322 Säter
☎ (225) 55190

Smedjebacken
Bäverstigen
S-77781 Smedjebacken
☎ (240) 60145

Söderbärke
Malingsbo 8100
S-77020 Söderbärke
☎ (240) 35098

Arvidsjaur, the largest remaining Lapp church village in Sweden (Chapter 12)

A midsummer pole on the Åland Islands (Chapter 13)

A windmill in the Jan Karlsgården Museum at Sund, Åland Islands (Chapter 13)

The ferry from Överö, Åland Islands (Chapter 13)

12 • Swedish Lappland

This area comprises the whole of Norrbotten, the most northerly province of Sweden, and beyond. It borders on Norway to the north and west, Finland to the east and the Gulf of Bothnia to the south. It is the land across which the Lapp race have followed their reindeer regardless of national boundaries almost since time began. The rivers here are huge, not as rushing as before man harnesssed them for hydro-electricity, but broad, filling their valleys with water, quiet lazy lakes of rivers that squeeze sometimes into fish-full rapids. The Torneålven, Luleålven, Piteålven ... they all flow down to the sea, to the towns that grew at their river mouths. In the west, the great wilderness parks, Stora Sjöfallet, Padjelanta and the difficult and potentially dangerous Sarek, shelter potentially dangerous animals such as lynx and bear, wolverines and wolves. There are otters in the rivers and buzzards, merlins and the golden eagle in the sky. Of the three parks, Stora Sjöfallet has the easiest trails; Padjelanta requires mountain hiking experience, and Sarek with its sharp peaks and glaciers cut by deep valleys with swift streams should only be attempted by the most experienced. It has no tourist facilities, no paths, no cabins. Only the long distance trails, the Kungsleden and the Padjelanta, cut across its southern fringes. The season in these wilderness parks is a mere 6 weeks, from mid-July, when the rivers subside after the melting of the snows, to the end of August. For the average tourist there are easier nature reserves with paths that do not necessarily involve carrying food and sleeping bag on one's back, or day trips arranged by local tourist offices.

Naturally most pursuits in this area of forests, lakes, mountains and rivers are outdoor ones, the most widespread being fishing. Licences are bought at ticket machines beside lakes or rivers and there are often barbecues with ready-cut logs for that fresh-caught, fresh-cooked supper. Salmon, trout, grayling, whitefish ... they await the keen angler in all their Scandinavian abundance — as do the mosquitoes! A good repellent is essential equipment in the interior. Canoeing, rubber-rafting down rapids, horse-riding are all

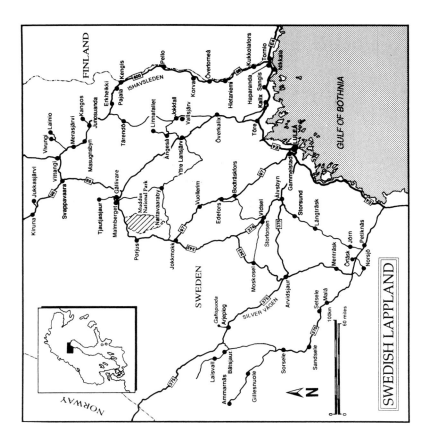

widely available and the whole inland area is also geared to winter sports for here snow and ice are guaranteed every year.

Being Sweden other more cultural activities are available too. In the ore areas there are mine tours as well as *kulturminne* round industrial remains. One can visit hydro-electric power plants, a Stone Age village, a number of interesting churches and museums and ride on the world's longest cableway. There is plenty of evidence of the Lapps too, in their characteristic houses and storehuts, their churches and museums, and their reindeer. A quarter of a million of these roam the area, treating the roads with total disdain. There is no need to seek them out. They browse the lush vegetation of the verges, sun themselves on sandy banks and on the minor roads of the interior are more frequent than other traffic. There are elk too in the south but they are shy, elusive creatures, despite their size. Perhaps this is

Reindeer roam freely in Swedish Lappland

because they are still hunted whereas the reindeer enjoy protected status, belonging solely to the Lapps. Reindeer meat is of course on restaurant menus, served often in thin strips in a cream sauce with berry preserve, but they are used to being herded and even harnessed and so are merely wary of the too curious photographer.

The main access points for this area are Kiruna in the north-west and Luleå in the south-east. Both have rail connections, the former across to Narvik in Norway and both south to Stockholm, including car sleeper facilities from Luleå, as well as airports connecting directly to Stockholm.

The northernmost through route in this area runs from Kiruna to the Gulf of Bothnia at Haparanda. Kiruna and nearby Jukkasjärvi are covered in chapter 5. Here it is proposed to describe the road from Vittangi, the Ishavsleden or Ice Sea Route, that begins on the border of Finland at Karesuando and follows the Torne river valley down to the sea. From its birth in the huge lake, Torneträsk, along whose shores both the Nordkalottan highway and the Narvik-Kiruna railway run, the Torne is a wide river, spreading itself wherever the land permits, as at Vittangi, to lake-like proportions.

It is a route with many interesting places to stop, all of them well-signed and with information boards in Swedish, Finnish and English. The first involves a 60km (37 miles) diversion there and back into the forests to **Lainio** — signed left about 10km (6 miles) south of Vittangi. Here a small museum at the Mariijgården *hytte* site is

The preserved watermill at Merasjärvi

displayed on request at the summer café near the self-operated chain ferry that goes across the river to further villages. Here one is in the centre of a Lapp trapping area, where small V-shaped pits were dug and covered with branches to trap reindeer. There are hundreds in the nature reserve near Lainio but they are difficult to find. It is far better to return to Vivungi (signed right on the way back) and follow the Fritidsområde sign. Take the orange-marked track to the picnic and bathing place on the shores of Lake Rahtusenjärvi, approaching the barbecue shelter cautiously — it is a favourite resting place for reindeer! From there a circular trail leads past trapping pits and ancient living places.

This is the only major diversion suggested. Most other points of interest are on or near the main road. For example, just beyond Merasjärvi, the Kvarnmiljö is a turbine-driven mill used by local villagers for grinding flour and sawing timber from the late nineteenth century to the early 1940s. It has now been restored with a picnic/barbecue site and a nature trail through the woods. At **Masugnsbyn,** follow the Sommarkafé sign for an ironworks *kulturminne;* a small museum of artefacts in a 1650 house and the restored buildings of the first inland mining village in Norrbotten. The old blast furnace is intact with rails and tubs. Here iron ingots were made and transported to Kengis for working into saleable wares. The Kengis works and the museum of ironware at Pajala are all along this same road. A trail leads past roasting pits, heaps of waste and picture

Blast furnace museum at Masugnsbyn

boards of birds and insects that may be seen. Plastic spoons mark the more unusual flora! Further south, at Junosuanda, turn left to **Kangos** and right just before the river bridge for the homestead museum. Here a dozen old wooden buildings surround a green yard where even if they are closed one can peer through the windows and picnic in total peace. From Junosuanda one is close to the Torne river for the rest of its length. At Tornefors there are minor rapids and a short culture trail of ironworks foundations. A kilometre or two further on the *kulturminne* to the Palokorva blast furnace ruins is more worth while, with recognisable remains at the end of the path. **Tärendö** a total diversion of 28km (17 miles) from Antinova, is worth visiting for the guided tour of their Homestead Museum. One sees farmhouse and outsheds, coolhouse, smithy and tar pit. The site comprises everything needed for a self-sufficient farm in days gone by.

Back on the Ishavsleden stop at the Röktfisk sign for fresh-smoked fish to eat at a riverside site that includes a small information office. Then take the road opposite, signed Erkheikki and follow the **Vasikkajoki** signs right and left (about 3km, 2 miles) for something different. The path from the parking leads to a lookout tower over a hay-making marsh where over seventy haymakers' huts have been restored. These wooden cabins were used by the workers during the hay-making season. A wooden walkway leads across the marsh to one of these but the workers harvested standing in water with their extra-long scythes and rakes. Returning the hay to the farms in autumn must have been more fun, hauling it on sledges once the marsh had frozen.

On then to **Pajala** for the iron museum (book at the tourist office) and soon afterwards to **Kengis**. Turn left (signed Kengisbruk) and left again where five blue 'sights' signs point to the remains of an old church and cemetery. These include the foundations of the vicarage where revivalist preacher Læstadius was the first vicar of the iron-works church. His sect still exists in Sweden today and a small museum in Pajala is dedicated to him. The best activity here is to follow the delightful footpath signed to Kengisbruk. It leads along-side the ever more swiftly flowing river as it speeds into the most powerful rapids of its whole length which is why the ironworks were built here — their force powered the machinery. The old factory site, and Sweden's northernmost manor house, are at the end of the path.

From here to Pello, where one can cross into Finland and on to the Arctic Circle, there is a landscape of farming villages, small barns in every field, set between areas of forest. The river is now the frontier and there is bathing in it at Juonsengi and white water canoeing on a tributary. Crossing the Arctic Circle is marked with blue sign-boards and a souvenir kiosk 1km ($^1/_2$ mile) further south.

From here to Övertorneå there are several interconnecting points of interest. North of Korva, where the Hietalas ecological and or-ganic farm board stands, a footpath up the hill leads to Antti Keksi's memorial. A Finnish poet in the seventeenth and eighteenth centu-ries, his oral verses picture life in the area. His most famous poem told of spring floods in 1677. The wooden cross on the river bank just before the Turistinform board) marks the site of the Särkalix chapel that was washed away in earlier spring floods in 1615. Seven years later its medieval wooden statues were recovered from the river and are now in **Övertorneå** church. They include a beautiful madonna that opens to reveal God the Father inside. Probably fifteenth-cen-tury German, it is one of only ten extant in the whole world. Also in Övertorneå church (red wood eighteenth-century cruciform by Hans Biskopp) one finds the oldest working organ in Sweden, dating from between 1608 and 1609, and an elaborate pulpit, a copy of that at Uppsala. Its belltower is also very decorative and typical of the period and area. Before leaving Övertorneå, visit the Folk Museum next to the swimming pool. The furnished farmhouse has interesting pictures and wall hangings, some of which are for sale.

South of Övertorneå, Luppioberget (Santa Claus Mountain) is worth visiting, not to see Father Christmas (his grotto is a bare cave;

The church and bell tower at Hietaniemi

his only presence a doll in the café window), but for the extensive if green views from the flagpole. Park at the 'café 200m' sign and walk from there. Another church worth visiting is at **Hietaniemi**, signed left at the end of Hedenäset. Probably also built by Hans Biskopp, the style is similar and so is the pulpit. The organ is also old as it is part of a seventeenth-century instrument built for a Stockholm church. The belltower, identical in shape to Övertorneå's, is open for viewing the bells and the vista of hay meadows and river from the windows. Along the outer wall, where one parks, note the rings for tethering horses years ago. Behind the church the path leads to a grassy mound where a market place existed for three centuries until destroyed by fire, possibly deliberately by rival merchants from Övertorneå. Here also are pagan graves from as late as the seventeenth century. Frontier cairn number 44 determines the exact position of the border in the river, one of sixty-seven that were placed along the valley in 1810.

Continuing south the valley broadens with more extensive farmlands dotted with storehouses. At **Kukkolafors** there are wide rapids which one can shoot on rubber rafts twice a day. Walkways are built out over the rapids for fishing. The last week of July to 10 August is the peak season for whitefish which are dipped with nets, scooping them out of the hollows in which they rest between bursts up river. The whole area is also a *kulturminne* with preserved sheds and storehouses. One sports a clocktower so the working fishermen could check the time of their shifts. There is also a flourmill, sawmill,

The international distance post at Haparanda

and the electric power plant that once provided all Kukkola with direct current. A good fishing museum and aquarium completes what is a very interesting site.

The Ishavsleden ends at the twin towns of Haparanda in Sweden, founded after the Torneå river boundary was drawn and Tornio, in Finland. **Haparanda** has interesting old buildings like the Kopukka property from 1796, and the courtyard property of the Hermansson family that is still a shop, with an interior from the 1930s. The railway bridge has both Swedish standard and Russian broad gauge tracks across it. This was the route by which Lenin returned to Russia from Switzerland in 1917 and also by which some German troops passed into Finland in World War II. There is also a modern church with a copper exterior to make sure it never burns down and a distance post outside the tourist office giving the distance to London and New York as well as Timbuctoo and Samarkand!

While in Haparanda, why not slip across the border on the E4 and spend an afternoon in Tornio? One does not even need Finnish currency as they accept Swedish kroner just as readily. **Tornio** is the older town, the original city at the mouth of the Torne river. Founded

The restored interior of the Russian Orthodox church at Tornio

in 1621 by King Gustav II Adolf of Sweden it was lost when the boundary between Sweden and Finland was fixed as the middle of the Torne river. One can overlook the town from the café in the old water tower, or visit three interesting churches. Tornio church dates from 1686. Narrow, with high roofs, there are paintings round the 'domed' ceilings, an elaborate pulpit and pillars and pews painted with leaves and trees. Alatornio church is neo-Classical dating from 1797, with an interesting pulpit and altar. In contrasting style the tiny Orthodox church was built originally by the Russians for their soldiers and desecrated by the Finns after 1917. Restored to its original form, it looks brand new with its shining gold paint and locally produced icons. Lastly, there are botanical gardens, signed as an arboretum but containing herbaceous borders, rockery, roses and fuchsias, farmyard fowl, pond and a woodland walk. One word of warning: Finnish time is an hour ahead of Swedish, making churches and museums close prematurely!

One has now reached the sea, except that, as in Blekinge, the coast is elusive. Even the islands are so tree-covered that glimpses of the Gulf of Bothnia are rare. The main road along the coast is the E4, a good fast route which connects to other north/south roads, or through to Luleå. Sights along its way, like the 600m (660yd) long stone-arched bridge at **Nikkala**, are well signed. Finished in 1772, there is a monument to the villagers who built it and steps down to admire the mortarless construction of the arches. At **Sangis**, the grave mound on the former coastline is the most northerly in Sweden. **Kalix** church has suffered fire and plunder, yet retains a medieval triptych, the oldest pulpit in the diocese of Luleå, and two eighteenth-century oil paintings. The manor of Englundsgården, dating from the 1600s, is now a homestead museum. Beyond Kalix and the military restricted zone (drive straight through) one reaches **Töre**, where there are industrial remains, a nature trail, and a small hut museum. But the coastal area is not true Lappland. For that one needs to return inland.

The road north from Töre goes to **Överkalix**, whose church has a striking altar painting executed in 1943 and by the same artist a peace painting in 1945. There are views over the town from Brännaberget hill to the south. To the north there is a good waterfall on the Kalix river at Jokkfall. Take the main Pajala road to **Nybyn** where the Martingården is on the Jokkfall road. This farm museum includes two furnished houses and a variety of storehouses, one with sleighs, carriages and a boat. The 392 then follows the Kalix valley to Rödupp where there is a bright yellow motorised chain ferry to the far side. The Arctic Circle is crossed just past the Hotel Polarcirclet.

Jokkfall is an 8m (26ft) drop in the Kalix river, a wide fall with a salmon ladder, hiking trails, plus campsite and café. For a higher waterfall right out in the wilds, cross the bridge and go first left signed Vallsjärv, then first right. From Vallsjärv follow the Ängeså signs. This takes one through wooded countryside, past signed trails into the Svartberget nature reserve, into territory where reindeer are more common than motorcars. This is their breeding ground, so that one sees females with calves. After some 24km (15 miles) turn left into **Ängeså**, over the river and immediately right for **Linnafallet**. This is a further 13km (9 miles) away along a narrow unmade road but well worth the effort. Linnafallet is an 18m (59ft) high waterfall on the Ängesån. The Hängbro (a suspension bridge that bounces alarmingly under the feet) gives hiking access to the far side of the falls. Back at Ängeså turn right to join the 98 Överkalix to Gällivare road.

Another trip into the wilds can be made from here. Drive south to Yttre Lansjärv, then take the 813 towards Edefors. This unsurfaced numbered road passes various fishing lakes. After some 30km (19 miles) go left for Niemisel and 5km (3 miles) later left again for **Rikti Dokkas**. This is an old pioneer settlement set against a rocky hillside. There is a winter cottage and a much smaller summer cottage, a bake house, pump, sauna and various storehouses. In summer someone lives here. Beyond, a hilly, rocky nature path goes for a $1^1/_2$km (1 mile) circuit past lightning-blasted trees, old pines and a viewpoint. Unfortunately the explanatory boards about bark beetles and the life cycle of the pines, are in Swedish only.

From here, go north to **Nattavaaraby** where the pretty river Venetjoki has a picnic and bathing spot, to join the Gällivare-Jokkmokk road. **Gällivare** is certainly worth visiting for the number of attractions in the area. The homestead museum includes a specially built Lapp encampment with some English labelling. There is also the small and plain Lapp church, originally dubbed the one öre church because it was built from contributions of one öre from all over Sweden. Much more elaborate is the *Fjällnäs* 'Tree Castle' built by Englishman, Lieutenant Colonel Bergman in 1889. He sold his 211 mining concessions at Malmberget for 2,000,000 SEK and used 1,000,000 to build this Gothic wooden castle which is now a meeting place for the tenant owners' association.

Malmberget is the neighbouring town to the north, whose prosperity burgeoned from the iron ore mines, now owned by LKAB. They gave All Saints' Church to the town in 1944 (just as they built the Lapp church at Kiruna). The altar is cut from black iron ore but otherwise the influences are Lappish as in the riveted leather of the altar rail, the scenes on the silver baptismal basin and the figures in the stained glass windows. The gold altar painting was produced by two exiled Norwegians during World War II. To return to the mining industry, there are guided tours of the Vikefors and Aitik mines where tungsten and copper ore are also mined. A mining museum and, the shanty town of **Käkstan** which combines museum elements like Finn-Greta's log cabin, the Maplewood Inn and a teetotal café (with modern wares sold in the booths lining the Västerlånggatan) can also be visited. In Käkstan you can arrange to visit the Mariamine at Nautanen. Follow the Tjautjasjaur road out of Malmberget, past the statue of a miner pushing his ore tub at Koskullskulle until **Nautanen** is signed to the right. This is a *kulturminne* on a grand scale, covering the remains of the planned (as opposed to shanty-style) boom town that flourished here for just 9 years, from 1898 to 1907. Even when the Mariamine is closed, you can still feel the cold air emerging from the mine and read about the sites from the information boards. **Tjautjasjaur**, at the end of the road, is one of Swedish Lappland's many nature reserves. It includes trails suitable for pushchairs, bicycles or wheelchairs though you do need to boat across the lake in the first place! Enquire near the information board.

The next large centre is Jokkmokk, 105km (65 miles) south-west of Gällivare. The 88 goes all the way but on a clear day pause first for the

*Statue of a miner
pushing a tub at
Koskullskulle*

views from Dundrettoppstuga. Ignore the leisure complex signs for Dundret and continue for several kilometres south to find the signpost. The road goes right to the top for 110km (68 miles) of visibility in all directions. Further south the 88 skirts the northern edge of the Muddus National Park but there are no trails from this side, so continue to **Porjus**, where the striking 'power/strength/energy' monument stands above the old hydro-electric power plant. This now houses an underground power museum and a pictorial exhibition of the growth of this small community. This is the first of a series of power stations that harness the Stor Luleälven and guided tours are available via Jokkmokk or Gällivare tourist offices. Beyond the next (Harsprånget), the deep rocky gorge that the river once cut is impressive and the flat rocks above it invite picnics.

From the third power station, at Liggadamnen, one can reach Muddus National Park quite easily. Follow the signs from just before the bridge — there is a mere 13km (8 miles) of unmade road to reach the parking! The chief advantage of this reserve is this accessibility. So many of them involve travelling kilometres into the wilderness first, so that unless one is an outback enthusiast, fit and willing to camp in tourist huts, they are not a viable proposition, but at

*Walkway in the
Muddas National Park*

Muddus, the 100m (328ft) deep Moskoskorsu ravine is only 5km (3 miles) away along the river edge on a path that is fun, with plank walkways over marshes and bridges over the rivers. Alternatively a 7km (4 mile) trail leads northwards to the 42m (138ft) high Muddus waterfall. Wildlife in the park includes elk in the south, otters along river banks and bears in the west, but the daytime stroller is unlikely to encounter any of these. Longer trails include two circular routes, the shorter some 20km (12 miles) long, and overnight huts in two locations. The central lakes are bird sanctuaries with no access during the breeding season (15 March to 31 July) though there is a year round bird-watching tower overlooking them at Muddusluobbal, 12 to 15km (7 to 9 miles) into the reserve.

Seven kilometres (4 miles) north of Jokkmokk, the 805 heads for Kvikkjokk, 120km (74 miles) away, the gateway to the Sarek and Padjelanta national parks. It is worth exploring for a short way for its lake scenery. Nearer **Jokkmokk**, the Akkats Power Plant and Aquarium can be visited. Jokkmokk is a colourful town with flower displays, the Storknabben hill, giving good views from above, and a lake full of rainbow trout round which one can walk or jog. Closely connected with the Lapp or Sámi people, its name comes from a group of forest Sámi and means 'bend in the stream'. The settlement began in 1605 when King Karl IX chose the place for a market and a church in an attempt to civilise the Lapps. The market site was near the present Homestead Museum and the church where it still stands — though this is a modern replica, the original having burnt down in 1972. Externally it is a perfect reproduction including the wide timber 'wall' in which the coffins of people who died during the winter were kept until spring softened the ground enough to bury them! Internally modern Lapp tin thread embroidery decorates the altar and pulpit cloths. Ájtte is an imaginative Lapp museum, with full scale scenes from the Lapp way of life, wood models of their typical year, sound effects, and a slide show every hour.

For an interesting circular tour south of Jokkmokk, travel first on the 97 to Vuollerim. At Mattisudden, the Larveskogan on the right is a forestry area with long distance tracks. Just beyond, a timber floating dam (*Flottningsdamn*) has been reconstructed. These were used in the logging season to collect sufficient water in the side rivers for tree trunks to float down to the Lilla Luleälven, in the valley below. Where the road crosses the polar circle, the Skogsbruk information boards — displaying the life cycle of the trees and local flora and fauna — stand directly along the 66° 31' parallel, indicating clearly that it does not cross roads conveniently at right angles but is a true circle round the earth's surface. Beyond here cross a military zone with an airfield to reach **Vuollerim**. Turn into the village for the 6000-År complex about the discovery of a Stone Age settlement.

There is an exhibition and a 20-minute slide show in the small museum. To reach the sites, drive on; take the first left down and across the dam. At the T-junction beyond, go left and park at the toilet hut. Follow the track through the woods and down to river level to find the beautifully reconstructed site, its living tent covered with seventy elk hides and its chimney going right into the ground: they obviously had the world's first underfloor heating! There is also a hide canoe and all the paraphernalia necessary for Stone Age living. Visiting the reconstruction first enables one to understand the real site (park 200m [220yd] right from the T-junction: path left through trees) which is pegged out archaeological style with dips and pits and animal bones. The whole is well worth a visit but unfortunately is poorly signposted. Guided tours are arranged at the museum. While in Vuollerim, visit the church, prettily situated overlooking the lake, for the 'Life's Way' fresco that covers the altar wall. Now continue south to **Edefors** for walks beside the Luleålven. Here the English owners of the Gällivare mines started a canal to bypass the rapids so that their ore could travel downriver to the sea. They ran out of funds with the canal hardly begun and the rapids have been harnessed by the HEP industry. There are however several *kulturminnes* close by and short walks both here and round the lakes beside the Bodträskfors road. Follow this to reach the highest unexploited waterfalls in this part of Scandinavia. Right for Käbdalis, left for Vidsel, then right on the 374 brings one to **Storforsen** which is signed to the left on the Moskosel road. Storforsen is a wonderful area of rocks, walkways, bridges, boil holes, pools, and streams. The present falls which storm down the hillside for some 500m (550yd) were created by smoothing out the river bed so that timber could be floated on it. Although a major tourist attraction, even at the height of the season it is not over-crowded. Children can paddle in the pools and there is a specially built route for the disabled, a café and a nature path past buildings from bygone forestry days including a tar pit which shows clearly how pitch was made. From here return to Jokkmokk by the main road or continue south towards Älvsbyn. Passing after some 20km (12 miles), another fall on the Piteålven, the 11m (36ft) Fällforsen which stops salmon progressing any further up river. It is nothing by comparison with Storforsen, yet in its own right it is an impressive sight. Alternatively you could visit it from Älvsbyn, north on the Nystrand road, for you need to be south of the river to see it.

Another possible route from Storforsen is to continue cross country towards Moskosel. This is a good road, at least as far as the military airfield. Cross the river soon afterwards at Benbryteforsen where there is a map of all the rapids on the Piteålven. If you did not visit Storforsen then these would be a good substitute. Where road 88 is joined, old and new bridges cross the river side by side and here you can shoot the rapids on a rubber raft. If that does not appeal, go left to **Arvidsjaur**, which is a Lappish centre. Stop first at the old vicarage (Gamla Prastgården), an interesting homestead museum with lively English signs, lots of furnishings and old equipment. On into town and **Lappsteden** is signed to the left. This is the largest remaining Lapp church village in Sweden. A closely packed settlement of storehouses on stilts and low tent-shaped wooden living huts (one has to squat or lie down inside) they are still used by the Lapps on the occasion of church festivals. Some of the huts are opened up at lunchtime or in the evening for coffee. Nearby Arvas house specialises in Lapp dishes, sells their handicrafts, and arranges guided tours into Lapp territory, to join the reindeer herders for a day and watch roundups and the earmarking (literally) of the calves.

Road 95 through Arvidsjaur is both the Polar Road and the Silver Road, running from the coast at Skelefteå through the mountains to Bodø in Norway. It was opened in 1974, and its name refers to the silver that was mined at Nasafjäll in the seventeenth century, brought out by reindeer sledge and then transported down the waterways to the Gulf of Bothnia. On the way north it takes one to Arjeplog. Some 10km (6 miles) short of the town, watch for the Fornlämning sign marking the Rackträsk Lappish dwelling site, with trapping pits, hearths and a cooking place that make an interesting walk through light woodland. The Lucas Automotive sign one passes next refers to the fact that Arjeplog is now used in winter for testing car components in Arctic conditons — the lakes freeze up to a metre deep — a far cry from the silver industry of bygone years. Not silver but gold is the metal on the Galtispuoda road. This lovely road winds from island to island on causeways through the amazing scenario of lakes that surrounds Arjeplog. Follow the signs to the top of the 800m (2,624ft) mountain for a magnificent panorama. Water is everywhere, with a backdrop of rounded mountains and millions of fir trees. In winter cars drive over the frozen lakes and drag lifts bring the skiers to the top!

In **Arjeplog** the shingled church is a pretty pink outside and has a clear blue ceiling inside with the sun at its centre, and an altar painted in the eighteenth century by a 22-year old artist. The pulpit is from the original seventeenth-century church. The Silver and Lapp Museum next door contains Lapp costumes, artefacts and silverwork including five rare medieval collars and a sixteenth-century chalice from Nürnberg. Other displays include settlers' equipment, a schoolroom, and local birds and animals in natural surroundings.

For a pretty and interesting route that loops through the countryside from here to Sorsele, go north first on the 95, which gives good views of the many lakes. Turn left for **Laisvall** just after the Laisdalen information board but bypass the village and head straight for Gruva, a mine producing lead, zinc and silver where there are short guided tours three times a week. Return south, through Laisvall, to pick up the Slagnäs road. Soon after Bätsjaur it threads its way scenically on causeways between lakes. Cross the Laisälven beyond Marielund, where Sorsele is signed. Below here there is a series of very accessible rapids — Ågotsforsen, Batsaforsen and Trollsforsen. All are clearly signed to the left and within easy walking distance of

*A six-sailed wooden windmill
at the Ruovesi Museum,
Finland (Chapter 14)*

*Häme castle at Hämeenlinna ,
Finland (Chapter 14)*

Logs being towed down the Pielisjoki at Joensuu on the Finnish Lakes (Chapter 15)

The interior of the Lintulan Convent, Finnish Lakes (Chapter 15)

Lapp turf huts at Gillesnuole

the road. Some have barbecue sites; all are connected by a riverside path. Watch too for a *kulturminne* of reindeer pits and later the display board, map and reconstructed pit that effectively explains the trapping system that runs all along the valley.

There is another good viewpoint in this area, similar to Galtis-puoda, at Arjeplog. Called Naloverdo, it also has a road to the top, though its condition is abysmal. It gives extensive views over Storvindeln and hills beyond. It isn't many kilometres from here to Sorsele but, given good weather and an afternoon or more to spare, why not drive up the Vindel valley to Ammarnäs? For the energetic there is a 4km (2 mile) footpath from Vendelberga to the top of Kyrkberget, giving similar views to those from Naloverdo. The Gillesnuole Kapell, beyond **Gillesnuole** village, is an eighteenth-century Lapp chapel with a tiny cemetery and collection of Lapp buildings including two turf huts. Services are held there several times a summer. Approaching Ammarnäs one enters the Vinde-fjallens Naturreservat, an area of long distance trails, such as the one signed 25km (15^1/$_2$ miles) to the Viktoriakapellet. There are more rapids by the roadside at Järnforsen and Sjöforsen and even a sea-plane for sightseeing flights.

Ammarnäs, a mountain village used first by the Lapps but then settled in the nineteenth century, sprawls round the head of the 'lake'. The Lapps still have a church village here, less regimented than the one at Arvidsjaur, which they use three times a year — the

Sunday before Midsummer, the first Sunday in July, and the last Sunday in September. The early settlers are remembered in the Hembygdsgården and the potato hill. An unusual moraine mound, it was planted with potatoes by the very first settler, Nils Jensen, back in 1830 and so propitious a site is it that they still grow potatoes down its sides today. For overhead views of the valley, with its hay meadows, and the wilderness beyond, the gondola ski lift runs up Näsberget in the summer too. One could of course walk through the wilderness on one of the long distance trails that are signed at the Vindelåforsen bridge and from N Ammarnäs. The longest of them all, the Kungsleden path, passes close by. For a shorter walk, follow the $4^1/_2$km (3 mile) path from N Ammarnäs to Örnbo, an old mountain farm perched above the lake which has been restored and is open to visitors. Before returning to Sorsele, visit the Naturum which has excellent displays of flora and fauna and is also the tourist office.

From Sorsele, the 88/94 leads directly across country through Arvidsjaur and Älvsbyn to Luleå but Lappland does not stop just because one has crossed from Norrbotten into Vasterbotten. An interesting loop southwards can be made on the way to Luleå. Go south on the 88 Storumen road beside the Vindelålven, the same river as runs through Ammarnäs. Blattniksele is pleasantly situated on an islanded lake shortly before it ends in the Sandsele rapids. Turn right towards Malå, past more rapids here and again beyond Gargbro. There are two tiny Lapp settlements signed to the left soon after Bolheden. The first is **Koppsele**, a hut and two storehouses on the side of a hill a 3km (2 miles) walk away along a track. Remains of an irrigation system can be seen there too. The other, **Setsele**, is more accessible, a 1km drive to a hut and storehouse that are still used today. Alternately, in **Malå** another Lappish church village hides behind the industry at the foot of the hill. A mineral trail and nature paths on the hill itself start from the tourist office and lead up to a V-shaped channel in the rock down which, according to legend, Lapps used to send their aged relatives when they were too old for the annual migration north! There is also a homestead museum at the far end of the village.

South of Malå note the tall concrete posts that carried the Boliden Co's ore buckets on the world's longest cableway from 1943 to 1987. It was built because of wartime shortages of coal and oil as a winterproof and cheaper form of transport. A 13km (8 mile) stretch between Menträsk and Örträsk has been converted from ore buckets to gondolas and operates three times a day in each direction as a tourist attraction with a free bus to return passengers to their cars and the option of a 'cabin lunch' to eat aboard. **Menträsk** is the less popular starting point, probably because all the activities (museum, kiddies tub train ride, gold washing) are at **Örträsk**. Both are signed off the 370 between Lilhomträsk and Bjurträsk. The trip needs booking in advance. Allow a good 3 hours as it is a very leisurely ride.

While in the area, **Norsjö**, just to the south is worth visiting. Turn right at the end of the Gisströsk lake, right and left across the 365 following 'Norsjö', then right for Björknäs. This minor road circles the Norsjön, giving good views — follow the road with the street lamps at the first junction! Coming round the lake, turn right into Arnberg. The Halsöbrunn (spa), signed left, is a natural spring in a tiny pool of rust brown mineral water discovered by Norsjö's first chaplain in 1819. In Norsjö itself, Vajsjön is a bird reserve with a viewing tower. The church has an interesting painted ceiling in the chancel and the Ski Museum is well done with scenarios (look for all the tiny and amusing details) and a workshop demonstrating the making of skis. Also well worth visiting is the Dahlbergskagården at Bastutjärn where five generations of the same family lived from the early nineteenth century to 1979. They built the house and most of the furnishings, including the organ, were made on the premises.

From here for a good cross country route to Älvsbyn, go right on the 370 along the Skelefteålven and through the prettily situated village of Petiknäs. Head north then through Jörn for Långträsk, Storsund and Älvsbyn. There is nothing of special interest unless one counts a huge *minnesten* (memorial stone) to the men who built the railway in 1893, but the mixture of scenery is good — river crossings, lakes, comparatively open forest and a hilly, twisty section near the end that gives good longer views.

At **Älvsbyn** one is out of true Lapp territory and within easy reach of Luleå and its airport. There is a church village, this time built for the settlers and consisting of a mixture of tiny cabins and two-storey houses. The most impressive church village remaining of the seventy-two that once existed in the whole of Sweden is that at Gammelstad, which is the old town of **Luleå**. The original town was founded in the fourteenth century, the red and grey granite block church in the fifteenth century. The magnificent gilded wood altarpiece from Antwerp is also fifteenth century as are the frescoes in the chancel and the sculpted ends of the choir stalls. The sumptuous pulpit and the commemoration tablets are eighteenth century. In its early days it was stronghold as well as church, and loopholes can still be seen in the gatehouses. However, the present wall would be useless for defence — its earth covering is perforated with sand martins' nest holes! To explore the old town properly buy the guide from the on site tourist office and follow the suggested walks, otherwise the tiny streets and alleys may leave a confused impression. At the bottom of Gamla Hamngatan, a nature path leads into the wetland that was once Gammelstad's harbour. Now a bird paradise, there are three observation towers along the walk. To the left of this 'harbour', the Friluftsmuseum (or Hägnan Rural Heritage Park) contains preserved farm buildings where demonstrations of crafts and musical events take place at weekends. The church cottage at 253 Framlänningsvägen, is also open, showing its simple kitchen and bed-sitting room, all that was needed for a stay of just a few days. Conveniently close to Luleå, a visit to Gammelstad can easily fill in that odd half day hanging about for a flight back to Stockholm!

Further Information

— Swedish Lappland —

All times are for the summer season, usually June to August.

Ammarnäs
Hembygdsgården
Open: 6-8pm daily.

Linbanen (gondolas)
11am-5pm daily.

Naturum
Open: daily.

Arjeplog
Silver and Lapp Museum
Open: 9am-6pm daily.

Arvidsjaur
Arvas Lapp Centre
Open: 10am-8pm daily.
☎ (0960) 125 25 for special Lapp tours.

Gamla Prastgården
Open: Monday to Friday 10am-7pm. Saturday and Sunday 12noon-4pm.
Lapp village, Houses open: 11am-1pm and 6-8pm daily.

Gällivare
Lapp Church
Open: 9am-6pm daily.

Homestead Museum and Lapp Camp
Open: 10am-8pm daily.

Jokkmokk
Ájtte Lapp Museum
Open: mid-June to mid-August, Monday to Friday 9am-7pm. Saturday and Sunday 11am-7pm. After mid-August Monday to Friday 9am-4pm. Saturday and Sunday 12noon-4pm.

Akkats Power Plant and Aquarium
Open: mid-June to mid-August, 10am-4pm daily.

Homestead Museum
Open: 10am-5pm daily.

Lapp Church and New Church
Open: June and mid- to end August daily 8am-4pm. Beginning July to mid-August 8am-8pm daily.

Kalix
Church
Open: mid- to end June and August 9am-6pm. July 9am-7pm daily.

Englundsgården
Open: late June to mid-August 12noon-5pm daily.

Kukkola
Fishing Museum
Open: 10am-7pm daily. White water rafting at 1pm and 7pm.

Laisvall
Gruva Lead Mine
Guided tours Monday, Wednesday and Friday 12noon.

Luleå
Gammelstad Church Village
Church
Open: June and August 9am-6pm. July 9am-8pm daily except during services.

Church Cottage
Open: Monday to Friday 10am-6pm. Saturday and Sunday 10am-5pm.

Friluftsmuseum
Open: mid-June to mid-August 11am-5pm daily.

Malmberget
Aitik Mine Tour
Leaves Gällivare tourist office at 1pm, Monday, Wednesday, Thursday and Friday, late June to early August.

All saints Church
Open: Monday to Saturday 11am-6pm. Sunday 1-6pm.

Käkstan Shanty Town
Open: mid-June to early August 11am-7pm daily. Guided tours 1pm and 3pm. Tours of the Mariamine are arranged from here.

Mining Museum
Open: mid-June to mid-August 10am-5pm daily.

Vikefors Iron Mine
Leaves Gällivare tourist office at 9.45am, weekdays mid-June to early August.

Norsjö
Church
Open: 7am-4pm daily.

Dahlbergskagården
At Bastutjärn
Open: 12noon-6pm daily.

Ski Museum
Open: mid-June to mid-August, 11am-4pm and 5-7pm daily.

Nybyn
Martingården
Open: Monday to Friday 11am-6pm, Saturday and Sunday 12noon-6pm.

Örträsk and Menträsk
Linbana
Open: mid-May to late September.
For booking inquire Världens Langsta Linbana
Storgatan 52
S-93500 Norsjö
☎ (0918) 11390

Övertorneå
Church
Open: 9am-5pm or 6pm daily.

Folk museum
Open: mid-June to mid-August 9am-6pm daily.

Tärendö
Homestead Museum
Open: late June to early August. Monday to Saturday 11am-6pm. Sunday 1-4pm.

Tornio
Alatornio Church
Open: beginning June to mid-August, Monday to Friday 9am-3pm.

Alatornio Local Museum
Open: Monday to Friday 12noon-4pm.

Orthodox Church
Open: 10am-6pm daily.

Panorama Tower
Open: 9am-10pm daily.

Tornio Wooden Church
Open: Monday to Friday 9am-5pm.

Voullerim
6000-År
Open: 10am-6pm daily.

Tourist Information Centres

Älvsbyn
Storgatan 6
S-94200 Älvsbyn
Open: June to August.
☎ (0929) 17200

Ammarnäs
Ammarnäsgården
S-920 75 Ammarnäs
Open: June to August.
☎ (0952) 60132

Arjeplog
Storgatan 20
Torget
S-930 90 Arjeplog
☎ (0961) 11220

Arvidsjaur
Östra Skolgatan 18
S-933 00 Arvidsjaur
☎ (0960) 15800

Gällivare
Storgatan 16
S-972 00 Gällivare
☎ (0970) 16660

Haparanda
Storgatan 92
S-953 00 Haparanda
Open: June to August.
☎ (0922) 15804

Jokkmokk
Porjusvägen 4
S-960 40 Jokkmokk
☎ (0971) 12140

Kalix
Fritidskonteret
Parallelgatan 4
S-952 00 Kalix
Open: June to August.
☎ (0923) 65122

Kiruna
Hjalmar Lundboms-
vägen 42
S-981 85 Kiruna
☎ (0980) 18880

Luleå
Rådstugatan 9
S-951 31 Luleå
☎ (0920) 93746

Malå
Storgatan 13
S-930 70 Malå
☎ (0953) 11297

Överkalix
Wärdshuset Naisheden 1
S-95600 Överkalix
☎ (0926) 27031

Övertorneå
Matarengivägen 27
S-950 94 Övertorneå
Open: June to August.
☎ (0927) 10535

Pajala
Kirunagägen 3
S-970 40 Pajala
☎ (0978) 10015

Sorsele
Stationsgatan
S-920 70 Sorsele
Open: June to August.
☎ (0952) 11185

Tornio
Lukiokatu 10
SF 954 Tornio
☎ (9698) 40048

Vuollerim
Folkets Hus
S-960 30 Vuollerim
Open: June to August.
☎ (0976) 10645

13 • The Åland Islands

Åland is a collection of 6,000 islands and skerries set in the Gulf of Bothnia midway between Sweden and Finland. By language and culture they are Swedish but were lost to Russia in the 1808-9 war. When Finland declared its independence in 1917, the Ålanders demanded reunion with Sweden. Instead, the League of Nations awarded them to Finland but they were guaranteed their Swedish lifestyle and autonomy. Today they have their own parliament and regional citizenship, demilitarisation, a thriving cultural life and economic ties with both Sweden and Finland — though Finland retains overall responsibility for such things as taxation. Tourism is growing but they are largely unspoiled, offering 'away from it all' holidays rather than attractions in the normal tourist sense. The only town is Mariehamn. Even Eckerö, the nearest ferry port to Sweden, is little more than a dock. Transport to the islands is very easy and amazingly cheap, the rival lines making their money out of their duty-free shops and restaurants. The ferries, large and luxurious, arrive frequently from Stockholm, Kappellskär, and Grisslehamn in Sweden and from Turku and Naantali in Finland. There are also flights into Mariehamn.

The islands are divided into sixteen districts of which the ruling one is **Mariehamn** in the sense that the government buildings and consulates are there. Called the 'Town of a Thousand Linden Trees' for its avenues of limes, it is a spacious place of broad streets and individual buildings. Ferries from Sweden and Finland come and go at its busy port all day long and into the night. They bring the tourists who are the most rapidly expanding branch of the Åland economy, but shipping has always dominated her trade. This is reflected in the Maritime Museum. Most impressive is the entire front deck, with the captain's salon and quarters down below, preserved from the four-masted sailing barque, the *Herzogin Cecilie*. The museum also owns the *Pommern*, anchored in the harbour outside. Built in 1903 in Glasgow for a German shipping company, she is a four mast steel

247

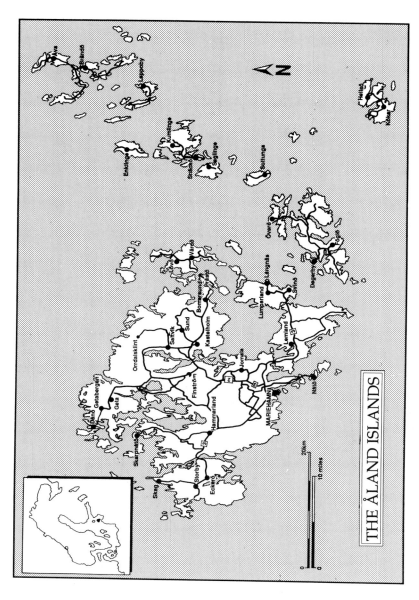

THE ÅLAND ISLANDS

barque with a total sail area of 3,160sq m (3,800sq yd) yet only a twenty-six man crew to work her on the wheat run from Australia to England. She was bought by an Åland shipping magnate in 1923 and pensioned off to the museum in 1952. There is also a town museum

The sailing ship Pommern *is now part of the Maritime Museum at Mariehamn*

with imaginative displays of Åland life from prehistory to recent times. The fishingscape is particularly well done with its different eye levels as is the house-moving scene with the cart surrounded by the carved wooden spindles that were traditionally given to Åland brides. There is also a chemist's shop and the Merchant's House by Tullarnsäng shows typical shop goods that were for sale in the nineteenth century. Tullarnsäng is a woody park which also contains metal figures, a mineral spring with a working pump, stone laby-rinth and the charming Lilla Holmen with its pond, collection of fowl, rabbits and guinea pigs, and its sandy bathing beach. Children can enjoy the Ålandparken's Tivoli-style activities while adults might prefer the trotting races held just north of the town.

Apart from what Mariehamn has to offer, there are very few of the normal tourist attractions for the delight of the Åland islands is their unspoilt peace and quiet. A good way to explore is by bicycle, on hire from various centres, as the terrain is only mildly hilly. There are kilometres of signed routes on the main island and special bicycle ferries to save one returning down long no-through roads as the motorist frequently must and one can island hop on the free car ferries. Kayaks are also for hire as are boats and fishing gear. The waters shelter a variety of fish and permits can be bought. Ask for advice or even a guide to help find the best places. Otherwise it is walking, swimming and sunbathing and doing one's own thing from one of the many holiday cottages available.

Travelling round the countryside the most striking sights are the midsummer poles. Decorated for the midsummer festival with green garlands and brightly coloured ribbons in stylized shapes, they are topped with a flag, a symbolic sun and four sailing ships (for seafaring) to power it round. Midsummer is celebrated with traditional dances round the pole and then it is left in place until the following June when it is lowered and redecorated. There are also small red windmills on many farms, once the means of self-sufficient grain-grinding. The older farmhouses are all built to a pattern. The central door is flanked by two gracious windows. Above, a row of little windows run beneath the roof, while a tall window in each end lights the upper rooms. Porches, that are often rooms in themselves, are later additions. Inside, the ground floor contains just two rooms, both large, high and light. One is the 'everything' room with huge fire-cum-oven for cooking, large table for preparing and eating, and two-tiered curtained beds for sleeping in the warmest place in the house. The other room is often an elegant best room. Upstairs are store places and workrooms for weaving and spinning. Most of Åland's districts have small museums some of which are these old farmhouses. Every district too has its church, most of them medieval edifices in the local red granite that outcrops through the surface wherever the soil is thin. All are worth visiting for their wooden sculptures and frescoes.

No routes are given in this chapter as the whole area is small and can be visited from any centre in any order. Instead each district will be described in turn, starting with Jomala which is north of Mariehamn. On the Eckerö road out of Mariehamn, Ramsholmen peninsula has a nature reserve with flowering meadows. The highest point here is Ingbyberget. Park on the old road at the Ingby crossroads and walk up the signed path. A different sight is to the north of Overby on the Jomala road. Called Ryss-Petters Brunn, it is a large wooden well, 3sq m (32sq ft) and 24m (79ft) deep. Lift the cover and look inside through the iron grill.

Hammarland is north-west from here. St Catherine's church is typical for Åland. Squat and pink, made of the red granite that

The church at Eckerö is shaped like a longhouse

underlies the soil, its oldest parts are medieval. It contains an early font, leaf-painted roof vaults with just the one picture of God holding a two-barred cross, an old pew front and an ornate nineteenth-century pulpit with delicate hourglass. A 32-mound Iron Age cemetery lies to the west of the church and individual church stables beyond that. The *fornborg* in the vicinity is an Iron Age hill fort. Travelling to Skarpnåtö the northernmost tip of the district, one passes the little Gårdsmuseum at Postad (open on request).

Skarpnåtö's museum is run as a family enterprise. The oldest storehouse is a salesroom for wooden and woollen handicrafts that have been made during the winter. Even the sheep and the wool factory belong to relatives. The farmhouse, the original family home, contains only articles that have always been there. Used for a film of one of Anni Blomqvist's stories, nine layers of wallpaper were stripped to reveal the painted patterns beneath. The bread hanging in the kitchen was made for the film in 1974. The bicycle ferry that goes from nearby is also family-run but motorists must return the way they came.

Eckerö is the westernmost district. Its church, shaped like a longhouse, contains some murals and several medieval statues, the most interesting being the Gotland Madonna and child with altered hairstyles to suit sixteenth-century ideals of fashion. Eckerö is of course a ferry port but it is not a town, although the post and customs house recalls the time when it had pretensions to grow into one. As

The café at Getabergen

the nearest point to Sweden it was an important stage in the mail route from Sweden to Finland. The island hopping was done by local farmers turned postmen who in winter had to push their rowboat across the ice on a journey from Stockholm to Turku that could take 23 days! A small museum features one of the old mail boats. At **Käringsund**, smooth rocks shelter the fishing harbour-cum-marina with typical Swedish boat sheds rimming the quiet water. There is also a wildlife park with deer.

Storby has a local museum too. One room contains Åland's first bank with wind-up telephone, early typewriter, adding machines, and a display of coins. There are also furnished rooms and a display of clothes. The black gown with matching boots was an 1840s wedding dress — not until the twentieth century did Åland brides wear white. There is also an Eckerö national costume and a case displaying the other district variations on dolls. At **Skag**, to the north, a 2.8km (2 miles) circular path goes from Uddens Stugby. Turn left at the end of the road following white marks over expanses of red granite past twisted pines and down to the coast. It is unbelievably peaceful.

Geta, on the northern part of this main island, also has its church, its walk and its local museum. The church has an old bell in the porch and the door opens with a tiny hand but inside it is plain: just a few faded frescoes and an interesting George and the Dragon sculpture. The walk goes from the viewpoint (a whole 99m, 325ft high) of Getabergen, that looks out over the western coast and seas. A white-marked trail leads from the cairn by the café to a cave 2km (1 mile) away. Take a picnic and admire the view — it is better than the cave — as the return walk, being uphill, feels longer! The small *hembygdsgård* is at Dånö.

Finström, in the centre, has one of the best churches with a quantity of frescoes containing unusual elements. For example there are two boats and also two very childish figures with birds and a very old wooden head stuck to the roof. There are many medieval wood sculptures and a large votive ship from 1688, the type of double-decked ship that served in Charles XIs navy. The 1768 organ in the porch is still used for concerts and at Christmas. Leaving Finström going east, you have to cross the Färjsund bridge. The last left before this, signed with a coffee cup, leads to parking and a walk up to the café that gives views over the sound. Descending, the Godby arboretum is opposite with a $1^1/_2$km (1 mile) trail through mixed woods with labelled trees — it helps to know the Latin names!

Beyond the bridge, **Saltvik** is the district to the north. Twelfth-century St Mary's Church contains some frescoes, a thirteenth-century crucifix and an interesting stone sculpture over the porch. There are also lots of prehistoric sites labelled *fornminne* or *fornborg* depending on whether they are grave sites or old forts. The most interesting place is Orrdalsklint, at 129m (423ft) the highest point on Åland. The red granite cliffs tower above the track that is driveable as far as the picnic place. Halfway there, the footpath labelled *grottan* leads for $1^1/_2$km (1 mile) through woods and across rocks — clearly marked again in white — to a large cave at the base of similar cliffs. From here a further $1^1/_2$km (1 mile) leads to Orrdalsklint.

The last 'mainland' district and the one with most of interest is **Sund** on the south-east corner. Here Kastelholm is the only Åland castle still in existence. Its exact origins and founder are unknown, the first reference to it being in 1388. It has been added to and altered since and is currently under longterm restoration by Finnish prisoners so one is not free to wander round. Instead there are six guided tours a day. A circular walk from the nearest parking goes between lake and castle to Jan Karlsgårdens *hembygdsgård*. This is an excellent collection of old buildings, labelled in English, with good information on such topics as the absolute necessity of possessing a 15-20cm stone when constructing a wattle fence! There are viewing doors into interiors and the main house has a drawing room beautifully painted with elegant townscapes. Circling back you pass the prison museum. It is an authentic jailhouse with warder's office, his family living quarters (which are almost as cramped as the prisoners' cells), and

The remains of the Crimean War fortress at Bomarsund

these latter furnished for four different periods. There are also some nasty-looking sets of chains, a wash house and an exercise yard. A completely different circular walk can be undertaken on the opposite side of the lake following the golf course signs. Some 300m (330yd) beyond the clubhouse there is a forest trail, 2.7km (2 miles) through woods and down to the lake.

The other main attraction in Sund is the Bomarsund fortress area where a major battle was fought in the Crimean War. The Russians had started fortifying this eastern corner of Åland in the 1830s but never finished and after capturing it, the French and British destroyed most of what remained so that what can be seen today is fragments of walls and towers. The site is clearly labelled and a good English leaflet is available from the Bomarsund Museum in the old pilot house across the bridge on Prästö. Three tower sites can be visited. Brännklintstornet has a section of wall complete with gun intact; Notvikstornet is the best preserved while Prästö is little more than rubble. Djävulsberget is a natural rocky outcrop within this area that the Russians never got round to fortifying. On the highest point, it gives the best views of the whole area. The military hospital was on Prästö and that fact plus cholera epidemics account for the large number of cemeteries to be found here. Because the Russian army was polyglot, different cemeteries were provided for the different religions. One walk passes the Orthodox cemetery to the Jewish and Muslim ones. The last has no visible graves left but the other two have some headstones with translations provided. The language used is interesting as are the Judaic dates. More recent graveyards exist too, as the local people are still buried here. If you want to visit more remains, there is an Iron Age hill fort on the Björby road and Sund church contains a stone cross with runic inscriptions from the grave of Archbishop Wenni who died in AD936.

Lemland and Lumparland, connected by causeways and bridges to the main island, are the gateway to the outer districts. One passes into **Lemland** over a canal — notice the old swing bridge now used by the roadside café as part of its outdoor seating. **Lemböte** chapel is a twelfth-century seafarers' chapel on the old route from Denmark to Russia. This seems impossible now, seeing how high it is above the water, but the sea level was higher then and the route is one of the earliest to be chronicled in northern Europe. In the sixteenth century it lost its importance as larger sailing ships had no need to island hop and the chapel fell into decay. It has now been repaired and is occasionally used for services. Beyond the chapel, above the sea, it is possible to find two split stone compasses and, on the highest point, a navigation cairn. There is also a path from Hellestorp to Kasberget the local high point, at 58m (190ft). Lemland church contains segments of wall high frescoes in a formal style with Roman and Byzantine borders between the pictures, medieval sculptures and a seventeenth-century ship model.

The delightful causeway road south of Mariehamn also counts as Lemland district. This area is rich in bird life and there is an interesting nature trail at Nåtö. Park if possible at the biological station. From there it is 2.4km ($1^1/_2$ miles) for the whole round route, with short cuts available. One passes through deciduous and pine woods, tiny meadows and out to the shore. The information boards are in Swedish but they do include pictures. The route is well-signed and boarded in the dampest places.

Beyond Lemland proper, one passes into **Lumparland** whose church is the oldest of the three wooden churches on Åland. Beautifully sited overlooking the water, its interior is dominated by a nineteenth-century Finnish altarpiece of Christ welcoming one into the church. The apostles on the gallery are eighteenth century — St Matthew, on one of the walls, was moved when the railing was shortened! Incidentally, in 1988 the parish of Lemland/Lumparland was the first in Finland to have a female priest. For exercise, there is a $2^1/_2$km ($1^1/_2$ mile) forest trail from Långnäsbyn Stugor near the ferry port of Långnäs.

The other districts are separate islands reached by the ferry serv-

The island of Föglö, reached by ferry from Lumparland

ices. These are free at present though there is talk of the Finnish government imposing a tax on them. Most can be pre-booked from abroad, otherwise queue early in the peak season. Caravans are discouraged by only taking them if the boat is not full with other vehicles. The ferries thread their way through the hundreds of rocky skerries that form the Åland archipelago, occasionally making unscheduled stops for deliveries. **Sottunga** is the smallest district. There is a red wood church and a forest trail and little else but then the pleasure of the smaller islands is in the opportunity to get away from it all, to swim, sunbathe and fish.

Kökar is a larger area that can be visited as a day trip from Långnäs. Once it was home to a Franciscan monastery. Later stones from the ruin were used to build the present church on the same site. Its interior is vivid with bright blue trims and it contains a variety of religious sculptures of different types and periods. Do not miss the unusual birds flying over the pulpit or the early chandelier. Nearby a small museum has been built into the old monastic cellar. Even older remains, from Otterböte's Bronze Age seal hunters' settlement lie at the end of a clear pathway, beneath a rocky outcrop that gives wide views. There are fishing harbours and long narrow inlets and in the museum at **Hellsö** an old boat along with fishing and bird hunting displays. Nothing is labelled in English but much is self-explanatory and the large collection of old photographs adds atmosphere.

From Svinö on Lumparland one can island hop, sampling some of the outer islands. The ferry takes you to **Föglö**, an island group linked by bridges and causeways. It arrives at **Degerby**, an attractive place with tree-lined streets running parallel with the shore. Just by the harbour one of the red wood sheds houses a small fishing museum. The one next door was once a customs house. Apart from Degerby and Föglö church, which is less interesting than most, there is nothing to 'do' here in the tourist sense. The roads link small farming communities lying between woods. It is a district above all of water and water-based activities. To leave, go north via an ordinary yellow ferry to Överö to catch the ferry to Snäckö on Kumlinge. Incidentally, you need to know the name of the ferry for the route you are travelling as they are not labelled with destinations and all leave from the same quay. Names are given in the ferry timetables available from the tourist office in Mariehamn, hotels, camp sites etc.

There is a yellow ferry from Snäckö to **Seglinge** if one wishes to explore this tiny island with its harbours, scattering of villages and pottery-cum-café at Skärvan. If not, **Kumlinge**'s main claim to fame is its beautifully decorated church. Franciscan style paintings cover the roof vaults and descend some of the walls. Other lower ones were lost when parishioners tried to clean off soot after Russian troops had used the church for stables and billets during the Great Northern War. Most are clearly etched and highly stylised but there is a delightful serpent's head trying to swallow Eve opposite the entrance. Also worthy of note are the mid-thirteenth-century reredos and the triumphal crucifix. One leaves Kumlinge from the north for Hummelvik on Vårdö.

Vårdö's church is much plainer. Its most interesting artefacts are a glass chandelier, an 1854 rug on the walls and the Byzantine style icons of saints on the gallery. Opposite, there is a short remaining stretch of post road that was used from 1638 to 1910 and beside the road to Mariehamn three old style kilometre posts have been restored. To the north at **Lövö**, Seffersmuseum is one of the old style farmhouses.

The remaining group of islands, out at **Brändö**, are a veritable chain, linked by causeway, bridge and ferry and surrounded by a wilderness of skerries that sport names not because anyone lives there but solely to identify them for navigational purposes. There is a nineteenth-century church at Brändö, an archipelago museum at Lappoby and a homestead museum at Ava. Brändö is much harder to reach than any other Åland district as the only way to do a day trip is by leaving at 4am or returning at midnight. Alternatively one could cross them from Finland on a free ferry route from the tiny port of Osnäs way out in the Finnish archipelago — just one last route for reaching these unspoilt island gems.

Further Information
— The Åland Islands —

Eckerö
Mailboat Museum
Open: June to August daily 9am-4pm.

St Lars Church
Open: June to August, Monday to Friday 10am-8pm. Saturday 10am-6pm. Sunday 12noon-6pm.

Storby Rural and Bank Museum
Open: June to August daily 9.30am-3.30pm.

Finström
St Michael's Church
Open: June to August, Monday to Friday 10am-4pm.

Föglö
Föglö Museum
Open: mid-June to mid-August, Tuesday to Sunday 12noon-2.30pm and 3.30-7pm.

Geta
Dånö Museum
Open: late June to mid-August, Tuesday, Thursday and Sunday 1.30-4.30pm.

St Gorans Church
Open: June to August, Monday to Saturday 10am-6pm. Sunday 12noon-6pm.

Hammarland
Skarpnåtö Museum
Open: June to August, Tuesday to Saturday 11am-3pm. Sunday 12noon-3pm.

St Catherine's Church
Open: mid-May to end August, Monday to Saturday 9am-4pm. Sunday 12noon-4pm.

Kökar
Hellsö Museum
Open: mid-June to mid-August daily 1-5pm.

St Anne's Church and Franciscan Cellar
Open: June to August daily 9am-9pm.

Kumlinge
St Anna's Church
Open: June to August, Monday to Saturday 10am-6pm. Sunday 12noon-6pm.

Lemland
St Birgitta's Church
Open: early June to early August, Monday to Friday 11am-3pm.

Lumparland
St Andrew's Church
Open: early June to early August, Monday to Friday 11am-3pm.

Mariehamn
Ålandsmuseum and Kunstmuseum
Open: May to August, Wednesday to Monday 10am-4pm, Tuesday 10am-8pm. September, Tuesday to Sunday 11am-4pm.

Ålandsparken
Open: May to August daily 10am-9pm. September, Saturday and Sunday 10am-9pm.

Merchant's House
Open: mid-June to mid-August, Monday to Friday 1-3pm.

Museum Ship Pommern *and Sjöfartsmuseum (Maritime)*
Open: May, June, August and September daily 9am-5pm. July daily 9am-7pm.

Saltvik
St Mary's Church
Open: June to August, Monday to Saturday 10am-4pm. Sunday 12noon-4pm.

Sund
Bomarsund Museum
Open: June to August, Tuesday to Sunday 10am-3pm.

Jan Karlsgårdens Hembygdsgård
Open: May to September daily 9am-9pm.

Kastelholm Castle
Open: early May to end August. Guided tours 10.45am-4pm.

St John the Baptist Church
Open: June to August, Monday to Saturday 9am-4pm. Sunday 12noon-4pm.

Vita Bjorn Prison Museum
Open: May to September daily 10am-5pm.

Vårdö
St Matthew's Church
Open: June to August, Monday to Saturday 10am-6pm. Sunday 12noon-6pm.

Tourist Information Centre

Ålands Turistinformation
Storagatan 11
SF-22100 Mariehamn
Åland
☎ 27300

14 • Finland's West Coast

Introduction to Finland

Finland is the most easterly of the Scandinavian countries. One can travel further east here than in any other European country, beyond the Balkans to a line of latitude running through Turkey. Geographically it resembles Sweden with its square kilometres of pine and birch and its thousands of lakes; ethnically it does not. Although ruled by Sweden for much of its history, only 6 per cent of the population, on the western seaboard, speak Swedish. The rest speak Finnish, a language so different from any European counterpart that a small dictionary is an essential part of the traveller's luggage. English language tourist information is available but unfortunately gives only the English translation for the attractions which does not help one find them when they are signposted in Finnish. To overcome this problem, the attractions here are given their Finnish names as well and to help with life in general here is a short list of useful words:

Hissi —	a lift
Kelirikko —	unsurfaced road
Keskuska —	town centre
Kiitos —	thank you
Kotiseutumuseo —	local museum
Laivalturi —	pier for lake cruises
Lountopolku —	trail
Ravintola —	restaurant
Satama —	harbour
Taide —	art
Torni —	lookout tower
Ulos —	exit
Vuori —	hill/fort

Driving in Finland is on the right and not difficult apart from in towns where everyone gives way to the right at junctions. In the countryside all main roads are surfaced and one can travel from town to town quickly and easily while keeping a weather eye open for elk. As large and heavy as a small horse and possessed of no traffic sense whatsoever, an adult male can cause a serious accident. Once embarked on crossing a road nothing deflects it from its purpose and the only way to avoid it is to pass **behind**. Injured elk **must** be reported to the police. Reindeer are found in the north while lynx and bears are mainly in the national parks. Most of the tourist attractions are in the towns and for this reason less country routes are given here than elsewhere. Some unsurfaced roads are used but they should cause no problems. Where routes cross ferries it is worth knowing that these are all free and operate shuttle services apart from four 12-minute coffee breaks a day. Hotels and restaurants do not always have English menus (another case for a good phrasebook) and it might be useful to know that most serve a salad starter as part of the price of the main course. In the evenings in the small towns there is often live music with the locals meeting for a drink and a dance.

For activities there is a wide variety of museums, including local ones generally close to the large wooden cruciform nineteenth-century churches. Most of these are extremely plain as befits the Lutheran religion. Certain areas also have Orthodox churches. There are a lot of domestic animal parks and entertainments for the younger children. In the countryside, hiking is the main activity with special government hiking areas with excellent trails. Those in the National Parks are rougher and intended mainly for the serious hiker, just as the long distance canoe routes are meant for the experienced canoeist. Shooting the rapids is possible in some places. The lakes offer bathing and cruises in the summer season. Worm fishing is available anywhere any time, but fly fishing requires a licence from the local post office (*postipankki*). In addition local permits must be obtained via tourist offices, holiday villages or campsites. Many towns also have their water tower café and there are lookout towers on high points throughout the country. Two last Finnish national pastimes are trotting races and sauna baths.

Finland's West Coast

When studying a map of the west coast of Finland, you can see that it is indented between headlands and studded with the islands of the Finnish archipelago. It is an attractive looking coastline but the main road number 8, a good quality arterial that links the larger towns, is rarely if ever in sight of the sea. Minor roads come closer but the coast is as elusive as Sweden's, hidden behind trees or houses. One can find it of course. Every little place has its *satama* or harbour. Archi-

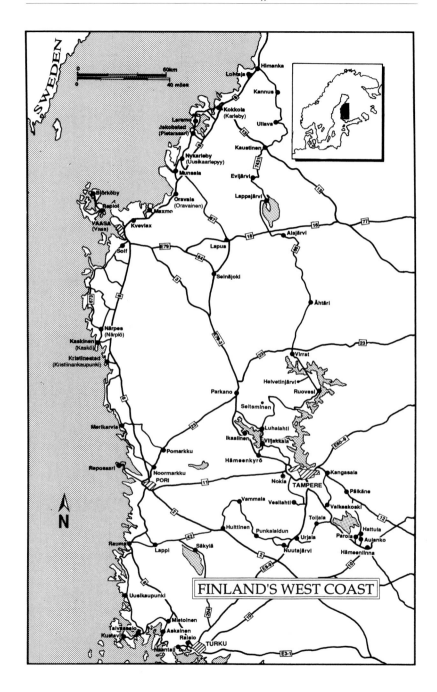

FINLAND'S WEST COAST

The marina and convent church at Naantali

pelago cruises are available from the main towns and sea-fishing or wind-surfing off good clean sand beaches are other leisure activities. Cruising, fishing and bathing are also available on the lakes which form part of the return itinerary to produce a loop starting and ending at Turku.

Turku is Finland's oldest and fourth largest town, a place that deserves a day's exploration in its own right with its castle, museums and botanical gardens. It can be reached by air direct from Denmark or Sweden and by internal flight from Helsinki. Alternatively there are day and night car ferries from Stockholm. If one arrives by this latter route the approach is through a myriad of leafy islands with wooden summer houses nestling among the trees. The medieval castle dominates one's first sight of Turku, begging to be visited, but if the intention is to head straight for the coast, then avoid the complications of the town by following the Pori signs from the dock.

Not far out of Turku, fork off the 8 for **Raisio**'s fourteenth-century greystone church. The tombstones in the entrance are even older, suggesting the existence of a previous church or maybe a cemetery. Inside, the medieval rood crucifix is magnificent; there are grey fresco decorations in the chancel and the pulpit is seventeenth-century Baroque. A little further on turn left for **Naantali**.

The centre of this little town is to the right of the main road where the huge convent church of St Birgitta stands on a rise overlooking the busy marina. From the lookout tower beyond, one can see the

Louhisaari Manor, Askainen

pontoon bridge to the pleasure island of Kailo and across the sound the grey tower of the President's summer residence, Kulturanta, set amid trees on Luonnonmaa. The town of Naantali grew up round the convent as long ago as the 1400s and although the present wooden buildings are late eighteenth and early nineteenth century, they still occupy the sites of the original medieval houses. Most of those by the water are now eating places but Hillola house on the main street is a museum.

Continuing over the new bridge onto Luonnonmaa island, another museum is to be found to the left at **Käkölä**. In a setting of old houses, farms and developing gardens, it contains over 1,000 rural and agricultural articles. **Luonnonmaa** is a typical offshore island, the farms forming oases of cultivation among the rocky wooded hills where pine and birch are the prevalent trees. Bridges lead onto the next island; follow the signs for **Merimasku**. A small red wood church with separate campanile and stocks inside its eighteenth-century porch stands above the yellow ferry that takes one north on the 193 to **Askainen**. Opposite Askainen church, turn left for Louhisaari Manor, the most impressive Dutch Renaissance style house in all Finland. Built in 1655 during the Swedish era, it has three floors of beautifully restored rooms with lovely painted ceilings and walls, period furniture and massive stoves. Most curious perhaps is the grotto room decorated with painted trees in seventeenth-century style. The park outside has wild flowers blooming in its grass, two summerhouses and a monument to Marshall Mannerheim, Finland's most famous general in the 1940s, who was born here. The 193 continues now towards Mietoinen. Go left at the crossroads for Kustavi. There are several interesting sights along the way: an old bridge on the right where one crosses the river in from the sea; a typical small red mill beside a farm; and Muntinsilta, a dry stone single arch bridge paid for by parishioners in 1860 although the style of it is 100 years older. On reaching **Taivassalo**, turn into the village for the greystone church with its beautiful murals on walls and ceiling vaults. Clear and bright, the reds complement the brick pillars. What a pity that the organ loft has been built right across those at the tower end obscuring them from view! Beyond here, the 192 threads its way over causeways and bridges to **Kustavi** where the red wood cruciform church contains various medieval wooden figures, a seventeenth-century pulpit and three men-o'-war hanging Swedish style from the roof.

Return to Taivassalo to join the 196 for **Uusikaupunki**, a pleasant coastal town. The long harbour shelters yachts now rather than ships but in the nineteenth century they possessed Finland's second largest sailing fleet. Warehouses from those days still exist on both shores. The seafaring connection is maintained too in the old church which has a 25m (82ft) long topsail yard outside and a ceiling curved like the upturned hull of a boat. The tiny pilot's cottage close by is a private museum to the pilot's trade. There are also seafaring objects in the cultural museum but a more modern association of Uusikaupunki is with the Saab motor industry. Both the factory and car museum can be visited. One last collection is the four unusual windmills standing in gardens on the hill at the foot of the water tower, which, like so many in Finland, can be climbed for the view.

North of Uusikaupunki on the 196 still, fork left for **Pyhämaa** where the seventeenth-century sacrifice church has wall and ceiling paintings. The path opposite, signed Kotiseutumuseo, leads past an old mill on a rocky hill down to the coast, where a line of old salt and net sheds, part shingled, part thatched, house the local fishing museum. Return to the 196 and head north through Pyharanta to the 8 and Rauma.

Rauma, like Naantali, developed in the Middle Ages around a monastic church, though its later progress owed more to the sea than to religion. Sixteenth-century shipbuilders designed the street layout that has been maintained in the old town and seafarers introduced bobbin lacemaking which became an important cottage industry. Both these facets can still be seen in Rauma today. The old

Windmills at Uusikaupunki

town with its 600 wooden buildings is one of the best preserved wooden towns in Finland. The old town hall houses the Rauma Museum where lacemaking demonstrations take place on Sundays and Prija's house is a specialist lace shop selling these delightful products. The seafaring interest is reflected in the shipowner's home, Marela, and sailor's home, Kirsti, a pair of contrasting museums showing the differing standards of living within this profession. The original monastery church of the Holy Cross has vibrant frescoes round the chancel and disappointingly mundane saints along the gallery and organ loft. There is also a modern water tower with a café giving extensive views over the blocks of modern Rauma. The coast beyond the industry looks pretty but the old town is lost from above. Outside the tower a world signpost decorates a rock and a water feature leads down past a superb modern sculpture of birds swooping through rings.

Leave town on the 42, signed Huittinen, as far as the 207 for Eurajoki. Immediately on turning left, **Lappi** church can be seen among the trees. A red painted wooden church, it also boasts neglected church stables and a stone barn (now a local museum) on the track past its small separate belltower. Follow the 207 towards Eurajoki, turning right just before reaching the 8 and right again for **Irjanne**. Here the eighteenth-century church and Agricultural Museum is worth visiting before joining the 8 for **Pori**, a typical Finnish town mixture of old wood and modern block. The most impressive street is Hallituskatu with some splendidly decorated stone houses one of which contains the Satakunta Museum with its reconstructions of trade shops and working class family home. There is also an art museum in a modernised warehouse.

An interesting trip from here, out along the islands to Reposaari, starts by following the Meri-Pori signs out of town. Turn left for **Yyteri** where plank paths lead over the dunes to a 4km (2 mile) stretch of sand round a large bay. In season it is a tourist spot with camping, café and children's activities. At **Kaanaa** on the same road the water tower/café is open for views in summer. Soon after the Yyteri road fork left over causeways for **Reposaari**. Once the deep water port for Pori and even suggested as a new capital for Finland during the Great Northern War (1700-21) its harbour now shelters only small craft and the town is a peaceful backwater of wooden houses on the traditional grid pattern. The Norwegian-style fjeld church is an elegant octagon in white and green, its ceiling decorated with twentieth-century paintings of Biblical seascapes. The model boat is a replica of Sir Francis Drake's *Golden Hind*. The other show place was the Villa Junnila which unfortunately burnt down in 1991 but one can still stroll through its small English-style park with lake, castellated cottage and ruin built of stones from the beach. For an alternate route back to Pori, turn left opposite the Yyteri road for Pihlava and Kyläsaari.

Continuing north now, by-pass Pori on the Vaasa 8/23 route, taking the 23 for Noormarkku where they split. **Noormarkku** possesses an open-air collection of farm buildings behind the Kotistudio and on the other side of the 23, a 1930s church that has replaced the eighteenth-century one that matched the belltower. It contains a full wall altar fresco, some stained glass and various paintings. Continuing north, the Isonevan Soidensuojelualue signed shortly before Pomarkku is a nature area of peat bogs with two short trails and a bird tower. **Pomarkku** has two churches standing side by side on the same hill. The new is similar inside to Noormarku's but in more luminous yellow tones. Beyond the church hill, the through road transforms back in time to a twisty village street looking much as it would have done centuries ago.

At the next crossroads, turn left, crossing the 23 to return to the coast on an undulating and twisty road with Lake Isojärvi hiding among the trees and homesteads punctuating the monotony of pine and birch. In Loväsjoen go left on the 260 and left again when signed for Lankosku. The attractions here are a few hundred metres to the left of the junction with the 8. They include an 1830s mill that is now a café; a two-arched stone bridge built in the 1880s on the medieval royal road; the fast-flowing river underneath; and a nature trail from the layby.

Return north from here on the 8 just briefly before forking left to Alakylä and **Merikarvia**. This pleasantly spacious town has the largest wooden church in Finland still in regular use. Kerimäki in the lake district (see chapter 15) claims the largest wooden church in the world. Continue on for **Siipyy**. The sea is not far to the left but it can only be glimpsed occasionally. More interesting are the old long-beam hoists for drawing water from the wells that still exist on a number of the farms. Go left when signed for Kilens *Hembygdsgård*, the Swedish name for the old harbour of Siipyy, an area now preserved as a museum with fishing sheds and a mill. This is a reminder that here in Vaasa province the long years of Swedish possession are still present in the names. Every place has two. For example, after Siipyy one joins the 660 for **Kristinestad/Kristiinankaupunki**. Every street here also has two names. It is a town that repays exploring. Wooden houses large and small line its grid-pattern streets. The Lebell Residence, a merchant's house from 1750, is now a museum, furnished in period. The name Lebell appears again on church stables at the eighteenth-century church. Beside it stands a 1720 toll cottage and there is also a windmill perched on the highest rocks, while below the streets the river flows wide out to sea.

Leave Kristinestad/Kristiinankaupunki past the town hall and the old church, forking left for Skrattnäs and on to the greenhouse land of Pjelax. Left and left again onto the 667 takes one on a causeway road to Finland's smallest town, **Kaskinen/Kaskö**. Only 200 years old, it has straight streets of wooden houses running parallel to the sea, two museums and a preserved windmill. Leave the town on the 676 for Narpes/Narpio through a broad farm belt of flat fields dotted with storage huts. Turn towards **Närpes/Närpiö** and almost immediately on the right there is the Viskogsparken museum with farm buildings, farmyard birds and animals, an open-air theatre and an old steam engine complete with bulbous funnel and a railvan. Närpes/Närpio also possesses rows of Swedish-style church stables (150 in all) and close by, the Jordbruks Agricultural Museum. Beyond the town centre, turn left for Korsnäs to eventually reach the town of Vaasa.

There are several places to visit on the way. For example, **Harrström**'s *fiskehamn* has lines of grey fishermen's sheds on the shore, two windmills and an 1898 bridge built of stones from the local forest. **Åminne**'s fish harbour is also extensive, sheds lining the river

The heathen cross at Korsholma Castle, Vaasa

mouth. Many are now used for summer craft though some fishing still takes place. Kvarkens boat museum is at the end of the road. At **Solf**, Stundars Craft Village has forty-three buildings, mainly workshops, from the eighteenth and nineteenth centuries like tinsmiths, cobblers and carpenters. There is also a printing museum and artists' workshop, a farm complex and exhibitions and demonstrations in the *Hemmersgården*.

Continue towards **Vaasa/Vasa**, turning right for Gamla Vaasa when signposted on a normal blue sign. The original town developed here in the Middle Ages around Korsholma Castle, which was then on the sea. Over the centuries it suffered a series of disasters; the town was twice destroyed in war; the shore area gradually silted up and finally in August 1852 the whole town burnt down. The area called Gamla Vaasa contains the ruins of this old town — the best immediately ahead at the T-junction. The ruins of St Mary's church are particularly impressive. Just up the road, the Court of Appeal, now the Mustasaari church, is one of the few buildings that survived the fire. Opposite, on the foundations of Korsholma Castle, stands the heathen cross, commemorating a fourteenth-century wooden cross placed there by Swedish seafarers. The present town of Vaasa was built 6km (4 miles) nearer the sea. It is a seemingly random mix of wood, stone and modern concrete block. The Swedish influence is obvious in the names but so is the Russian with an Orthodox church, minute in comparison to the Lutheran one. There are various museums including the open-air Bragegården which besides the normal farm complex has a troll's ring like the one at Vittaryd in Småland. It can be reached by walking out along the shore path (as well as by car). The shield-shaped motto over the farmhouse door here is in Swedish for when it was built the whole area was Swedish-speaking. Today only 6 per cent of the population still speaks Swedish as their native language. There is also the inevitable water-cum-lookout tower and a recreation centre for children, Vasalandia, that includes a log flume, laser show, 3-D film and all sorts of carousels. The Tropic Center contains tropical reptiles, birds and fish.

Leave Vaasa on the 724 for the Replot island complex, reached at the last by one of Finland's free yellow ferries plying a shuttle service across the final gap. **Replot** has a small homestead museum beautifully fitted inside with dummies of a family and lots of artefacts like bone skates and home-made rugs produced on looms in the loft. The furniture in the 'everything' room downstairs is amazingly compact with the two-storey bed end acting as a dresser and a clock built into the corner cupboard. The doorways are amazingly low too. There is also an eighteenth-century church, its pulpit and altar rescued from St Mary's in Gamla Vaasa. The harbour is typical with restored boatsheds on every available space. North of Replot, **Björköby** is a farming community with storage sheds on every old-fashioned strip of land. It too has a fishing harbour as have the villages to the south and west of Replot. From Kalvholm on the west coast, at **Bullerås Semesterby**, there is Granösunds Fiskeläge, fishing museum with boats and equipment including a fishermen's hut with bunks for four along one wall. At the north-west tip of the island Klobbskat is very much a working fishing harbour with seagoing boats. Nearby Kalle's Inn is a recreation centre.

On returning over the ferry, fork left for Jungsund and left again for Karpero on a dirt road through farming scenery. Left at a T-junction and right again takes one to **Kvevlax** and its late seventeenth-century church. The parish storehouse next door is a museum. Turn left round the church for Petsmo, then straight on for Hankmo. Cross the river and go left towards **Västerhankmo** which is a well-maintained farming milieu described by the local tourist office as a typical centuries-old peasant culture. There is a windmill in the centre of the settlement. After this short diversion return to Kvevlax and the 8 for Kokkola/Karleby. Beyond the Vassorfjörden, divert into **Maxmo** for the early nineteenth-century church with its wooden statue for collecting monies for the local poor. This is the first such statue on this route but it heralds an area where most churches have retained them.

All are different and they are often more interesting than the plain Lutheran churches outside which they stand. Follow the Karklax road out past the Sunday school museum, a tiny furnished cottage and two storehouses in a pretty little garden. Where this road rejoins the 8, a new development is the *Klemetsgårdarna*, a restored café with a historical trail behind it to such places as Viking graves. Guided walks are available but the route is signed and accessible at all times. Continue towards **Oravais/Oravainen**. The museum road signed to the right dates from the sixteenth century. Opposite the information board climb to the monument on the hill where the 'Bloody Day in Oravais', a crucial battle that resulted in the loss of Finland to Russia after 600 years of Swedish rule, is fought out blow by blow in English.

Rejoin the 8 in Oravais for some 10km (6 miles) before forking left on the 727 for Nykarleby/Uusikaarlepyy, past Svedberg's school museum. **Munsala** has a local museum on the road in and a truly massive stone church capable of seating 1,500. The oldest artefact inside is a medieval sculpture of Bishop Henrik. Otherwise the interior is plain with just a painted pulpit and altarpiece. Outside there is another of the almost lifesize collecting figures. **Nykarleby/ Uusikaarlepyy** itself has a panorama café, a local museum and also Topelius' childhood home, a small manor with cottage, summer-house and wagonsheds also. Topelius, although writing in Swedish, is regarded as the father of the Finnish historical novel. Beyond the town, fork left for Soklot and Grisselören, then right on the minor road for Nabba. After the fishing lakes, turn left for **Pörkenäs** along the coast and follow the through road until reaching the Nanoq Arctic Museum. Designed like a Greenland house, covered with earth and peat for insulation, this unusual museum contains local explorer Pentti Kronqvist's collections about Greenland's Eskimos. Shortly afterwards, Fäbodä to the left is a bay with sandy beaches and bathing. The road now leads directly into **Jakobstadt/Pietarsaari**.

This town, founded in the seventeenth century by Countess Ebba Brahe, was originally named Jakobstadt in memory of her husband, a famous Swedish soldier. Although it was destroyed during the Russo-Swedish wars of the early eighteenth century, its replacement can still be seen in the narrow streets of Skata where 300 or so wooden houses are preserved. The nineteenth century brought industry, including Europe's oldest tobacco factory, dominated by the largest clock in Finland. Today it also houses a tobacco museum and there is a motorcycle museum next door. Close by a botanical garden contains 1,000 different species of plants. By the old harbour a full-sized replica of one of the eighteenth-century galleons that used to ply out of Jakobstadt is being built which will both take cruises off the coast and be the centre of a new shipping museum area. Nearby a Fanta Sea park for children is also being developed while adult fitness fanatics can attempt a jogging-cum-exercise trail. On leaving the old harbour, go left and right for Luoto to pass Runeberg's cottage, the childhood home and first school of this greatest of Finnish poets. Though he too wrote in Swedish, his poems show great sympathy for the plight of the Finnish peasant and one of them, *Vårt land*, was adopted as the Finnish national anthem. Now join the 749 Seven Bridges Archipelago Road for Kokkola/Karleby. On the way, one passes **Larsmo Kirkeby** with its church dating from 1789 and a local museum, Björgas Hembygdsgård.

Kokkola/Karleby is a developing industrial town with a commercial port and summer ferry connections to Skellefteå in Sweden. It also has its museums. In the same street one may find the K.H. Renlund Art Gallery, a nature museum and Lassander's house, now a historical museum with exhibition rooms. One can walk through the old wooden town behind the latter to the English longboat from the Crimean War that rests in a special 'house' near the river. It was part of a raiding party against the Russians that went wrong and is the only war trophy Finland has ever taken from the Royal Navy. From here one can walk back into the town centre along the river. Out at Karleby Kirkonmäki there is also a large open-air museum behind the fifteenth-century stone church. From here join the 8 for Oulu. Watch out for the zoo signs on the right soon after entering **Kälviä** district. It is a domestic animal park, not a collection of lions and tigers. Next turn into **Lohtaja** (it has a local museum behind the regimental statue in the church car park) for a diversion up to the fishing village of **Ohtakari**, with its dunes, beaches, bird tower, café and fishing cabins. Out of season it is a ghost village with only a few fishermen about. In season the cabins fill with holidaymakers and the harbour with pleasure craft. The small museum shows the original furnishings of one of the older cabins and storesheds. The wooden lighthouse tower gives views over village, coast and the open sea.

Returning, go left at the T-junction to rejoin the 8 via a twisty unsurfaced forest road. At **Himanka**, the local museum stands apparently in the middle of a field as one reaches the town — the entrance is from the road behind. Raumankari, signed in the village, is a stone bridge with a wooden centre span over the Lestijoki as it hastens to the sea. The road on the far side follows it out along the coast but one must eventually return the same way. This is the

One of the buildings at the Pauanne Finnish cultural area, near Kaustinen

farthest north point on this coastal tour. Turn inland from here, following the river valley towards Kannus, in order to return to Turku on a more inland route. Some of the early stretches are flat and dull, but you soon discover lake views and undulating roads. By the time places like Virrat and Ruovesi are reached, it is more scenic than parts of the coastal plain already traversed. In Kannus cross the river, then go left past the church and right when signed for Ullava. At the T-junction here, follow the Kaustinen signs taking the 755 past Ullavanjärvi. **Kaustinen** has a local museum next to the church but its main interests are musical. There is a special arena in the centre for staging musical events and nearby are the Folk Musicians' House and the museum of musical instruments. Music also plays its part out at the Pauanne Finnish cultural area off Teerijärvanti in the Puhkionkallio forest. Interesting-shaped buildings, designed by a television and radio engineer as an expression of communion with nature, dot the rocky landscape. Light refreshments are available and weddings and special events are held here. Although not as high as the ski jump, clearly visible across the treetops, the site gives good views over the surrounding area.

Continue on road 740 for Evijärvi, past various small lakes then turn right for Inankylä on the road that crosses the top of Lake Evijärvi. Eventually, at a T-junction, go right to **Väinöntalo** open-air museum. The large farm once housed two families with up to ten children each. Just count the beds and note how few stoves there are to keep them warm. The site also includes twenty outbuildings, mainly from the early eighteenth century. Now head south for Evijärvi, Lappajärvi, then Kauhava and Alajärvi, circling the lake along the western side, to reach **Alajärvi**. Here the work of two very different Finns is represented. The artist Nelimarkka is remembered in a modern museum of that name dedicated not only to his work but to nineteenth- and twentieth-century Finnish artists in general. The architect Alvar Aalto, whose working career spanned six decades of this century, was responsible for several buildings in the town. Two stand on the road beside the church, but some might prefer the 'flying' maiden in the churchyard to their solidity. Heading south again round the lake, take the 714, then the 706 to Lehtimäki; then follow the Ähtäri signs. There are lots of attractions in and around **Ähtäri**; from a homestead museum, to a car museum containing everything from a '59 Chevrolet and two Russian cars, to radios, gramophones and an old-fashioned shop. Several kilometres further on, the zoo with narrow gauge railway and the Mini-Finland theme park will appeal to children, as will the Kotieläinpuisto, a domestic animals park. There is also a new wild west feature nearby. Return then to Ähtäri and continue south on the 349 for Virrat. This is a pretty road, affording views of the lakes and rivers it passes.

Virrat is a pleasant town on the shores of Lake Torsvesi. The natural harbour at the lake end is delightful, with gardens created along the shore. From the quay one can cruise along the Poet's Way to Tampere, a journey that takes the best part of a day (the poet is Runeberg). Virrat's most popular attraction, 3km (2 miles) north off the 66, is the traditional village of Perinnekylä. Here in the collection of nineteenth-century buildings there are museums and craft workshops separated by traditional birch fences. A six-bladed windmill, its sails resembling the petals of a flower, stands by a path. The church boat, 17.5m (57ft) long with twenty wooden rowlocks, was once used for carrying the villagers along the lake to church in Virrat. There is also a country path trail with points of interest like old-fashioned traps and metal statues of birds and fish. Return on the 66 past Virrat to the Toriseva lakes for some interesting walks. Park at the information board and head for the café. Behind the buildings, follow the red-marked posts to the signpost. Left leads to one of the three lakes and all the way back to Perinnekylä. Right leads to another and one could walk its length and circle back via Lahari to the signpost. Virrat tourist office can supply maps. The main feature of the lakes is that each is set in a deep narrow ravine with the paths passing high along their upper edges.

A collecting figure at Ruovesi church

Further walks are possible in the Helvetinjärven National Park. The most impressive viewpoint is the precipice Helvetinkolu where one descends through a cleft into Hell Canyon. To reach this continue from Toriseva turning right for Pohtio where signed. Helvetinkolu is 3km (2 miles) from the parking place along a forest path that needs walking boots. There are elk, bears and lynx in the park though the chances of seeing any in broad daylight are slim. Route 66 continues to **Ruovesi** where one can find Runeberg's spring which bubbles up through sand in a woodland pool. There is also a museum on a hill with an old timber farm and another six-bladed mill. At the church there is an even longer church boat with rowlocks for thirty oarsmen. Two others are in the museum by the lake and one, for just fourteen, is still used in summer.

Leave on the Kuru road and left again onto the museum road (Museotie). This has been in existence since at least 1790 and still follows its original route which makes it more scenic than the 337 which it eventually rejoins. From Kuru take the Parkano road for the

41sq km (15sq miles) of the Seitseminen National Park. One can drive right round this, stopping at various parking places for walks. Enter where the park is signed on the road to Kovero and go first to the information centre with its exhibition hall of native fauna. Maps of the park are available and every path is well-signed with distance posts. Kovero is an old farm. At the crossroads beyond here go left towards Jauli and park at Multiharju for a 2km (1 mile) long nature trail. It is an interesting and dry path through the forest way-marked with picture boards, though the text is only in Finnish. This is the easiest walk to do as it is circular. Return then to the crossroads and go left to leave the park. Just after Sisätto, watch for a small blue sign for Vahonkoski to the left. These narrow rapids lead into a gentle river lined with kingcups in springtime. Back from this short diversion, continue to Lukalahti where there is a possible choice of routes. Finland's third largest town, Tampere, is not far away to the south and it would be possible to make this a base for several days, cutting south from here and treating the circle round Kyrosjärvi, described here, as a trip out from Tampere.

Circling to the north on the 276, watch first for another small blue sign this time reading Arasalon Linnavuori. The road passes first through the old-fashioned village of Iso-Röyhiön Alaskylä before deteriorating on towards Arasalon. Translated *linnavuori* is a castle mountain, one of those rocky outcrops that were used centuries ago as strongholds and places of refuge. This one is a steep rocky hill ending in cliffs that gives views through the trees of lakes in most directions. Now continue round Kyrosjärvi, cutting through to Riitala and the 3/E79 for **Ikaalinen**. Here the Kylpylä signed just before the town is an ultra-modern spa with three hotels, mud baths, saunas, tennis, a golf driving range and many other facilities. It is 10 minutes by boat from the town or, in winter, a walk across the ice of the frozen lake, something which is hard to picture in summer but fits with the snow poles by minor roads and the ski jump in Kaustinen. Ikaalinen celebrated its 350th anniversary in 1991 but not a lot of the original town remains. The church is early nineteenth century with a local museum behind it. There is an old town gate, simply a decorative wooden arch across the road, which seems surprising until one remembers that wood was the all-pervading building material. Wide lime avenues lead down towards the water but only one side of the street and some larger houses near the lake are wooden. One unusual attraction here is Finland's baseball museum and there is a baseball diamond at the bottom of the street. Round the corner and across the causeway, Tolveolansaari island is a more relaxing place with beaches, walks and two more church boats in a shed by the water.

Pick up the main road again for Hämeenkyrö. Here, on the outskirts, the Mannanmäentie Näkätorni is a World War I battle memorial with a tower on top. It looks in rather battered condition but appears to open for viewing at weekends. Turn left for **Kyröskoski** for the Hämeen Hälläpyrörä rapids of saga fame. Although heavily industrialised there is still an impressive fall of water and an interesting circular path from the parking place. The best time to see them is the spring flood season from mid-April to mid-May but unfortunately most other attractions are not open that early in the year. Go back into town from here and cross the 3 for **Kyröspohja**, where the local museum beside the church looks like a huge brick prison. Rejoin the 3 going right past the commercial herb garden that sits beside the bridge. It runs courses on health foods and natural healing as well as selling its plants. The next left takes one to **Viljakkala**. Ignore the Keskusta sign and turn left soon after for the Haverin Gold Mine complex. Closed since 1960 it is now a museum and recreation area with old cottages, mining pit, open quarry, domestic animal zoo and a beach. A little farther on the Inkula stone bridge gives good views along the lake to either side. From here Lukalahti is but a few kilometres north to complete the circle, or Tampere is to the south via Ylöjärvi.

Tampere is too large a town to be off the beaten track but it is certainly a good base with its many attractions. The tourist office can provide detailed maps and information about these. Here a circular route round the south of the town is suggested before heading for the coast again at Turku.

Leave Tampere in the Turku direction just as far as **Nokia** where the lake has fountains and swimming. Follow the Turku signs through, rejoining the 41 briefly, then going left for Sorva on a country road that on its later stretches passes close to the Sorvanselkä. Turn left for Tottijärvi and continue south to pick up the Klaus Kurki road, a Finnish historical/cultural route with hanging signboards at points of interest. The first, just a short diversion down the Hinsala road is Laukka Manor (private), famous for its trotters. Horses of all ages fill the paddocks round the manor and its extensive farm buildings. Continuing on the through road, just beyond the Narva turning, the *kotiseutumuseo* is a tenant farm showing the old way of life, with handicrafts for sale in the dairy. Beyond the Punkalaidun turning, Hurskasvuori is a partly restored 1916 fortification 200m (220yd) up the hill. It has an extensive trench system and

Trotting horses at Laukka Manor

there is a signed walk round the area. Continue to beyond the inlet of the lake, then go left signed Suomela. The monument is to the Whites in the Russian Civil War of 1918 — just up the road you have left there is a monument to the Reds. The road now circles round to **Vesilahti** whose cruciform church has a separate fifteenth-century stone vestry that must have been very dark, possessing only one small grating to let in the light. The Tapola at the end of the village is a handicrafts shop. Rejoin the main road going left for Lampaala, then left again for Kaakilaniemi. Kaakila is a refuge fortress rock like the one at Arasalon but it is poorly signed and the road deteriorates badly along the way. Better perhaps to stop at the Kotielainpiha on the same road for the domestic animal park and the Satumetsan trail aimed at younger children.

This is the end of the Klaus Kurki road. Continue towards Lempaala, then right through Koskenkylä to reach Viiala. Take the Varrasniemi road there for an area of rapids and bridges where the river has been channelled through several different routes. The new road bridge rather spoils the site but it is still fun for children. Continue on to **Toijala** where there is the Veterimuseo (Railway Museum). The church is also well worth finding. Unlike the usual plain interior, this was painted in the 1930s by graphic artist Kalle Carlstedt with representations of the four gospel writers, angels and flower patterns. In the entrance there are wooden plaques from previous churches and a small museum.

Leave on the Hämeenlinna road which passes the Emil Wikström museum (with over 100 of his sculptures on show) shortly before joining the E79/3 for Valkeakoski across a series of bridges. Turn right into **Sääsmäki** for the fourteenth-century stone church with interior paintings in the same style as Toijala's, modern stained glass and two medieval wooden figures in glass cases. Continue towards Valkeakoski, passing two attractions together at Voipaala. One is an art centre with sculpture studio and National Art Exhibition; the other a prehistoric hill fort, *Rapola Linnavuori* with good English explanations and a trail round its fortifications and burial mounds. At **Valkeakoski** the watertower gives good views over the surrounding lakes — if one ignores the local factory belching out pollution). The historical side of the town's industry has been preserved. On the left before the bridge, the Kauppilamäki museum shows life and housing conditions for mill workers. Beyond the bridge the Myllysaari industry museum shows the development of a mill village into an industrial town.

Leave on the Kangasala road. This is an interesting area just east of Tampere. It has a military vehicle museum (Historiallinenmuseo) in an old quarry just off the road into Tampere. It is also worth continuing back towards Tampere to **Kaukajärvi** for the museum area here at Haihara. The Nukkemuseo (Doll Museum) is the one signed but the site also includes a cave, granary, smithy, Runeberg's house, carriage shed and handicrafts exhibition as well as lively metal statues outside the costume museum. Back in **Kangasala**, their museum is opposite the stone church. From here follow the Huutijärvi signs up onto the Kuohunharju ridge for views over lake Vesijärvi to the north. These *harjus* or ridges are relics of the Ice Age, and a typical feature of Finnish lake scenery. Descending from this one, right and right again following 'Lahti' brings one along the edge of another to the Automuseum at **Vehoniemi**. This is well done with figures like garage hands and fuel pump attendant. There is also a purpose-built wooden tower overlooking the lakes and a nature trail from the car park. Continuing south to **Pälkäne** one can drive up the Syrjänharju which also has a tower, doorless so open all hours, but perfectly safe, with three separate levels for viewing. Apart from lakes on either side one can see the ruins of the early sixteenth-century church beyond the 12. Pälkäne also has ruins of early eighteenth-century fortifications on the Kostia stream (just before the bridge). The 1713 battle in the Great Northern War between Russia and Sweden is vividly described on a picture board in the fort. Join the 12 then and soon the 57 for Hämeenlinna.

The Hämeenlinna area contains much of interest to suit all tastes. Turn left where signed and one arrives first at **Aulanko**. Here Colonel Hugo Standertskjöld, an arms manufacturer who made a fortune in Russia, created a forested park containing unusual species and romantic buildings. Taken over by the state, it is now open to visitors any time. A one-way road system (*puistometsa*), operates with parking places near the main attractions. Chief of these is the solid tower with its display of nature photographs. The lookout platform at its foot has a hunting fresco below. The 322 stone stairs down from here lead to the bears' cave with its life-like statue of a bear family and beyond to the lakeside — a curving footpath provides an alternate route. Back at the top there are two artificial ponds inhabited by ducks, swans and the inevitable gulls; also a ruined fortress which was of course built that way!

Beyond the park, sitting incongruously beside the modern Aulanko hotel with its golf course and recreational facilities, the wooden Silk House is a treasure trove of silk products, much of it for sale. It also tells the story of silk by video, butterflies and cocoons, and, usually, live silkworms. Continuing on towards **Hämeenlinna**, one of the best views of the fourteenth-century brick castle that gives the town its name is across the water from Rautatienkatu — sharp right at the start of town. In its long history, Häme Castle has been fortress, granary, prison and offices and is now a tourist attraction as well as a stage for concerts and exhibitions. Hämeenlinna is also Jean Sibelius' birthplace and the inspiration for his *Finlandia*. The house is open for visitors or for those who prefer cars, the Ahvenisto Formula 3 race track has a motor museum.

Continue north on the 305 towards **Hattula** for the fourteenth-century Tyrvanto church, a medieval treasurehouse. The walls, ceilings and even the ancient vestry are covered with frescoes; there are numerous wooden sculptures, both singly and in groups and even a fantastic seventeenth-century pulpit supported on the head and torso of a man. A detailed English booklet on loan from the desk enumerates every painting and statue. The nearby stone granary is now a bee museum with collections of bee-keeping equipment, hives and combs. Turn left then into **Parola** for one last attraction in this varied area. This is the Panssarimuseo (Panzer Museum) with its armoured train, tanks, lorries and assorted military hardware.

Continuing this outer loop, join the 3 towards Tampere but turn left into **Iitala** for its glass factory which produces both blown and crystal glass. There are guided factory tours or the shop area is open daily with a glass-blowing workshop where one can have a go.

The fourteenth-century church at Hattula is a treasurehouse of medieval frescoes

Continue past the church and local museum next door until the Forssa road is reached just before a railway crossing. You are cutting across country to Vammala here. The first section of the road is unsurfaced and gradually deteriorates as you turn right for Annula. Go left at the end onto the surfaced 2847 past Urjala (one can reach the same point on a surfaced road via Toijala and the 2847). Cross the E80 Turku road onto the 247 for about 4km (2 miles) to the Urjalan farm museum. Just past it the stone vestry by the river is all that remains of the old church. One can then follow the road to Punkalaidun. Alternatively you could go left on the E80 and right for **Nuutajärvi** glassworks and museum. One passes first the Vanhotalli (old stables), now a café and handicrafts centre. The Lasikylä (glassworks) is similar to that at Iitala with glassblowing every day but no factory tours. This road continues to join the 230 for **Punkalaidun** where the Talonpolkaismuseo on the outskirts is a typical collection of old buildings. From here the 252 twists through farming villages to Vammala.

Vammala possesses varied attractions. If one follows the Ojansuunkatu signs from the centre round onto the old road for Tampere, a kilometre or two out of town there is a short nature trail round a small headland (Vehmaanniemi). It is a pleasant half hour stroll through wild flowers and anthills with ten nature boards en route. Returning and crossing the river, fork right, following the Tervakallio camping signs. On the edge of the site a red building houses a tractor collection (Traktor-Näyttely). Further to the right off the Hämeenkyrö road, **Tyrvää** old church is another medieval church worth visiting, this time for its post-medieval interior. The wooden floor is sixteenth century and parts of it feel it! The pulpit and carving on the pews near the altar are seventeenth century and the painted galleries, one running the length of the church, are eighteenth century. All evoke the atmosphere that must have prevailed here in the past as does the wooden 'hammer' for waking up any Finns who fell asleep during the long Latin/Swedish services! The beautiful shingled roof outside is also eighteenth century. There is another even older medieval church 4km (2 miles) further out at Sastamala but it is much plainer and so less interesting. Returning, to the north of the bridge one finds the Seudanmuseo or Tyrvää town museum. Here one has completed the outer loop south of Tampere and it only remains to return to Turku.

Follow the 249 Ætsa road first with good views of both river and power station there. Cross the river and go south to **Huittinen** whose stone church also dates back to the fourteenth century though its shape has been much altered over the years. A restoration in the 1950s has brought back fresco friezes and an old pulpit and altar. The storehouse opposite is a museum. Leave on the 42 towards Rauma as far as the edge of Eura. Here turn left for Kauttua. The Käräjämäki signed off is a hill with paths. Go left on the 211 towards Yläne and first right over the railway for the shore road along Pyhäjärvi to Säkylä. Beyond the sandy bathing beach it becomes a scenic lake road. After **Säkylä**'s red wood church and matching windmill rejoin the main road for Turku and the completion of this west coast circuit.

Further Information
— Finland's West Coast —

Ähtäri

Car Museum
Open: May to late June and August 10am-6pm. Late June and July 10am-8pm.

Farm Animal Park
Open: mid-May to early June 10am-4pm. Rest June to early August 10am-6pm.

Local Museum
Open: June to mid-August, Tuesday to Saturday 2-6pm. Sunday 11.30am-3pm.

Mini Finland
Open: early May to late June and August, 11am-6pm. End June and July 11am-8pm.

Narrow Gauge Railway
Open: early June to early August, 11am-7pm.

Zoo
Open: May and late August, 10am-6pm. June, July and early August 10am-8pm.

Alajärvi
Nelimarkka Museum
Open: Sunday, Tuesday to Friday 12noon-6pm. Saturday 12noon-4pm.

Askainen
Louhisaari Manor House
Open: mid-May to August, 11am-5pm. September, Saturday and Sunday 11am-5pm.

Aulanko
Silk House
Open: June to mid-August 11am-7pm. Late August to October, Tuesday to Thursday 3-7pm. Saturday and Sunday 11am-3pm.

Tower
Open: June to mid-August, Monday to Friday 9am-7pm. Saturday and Sunday 11am-7pm.

Hämeenkyrö
Mannanmäentie Näkätorni
Open: Friday, Saturday and Sunday, 12noon-6pm June to mid-August.

Hämeenlinna
Ahvenisto Car Museum
Open: May to August 11am-6pm.

Häme Castle
Open: May to August 10am-6pm.

Sibelius' Childhood Home
Open: May to August 10am-4pm.

Hattula
Bee Museum
Open: Monday to Saturday 12noon-6pm. Sunday 11am-6pm.

Tyrvanto Church
Open: early May to end May 9am-5pm. June to mid-August 10am-5pm. Late August, 12noon-4pm.

Himanka
Museum
Open: 8am-3.30pm.

Huittinen
Church
Open: 9am-8pm.

Museum
Open: Monday to Friday 12noon-6pm. Saturday and Sunday 12noon-4pm.

Iitala
World of Crystal
Open: 9am-8pm. Factory tours Monday to Friday 11am, 1pm, and 3pm.

Ikaalinen
Local Museum
Open: 10am-1pm.

Irjanne
Agricultural Museum
Open: June to August 9am-5pm.

Jakobstadt/Pietarsaari
Motor Cycle Museum
Open: Monday to Friday 12noon-5pm. Saturday and Sunday 12noon-4pm.

Kaanaa
Watertower
Open: 12noon-midnight.

Kälviä
Domestic Animal Park
Open: June to August, Sunday to Friday 10am-8pm. Saturday 10am-6pm.

Kangasala
Local Museum
Open: June to late August 11am-5pm.

Military Vehicle Museum
Open: June to mid-August 11am-6pm daily.

Kaskinen/Kaskö
Fishing Museum
Open: 2-4pm mid-June to mid-August.

Town Museum
Open: Wednesday, Sunday 2-5pm,
mid-June to mid-August.

Kaukajärvi
Nukkemuseo (Doll Museum)
Open: mid-April to end September,
Saturday to Thursday 12noon-6pm.

Kaustinen
Folk Music Museum
Open: June to August 10am-2pm.

Kokkola/Karleby
Art, Nature and History Museums
All open: Tuesday to Friday 12noon-
3pm. Thursday 6-8pm. Saturday and
Sunday 12noon-5pm all year.

Local Museum
Open: May to August, Tuesday to Sunday 12noon-6pm.

Kristinestad/Kristiinankaupunki
Lebell Residence
Open: summer, 12noon-4pm.

Kustavi
Church
Open: June to August 10am-6pm.

Lohtaja
Museum
Open: June to August, Monday to Saturday 12noon-4pm. Sunday 11am-
5pm.

Maxmo
Klemetsgårdana
Open: Monday to Friday 1-9pm. Satur-
day and Sunday 11am-9pm.

Naantali
Käkölä Farm Museum
Open: Sunday 12noon-6pm.

Kulturanta
Gardens open: Friday 6-8pm or June to
August guided tours daily 3.30pm
from tourist office.

Museum
Open: mid-May to August, 12noon-
6pm.

Närpes/Närpiö
Viskogsparken
Open: 10am-4pm mid-June to mid-
August.

Noormarkku
Church
Open: June to August 9am-6pm.

Nuutajärvi
Glassworks
Glassblowing 7-11am and 11.30am-
3.30pm daily. *Museum* 9am-8pm.

Nykarleby/Uusikarlepyy
Topelius Childhood Home
Open: Tuesday to Sunday.

Tower
Open: Monday to Friday 10am-4pm.
Saturday and Sunday 12noon-6pm.

Town Museum
Open: May 10am-3pm. June to August
12noon-5pm.

Parola
Panzer Museum
Open: May 9am-6pm. June to August
10am-7pm. September, Saturday and
Sunday 10am-4pm.

Pori
Satakunta Museum
Open: Tuesday to Sunday 11am-5pm.

Punkalaidun
Talonpolkaismuseo
Open: June to August 10am-5pm.

Pyhämaa
Local Museum
Open: July, August, Sundays 11am-
2pm.

Sacrifice Church
Open: Monday to Saturday 9am-6pm.

Rauma
Kirsti (Sailor's Home)
Open: mid-May to mid-August, 10am-4pm.

Marela (Shipowner's Home) *and
Rauma Museum*
Open: mid-May to mid-August 10am-6pm.

Tower
Open: 10am-8pm, mid-May to mid-August.

Replot
Museum
Open: June to mid-August, Wednesday, Saturday and Sunday 12noon-4pm.

Ruovesi
Museum
Open: June to mid-August daily.

Sääsmäki
Emil Wikström Sculpture Museum
Open: May to September, Monday 11am-5pm. Tuesday to Sunday 11am-7pm.

Seitseminen
National Park Information Centre
Open: 10am-6pm.

Siipyy
Kilens Hembygdsgård
Open: beginning to mid-June and beginning to mid-August, 10am-6pm. Mid-June to end July 10am-8pm.

Solf
Stundars Craft Village
Open: 12noon-6pm July to August.

Toijala
Church and Museum
Open: Monday to Friday 1-3pm.

Veterimuseo (Railway Museum)
Open: late May to late August 12noon-4pm.

Urjala
Museum
Open: June to August, Friday, Saturday and Sunday 12noon-6pm.

Nykarleby/Uusikaupunki
Culture Museum
Open: 12noon-3pm Saturday, Sunday. June to mid-August Tuesday to Friday 10am-5pm.

Pilot Museum
Open: 12noon-3pm, Saturday, Sunday, May to August and June to mid-August also Tuesday to Friday 11am-3pm.

Saab Car Factory
Open: Tuesday, Thursday 12noon-7pm (not in July).

Saab Car Museum
Open: Tuesday to Thursday, Saturday and Sunday 12noon-6pm all year.

Tower
Open: Monday to Friday 10am-6pm June, July and August.

Vaasa/Vasa
Bragegården
Open: June to August, Tuesday to Friday 1-7pm. Saturday and Sunday 12noon-4pm.

Vasalandia Holiday Centre
Open: 1-8pm May to late August.

Väinöntalo
Museum
Open: May to August, 10am-6pm.

Valkeakoski
Jyraanmäki Tower
Open: Wednesday to Sunday 11am-6pm.

Industry Museum
Open: May to mid-August, Monday to Thursday 11am-6pm. Sunday 12noon-4pm.

Kauppilemöki (Papermill Workers' Museum)
Open: Monday to Friday 11am-3pm. Sunday 11am-6pm.

Vammala
Seudanmuseum
Open: 12noon-4pm.

Traktor-Näyttely (Tractor Exhibition)
Open: June to August, 1-2pm and 5-6pm.

Tyrvää Old Church
Open: Monday to Saturday 10am-4pm. Sunday 12noon-6pm June to late August.

Vehoniemi
Car Museum
Open: April 12noon-4pm. May to August 10am-6pm.

Vesilahti
Domestic Animal Park
Open: June to August 9am-6pm mid-May to end August.

Virrat
Perinnekylä Museum
Open: mid-May to end Aug 10am-6pm.

Voipala
Art Centre
Open: mid-May to mid-Aug 11am-6pm.

Tourist Information Centres

Ähtäri
Laajantie 5
SF-63700 Ähtäri
☎ 6537109

Hämeenlinna
Palokunnankatu 14
SF-13100 Hämeenlinna
☎ 17202388

Jakobstadt/Pietarsaari
Storgatan 11
SF-68600 Jakobstad
☎ 6731796

Kokkola/Karleby
Kaarlelankatu 21
SF-67100 Kokkola
☎ 68311902

Naantali
Puistotie 24
SF-21100 Naantali
☎ 21755388

Pori
Antinkatu 5
SF-28100 Pori
☎ 39335780

Rauma
Eteläkatu 7
SF-26100 Rauma
☎ 38224555

Tampere
Verkatehtaankatu 2
PB 87
SF-33211 Tampere
☎ 31126652

Turku/Äbo
Käsityöläiskatu 3
SF-20100 Turku
☎ 21336366

Uusikaupunki
Levysepänkatu 4A
SF-23500 Uusikaupunki
☎ 221551

Vaasa/Vasa
Raastuvankatu 30
PB 3
SF-65101 Vaasa
☎ 61251145

Valkeakoski
Valtakatu 20
SF-37600 Valkeakoski
☎ 3746997

Virrat
Kaupungintalo
SF-34800 Virrat
☎ 34512 276

15 • The Finnish Lake District

The Finnish Lake District or Saimaa Lakeland is the largest lake district in Europe. The thousands of lakes, of which Saimaa is the biggest, have 50,000km (31,000 miles) of shoreline and shelter some 33,000 islands. They contain abundant fish and the summertime temperature of the water is around 20°C (68°F) making swimming a pleasure. The lake steamer, operates from the *laivalturi* of most towns, offering a varied programme of cruises throughout the season. One can also canoe or windsurf but all these watery activities carry their own special hazard, the native mosquito. A good repellent is an essential item in the tourist's kitbag. Although there are no mountains here, the land is by no means flat. Fells go up to 347m (1,138ft) and Ice Age ridges run through the lake system. Where there are no natural high points towers give panoramic views. The most easterly part of the region, lying further east than Leningrad or the Balkans, is north Karelia where west meets east. The Lutheran religion lives side by side with the Orthodox: the Russian border is often only a few kilometres away. The borderzone atmosphere is represented in the World War II trench systems, weaponry that has been preserved and in the 3km (2 miles) no-go area still maintained by the Finns on their side of it.

The watery topography of this area, resembling a gigantic wheel, makes it hard to produce a logical itinerary. One can drive right round the rim or venture up spokes to the hub. The itinerary followed here nearly meets in the centre on several occasions allowing individual flexibility to design one's own route. There are excellent main roads linking the major towns and a network of minor, sometimes unsurfaced ones in between. Most of the attractions are in the towns so main roads are often suggested as the most sensible route. Smaller roads are not necessarily more scenic and it seems unreasonable to use them just for the sake of doing so.

Lahti, just 103km (64 miles) from Helsinki with its air and ship links with the wider world, has been chosen as the starting point.

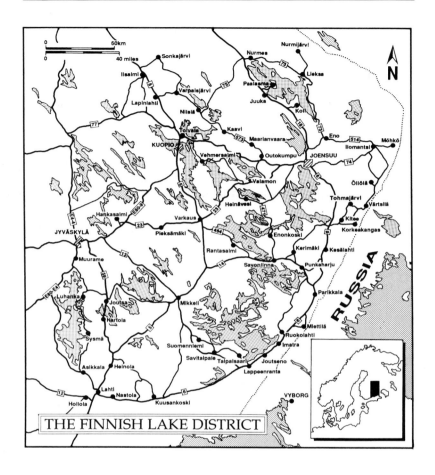

THE FINNISH LAKE DISTRICT

Historically it is a young town, founded in 1905. The historical museum is in one of the oldest buildings, the elegant Lahti manor. There are also museums of art, military medicine, and if you are there on a Sunday afternoon, broadcasting! The ski museum is at the modern sports centre along with a viewing platform at the top of the ski-jump. There is a second observation tower in the centre and the Church of the Holy Cross was designed by famous architect, Alvar Aalto. For small children the Laune family park provides play areas or you could catch the steam train to Heinola and return by boat.

Heinola is only 47km (29 miles) to the north on the 5 but for a more circuitous approach with points of interest along the way, leave Lahti on the 12 towards Kuovola. At **Nastola**, Fundart and Taaresti are both art galleries. Beyond there road 12 goes through trees along the

Salpausselka ridge. At the end, turn left for Sitikkala. This diversion takes country roads passing over dams where the Mankala rapids used to flow, past the ferry to Mankala AS, along a ridge and then right for Kymentaka and right again for Iitti Kyrkonkylä. One passes through forests, past lakes and old farms eventually crossing the Virransilta suspension bridge into Iitti. These are narrow unsurfaced roads and if that is daunting Iitti can also be reached from Kausala off the 5. At **Iitti/Kyrkonkylä** there are a number of nineteenth-century wooden houses (see plan opposite the church) and a local museum.

Follow the signs now to **Kuusankoski** where on a hill to the right there is a local museum and a mill workers' home museum. This is quite new as is the Fire Service Museum in a civil defence shelter near the town centre. The 1920s church is worth looking into for its wealth of Christian symbols — the twelve apostles painted along the nave, glass paintings and even illustrations in the porch. For the sport-minded, Kuusankoski also has an international standard 18-hole golf course. Leave on the 60 towards Jaala, past the piles of logs at the factories that make the town Finland's largest paper producer. An older mill, that produced ground wood pulp and board until 1961, has been restored as a museum at **Verla**, 7km (4 miles) to the right. A visit includes a film of how the work was done, shot in the last few days before it closed.

Continue then through Heinola Mlk to **Heinola** itself. An interesting walk is possible here. Follow the Lintutarhat signs and park here. This is a bird sanctuary receiving some 300 injured birds a year, not all of which can be returned to the wild. From here walk past the round pond to the observation tower where taped birdsong is played to a background of nesting boxes and bird pictures. Continue across the next road past the old spa pavilion, now a restaurant, and drop onto the railway bridge. The path beside the track gives excellent views over Lake Ruotsalainen. Descend at the far end and turn underneath for Forskulla manor which has art exhibitions and a waterside café. Return over the footbridges past Lohiapaja, a pond where one can fish for rainbow trout and under the road to the end of the harbour where cruise boats ply along the lake. In the riverside park, the many-trunked tree is the Czar's poplar, the largest of its kind in Finland. Turn right opposite the harbour building and right again along Kauppakatu. The Taidemuseo holds art exhibitions and the city museum is just beyond the square. At the end of the road go left and right to the tiny church, through its grounds and out onto Harjukatu. The tower is immediately in front but the car park is left and right beyond the round pond.

Return from Heinola north on the 5 towards Mikkeli, then left for
Hartola on the 59. The Nukketalo one passes is a puppet house
planned with children in mind. One leaves one's shoes inside the
door and whispers to avoid waking the wicked witch! Some 300
slightly grotesque puppets are on display and there are two theatres
— one for exhibitions and one with puppets that children can operate
themselves. On reaching Hartola turn right at the garage into the
town. The Ita-Hämeen museum is marked by a row of upright boat
halves outside the windmill. Over the river behind, a wooden suspension bridge sways precariously tempting the daring to cross!
Continue through rejoining the 59 towards Joutsa. Kotilainpiha,
signed to the right, is a domestic animal park down a long forest road.
Bypass Joutsa to take the 610 for an 'off-the-beaten-track' treat. After
8 to 10km (5 to 6 miles) go right signed on a small black village post
to Tammimäki, heading for the Näkötorvill. This steeply laddered
watchtower on the highest point around 241m (790ft) gives a 360°
panorama of surprising length. Continue and circle right to return to
the 610 and Joutsa. Bypass it again, this time on the Pertunmaa road.
At Viheri an old wooden bridge stands beside the new. Turn left for
Marjotaipale and cross the chain ferry at Ollinsalmi. Two older
ferries lie on the far shore behind the huts. Beyond Marjotaipale turn
right for Hirvensalmi and eventually left for Mikkeli. You do not see
much of the many lakes along the way but there are some good views
where you cross their tips.

Mikkeli is a typical Finnish town as revealed from its water tower,
unattractive in its buildings yet with plenty of attractions within its
boundaries. There are two excellent military museums: one about
life in the infantry illustrated with dummies in room settings; the
other, the Headquarters museum, the restored operations room of
Marshall Mannerheim from World War II when the Finns fought the
Russians. Marshall Mannerheim also graces the waxworks at the
Visulahti holiday centre along with a dinosaur park, domestic animals zoo, car racing track for chidren, car museum and miniature
town. Closer into the centre Kalevankangas park has a $2^1/_2$km ($1^1/_2$
miles) nature trail around Hankilampo lake (English booklet available at the tourist office). Finland's third largest Devil's Churn is also
within the town, sitting incongruously in a factory yard in Pursiala
Industrial Estate on the Lapeenranta road out — turn left for
Puumala and first left. Return and cross the Puumala road onto the
Museotie. This is a sixteenth-century summer road fought over in
1789 by the Swedes and Russians. It passes Porrassalmi manor set
picturesquely above the lake. Rejoin the main road south, past

The watchtower at Tammimäki

Ristiina and then left for Suomenniemi and left again for Savitaipale. This twisty hilly route crosses an old stone bridge over rapids at the start of Partakoski. Soon after the massive remains of Kärnäkosken Linnoitus appear on the left. Built in 1793 as part of a defence system against Catherine the Great's Russia, it is now home to wild flowers and sheep. **Savitaipale** is a small town with several attractions. The red granite church has vivid round stained glass windows. There is a church museum in the clockless clock tower and an open-air museum (*talomuseo*) on the hill above the churchyard with a very low-sailed windmill. The Etelä-karlajan Kuvakeskos on the harbour road houses art exhibitions.

Return and take the Taipalsaari road which leads eventually through a series of lakes to **Lappeenranta**. Turn left immediately on entering the town into the Linnuitus fortress. Dating from the Russian period in the eighteenth century, the buildings now house museums, art galleries, handicrafts workshops and a café as well as the Orthodox church built by Russian soldiers in 1785, with its many icons, both painted and in precious metals. In the town itself the Lappee wooden church is unique in that it is a double cross, one inside the other, the brainchild of the farmer from Savitaipale who designed it. The water tower contains a radio, telephone and gramophone collection in its café and signs on the windows point one towards the Russian border 21km (13 miles) away and Viborg another 26km (16 miles) into Russia. One possible cruise from Lapeenranta is through the Saimaa canal to Viborg. A day trip is visa free but so popular that it must be booked at least 8 days in advance. The only drawback to it is that the sight-seeing tour of Viborg is conducted in Finnish. For longer trips visas are needed. Part of the Saimaa canal can be seen by following the Saimaa kanava signs off the Imatra road out. On the way to Imatra one passes through **Joutseno** whose dramatic statue commemorates the great storm of 1972 which destroyed 30 per cent of the local forests and damaged 517 farms. Joutseno also possesses a water tower and a home museum where barley bread is baked on Fridays.

The next stop is **Imatra** where there is a very special display. The rapids on the Vuoksi river that Catherine the Great of Russia visited in 1772 and that Nicholas I declared a crown park in 1842 have been dammed so that all one normally sees is a rocky river bed but once every day in summer the waters are released for just half an hour, filling the chasm with a raging torrent. There are walks through the park beside it and also beyond the dam to the historical museum, 1km (half a mile) away. There is also an industrial workers' museum (Asuntomuseo) in the town. On the way out, just off the 6 (for Joensuu) the church of the Three Crosses (by Alvar Aalto again) has a slender belfry like an arrow plummeting to the ground and 103 windows of which only two are identical. He also designed the stained glass on the ceiling.

Leave the 6 on the 62 for **Ruokolahti** whose church hill is claimed to be the most beautiful in Finland with its white and green church sitting above the lake, its shingled campanile, a regional museum in the old barn and a traditional Karelian farm.

For something more modern, a 20km (12 mile) diversion up the road leads to **Syyspohja** where there are extensive remains of a World War II trench system with bunkers, dugouts and tank traps. Return to the 62 and cross it onto the 4061, a country road that returns across the 406, to the 6. Go left a little way, then right onto the 399, the border route. At **Rautjärvi Kko** there is a church with a parish house museum of local culture. Further on at **Miettilä** the Hammashuitola sign points to a historical barracks dating from 1790 when a Russian battalion was based here. It was last used in World War I as a prisoner-of-war camp.

The Russian border is very close here. Most side roads lead to it but there is no point in taking any as the Finnish border zone is 3km (2 miles) wide — a no-go area with warning signs, guardposts and watchtowers. One needs a permit to enter. On meeting the 6 again, cross it onto the unsurfaced road opposite. Almost immediately on the right there is a mark indicating the boundary set by the Peace of Uusikaupunki (Nystadt) in 1721 that ended the Great Northern War. Following this unsurfaced road through the Finnish countryside will eventually bring one to another set of border posts at Haukkavuori (signed in black to the right). It is just possible to drive up this side road to the picnic place and then walk up the hill to reach the markers. Returning, continue to Simpele, through the Keskusta to join the 6. If 27km (17 miles) of unsurfaced road is too much, the first mark is only just off the 6, then follow that instead.

On the 6 past Simpele, **Koitsanlahti** has a museum in an old house (Kartanomuseo). Just beyond there is a watch tower as one here is driving within the 3km (2 miles) border zone. Cross the water and turn left for Ristimäki, to arrive directly at **Parikkala** church on the shores of Simpelejärvi. Rejoin the 6, then the 14 for **Punkaharju**. One is travelling on a narrow neck of land here between lakes and even the main road gives good views but the best are found by following the Harjualue sign along the 7km (4 miles) Punkaharju ridge. At the far end the Valtionhotelli is possibly Finland's oldest tourist business. This area enchanted Czar Alexander I in 1803 so much that he ordered it to be preserved. State-owned from 1845, a gamekeeper's cottage was built at the top of the ridge. It was enlarged three times in the nineteenth century and so popular that the matching Villa Serena was built nearby. It is now a historic hotel serving Finnish and Russian specialities, with such facilities as boats and bicycles for hire and tennis in the grounds. A lake steamer calls four times daily in the high season and there are sandy beaches and a nature trail too. Just up the road the **Retretti** Art Centre is the largest in the three Nordic countries with special exhibitions and underground displays and Kesamaa, a pleasure park for children. From here Kerimäki and Savonlinna are not far to the north for this is where routes nearly meet and alternatives are possible. The itinerary followed here returns on the 14 past the old railway station — now a handicrafts workshop (*asema-atelje*) — to take the 479 through Punkasalmi to **Kesälahti**. Here the Savupirrti Myllytupu is an open-air museum with ten buildings including another low-sailed windmill.

Return to the 6 and head for **Kitee**. There is a *kotiseutumuseo* in a 1773 barn on the way in. Behind this, in the back of the municipal offices, Pienoisrautatie is the largest model railway in Finland with 200m (656ft) of track. The trains run for 15 minutes on the hour and half hour. Turn left onto the Korkeakangas road which runs briefly right beside the water. Follow Uusi-Värtsilä when signed. At the T-junction here, **Tohmajärvi** is 9km (6 miles) to the left with a pharmacy museum in Nymans house (follow *keskusta* past the *postipankki* and it is in beside the tennis courts) with a home museum on the same site. This road leads on to **Kirkonniemi** where the oldest wooden church in North Karelia stands beside the lake. Return now through Uusi-Värtsilä for **Värtsilä**. On the left over the railway the Kaurilan Koulomuseo is a former school, now a museum. Beyond there where the railway opens out into broad marshalling yards is the goods checkpoint for railway traffic to Russia. The road straight ahead also crosses into Russia but one is stopped short as always at the 3km (2 mile) mark and there is no view of the border itself. Turn instead into Värtsilä for the 500, the border road. Here it is inside the 3km (2 mile) zone and there are yellow-topped posts beside the road and regular signs warning one off. On the left at the start of Värtsilä, the Myllymuseo is a museum in an old mill. The church was built between 1948 and 1950 with the help of donations from American Lutheran parishes. It is clad with pine inside, with an old bell gracing the vestibule by the memorial wall. Further on the Lintutorni signed to the right is a birdwatching tower 800m ($^1/_2$ mile) away on the edge of the lake. Follow the Ilomantsi signs on, past lakes, watching the border marks come and go depending how close the no-go zone is. At one point the trees are ringed with yellow — another warning sign not to penetrate — and there is a watchtower among them. This is the best stretch of road for getting the full impact of Finnish wariness of the Russians beyond their frontier. Further on the 500 becomes uninteresting so turn left for **Öllölä** instead where Koskenniska mill and inn is now a museum. From here follow the 498 through Haukivaara to Ilomantsi.

Here one is in that most easterly province of Finland mentioned earlier. **Ilomantsi** is farther east than Leningrad. On the outskirts a cluster of attractions on Runolaulajan Pirtti (Parpperi Hill) include the Kalevala house where rune singing is still performed; a café serving Karelian delicacies; a museum and the field headquarters of Major General Raappana from World War II. In the town there is an Eläinmuseo with some 1,000 stuffed animals of 100 different species; an Orthodox church, airy and light with icons all round; and a watertower.

Further east still, off the road to Möhkö, the Petkeljärvi National Park contains partly restored dugouts and trenches from 1941 and a 6km (4 mile) nature trail (leaflet from the information) for which boots are not needed in dry weather. **Möhkö** itself has an excellent ironworks museum which also includes a war history room, lumberjack museum, sawmill, barge, smithy etc. The only snag with this excursion is that the road leads only to the border so one must return the same way. From Ilomantsi the 74 is a fast road back to Joensuu and the lake district proper.

This next section describes a circle round Lake Pielinen from **Joensuu**, a pleasant town of tree-lined streets. Kirkokatu runs between the Orthodox and Lutheran churches. Parallel to it, alongside the river (which is a log-towing route), Rantakatu has old wooden houses at one end. The island in the middle, Ilosaari, is home to the North Karelian Museum. Beyond the trotting track lie the university botanical gardens with flourishing greenhouses and the Art Nouveau Vainoniemi Huvila, a wooden villa overlooking the lake. Leave town via Rantakylä, following the river past Utra's tiny church. Keep right before the railway to join the 18 and then the 73 towards Eno. Go right again at the start of Jakokoski, signed Kanavamuseo. The far side of the ferry takes one round to the canal museum. With old tugs on the side of the canal that one can climb aboard, bridges to cross, walks the length of the locks, it is a very worthwhile museum. On leaving, circle left via Pikkasuo to Eno. Go straight through, over the bridge and left and right across the 18 onto the 518 for Ahveninen and Lieksa. Beyond the bridge, from the causeways, the high land visible across the lake is Koli which will be visited later. Now follow the Museotie, an old road built spectacularly along a narrow ridge between lakes. The Russians forced local peasants to build it during the Russo-Swedish war of 1741-3. Continue through towards Vuonislahti where Koli is again clearly visible from the bridge. Beyond Vuonislahti, Eva Ryynäsen's studio-workshop is on the right. She is a wood sculptress, some of whose work can also be seen in the ultra-modern church in **Lieksa**. On arriving here one passes first the huge Pielinenmuseo (Outdoor Museum) with some ninety sights. The new church is just beyond the bridge (go right and under to reach it). Also in the church park is a tiny Orthodox *tsasouna* or chapel. The town's watertower has no lift. The 244 steps up the hollow interior are not for the faint-hearted nor the vertiginous but the view over the leafy town is good.

Two diversions are possible from Lieksa. The first, just before the

View over Lieksa from the watertower

town, is 30km (19 miles) to the **Ruunaa** rapids which one can shoot in organised parties (book first). There is also a government hiking area. Park at the Neitikoski information for map leaflets and a 650m (700yd) plank walk, suitable for wheelchairs, to the Neitikoski rapids. There are also short trails suitable for families from the Siikakoski parking. Return on the same route. The other diversion is beyond Lieksa off the 73 Nurmes road. Take road 524 for 26km (16 miles) to Nurmijärvi and another 5km (3 miles) up the border road towards **Kivivaara** which saw battles in the 1939-40 Winter War against Russia. The battlelines, trenches, tank barriers and the three storey machine gun nests in Vornanen cave have been restored. The return can be made on road 526 to Vieki and Nurmes. If neither diversion appeals, follow road 73 direct to **Nurmes**.

Here the Bomba village on the outskirts is a purpose-built tourist village, hotel, restaurant, cabins, in the old Karelian style, worth exploring if only because it is so different from what one sees in the countryside. Nurmes is built on a peninsula with a ridge along its back lined with double rows of birches and wooden houses. Its square is graced by a most striking monument to composer P. J. Hannikainen. This is the work of Eva Rynäsen and is a genuine dead pine cast into bronze. Beyond the main town and over the main road crossroads, the first right leads to Ikolanmuseo, a homestead museum in reds and browns. Leave on the Kajaavi road, turning left for Kynsiniemi, then straight on for Lukanpuro to join the 18 south.

Shortly before Juuka go left for **Paalasmaa**, a short diversion that takes you right out into the lake. Beyond the ferry a series of causeways gives the best views of Pielinen from anywhere in the area. Return then to **Juuka**. The Puujuuka signs lead into the old wooden centre where there is a mill museum. On the way back out, along a tiny right just before rejoining the 18, the Pitäjäimuseo is a large barn divided into workshops and even a telephone operator's room.

Now one has almost reached **Koli** which at 347m (1,138ft) is the highest fell in Finland. Follow the Ukko-Koli signs up to the hotel. From here 156 steps lead the last 300m (186ft) to the top from where one can see the whole of Pielinen spread out like a map. There are also five different trails from here varying from 3 to 8km (2 to 5 miles) in length. The hotel has maps and leaflets and there is English information on the flora on the noticeboards. Take the Harivaari road back to the 18 and continue south. Just before Kontiolahti a sign points 11km (7 miles) up the Heinävaara road to the **Kolvanan Uuro**, yet another possible diversion. This is a canyon with a 5km (3 mile) nature trail in it that is for good walkers only. **Kontiolahti** itself has a homestead museum and a small Orthodox log church with the distinctive patriarchal cross and onion dome on its roof. From here it is not far on the 18 back to Joensuu.

Another loop is possible from Outokumpu. To reach here leave Joensuu on the 17 towards Koupio. There is a car museum 1km ($^1/_2$ mile) to the right along the 502 and shortly afterwards a clutch of small museums at Liperi to the left. In **Liperi** turn right onto the 482 and the Museot are signed first left. Close together one finds a collection of old buildings (*ulkomuseo*); a home museum with domestic items (Enwald-kotimuseo) and the Maatalomuseo of agrarian equipment. Back on the 17 another *ulkomuseo* is signed at **Kompero** before one arrives at **Outokumpu**, a town whose chief claim to fame is the large mining museum complex. Here are displayed original equipment, miniature models, safety methods, a mine worker's home from the 1930s and the old mining tower plus a multi-vision theatre and playground.

Leave Outokumpu on the 573 for Kaavi for a loop north and west. This is hilly country. **Maarionvaara** is a skiing area though Finnish downhill routes are nothing compared to the Alps. They do far more crosscountry skiing. One passes signs to more rapids — 13 and 21km (8 and 13 miles) away on the Vaikonjoki river — which one can shoot in parties. Book in advance. **Kaavi** has a very modern church, light and airy. Beyond there, bypass Juankoski, taking the 570 for Säyneinen, a pleasantly varied route with farming and open lake

views. After Lake Vuotjärvi take the 5701 towards Nilsiä. Just before
the district name, follow the small black **Pisa** sign to the right. Park
after about 2km (1 mile) where a signed path heads for this 271m
(889ft) hill. Although the post says 1¹/₂km (1 mile) allow 40 minutes
to reach the top as the way is rough in parts and steep in others and
there are signboards to study about the flora and fauna. Follow the
Pisa signs and the blue marks. The *kaivo* one passes is a well with
drinking bowl. The Näköalapaikka which one reaches in half the
time gives the best views. Beyond here the path climbs steeply past
the quartz outcrop to the 1595 boundary mark with its three crowns
and four sets of initials at the highest point. The views here are
obscured by trees and one may prefer not to make this final ascent.

From Pisa continue towards Nilsiä and **Varpaisjärvi** which has a
home museum, an evocative statue to Ruuna Reipas (a famous local
trotter) and a twentieth-century black granite church in the Jugend
style. Asymetric not cruciform, it contains an altar window of coloured glass and a large mural of the *Last Supper*. With a good map
you can find the way north from here to **Sonkajärvi** for its
Pullomuseo (International Bottle Museum) but if that does not appeal the 582 carries one west to **Lapinlahti**. This is a cultural centre
with concerts, music camps and two art museums, one dedicated
solely to the works of sculptor Emil Halonen. From there one can
cross by ferry and causeway to join the 564 south towards Kuopio.
Alternatively **Iisalmi**, 25km (15¹/₂ miles) north on the 5 is interesting
and one can return south on the 564 from here. Iisalmi can also be
reached on the 87 from Sonkajärvi. This brings one directly north of
Iisalmi to the Koljonviria area where an important battle was fought
between Finns and Russians in 1808. The Dolgorukin monument to
the right of the road is a memorial in Russian raised by the relatives
of this prince who was killed in the fighting. The museum behind it
is the childhood home of Finnish writer Juhani Aho and even this
saw some of the fighting, for the granary has bullet holes in one end.
Beyond the new bridge the campsite has a 2¹/₂km (1¹/₂ mile) trail
round the battlefield with information boards as well as rowing
boats, canoes and surfboards for hire. Further on, Colonel Sandels
monument marks where his headquarters was in this battle. Return
from here into Iisalmi. The old church is more decorative than most
with friezes and oval paintings on the galleries. There is also a
Panimomuseo (Brewing Museum) all casks and machines, upstairs
in a café on the waterfront and beyond the Paloisvirta bridge, a local
museum. This road continues through, third left across the railway,
second right, to Peltosalmi and the 564 south beyond the next bridge.

On reaching road 77 there are several water treats in store. Go right for just a few kilometres and right again signed **Korkeakoski**. Park at the information and walk into the woods. Beyond the bridge go right for a viewing platform over Finland's highest wild waterfall, a narrow river tumbling almost vertically down for 46m (151ft). Left leads to a long shallow staircase to the bottom. Returning along the 77, the Tuovinlanlahti area has more to offer: first a birdtower (*lintutorni*) to the left just after crossing a marshy river; then, just beyond the Martikkala turning, a disused canal, followed by rapids tumbling through sluices. Ahkiolahden kanavat is a new canal area which one can walk around from the parking by the bridge. It is amazing just how many canals and rivers the road crosses in this short area. There is also another birdtower beyond Maaninka just after the Alapitkä turning. From here, join the 5/E80 for Kuopio.

Kuopio offers many attractions. There is the Puijo tower with its slowly revolving panorama restaurant, 224m (735ft) above Lake Kallavesi, giving excellent views in all directions. One can even look down on summer ski-jumpers taking off from ice and landing on plastic. In winter it would be snow-covered — as would the lake where there is a signpost pointing skiers across the water. There is a steam exhibition in the old customs warehouse at the quay. In summer cruises round the island-dotted waters leave from here and there are evening markets every day. One tiny offshore island sports a windmill while in the lakeside gardens a brick factory chimney has been preserved as an industrial monument. Two cathedrals, an art gallery, the university botanical gardens and several museums can also be visited.

Leave on the motorway towards Jyväskylä then left on the 537 for Vehmersalmi, a route across the lake involving two ferries. As one leaves the second, there is a museum on the first road right and a handicrafts workshop on the edge of the first estate. There is bathing in the lake and a church with friezes, an interesting stained glass window but one of the gloomiest altar paintings ever! Take the Heinävesi road out (539) across causeways at first, following it all the way to **Palokki**. It is a long run, not all of it surfaced, but there is lots to do once one arrives. Lintulan Luostari is an Orthodox convent with a beautiful church, a café in the former manorhouse and a souvenir shop where you can buy your own icon. Here too all the candles used in Finnish Orthodox churches are made. Down the road at **Varistaipale** the tallest canal in the Nordic countries raises boats $14^1/_2$m (48ft) through a staircase of locks. The canal museum contains photographs of the construction from 1911 on, and tools in

The Finnish Orthodox monastery at Valamon

the loft. English notes describe it all. Left beyond the canal bridge takes one through to Valamon Luostan, Finland's main Orthodox monastery. There is a hotel on the site and courses are run (in English) on Orthodoxy, iconography and herbal gardening. The church houses the miraculous icon of the Mother of God of Konevitsa among other treasures. Guided tours in English are available. Follow the road down to the 23 and go right to **Karvio** where another canal bypasses rapids as the Varisvesi joins Kermijärvi lake. Circle this latter to **Heinävesi** on the opposite shore. The church is so high on a hill above the town that the first nineteenth-century one was struck by lightning during a service and burnt down. There are good views over the lake from its replacement. A local museum sits beside the one way road off the hill. The 476 continues to Kerma where one passes the rapids and canal out of this side of the lake, reminding one that many of these lakes serve as waterways for both pleasure and commerce. Perhaps the most spectacular form of commerce is the giant log-trains that pass through some of the lakes. Towed by a

Olavilinna Castle, Savonlinna

single tug, several thousand logs trail behind, shepherded by a second tug that prods and pushes them into the right channel. These can sometimes be seen here on the 471 route to Enonkoski where they can hold the ferry up for a good half hour while they chug slowly past on their way to the factories at Varkhaus. **Enonkoski** has an old single-span bridge that cost 300 marks for a single householder to build from boulders off the local fields, and a *pitäjämuseo* (parish museum) just behind the church.

Continue south but take the 4712 left for Kerimäki as a loop before going to Savonlinna. **Kerimäki** is well worth visiting. Not only has it the largest wooden church in the world, using two tiers of galleries to pack 3,300 people in, but one can climb the belltower by way of steep high-stepped ladders for views over the church and Lake Puruvesi. Finland's freshwater Fishing Museum is by the lake. For two different attractions head first for the Herttua hotel, on the Kala satama road where 1940s ordnance is displayed in the grounds along with dugout, tent HQ and a 500m (1,640ft) trench system. An indoor weapons and uniforms section can be visited via reception. The road beyond is a picturesque ridge run out to Hälvä Island. Just before the last causeway one can hire rowing boats to cross to Hyteerman island. Return by the same route and take the 71 to Savonlinna.

Savonlinna developed originally as a trading settlement around its spectacular Olavilinna Castle. Built in 1475, it is one of the best preserved medieval castles in northern Europe. The Savonlinna

Boat leaving the canal at Varkaus

opera festival is held here every year as are conferences and festive occasions but it is a tourist attraction too with 50 minute guided tours in English every hour on the hour. The massive square building nearby houses the provincial museum and moored beyond are three museum ships with displays inside. Continue through on the 14 towards Mikkeli, then right on the 464 for Varkaus. At **Rantasalmi** a group of islands in the lake form the Linnansaari National Park. The information office at the camping here gives details of boat connections and access to the home museum behind the trees. On approaching **Varkaus**, the mechanical music museum, voted Finland's best tourist attraction in 1988, traces this form of entertainment from the eighteenth century to the present day. Practical demonstrations enliven one's visit. Another museum is the National Central Canal at Taipale on the 23 towards Joensuu. Between the two one can find town and art museums, the latter beside the watertower with its observation platform, and both Lutheran and Orthodox churches.

Leave on the 23 towards Jyväskylä on a last lap back to Lahti. Turn right for Jäppilä when signed on a scenic route along the Syrjäharju ridge. The centre of **Jäppilä**, called Kyrkonkylä, boasts a small church and a parish museum that opens on Sunday afternoons. Return to the crossroads and go right for **Pieksämäki**. The tourist office here can provide a town walk that takes in all the sights including the Nukkekoti (Dolls Home), a tiny villa inhabited now by

The tower of the ski-jump at Jyväskylä

puppets and providing a play house for smaller children. The suburban parish church has eighteenth-century paintings round the galleries. An 8km (5 mile) nature trail sets off from here or there is a 5km (3 mile) one from Metsäopisto by Lake Kukkarojärvi — details of both from the tourist office. Take the 23 on towards Jyväskylä and either go directly there or, for a 23 building museum, follow the signs to **Hankasalmi** where it is beside the church and rejoin the 23 at Niemisjärvi.

Jyväskylä is a large town based around the Harju ridge, where the Vesilinna watertower has two observation levels over the town. For even more spectacular views, follow the Laatavuori signs and then Näkötorni for the lift up the ski-jump. One emerges onto a tiny platform above the highest level. The town is full of museums ranging from the Finnish handicraft museum to one devoted to municipal engineering and one to Jyväskylä's most famous son, architect Alvar Aalto. Thirty buildings in the city were designed by him, covering the whole range of his career from the 1920s to the 1980s.

A lock on the canal at Vääksy

There are also lake cruises, both day and evening, or one could wander round Finland's largest garden centre, Viherlandia. The city tourist office can provide details and maps of all this and more.

Leave Jyväskylä on the Lahti road. At **Muurame** there is a unique attraction — a Sauna Museum. The use of a sauna or perspiration bath is traditional in Finland from ancient times to the present day. Finnish saunas are unusual in that the dry hot air is alternated with steam by throwing water onto the hot stones of the stove. Twenty-three saunas are collected together here, with regional or age variations, including wartime saunas in hit-proof dugouts. The admission fee includes a comprehensive booklet in English and groups can take a perspiration bath together in the sauna of their choice! Muurame's other attraction, especially after Jyväskylä, is its 1929 Alvar Aalto church from his Italian period — note its campanile and small high windows. The inside is light with white paint and golden wood, an unusual altar painting and an interesting ceiling.

Rejoin the Lahti road until signed left on the 610 for Joutsa. This is one of the best scenic routes in the lake district. Points of interest along the way include a summer café in an old mill and then, 2km (1 mile) into **Tammijärvi**, the Mäkitupalaismuseo — an old cottars settlement still on its original site. Each tiny building has a separate use and there is even a sauna. Return and take the Luhanka road. At Sysma follow the Suopelto road to the right and after 5km (3 miles) the Päijäisalo signs for a 2 to 3km (1 to 2 mile) nature path from the parking through woods to a birdtower overlooking the lake. Return and follow Heinola and then the 314 Vääksy road. This brings one onto the 8km (5 mile) long Pulkkilanharju ridge with a nature trail, walks and fauna boards at the information kiosk just before the 1970 bridge. Beyond the ridge in **Asikkala** the local museum is in two sections, one in the storehouse by the church, the other, a small farm, down the track opposite. On reaching **Vääksy** ignore the first Lahti sign and proceed into the town over the canal. Just beyond it the D. Kalmarin museum in an old yellow villa houses art exhibitions. Follow the next Lahti sign. Soon after joining the main road the Talluka Automuseum appears on the right just before the Talluka hotel. It combines an art section with its historic cars. This effectively returns one to the starting point of Lahti though Hollola on the opposite shore of the lake to Vääksy deserves a visit.

On the way here from Lahti one passes the Messilä slalom ski area with its bobsleigh run, watersplash, dodgem boats, pony riding and other fun for children. **Hollola** itself possesses a medieval greystone church built on boulders with deep embrasures for doors and windows. Beyond the church there are both parish and open-air museums. The walk signed Linnamäki leads up to Kappatuosia hill fort where archaeological excavations show Stone Age occupation though its chief period of activity was early medieval. Oriental coins and a knight's spur are among finds from the digs. The wooden tower on top gives superb lake views which is the right memory with which to leave this scenic area of Finland.

Further Information
— The Finnish Lake District —

Museum denotes local museum in storehouse or farm buildings.

Asikkala
Museum
Open: late May to mid-August, Tuesday to Saturday 12noon-4pm.

Enonkoski
Pitäjämuseo (Parish Museum)
Open: June to August, Saturday and Sunday 11am-4pm.

Hankasalmi
Museum
Open: beginning June to end August, 12noon-7pm.

Hartola
Kotiseutumuseo (Domestic Animal Park)
Open: beginning June to mid-September, Monday to Saturday 12noon-8pm.

Ita-Hämeen-Museum
Open: mid-May to early August 11am-6pm.

Heinola
Taidemuseo
Open: Sunday to Friday, 11am-6pm. Saturday 11am-2pm.

Aviary and Watertower
Open: 11am-6pm.

City Museum
Open: Tuesday to Sunday, 12noon-4pm.

Forskulla Art Centre
Open: summer, Sunday to Friday 10am-8pm. Saturday 10am-4pm.

Musta-Ratsu Nukketalo (House of Puppets)
Open: June to August daily 12noon-4pm.

Hollola
Messilä Holiday Centre
Open: early May to mid-August, 10am-7pm.

Museum
Open: mid-May to early August, 11am-6pm.

Iisalmi
Paninomuseo (Brewery Museum)
Open: 10am-8pm.

Juhani Aho Museum
Open: beginning May to end August 9am-1pm and 2-6pm.

Museum
Open: 12noon-8pm.

Old Church
Open: 11am-6pm.

Iitti/Kyrkonkylä
Museum
Open: Sunday to Friday 11am-7pm. Saturday 11am-3pm.

Ilomantsi
Eläinmuseo (Zoological Museum)
Open: June to mid-August 10am-5pm.

Orthodox Church
Open: June to early August, Monday to Saturday 10am-6pm. Sunday 12noon-6pm.

Parpperi Hill Attractions
Open: 1 June to mid-August 9am-8pm. Rest of August 10am-6pm.

Imatra
Farm Museum and Industrial Workers Museum
Open: May to August, Tuesday to Sunday 10am-6pm.

Rapids
Open: beginning June to early August, Monday to Saturday 7pm. Sunday 3pm.

Joensuu
Botanical Gardens
Open: Wednesday to Monday 10am-6pm.

Lutheran Church
Open: 10am-6pm.

Orthodox Church
Open: Monday to Friday 10am-1pm and 2-6pm.

Pohjois Karjalan Museum
Open: Tuesday, Thursday and Friday 12noon-4pm. Saturday 10am-4pm. Sunday 10am-6pm.

Joutseno
Museum
Open: Monday to Thursday 12noon-6pm. Friday 8am-6pm. Saturday and Sunday 11am-3pm.

Water Tower
Open: Monday to Friday 1-7pm. Saturday and Sunday 11am-3pm.

Juuka
Museums
Open: beginning June to end August, Tuesday to Sunday 10am-5pm.

Jyväskylä
Finnish Handicrafts Museum
Open: Tuesday to Sunday 11am-6pm.

Laajavuori Ski-jump
Open: 11am-7pm.

Vesilinna Watertower
Open: beginning to end May and mid- to end August, 10am-6pm. Beginning June to mid-August, 10am-8pm.

Viherlandia
Open: May to August, Monday to Friday 9am-8pm. Saturday 9am-6pm,

Sunday 10am-6pm. Also open rest of year Monday to Friday 9am-8pm. Saturday 9am-4pm, Sunday 11am-6pm.

Kerimäki
Church
Open: June to mid-August, Monday to Friday 9am-8pm. Saturday 9am-6pm. Holidays 11am-8pm.

Fishing Museum
Open: mid-May to mid-June and August, 12noon-3pm. Mid-June and July 11am-6pm.

Herttua Hotel Ordnance Museum
Open: 9am-8pm.

Kitee
Pienoisrautatie (Model Railway)
Open: Monday to Friday 10am-4pm. Saturday 10am-2pm. Sunday 12noon-4pm.

Koitsanlahti
Kartanomuseo
Open: June to August, 10am-6pm.

Kompero
Museum
Open: mid-June to mid-August, Tuesday to Sunday 1-5pm.

Kuopio
Art Museum
Open: Monday to Saturday 9am-4.30pm. Sunday 11am-6pm. Wednesday 4.30-8pm.

Botanical Gardens
Open: Tuesday to Sunday 12noon-3pm. Tuesday and Sunday 3-7pm.

Cathedral
Open: June to August 10am-5pm.

Puijo Tower
Open: 9am-1am.

Steam Exhibition
Open: 1-9pm.

Kuusankoski
Fire Service Museum
Local and Mill Workers' Museum
Open: May to September, Monday 12noon-4pm. Tuesday, Wednesday, Thursday and Sunday, 12noon-6pm.

Lahti
Hennala Military Medicine Museum
Open: May and mid-August to end September. Thursday, Saturday and Sunday 11am-3pm. June to mid-August, Tuesday to Friday 12noon-5pm. Saturday and Sunday 11am-3pm.

History Museum
Tuesday to Sunday, 12noon-4pm. Thursday 6-8pm.

Ski-jump Viewing Platform
Open: June and July, Monday to Friday 11am-6pm. Saturday and Sunday 10am-5pm.

Lappeenranta
Cruises to Viborg. Saimaa Lines
☎ 95353300

Lappee Wooden Church
Open: June to mid-August, 10am-5pm.

Linnuitus Museums, Orthodox Church
All open: Tuesday to Sunday 11am-5pm. Thursday 11am-8pm.

Watertower
Open: June to August, 11am-7pm.

Lieksa
Church
Open: June to mid-August, 11am-7pm.

Orthodox Chapel
Open: mid-June to early August, Sunday 11am-3pm.

Pielinenmuseo (Outdoor Museum)
Open: mid-May to mid-August, 9am-6pm. Mid-August to mid-September 10am-6pm.

Watertower
Open: June to mid-August, 12noon-6pm.

Liperi
Automuseum
Open: mid to end May and early September, Saturday and Sunday 11am-7pm. June to August 11am-7pm.

Museums
Open: early June to mid-August, Tuesday to Sunday 12noon-5pm.

Mikkeli
Headquarters Museum
Open: mid-May to end August, 11am-5pm.

Infantry Museum
Open: mid-May to mid-June and mid-August to mid-September, Tuesday to Sunday 11am-6pm. Mid-June to mid-August 11am-6pm.

Naisvuori Tower
Open: June to mid-August, 10am-9pm.

Visilahti Holiday Centre
Open: June to mid-August daily 10am-7pm.

Möhkö
Ironworks Museum
Open: June to mid-August, Sunday to Friday 10am-6pm. Saturday 10am-4pm.

Muurame
Alvar Aalto Church
Open: 9am-6pm.

Sauna Museum
Open: June to August, 10am-6pm.

Nurmes
Museum
Open: June to August, Tuesday to Sunday 12noon-6pm.

Outokumpu
Mining Museum
Open: daily June to August 10am-6pm.

Palokki
Lintulalan Luostari (Convent)
Open: 10am-6pm.

Pieksämäki
Church
Open: 10am-4pm.

Nukkekoti (Dolls Home)
Open: early June to August, 10am-6pm.

Punkaharju
Kesamaa Adventure Park
Open: mid-May to mid-August.

Retretti Art Centre
Open: 10am-7pm daily all year.

Ruokolahti
Museum
Open: Monday to Friday 12noon-6pm. Saturday 12noon-4pm. Sunday 11am-4pm.

Ruunaa
Rapids
☎ 97533111

Savitaipale
Art Exhibiton
Open: Monday to Friday 12noon-7pm. Saturday 10am-3pm. Sunday 11am-6pm.

Church
Open: 11am-6pm.

Museums
Open: Tuesday to Sunday 12noon-6pm.

Savonlinna
Olavilinna Castle
Open: June to mid-August, guided tours on the hour 10am-5pm.

Provincial Museum
Open: late June to early August, 10am-8pm. Rest of year Tuesday to Sunday 11am-5pm.

Sonkajärvi
Pullomuseo (International Bottle Museum)
Open: June to August, 10am-8pm.

Tammijärvi
Mäkitupalaismuseo (Cottars Museum)
Open: June to mid-August 12noon-7pm.

Tohmajärvi
Nyman House Pharmacy Museum
Open: mid-June to mid-August, Monday to Friday 9am-3pm.

Vääksy
Tallukka Automuseum
Open: Monday to Saturday 12noon-6pm. Sunday 11am-4pm.

Valamo
Monastery
Open: 10am-6pm daily, all year.

Varistaipale
Canal Museum
Open: mid-June to mid-August 10am-6pm.

Varkaus
Mechanical Music Museum
Open: June, August, September, Tuesday to Sunday 11am-7pm. July 9am-9pm.

Watertower
Open: June to mid-August, Monday to Friday 10am-8pm. Saturday 9am-5pm. Sunday 12noon-8pm.

Värtsilä
Church
Open: June to August, Sunday to Thursday 9am-4pm.

Kaurilan Koulomuseo (School)
Open: Tuesday to Thursday 12noon-4pm. Mid-June to mid-August.

Myllymuseo (Mill Museum)
Open: Sunday 12noon-3pm.

Verla
Mill Museum
Open: mid-May to end August, 10am-12noon and 1-5pm.

Vuonislahti
Eva Rynäsan Sculptures
Open: June to August, 11am-6pm.

Tourist Information Centres

Heinola
Torikatu 8
SF18100 Heinola
☎ 1058444

Iisalmi
Kauppakatu 14
SF-74100 Iisalmi
☎ 7722346

Imatra
Keskusasema
PB22
SF-55101 Imatra
☎ 5467988

Joensuu
Koskikatu 1
SF-80100 Joensuu
☎ 73201362

Jyväskylä
Vapaudenkatu 38
SF-40100 Jyväskylä
☎ 41294083

Kuopio
Haapaniemenkatu 17
SF-70100 Kuopio
☎ 71182584

Kuusankoski
Kuusankoski-talo
Kymenlaaksonkatu 1
SF-45700 Kuusankoski
☎ 51404336

Lahti
Torikatu 3B
PB175
SF-15111 Lahti
☎ 18182580

Lapeenranta
Bus Station
PB113
SF-53101 Lapeenranta
☎ 5318850

Lieksa
Pielisentie 7
SF-81700 Lieksa
☎ 7520500

Mikkeli
Hallituskatu 3a
SF-50100 Mikkeli
☎ 55151444

Nurmes
Kirkkokatu 12
SF-75500 Nurmes
☎ 7621770

Outokumpu
Sepankatu 6
SF-83500 Outokumpu
☎ 7354793

Pieksämäki
Torikatu 14
SF-76100 Pieksämäki
☎ 95813613

Savonlinna
Puistokatu 1
SF-57100 Savonlinna
☎ 5713492

Varkaus
Ahsltröminkatu 11
SF-78250 Varkaus
☎ 72292383

Index

Accommodation and Eating Out

English is widely spoken in all four countries. Hotels and restaurants can usually provide an English menu — if not, one of the waiters will usually be able to translate. Alternatively a good pocket dictionary or phrasebook should include a section on restaurant food. Service charges are already included on most bills.

Drink/drive laws are very strict in all four countries. 0.05 per cent alcohol is the legal limit. It is safest not to drink at all when driving. In Norway there are also banned substances for drivers which include some medicines available on prescription outside Norway.

Currency

Norway

Norwegian currency is the *Krone* or NOK. One *Krone* subdivides into 100 *øre* though only 10 and 50 *øre* coins exist. *Kroner* come in 1, 5, and 10 value coins and notes of 50, 100, 500 and 1,000 NOK. Foreign currency and travellers' cheques can be exchanged at many hotels as well as banks. The latter exist in all towns and many large villages but only open Monday to Friday. All major credit cards (Eurocard/Mastercard, Visa, American Express, Diners) are generally accepted in hotels, restaurants, garages, tourist shops and large stores but smaller places, particularly off the beaten track, prefer cash. British cheques backed by a Eurocheque card can be cashed at leading banks.

Sweden

Swedish currency is the *Krona* or SEK which also subdivides into 100 øre. There is a 50 øre coin, also 1, 5 and 10 SEK coins. Notes are in values of 20, 50, 100, 500 and 1000 SEK.

Foreign currency and travellers' cheques can be exchanged at many hotels as well as banks. The latter only open Monday to Friday. All major credit cards (Eurocard/Mastercard, Visa, American Express, Diners) are generally accepted in hotels, restaurants, garages, tourist shops and large stores but smaller places, particularly off the beaten track, prefer cash. British cheques backed by a Eurocheque card can be cashed at leading banks.

Telephone Services

Norway

To telephone Norway the international dialling code is: from the USA and Canada (011) 47, UK (010) 47 and Australia (0011) 47.

The international code for dialling out from Norway is 095, followed by your own country's national code. English language operator assistance can be reached by dialling 093.

Sweden

To telephone Sweden from your home country dial the international code first, followed by the national code for Sweden which is 46. The international code for dialling out from Sweden is 009, followed by your own country's national code.

Tipping

Sweden

Tips are included in hotel and restaurant bills but taxi drivers expect 10-15 per cent.

Tourist Information Offices

Norway

UK
Norwegian National Tourist Office
Charles House
5 Lower Regent Street,
London SW1Y 4LR
☎ 071 839 2650

USA and Canada
Norwegian Tourist Board
655 Third Avenue
New York
NY 10017
☎ (212) 949 2333

Denmark

UK
The Danish Tourist Board
169 Regent Street
London W1R 8PY
☎ 071 734 2637

USA
The Danish Tourist Board
655 Third Avenue
18th floor
New York
NY 10017
☎ (212) 949 2333

Canada
The Danish Tourist Board
PO Box 115, Station 'N'
Toronto,
Ontario M8V 3SA
☎ (416) 8239620

Sweden

UK
Swedish Travel & Tourism Council
73 Welbeck Street
London W1M 8AN
☎ 071 935 4130

USA
Swedish Tourist Board
(Head Office USA)
655 Third Avenue
18th floor
New York
NY10017
☎ (212) 9492333

Finland

UK
Finnish Tourist Board UK Office
66/68 Haymarket
London SW1Y 4RF
☎ 071 8394048

USA
Finnish Tourist Board
655 Third Avenue
New York
NY 10017
☎ (212) 949 2333

Accommodation and Eating Out

❋❋❋ Expensive
❋❋   Moderate
❋   Inexpensive

All the hotels listed below include
restaurants, unless stated otherwise.

Norway

There are several hotel schemes available that offer reduced prices in first class
hotels in the summer season. The largest is the Fjord Pass which covers 294 Norwegian hotels divided into four price categories. If one is visiting just Norway, this is
the most attractive option. Other schemes offer a selection of hotels in the whole
Scandinavian area. These include Best Western Hotelcheque Scandinavia (BWN);
Scandinavian Bonuspass which uses Inter Nor Hotels; and the Scandic Hotel
MiniPas which covers Norway and Denmark. A hotel booklet containing information on some 870 hotels is available on request from the Norwegian tourist board.
Addresses for further information.

Fjord Tours A/S
PO Box 1752 Nordnes
N-5024 Bergen
Norway

Best Western Hotels
Storgt, 117
PO Box 25
N-2601 Lillehammer
Norway

Inter Nor Hotels
Dronningensgt 40
N-0154 Oslo
Norway

Scandic Booking Service
Parkvn 68
N-0254 Oslo
Norway

Chapter 1 •
Vestfold and Telemark

Åsgårdstrand
Åsgårdstrand Hotell ❋❋
Strandpromenaden
N-3155 Åsgårdstrand
☎ 033 81 040

Brevik
Korvetten Hotell ❋❋
N-3950 Brevik
☎ 03 57 11 66

Horten
Grand-Ocean Hotell ❋❋❋
Jernbanegt 1
N-3190 Horten
☎ 033 41 772

Hovden
Hovdestøylen Hotell og Hyttetun ❋❋❋
N-4695 Hovden
☎ 043 39 552
BWN/Fjord Pass

Kongsberg
Gyldenløve Hotell ❋❋
Herm Fossgt 1
N-3600 Kongsberg   ☎ 03 73 17 44
BWN/Fjord Pass

Kviteseid
Kviteseid Hotel A/S ❋❋❋
N-3850 Kviteseid
☎ 036 53 222

Langesund
Skjærgården Hotell og Badepark ❋❋❋
Stathelleveien 35
N-3970 Langesund
☎ 03 97 30 11
Fjord Pass/Scandinavian Bonuspass
Expensive to very expensive. Includes
tropical bathing park.

Larvik
Inter Nor Grand Hotel ❋❋
Strogt 38/40
N-3250 Larvik   ☎ 034 87 800
Scandinavian Bonuspass

Rauland
Rauland Høyfjellshotell ✳✳
N-3864 Rauland
☎ 036 73 222
Fjord Pass

Rjukan
Gaustablikk Høyfjellshotell Appartment og skisenter ✳✳
N-3660 Rjukan
☎ 036 91 422
BWN/Fjord Pass

Sandefjord
Granerød Hotell ✳
Krokemovn 41
N-3200 Sandefjord
☎ 03477 077
Fjord Pass

Skien
Høyers Hotell ✳✳
Kongensgt 6
N-3724 Skien
☎ 03 52 05 40
Rainbow Hotel

Stavern
Wassilioff Hotel ✳✳
Havnegt 1
N-3290 Stavern
☎ 034 98 764
Romantik Hotel

Tønsberg
Grand Hotel A/S ✳✳✳
Øvre Langgt 65
N-3100 Tønsberg
☎ 033 12 203
BWN/Fjord Pass

Valle
Bergtun Hotel ✳
N-4690 Valle
☎ 043 37 270

Vrådal
Straand Hotel ✳✳
N-3853 Vrådal
☎ 036 56 100
Fjord Pass

Chapter 2 •
Glaciers and Mountains

Årdalstangen
Klingenberg Fjord Hotell ✳✳✳
N-5875 Årdalstangen
☎ 056 61 122
fjordpadd

Bøverdalen
Juvashytta ✳
N-2687 Bøverdalen
☎ 094 90 945
At top of toll road up Juvashytta.
Specialises in mountain activities.

Fjærland
Fjærland Fjord Hotel ✳✳
N-5855 Fjærland
☎ 056 93 161

Leikanger
Leikanger Fjordhotell ✳✳✳
N-5842 Leikanger
☎ 056 53 622

Loen
Alexandra Hotel ✳✳✳
N-6878 Loen
☎ 057 77 660
Expensive to extremely expensive! It is *the* hotel to stay in at Loen for the Briksdal glacier trip.

Richards Hotell ✳
N-6878 Loen
☎ 057 77 661
Inexpensive and perfectly adequate alternative. You pay for the cachet at the Alexandra.

Lom
Spiterstulen ✳
Jotunheimen
N-2686 Lom
☎ 062 11 480
At end of the toll road.
Specialises in mountain activities.

Olden
Olden Fjordhotell ✳✳✳
N-6870 Olden
☎ 057 73 400
Fjord Pass/BWN

Yris Hotell ✳✳
N-6870 Olden
☎ 05 12 54 85
Fjord Pass

Solvorn
Walaker Hotell ✳✳
N-5815 Solvorn
☎ 056 84 207
Fjord Pass

Skjolden
Skjolden Hotel ✳
N-5833 Skjolden
☎ 056 86 606

Stryn
Stryn Hotel ✳✳
Visnesveg 1
N-6880 Stryn
☎ 057 71 802
Fjord Pass

Chapter 3 •
The Coast from Florø to Hitra

Ålesund
Rica Parken Hotel ✳✳
Storgt 16
N-6002 Ålesund
☎ 071 25 050
Fjord Pass

Åndalsnes
Grand Hotel Bellevue ✳✳
Åndalsgt 5
N-6300 Åndalsnes
☎ 072 21 011
Fjord Pass

Florø
Victoria Hotel A/S ✳✳✳
Markegt 43
N-6900 Florø
☎ 057 41 033
Fjord Pass

Fillan
A/S Gjestehuset Hjorten ✳
Postb 120
N-7240 Fillan
☎ 074 41 250

Kristiansund
Baron Hotel Kristiansund ✳✳✳
Hauggt 16
N-6500 Kristiansund
☎ 073 74 011
BWN

Måløy
Kaptein Linge Hotel ✳✳
Gate 1
N-6700 Måløy
☎ 057 51 800
Inter Nor Hotel/Scandinavian
Bonuspass

Molde
Hotell Molde ✳✳
Storgt 19
N-6400 Molde
☎ 072 15 888
Fjord Pass

Inter Nor Alexandra Hotell ✳✳
Storgaten 1-7
N-6400 Molde
☎ 072 51 133
Scandinavian Bonuspass

Nordfjordeid
Nordfjord Hotell ✳✳
N-6770 Nordfjordeid
☎ 057 60 433
Fjord Pass

Runde
Christineborg Turisthotel ✳✳
N-6096 Runde
☎ 070 85 950
Fjord Pass

Sandane
Gloppen Hotel ✳
N-6860 Sandane
☎ 057 65 333
Fjord Pass

Selje
Selje Hotel A/S ✳✳✳
N-6740 Selje
☎ 057 56107

Sunndalsøra
Hotell Sunndal ✳
N-6600 Sunndalsøra
☎ 073 91 655

Surnadal
Surnadal Hotell ✳✳
N-6650 Surnadal
☎ 073 61 544
Fjord Pass
BWN

Sykkylven
Sjølyst Hotell A/S ✳
N-6230 Sykkylven
☎ 071 57 500

Ulsteinvik
Inter Nor Ulstein Hotell ✳✳
Varleite
N-6065 Ulsteinvik
☎ 070 10 162
Scandinavian Bonuspass

Valldal
Muri Kro og Motell ✳
N-6210 Valldal
☎ 071 57 500

Volda
Volda Turisthotell ✳
Postb 187
N-6101 Volda
☎ 070 77 050
Eurohotel

Chapter 4 •
The Lofoten and Vesterålen
Islands

Andenes
Søylen pensjonat & camping ✳
Bleiksv 39
N-8480 Andenes
☎ 088 41 412

Harstad
Grand Nordic Hotell ✳
Strandgt 9
N-9400 Harstad
☎ 082 62 170
Fjord Pass

Kabelvåg
Lofoten Rorbuferie ✳✳
Boks 185
N-8310 Kabelvåg
☎ 088 71 200

Nyvågar Rorbu-og-aktivitetssenter ✳✳✳
Storvågan
N-8310 Kabelvåg
☎ 088 78 900
These two hotels offer *rorbu* (converted fishermen's cabins) for visitors, but with restaurant facilities on site.

Melbu
Melbu Nye Hotell A/S ✳✳
N-8490 Melbu
☎ 088 57 000
BWN

Sortland
Sortland Nordic Hotel ✳
Verterålsgt 59
N-8400 Sortland
☎ 088 21 833

Stamsund
Stamsund Lofoten Hotell ✳✳
N-8340 Stamsund
☎ 088 89 300

Svolvær
Vestfjord Hotel ✳✳
Havna
Boks 386
N-8300 Svolvær
☎ 088 71 200
Fjord Pass

Chapter 5 •
The Arctic Circle Tour

Alta
SAS Alta Hotel Løkkeveien ✳✳✳
N-9500 Alta
☎ 84 35 000

Alta Motel ✳✳
Bossekop
Postb 15
N-9500 Alta
☎ 084 34 711

Bakkehaug
Rundhaug Hotell ✳✳
N-9230 Bakkehaug
☎ 089 37 311

Bardu
Bardu Motor Hotel ✻✻
Setermoen
N-9250 Bardu
☎ 089 81 022

Hammerfest
Rica Hotel Hammerfest ✻✻✻
Sørøygt
N-9600 Hammerfest
☎ 084 11 333
Rica Hotels

Hammerfest Hotel ✻✻
Strandgt 2-4
N-9600 Hammerfest
☎ 084 11 622

Håpet
Scandic Hotel Tromsø ✻✻
Langes
N-9014 Håpet
☎ 083 73 400
Scandic Hotels

Honningsvåg
SAS Nordkapp Hotell ✻✻
Storgt 4
N-9750 Honningsvåg
☎ 084 72 333

Hotel Havly A/S ✻✻
Storg 12
N-9750 Honningsvåg
☎ 084 72 966
Norstar hotel

Inari
Inarin Kultahovi ✻✻
SF-99870 Inari
☎ 697 51 221
Finlandia Hotels/Finncheque

Ivalo
Ivalo Hotel ✻✻
Ivalontie 34
SF-99800 Ivalo
☎ 697 21 911
Finlandia Hotels/Finncheque

Karasjok
SAS Karasjok Turisthotell ✻✻✻
Postb 94
N-9730 Karasjok
084 67 400

Kiruna
Reso Hotel Ferrum ✻✻✻
Lars Jannssonsg 15
S-981 Kiruna
Pro Scandinavia Voucher

Luleå
Scandic Hotel Luleå ✻✻✻
Mjölkudden
S-951 Luleå
☎ 920 283 60

Narvik
Inter Nor Grand Hotel ✻✻
Kongensgt 64
N-8500 Narvik
☎ 082 41 531
Scandinavian Bonuspass

Rovaniemi
City-Hotelli ✻✻
Pekankatu 9
SF-96200 Rovaniemi
☎ 60 314 501
Finlandia Hotels/Finncheque

Sodankylä
Arctia Hotal ✻✻✻
Unarintie 15
F-99600 Sodankylä

Sørstraumen
Kvænangsfjell Gildetun ✻
N-9092 Sørstraumen
☎ 083 69 958

Tromsdalen
Tromsdal Gjestgiveri ✻✻
Tyttebærvn 11
N-9020 Tromsdalen
☎ 083 39 900
Has a café rather than a restaurant.

Tromsø
Grand Nordic Hotel ✻✻✻
Storgt 44
N-9000 Tromsø
Fjord Pass

Polar Rainbow Hotell ✻
Grønnegt 45
N-9000 Tromsø
☎ 083 86 480
Rainbow Hotels

Denmark

Several cheque systems are available in Denmark for reducing prices to tourists in the summer season. The three most widespread schemes are Best Western Hotel Cheque Scandinavia, ProSkandinavia Hotel Check System and Scandic Hotels MiniPas all of which cover other Scandinavian countries as well as Denmark. Inn Cheques cover Danish Kros (inns) belonging to the Danske Kroferie scheme. A hotel booklet including hotels, pensions, inns and holiday centres is available on request from the Danish Tourist Office.

Useful addresses are:
Best Western
Vodroffsvej 44
DK-1900 Frederiksberg

Haman Scandinavia UK Ltd
Unit No 4
4 Crawford Avenue
Wembley, Middlesex HA0 2UU
England

Inn Cheques from:
Danske Kroferie, Søndergade 31
DK-8700 Horsens
☎ 75 62 35 44

Scandic MiniPass via travel agents

Chapter 6 • North Jutland

Ålestrup
Hotel Hvide Kro
Jernbanegade 7
DK-9620 Ålestrup
☎ 98 64 14 33
Inn Cheque

Års
Års Hotel
Himmerlandsgade 111
DK-9400 Års
☎ 98 62 16 00
Inn Cheque

Brovst
Kokkedal Slot ✳✳✳
Kokkedalsvej 17
DK-9460 Brovst   ☎ 98 23 36 22
Moated castle.

Frederikshavn
Hotel Jutlandia ✳✳✳
Havnepladsen 8E
DK-9900 Frederikshaven
☎ 97 96 10 44
Danway Hotels

Hantsholm
Golf Hotel Hantsholm ✳✳
Byvej 2
DK-7730 Hantsholm
☎ 97 96 10 44

Hirtshals
Danland i Hirtshals ✳✳
Feriefotel Fyrklit
Kystevejn 10
DK-9850 Hirtshals
☎ 98 94 20 00

Løgstør
Hotel du Nord ✳✳
Havnevej 38
DK-9670 Løgstør
☎ 98 67 17 11
Inn Cheque

Nykøbing Mors
Hotel Pakhuset ✳✳
Havnen
DK-9700 Nykøbing Mors
☎ 97 72 33 00

Outrup
Outrup Hotel ✳
Jernbanegade 2
DK-6855 Outrup
☎ 75 25 10 13

Skagen
Hotel Skagen ✳✳✳
Gl Landevej 39
DK-9990 Skagen
☎ 98 44 22 33
Best Western

Skørping
Hotel Rebild Park ✳✳
Jyllandsgade 4
DK-9520 Skørping
☎ 93 39 14 00
Inn Cheque

Spøttrup
Spøttrup Kro *
Østergade 6
Rødding
DK-4780 Spøttrup
☎ 97 56 10 75

Strandby
Strandby Sømandshjem **
Havnevej 11
DK-9970 Strandby
☎ 98 48 10 27

Thyholm
Tambohus Kro *
Tambogade 29
Tambohus
DK-7790 Thyholm
☎ 97 87 53 00

Thisted
Hotel Thisted **
Frederiksgade 16
DK-7700 Thisted
☎ 97 92 52 00

Tylstrup
Tylstrup Kro **
Tylstrupvej 36
DK-9382 Tylstrup
☎ 98 26 15 66
Inn Cheque

Vinderup
Sevel Kro *
Søgårdvej 2
Sevel
DK-7830 Vinderup
☎ 97 44 80 11

Chapter 7 •
Funen and Islands to the South

Ærøskøbing
Hotel Ærøhus
Vestergade 38
DK-5970 Ærøskøbing
☎ 62 52 10 03
Inn Cheque

Assens
Marcussens Hotel
Strandgade 22
DK-5610 Assens
☎ 64 71 10 89

Bogense
Bogense Hotel
Aldegade 56
DK-5400 Bogense
☎ 64 81 11 08

Broby
Brobyværk Kro ***
Marsk-Billesvej 15
Brobyværk
DK-5672 Broby
Inn Cheque

Fåborg
Hotel Fåborg Fjord ***
Svendborgvej 175
DK- 5600 Fåborg
☎ 62 61 10 10

Kerteminde
Ulriksholm Slot
Ulriksholmvej 96
Kølstrup
DK-Kerteminde
☎ 65 39 15 44

Tornøes Hotel **
Strandgade 2
DK-5300 Kerteminde
☎ 65 32 16 05

Marstal
Hotel Marstal *
Dronningestræde 1A
DK-5960 Marstal   ☎ 62 53 13 52

Middelfart
Cassiopeia-Middelfart Park Hotel
Karensmindevej 3
DK- Middelfart
☎ 64 41 29 69

Millinge
Falsled Kro ***
Assensvej 513
Falsled
DK-5642 Millinge
☎ 62 68 11 11
Relais and chateaux.

Munkebo
Munkebo Kro
Fjordvej 56-58
DK-5330 Munkebo
☎ 65 97 40 30
Inn Cheque

Rudkøbing
Hotel Rudkøbing Skudehavn ✳✳
Havnegade 21
DK-5900 Rudkøbing
☎ 62 51 46 00

Svendborg
Hotel Royal ✳✳
Tolbodvej 5
DK-5700 Svendborg
☎ 62 21 21 13

Hotel Troense ✳✳
Strandgade 5-7
Troense
DK-5700 Svendborg
☎ 62 22 54 12
Inn Cheque

Restaurant Valdemars Slot ✳✳✳
Slotsalleen 100
Troense
DK-5700 Svendborg
☎ 62 22 59 00
You pay for staying in a showpiece
castle with a much advertised restau-
rant.

Tranekær
Concordia ✳
Østerhusevej 24
Lohals
DK-5953 Tranekær
☎ 62 55 14 00

Tranekær Gæstgivergård ✳✳
Slotsgade 74
DK-5953 Tranekær
☎ 62 59 12 04

Vissenbjerg
Visenbjerg Storkro ✳✳
Søndersøvej 30
DK-5492 Vissenbjerg
☎ 64 47 38 80

Chapter 8 •
Storstrøm County

Eskilstrup
Hotel Højmølle Kro ✳✳
Nykøbingvej 112
DK-4863 Eskilstrup
☎ 53 83 63 06

Fakse Ladeplads
Samklang-ved havet ✳
Klintevej 19
DK-4654 Fakse Ladeplads
☎ 53 71 60 12

Gedser
Danland i Gedser-Feriehotel Gedser
Vestre Strandevej 2
DK-4874 Gedser
☎ 53 87 99 99
Danland Hotels.

Guldborg
Motel Guldborg ✳✳
Guldborgvey 284-286
DK-4862 Guldborg
☎ 53 89 01 13

Haslev
Dalby Hotel ✳✳✳
Vordingborgvej 425
Dalby
DK-4690 Haslev
☎ 53 69 81 06

Maribo
Hotel Dana ✳
Suhrsgade 13
DK-4930 Maribo   ☎ 53 88 17 11

Nakskov
Hotel og Restaurant Skovridergården ✳
Svingelen 4
DK-4900 Nakskov
☎ 53 92 03 55
Inn Cheque.

Næstved
Menstrup Kro and Gæstgiveri
Menstrup DK-4700 Næstved
☎ 53 74 33 63
Inn Cheque.

Nykøbing Sjælland
Hotel du vest ✳✳
Algade 1
DK-4500 Nykøbing Sjælland
☎ 53 41 12 38

Nysted
Den Gamle Gaard ✳✳
Stubberupvej 17
DK-4880 Nysted
☎ 53 87 15 50

Præstø
Hotel Frederiksminde
Klosternakken 8
DK-4720 Præstø
☎ 53 79 10 42

Rødby
Euro Hotel E4 ✳✳
Maribo Landevej 4
DK-4970 Rødby
☎ 54 60 14 85

Danhotel ✳✳
Havnegade 2
Rødbyhavn
DK-4970 Rødby
☎ 54 60 53 66

Rødvig Stevns
Rødvig Kro ✳✳
Østersøvej 8
DK-4673 Rødvig Stevns
☎ 53 70 60 98

Stege
Hotel Stege Bugt
Langelinie 48
DK-4780 Stege
☎ 55 81 54 54
Dansk Familie-Hotel

Præstekilde Kro and Hotel ✳✳✳
Klintevej 116
Keldby
DK-4780 Stege
☎ 55 81 34 43
Inn Cheque.

Stubbekøbing
Elverkroen Hotel-Restaurant
Vestergade 39
DK-4850 Stubbekøbing
☎ 53 84 12 50

Vordingborg
Hotel Kong Valdemar ✳✳✳
Algade 101
Slotstorvet
DK-4760 Vordingborg
☎ 53 77 00 95

Sweden

There is a very wide choice of hotel chains available in Sweden offering discounts to summer tourists. The largest is Sweden Hotels whose pass entitles one to a 50 per cent discount on normal bed and breakfast prices. This pass cannot be bought in Sweden but is obtainable through specialist travel agents in Europe and America. Other schemes include Best Western Hotelcheque Scandinavia, Scandinavian Bonus Pass, Scandic cheques and the Proskandinavia hotel cheque system, all of which include hotels all over Scandinavia. A hotel booklet containing details of nearly 1,000 hotels is available on request from the Swedish Tourist Board.

Useful addresses are:
Best Western Hotels Sverige
Box 6898
Salt Mätargatan 5
S-113 86 Stockholm
☎ 46-8 30 04 20

Countryside Sweden
Grand Hotel Saltsjöbaden
S-133 83 Stockholm
☎ 46-8 717 09 29

Scandic Hotel AB
Reservation service
Box 6197
S-102 33 Stockholm
☎ 46-8 610 50 50

Scandinavia Bonus Pass
SARA booking
Svärdvägen 23
S-182 84 Danderyd/Stockholm
☎ 46-8 753 73 50

ProSkandinavia
c/o Haman Scandinavia AB
Box 2009
S-103 22 Stockholm
☎ 46-8 14 34 10

Sweden Hotels
Kammakargatan 48
S-111 60 Stockholm
☎ 46-8 20 43 11

Chapter 9 •
South-East Sweden

Ljungby
Hotel Terraza ✳✳✳
Stora Torget 1
S-341 30 Ljungby
☎ 0372 135 60

Kalmar
Kalmarsmund Hotell ✳✳✳
Fiskaregatan 5
S-392 32 Kalmar
☎ 0480 181 00
Sweden Hotels

Kalmar Stadshotell ✳✳✳
Storgatan 14
S-392 32 Kalmar
☎ 0480 151 80
Best Western

Scandic Hotel Kalmar ✳✳ (SAB)
Dragonv 7
S-392 39 Kalmar
☎ 480 223 60

Karlshamn
Hotel Carlshamn AB ✳✳
Varvsgatan 1
S-374 35 Karlshamn
☎ 0454 890 00
Sweden Hotels

Scandic Hotel Karlshamn ✳✳✳ (SAB)
Jannebergsvägen 2
S-374 32 Karlshamn
☎ 0586 504 60

Karlskrona
Hotell Angöringen Carlskrona ✳✳
August Palmgrens Väg 3
S-371 61 Karlskrona
☎ 0455 246 00

Hotell Siesta ✳✳
Borgmästereg 5
S-371 31 Karlskrona
Breakfast only.

Mörrum
Hotel Walhalla ✳✳
Stationsv 24
S-375 00 Mörrum
☎ 0454 500 44

Nybrö
Stora Hotellet ✳✳
Stadshusplan/Mellang 11
S-383 00 Nybrö
☎ 0481 119 35

Örland
Haltorps Gästgiveri ✳✳✳
Högsrum
S-387 92 Borgholm
☎ 0485 850 00
Countryside Sweden.

Ronneby
Grand Hotel ✳✳
Järnvägsg 11
S-372 37 Ronneby
☎ 0457 268 80
Breakfast only.

Ronneby Brunn AB RESO Hotels ✳✳✳
S-372 22 Ronneby

Sölvesborg
Pensionat Hälleviks Havsbad ✳
S-294 00 Sölvesborg
☎ 08 762 32 98

Växjö
Hotel Royal Corner ✳✳✳
Liedbergsgatan 11
S-352 46 Växjö
☎ 0470 100 00
Best Western

Scandic Hotel Växjö ✳✳✳
Hejareg 19
S-352 46 Växjö
☎ 0470 220 70

Chapter 10 •
Värmland

Arvika
Hotel Oscar Statt ✳✳ (SH)
Torggatan 9
S-671 22 Arvika
☎ 0570 222 22

Ekshärad
Hedegårds Pensionat ✳
Harat
S-680 50 Ekshärad
☎ 0563 400 24

Wärdshuset Pilgrimen ✳
Klarälvsv 35
S-680 50 Ekshärad
☎ 0563 405 90

Hagfors
Hotel & Restaurang Jonte ✳
Folkets Väg 1
S-683 01
Hagfors
☎ 0563 141 50

Filipstad
Hennickehammars Herrgård ✳✳✳
S-682 00 Filipstad
☎ 0590 125 65
Countryside Sweden.

Scandic Hotel Filipstad ✳✳
John Ericsson 8
S-682 00 Filipstad
☎ 0590 125 30

Karlskoga
Brogårdens Hotell o Gästigiveri ✳✳
Kanalvägen 1
S-691 53 Karlskoga
☎ 0586 305 20

Scandic Hotel Karlskoga ✳✳✳
Hyttåsen
S-691 33 Karlskoga
☎ 0586 504 60

Karlstadt
Hotel Gösta Berling ✳✳
Drottningg 1
S-652 24 Karlstadt   ☎ 054 15 01 90
Sweden Hotel

Stadshotellet ✳✳✳
Kungsg 22
S-651 01 Karlstad   ☎ 054 11 52 20
Best Western.

Kristinehamn
Gastivargården Carlslund ✳✳
Värmlandsäby
S-681 00 Kristinehamn
☎ 0551 102 80

Munkfors
Wärdshuset Munken ✳✳
Munkeruds väg 6
S-684 00 Munkfors
☎ 0563 522 35

Säffle
Scandic Hotel Säffle (SAB) ✳✳✳
Olof trätäljagatan 2
S-661 00
Säffle
☎ 0533 126 60

Stollet
Stöllets Gästgivaregård ✳✳
S-680 51 Stollet
☎ 0563 811 50

Sunne
Broby Gästgivaregård ✳✳
Långgatan 25
S-686 00 Sunne
☎ 0565 133 70

Sysslebäck
Långbergets Hotel ✳✳
S-680 60 Sysslebäck
☎ 0564 260 50

Chapter 11 •
Dalarna

Älvdalen
Hotell Älvdalen ✳
Dalgatan 77
S-796 01 Älvdalen
☎ 0251 110 70

Avesta
Star Hotel ✳✳ (SH)
Marcustorget 1
S-774 23 Avesta
☎ 0226 560 00

Borlänge
Hotel Brage ✳✳✳
Stationsgatan 1-3
S-781 30 Borlänge
☎ 0243 241 50
Sweden Hotel

Scandic Hotel Borlänge ✳✳✳
Stationsgatan 21
S-781 50 Borlänge
☎ 0243 281 20

Dala-Floda
Värdshuset i Dala-Floda ✳✳
Badvägen 6
S-780 44 Dala Floda
☎ 0241 220 50

Falun
Hotel Bergmästaren ✳✳✳
Bergskolegränd 7
S-791 26 Falun
☎ 023 636 00
Sweden Hotel.

Scandic Hotel Falun ✳✳
Kopparvägen/Norslund
S-791 05 Falun
☎ 023 221 60

Grängesberg
Vardshuset Stopet ✳✳
Kopparberget 60
Grängesberg
☎ 0240 220 00

Idre
Lövåsgården Fjällhotell ✳
S-790 91
Idre
☎ 0263 290 29

Långshyttan
Långshyttan Brukshotell AB ✳✳
Holmg 4
S770 70 Långshyttan
☎ 0225 600 54

Leksand
Hotell Korstäppan ✳✳✳
Hjotnäsv 33
S-793 31 Leksand
☎ 0247 100 37

Ludvika
Grand Hotel
Eriksgatan 6
S-771 00 Ludvika
☎ 0240 182 20

Mora
Mora Hotell ✳✳✳
Strandg 12
S-792 01 Mora
☎ 0250 117 50
Best Western.

Orsa
Fryksås Hotell ✳✳
Fryksås
S-794 00 Orsa
☎ 0250 460 20
Countryside Sweden,

Rättvig
Scandic Hotel Lerdalshöjden ✳✳✳
S-795 00 Rättvik
☎ 0248 111 50

Särna
Knappgårdens Kurs o Friluftsgård ✳
Särnaheden
S-790 90 Särna
☎ 0253 180 60

Smedjebacken
Vanbo Herrgård ✳✳
S-777 91 Smedjebacken
☎ 0240 765 00

Tällberg
Romantik Hotel Åkerblads i Tällberg ✳
S-793 70 Tällberg
☎ 0247 508 00

Chapter 12 •
Swedish Lappland

Ammarnäs
Ammarnäsgården ✳✳
S-920 75 Ammarnäs
☎ 0950 600 03

Arjeplog
Silverhatten Hotell ✳✳✳
S-930 90 Arjeplog
☎ 0961 112 10

Arvidsjaur
Laponia Hotel ✳✳✳ (SH)
Storgatan 45
S-933 00
Arvidsjaur
☎ 0960 108 80

Gällivare
Nya Dundret AB ✳✳✳
S-982 21 Gällivare
☎ 0970 145 60

Jokkmokk
Hotel Gästis ✳
Herrevägen 1
S-960 40 Jokkmokk
☎ 0971 100 12

Hotel Jokkmokk ✳✳✳
Solgatan 45
S-960 40 Jokkmokk ☎ 0971 113 20

Kalix
Hotell Valhall ✳✳
Strandg 21
S-952 00 Kalix
☎ 0932 121 90
Sweden Hotel

Kiruna
RESO Hotel Ferrum ✳✳✳
Lars Janssonsg 15
S-981 31 Kiruna
☎ 0980 186 00

Luleå
Luleå Stads Hotell ✳✳✳
Storg 15
S-951 31 Luleå
☎ 0920 283 60
Best Western

Scandic Hotel Luleå ✳✳✳
Mjölkudden
S-951 56 Luleå
☎ 0920 283 60

Överkalix
Hotel Överkalix ✳✳✳
Skolgatan 4
S-956 00 Överkalix
0926 118 00

Polcirkelgård Turistani o Hotell Polcirkeln ✳
Polcirkelgården 3898
S-956 91 Överkalix

Övertorneå
Hotell Tornedalia ✳✳
S-950 22 Övertorneå
☎ 0927 115 50

Sorsele
Hotel Gästis ✳✳
Hotellg 1
S-920 70 Sorsele   ☎ 0950 107 20
Sweden Hotel

Tornio
Kaupunginhotelli ✳✳
Itäranta 4
SF-95400 Tornio   ☎ 698 43311
Finncheque

Finland

The best way to book hotels in Finland is to use the Finncheque scheme. This covers a wide range of hotel chains and gives a choice of 252 hotels all over Finland, divided into three price categories. In the most expensive category there is a surcharge over the cost of the Finncheque; in the cheapest a packed lunch is provided as well. The cheques are bought from specialist travel agents outside Finland. A hotel booklet covering most of the country's hotels is available on request from the Finnish National Tourist Board.

Chapter 13 •
The Åland Islands

Brändö
Brändö Hotel
SF-22920 Brändö

Godby
Godby Congress Hotel
SF-22410 Godby
Finström
☎ 28 41 170

Mariehamn
Arkipelag Hotell
Strandgatan 31
SF-2210 Mariehamn
☎ 28 24 020

Cikada Hotel ✳
Hamngatan 1
F-22100 Mariehamn
☎ 28 16 333

Hotel Pommern
Norragatan 8
SF-22100 Mariehamn
☎ 28 15555

Hotel Savoy
Nygatan 12
SF-22100 Mariehamn
☎ 28 15 400

Kökar
Brudhäll Hotel and Restaurant
Karlby, SF-22730 Kökar
☎ 28 55 955

Kumlinge
Remmaren Inn ✳
SF-22820 Kumlinge
☎ 28 55 402

Pålsböle
Bastä Hotel
SF-22310 Pålsböle
Finström
☎ 28 42 382

Storby
Eckerö Hotell & Restaurang
P1175
SF-22270 Storby
☎ 28 38447

Hotell Havsbandet
SF-22270 Storby
Eckerö
☎ 28 38 305

Chapter 14 •
Finland's West Coast

Ähtäri
Mesikämmen ✳✳
SF-63700 Ähtäri
☎ 65 391 111
Finncheque

Hämeenlinna
Rantasipi Aulanko ✳✳
SF-1499 Hämeenlinna
☎ 17 29 521
Finncheque

Cumulus Hämeenlinna ✳✳
Raatihuoneenkatu 16-18
☎ 17 28 811
Finncheque

Ikaalinen
Ikaalinen Spa ✳✳✳
SF-39510 Ikaalinen
☎ 33 60 451

Ikahovi ✳✳
Keturinkatu 1
SF-39500 Ikaalinen
☎ 33 6325
Finncheque

Jakobstad/Pietarsaari
Fontell ✳✳
Kanalesplanaden 13
SF-68600 Jakobstad/Pietarsaari
☎ 67 30 366
Finncheque

Kaskinen
Kaske ✳✳
Raatihuoneenkatu 41-43
SF-64260 Kaskinen
☎ 62 27771
Finncheque

Kokkola
Vaakuna ✳✳
Rantakatu 16
SF-67100 Kokkola
☎ 68 15411
Finncheque

Kristinestad/Kristiinankaupunki
Kristina ✳✳
Suurtori 1
SF-64120 Kristinestad/
   Kristiinankaupunki
☎ 62 12555
Finncheque

Naantali
Naantalin Kylpylä ✳✳✳
Kalevanniemi
SF-21100 Naantali
☎ 21 857 711
Finncheque

Pori
Cumulus Pori ✳✳
Itsenäisyydenkatu 37
F-28100 Pori
☎ 39 828 299
Finncheque

Rauma
Cumulus Rauma ✳✳
Aittakarinkatu 9
SF-26100 Rauma
☎ 38 221 122
Finncheque

Tampere
Cumulus Koskikatu ✳✳
Koskikatu 5
SF-33100 Tampere ☎ 31 35 500
Finncheque

Victoria Hotel ✳
Itsenäisyydenkatu 1
F-33100 Tampere
☎ 31 2425 111
Finncheque

Turku
Cumulus Turku ✳✳
Eerinkinkatu 28
SF-20100 Turku
☎ 21 514 111
Finncheque

Park Hotel ✳✳✳
Rauhankatu 1
SF-20100 Turku
☎ 21 617 000
Best Western

Scandic Hotel Turku ✳✳
Matkustajasatama
F-20100 Turku
☎ 21 302 169
Finncheque

Uusikaupunki
Aquarius ✳✳
Kullervontie 11B
SF-23500 Uusikaupunki
☎ 22 13 123
Finncheque

Vaasa
Royal Waasa Hotel ✳✳✳
Hovioikeudenpuistikko 18
F-65100 Vaasa
☎ 61 123 861
Finncheque

Valkeakoski
Waltikka ✳✳
Hakalantie 6
SF-37600 Valkeakoski
☎ 37 7711
Finncheque

Virrat
Tarjanne Hotel ✳✳
Virtaintie 35
F-34800 Virrat
☎ 34 554 54

Chapter 15 •
The Finnish Lake District

Heinola
Kumpeli ✳✳
Muonamiehenkate 3
SF-18000 Heinola
☎ 58214
Finncheque

Iisalmi
Koljonvirta ✳✳
Savonkatu 18
SF-74100 Iisalmi
☎ 77 23511
Finncheque

Imatra
Valtionhotelli ✳✳
Torkkelinkatu 2
SF-55100 Imatra
Finncheque

Vuoksenhovi ✳✳
Siitolankatu 2
SF-55120 Imatra
☎ 54 25011
Finncheque

Joensuu
Karelia Hotel ✳✳✳
Kauppakatu 25
F-80100 Joensuu
☎ 73 24 391

Jyväskylä
Alexandra ✳✳
Hannikaisenkatu 35
SF-40100 Jyväskylä
☎ 41 212 611
Best Western, Finncheque

Kerimäki
Herttua ✳✳✳
SF-Kerimäki
☎ 57 541 301
Finncheque

Kuopio
Cumulus Kuopio ✳✳
Asemakatu 32
SF-70100 Kuopio
☎ 71 123 555
Finncheque

Kuusankoski
Sommelo ✳✳
Pallokentäntie 2
SF-45700 Kuusankoski
☎ 51 491 910
Finncheque

Lahti
Sokos Hotel ✳✳
Hämeenkatu 4
F-15110 Lahti
☎ 18 89 721
Finncheque

Lappeenranta
Cumulus Lappeenranta ✳✳✳
Valtakatu 31
F-53100 Lappeenranta
☎ 53 57 81
Finncheque

Lieksa
Puustelli Hotel ✳✳✳
Hovileirinkatu 3
F-81700 Lieksa
☎ 75 25 544
Finncheque

Mikkeli
Cumulus Mikkeli ✳✳✳
Mikonkatu 9
F-50100 Mikkeli
☎ 55 20 511
Finncheque

Outokumpu
Malmikumpu Hotel ✳✳
Asemakatu 1
F-83500 Outokumpu
☎ 73 550 333
Finncheque

Punkaharju
Valtionhotelli ✳✳
F-58450 Punkaharju 2
☎ 57 311 761
Finncheque
Possibly Finland's oldest hotel

Savonlinna
Tott Hotel ✳✳✳
Satamakatu 1
F-57130 Savonlinna
☎ 57 514 500

Vääksy
Talluka ✳✳
Tallukaantie 1
SF-17200 Vääksy
☎ 18 68611
Finncheque

Varkaus
Keskus-hotelli ✳✳
Ahlströminkatu 18
F-78250 Varkaus
☎ 72 27 994
Finncheque

A Note To The Reader

The accommodation and eating out lists in this book are based upon the authors' own experiences and therefore may contain an element of subjective opinion. The contents of this book are believed correct at the time of publication but details given may change. We welcome any information to ensure accuracy in this guide book and to help keep it up-to-date.
Please write to The Editor, Moorland Publishing Co Ltd, Moor Farm Road, Airfield Estate, Ashbourne, Derbyshire, DE6 1HD, England.
American and Canadian readers please write to The Editor, The Globe Pequot Press, 6 Business Park Road, PO Box 833, Old Saybrook, Connecticut 06475, USA.

MPC

The Globe Pequot press